Empowering Affected Interests

Many demands for democratic inclusion rest on a simple yet power-ful idea. It's a principle of affected interests. The principle states that all those affected by a collective decision should have a say in making that decision. Yet, in today's highly globalized world, the implications of this "All-Affected Principle" are potentially radical and far-reaching. *Empowering Affected Interests* brings together a distinguished group of leading democratic theorists and philosophers to debate whether and how to rewrite the rules of democracy to account for the increasing inter-dependence of states, markets, and peoples. It examines the grounds that justify democratic inclusion across borders of states, localities, and the private sector, on topics ranging from immigration and climate change to labor markets and philanthropy. The result is an original and import-ant reassessment of the All-Affected Principle and its alternatives that advances our understanding of the theory and practice of democracy. This title is available for Open Access on Cambridge Core.

Archon Fung is the Winthrop Laflin McCormack Professor of Citizenship and Self-Government and directs the Roy and Lila Ash Center for Democratic Governance and Innovation at the John F. Kennedy School of Government, Harvard University.

Sean W. D. Gray is Assistant Professor of Political Science at Memorial University of Newfoundland and Labrador, Canada.

Empowering Affected Interests

Democratic Inclusion in a Globalized World

Edited by

ARCHON FUNG
Harvard University

SEAN W. D. GRAY
Memorial University

Shaftesbury Road, Cambridge CB2 8EA, United Kingdom

One Liberty Plaza, 20th Floor, New York, NY 10006, USA

477 Williamstown Road, Port Melbourne, VIC 3207, Australia

314–321, 3rd Floor, Plot 3, Splendor Forum, Jasola District Centre,
New Delhi – 110025, India

103 Penang Road, #05–06/07, Visioncrest Commercial, Singapore 238467

Cambridge University Press is part of Cambridge University Press & Assessment,
a department of the University of Cambridge.

We share the University's mission to contribute to society through the pursuit of
education, learning and research at the highest international levels of excellence.

www.cambridge.org
Information on this title: www.cambridge.org/9781009454018

DOI: 10.1017/9781009453981

© Cambridge University Press & Assessment 2024

First published 2024

A catalogue record for this publication is available from the British Library

A Cataloging-in-Publication data record for this book is available from the
Library of Congress

ISBN 978-1-009-45401-8 Hardback
ISBN 978-1-009-45400-1 Paperback

In memory of
James Bohman
1954–2021

Contents

Contributors

Joseph H. Carens, Professor of Political Science Emeritus, University of Toronto.

Thomas Christiano, Professor of Philosophy and Law, University of Arizona.

Archon Fung, Winthrop Laflin McCormack Professor of Citizenship and Self-Government, and Director, Roy and Lila Ash Center for Democratic Governance and Innovation, John F. Kennedy School of Government, Harvard University.

Robert E. Goodin, Distinguished Professor of Philosophy Emeritus, Australian National University.

Carol C. Gould, Distinguished Professor of Philosophy, Hunter College, and Director, Center for Global Ethics and Politics, Ralph Bunche Institute for International Studies, City University of New York.

Sean W. D. Gray, Assistant Professor of Political Science, Memorial University of Newfoundland and Labrador.

Clarissa Rile Hayward, Professor of Political Science, Washington University, St. Louis.

Melissa Lane, Class of 1943 Professor of Politics and Director, University Center for Human Values, Princeton University.

Terry Macdonald, Associate Professor in International Relations, University of Melbourne.

Tomer J. Perry, Assistant Professor of Social Sciences and Philosophy, Minerva University.

Rob Reich, Professor of Political Science, and Faculty Director, Center for Ethics in Society, Stanford University.

Jennifer C. Rubenstein, Associate Professor of Political Science, University of Virginia.

Emma Saunders-Hastings, Assistant Professor of Political Science, Ohio State University.

Anna Stilz, Laurance S. Rockefeller Professor of Politics and the University Center for Human Values, Princeton University.

Laura Valentini, Professor of Political Science and Political Theory, Ludwig Maximilian University of Munich.

Mark E. Warren, Professor of Political Science Emeritus and Harold and Dorrie Merilees Chair in the Study of Democracy Emeritus, University of British Columbia.

Melissa S. Williams, Professor of Political Science, University of Toronto.

Acknowledgments

This volume has its origins in a series of informal conversations that began between the coeditors at the Harvard Kennedy School in early 2016. There was a feeling at the time that democratic theory had come to an impasse in trying to account for new demands for democratization that outstripped the capacities of the nation-state to deliver, including in immigration, climate governance, and international trade and finance, and in domains ranging from the domestic workplace to the World Bank. The idea for a workshop was floated, and we soon assembled a stellar team of workshop organizers who met over the next few months: Danielle Allen, Archon Fung, Sean Gray, and Tomer Perry.

Given the ambitious scope of this project, we knew from the get-go that we needed the input and perspectives of a diverse team of leading scholars. We also knew that the format of our meetings had to be somewhat unconventional if we were going to genuinely break new ground. The strategy that we hit upon was to organize two in-person workshops – held approximately six months apart – so that our invited participants could submit shorter "think pieces" and receive feedback, before committing to a more substantial chapter-length contribution. In between these in-person meetings, we organized two online brainstorming sessions, with participants gathering in small thematic working groups. This had the bonus of ensuring the conversations and debates that emerged over the course of the workshops were captured in the papers that were eventually submitted, as our participants tested their ideas and arguments and learned from one another.

The first in-person workshop was held over two days at Harvard University in December 2016, and the second in-person workshop took place over two days in June 2017. We invited sixteen participants to develop papers: Joseph Carens, Thomas Christiano, Robert Goodin, Carol Gould, Sean Gray, Clarissa Hayward, Hélène Landemore, Melissa Lane, Terry Macdonald, Tomer Perry,

Rob Reich, Jennifer Rubenstein, Emma Saunders-Hastings, Anna Stilz, Laura Valentini, and Mark Warren. Each paper was paired with an expert commentator who was tasked with providing constructive feedback on the same paper over successive drafts. For their willingness to serve as commentators, and their critical feedback throughout the process, we wish to thank Arash Abizadeh, Danielle Allen, Arthur Applbaum, Eric Beerbohm, Gerald Frug, Archon Fung, Mathias Koenig-Archibugi, Jane Mansbridge, Christopher Robichaud, Nancy Rosenblum, Lucas Stanczyk, Dennis Thompson, Melissa Williams, and Annette Zimmerman.

In addition to the Harvard workshops, a set of panels was organized for the 2017 American Political Science Association Annual Meeting in San Francisco to publicly showcase our works-in-progress. We are indebted to the presenters and audiences who participated in this event. We also gratefully acknowledge the financial and logistical support provided by the Harvard Kennedy School's Roy and Lila Ash Center for Democratic Governance and Innovation, and the Edmond and Lily Safra Center for Ethics, Harvard University. The project would not have gotten off the ground were it not for the advice and dedication of several Ash and Safra Center staff, including Tim Glynn-Burke, Hannah Hilligoss, Nadia Chavez, Jose Martinez, Jess Miner, Maggie Gates, and Susan Cox.

Robert Dreesen, editor at Cambridge University Press, was enthusiastic about the project from the moment we approached him. We would like to thank Robert and the rest of the Cambridge University Press team – especially, Sable Gravesandy, Becky Jackaman, and Balaji Devadoss – for their suggestions and guidance throughout the publication process. Moira Eagling completed the final copyediting of the manuscript with great care, and Victoria George prepared the index with diligence and speed.

Our work on the volume was delayed by the COVID-19 pandemic, which continues to impact millions around the globe at time of writing. Many people were sick, lost their lives, or know people who were sick and lost their lives. Governments closed economies and suspended travel. There was a scientific arms race to produce test kits and distribute vaccines to halt the spread of the virus. Countries and jurisdictions openly competed with one another for scarce resources to prop up their overburdened health and welfare systems. And, as is almost always the case, it is the most vulnerable who are most affected. Though the chapters in this volume were written before the pandemic, the need to rethink the boundaries of democratic inclusion in domestic and global policymaking couldn't be more urgent.

Finally, the coeditors would like to dedicate this volume to the memory of James Bohman, whose extraordinary contributions to deliberative democracy and global political theory paved the way for rethinking the possibilities for democracy across borders. Jim would have been a contributor to this volume, and we continue to feel the loss of his friendship, wisdom, and kindness.

The All-Affected Principle

A Pathway to Democracy for the Twenty-First Century?

Archon Fung and Sean W. D. Gray

In Neal Stephenson's 2021 novel *Termination Shock*, a billionaire using the pseudonym T. R. McHooligan takes it upon himself to single-handedly address global climate change by launching projectiles from a base in Texas using "the biggest gun in the world."[1] His high-tech cannonballs spread a layer of sulfur into the atmosphere that cools the earth by reflecting the sun's radiation back into space. This general approach, called solar geo-engineering, is actually an active area of research that is promoted by, among others, Harvard scientist David Keith.[2] In the novel, McHooligan's geo-engineering project creates winners and losers all over the world, as actual geo-engineering would. Some people live in places where the climate becomes milder and more conducive to their economic and social activities. Others are spared the destruction from sea level rise. But still other places suffer more frequent and severe storms and the climate becomes less hospitable.

Who, other than T. R. McHooligan, should have a say over whether his geo-engineering project goes forward? As a citizen and a person operating in the United States, he should be subject to that country's laws. In Stephenson's speculative fiction, the state of Texas is too libertarian to care. For its part, the United States government is too dysfunctional to notice, much less regulate, McHooligan. But suppose that the United States was well governed, and that its people judged that the United States would be a net beneficiary of geo-engineering, and so fully supported McHooligan. Should people in other countries – those who are net losers from geo-engineering – have any say?

In *Termination Shock*, governments and other organizations from far-off places send covert spies to Texas to protect their interests. One country goes so far as to send soldiers in the name of "climate peacekeeping." In other words, they invade the United States to stop McHooligan. They feel that they should have a say because their interests are profoundly affected, but the state-based, territorial structure of this democracy provides no democratic avenue for them to exercise influence to protect their interests.

Many theories of democracy presume that democratic authority governs a fixed set of people – citizens – who reside in a fixed territory, usually a sovereign state. The authors of this volume explore a different starting point for democracy: the All-Affected Principle (AAP).[3] That principle states that *everyone who is affected by a decision should be able to influence that decision.* According to the AAP, everyone in the world – not just the citizens of Texas or the United States – should have a say over T. R. McHooligan's geo-engineering project because his decisions affect everyone in the world.

Turning to actual events rather than speculative fiction, politics in the streets and in parliaments over the last decade evince widespread disappointment and anger at the reality of the territorially organized liberal democracies that reigned hegemonic at the beginning of the twenty-first century. The Indignados in Spain and #Occupy movements in major cities like New York, London, Paris, and Toronto highlighted the failure of liberal democracies to advance distributive justice after the Great Recession of 2007–2009. Extinction Rebellion, Sunrise, and other movements press societies to face up to the existential threat of climate change. Populist leaders and movements – marked by the victories of Brexit in the United Kingdom and then of Donald Trump in the 2016 United States presidential contest – rode waves of disaffection with liberal democracy. In the COVID-19 pandemic, this disaffection transmogrified into the dysfunctions that come from institutional distrust and illegitimacy, leading to violent conflicts about social distancing and massive vaccine skepticism in many parts of the world.

Perhaps these challenges to the existing political order in the democratic precincts of the world need not trigger deeper normative reconsideration. It may be that this turbulence is a failure of politics, not of democratic theory. Perhaps we should strive more vigorously in light of these failures to achieve what many normative political views already recommend: liberal democracies of free and equal citizens governing themselves through the powers of territorially bounded nation-states that hierarchically rule over not just the citizens, but the corporations and civic organizations, in those territories (see Macdonald, this volume).

The authors of this volume take a different path. We explore a whether the very different normative starting point of the AAP can provide a useful guide to assessing our practices of governance, designing institutions, and justifying democracy. As Melissa Lane (Chapter 12) describes, the AAP has ancient origins in Western thought, tracing back to the Codex of Justinian in the fifth century: *"quod omnes similiter tangit, ab omnibus comprobetur"* ("What touches all similarly must be approved by all"). Many attribute contemporary usage of the principle to Robert Dahl. Dahl offered this formulation:

Everyone who is affected by the decisions of a government should have the right to participate in that government.[4]

Dahl insisted that this is "very likely best general principle of inclusion that you are likely to find" for democracy. He saw it driving democratic slogans and intuitions like "No taxation without representation."[5] Almost in the very next breath, however, Dahl noted that the principle may have absurd, or at least troubling, implications. In the very same city, three people might be affected in one way by decisions around education, and in a very different ways by zoning decisions; should two be enfranchised in one set of decisions but disenfranchised on the other one? Moreover, the AAP suggests proportionality rather than equality; should those who pay greater taxes be afforded more voice because they are *more* affected? And then, Dahl observed that the principle

forces us to ask whether there is not after all some wisdom in the half-serious comment of a friend in Latin America who said that his people should be allowed to participate in our [U.S.] elections, for what happens in the politics of the United States is bound to have profound consequences for his country.[6]

In the face of some of the serious twenty-first-century challenges to democracy, however, some of the drawbacks of the AAP may be points of departure that better address difficulties that arise from more conventional, nation-state-centric conceptions of democracy. Some of these difficulties include the treatment and standing of immigrants; cross-border problems such as trade, pollution, and climate; the inability of national governments to effectively regulate economic and civic organizations; and, importantly, the unequal power of individuals and organizations within states. In other words, what Dahl took to be the "absurd" aspects of the AAP may in fact turn out to be positive features.

VARIETIES OF THE ALL-AFFECTED PRINCIPLE

The All-Affected Principle can be interpreted in many different ways. The authors of this volume explore alternative formulations of the principle and they offer various reasons to support and reject the principle itself. In particular, formulations of the principle that *everyone who is affected by a decision should have influence on that decision* can vary according to:

1. The organization making the decision
2. What type of decision
3. Ways having influence
4. Allocation of influence
5. Conceptions of affectedness
6. Weak and strong normative uses of the AAP

In Dahl's formulation above (and also Robert Goodin's formulation in Chapter 1 of this volume), the organizational scope of the All-Affected Principle is limited to *governments*. But most of the other authors expand the AAP to include decisions by other entities such as companies, philanthropic organizations, civic organizations, voluntary associations, and even individuals themselves. One straightforward interpretation of the AAP is that it should regulate explicit decisions such as the policies made by legislators or public and private leaders. But decisions always occur in a broader context of agendas that pre-scribe options, institutions, and resources that make some options more and less available. Thus, several authors in this volume argue that the AAP should track "power not [only explicit] decisions" (e.g. Gray, Hayward) and so be attentive to the background conditions that shape decision making. Other authors (e.g. Lane, Christiano) highlight how the AAP ought to be attentive to resources – for instance, time, money, or information – because resources often dictate available choices.

Formulations of the AAP specify different ways of having influence. In the democratic context, the most common method of exercising influence is vot-ing. From that point of departure, the question of influence is who should be given a vote over some decision. So, in an influential contemporary argument for the AAP, Goodin answers that everyone in the world should be enfran-chised by having a vote – through representatives – on every decision that possibly affects them.[7] But the vote is not the only way to confer influence. Standing to speak in a public deliberation or council – such as a city council meeting or at the United Nations – also constitutes influence, as does partic-ipating in a protest march or writing an opinion piece. A worker who is rep-resented by a labor union is likely to have more influence over his employer's decisions about compensation and workplace conditions than one who does not have a union (Christiano, this volume). All of these are active forms of influence, but there may be passive forms of influence available as well. For example, decision makers can be obliged to review the effects of their deci-sions on the interests of those who are affected, because of background laws and regulations. Though a "weaker" empowerment than (say) voting, such requirements may nevertheless ensure that the interests of those affected are considered.

The allocation of influence is another variation within the AAP. In demo-cratic political setting, the moral equality of citizens is often translated into an equal opportunity for influence through enfranchisement: one person, one vote. The AAP could be similarly formulated: so long as a person's interests are affected above some threshold, that person is given a vote equal to the vote of others who are affected in the same way. A more natural, if less easily imple-mented, interpretation of the AAP is for influence to be allocated in proportion to affectedness.[8] On this account, influence proportional to affectedness flows from the moral equality of individuals in a democracy. It requires treating each as a free equal, rather than just treating each equally. Even if morally attrac-tive, allocating influence proportionally might seem institutionally unworkable compared to the simplicity of a general election. But it turns out that many actual practices of governance already approximate, and indeed are motivated by, the intuition that influence over decisions be weighted. Membership in a school's Parent–Teacher Association, for example, is normally open to parents (and teachers) at that school, who are presumably more affected than others in the neighborhood or elsewhere in the nation (see Warren's chapter). In his

1970 exploration, Dahl wrote that "this tendency helps explain why there were 1,467 distinct political entities in the New York Metropolitan Region and why the citizens of Fridley, Minnesota, labored beneath eleven different layers of government."[9]

Another key question is what counts as being "affected" according to the AAP. At one inclusive end of the spectrum, one should have influence over decisions that possibly affect any interests that one may have. In more limited formulations, influence accompanies decisions that affect particularly important, fundamental, or justice-based interests. Patterns of repeated interaction, decision making, and effect – as with coresidents or cooperators in firms and other associations – may indicate the kind of relationship that ought to confer influence over decisions. And nondecisions and hidden structures of power can produce effects on people's interests that trigger the democratic concern for voice and control that motivate the AAP.

Beyond these conceptual challenges, there are also a range of normative applications – or levels of ambition – for which the AAP might be employed. Modestly, the AAP might be deployed as a democratic tripwire – a kind of early warning system that triggers cause for normative concern and investigation. When we notice that someone's (important) interests are being adversely affected, and that they have no influence to redress this concern, this might alert us to the existence of a democratic deficit. Upon further investigation, it may turn out that the problem is better accounted for by some other theory of democracy or justice (Carens, this volume). A problem that appears to be a violation of the AAP might, for example, turn out to be better understood, and redressed, as a denial of fundamental rights (Stilz, this volume) or equal citizenship in a national democracy. More strongly, the AAP could be deployed as a middle-level principle, a normative yardstick to judge and design processes of governance and decision making. In Chapter 9 of this volume, Carol Gould writes that "the main function of the All-Affected Principle is to address just these sorts of exogenous impacts of decisions. It demarcates the affected others, and argues for the need to give them democratic input to these decisions, if not fully equal participation rights."[10] Christiano, Rubenstein, and Lane use the AAP in this middle-level fashion in their respective chapters. Most ambitiously from a normative perspective, the contributions of Goodin, Warren, and Gray explore the AAP as a fundamental principle to justify democratic arrangements, while the chapters by Stilz, Valentini, and Williams present various arguments against grounding the AAP at this deeper level.

Even if one rejects the AAP as a justification of ideal political institutions, it might nevertheless be a useful guide to democratic action, responsibility, and reform in the face of structural injustice, pervasive inequality, and technocratic and authoritarian governments. On this view, the AAP provides a means of coping with what are essentially nonideal conditions. If you are a democrat, for example, but the world is such that kings will rule for a long time, what do you have to say about the accountability, rights, and obligations of kings to their subjects? More immediately, if you don't think billionaires should exist at all, but there are a lot of billionaires, and they will be around for some time, what are their obligations? The contributions to this volume by Macdonald, Hayward, Saunders-Hastings and Reich, and Rubenstein explore the AAP as a response to the many injustices of our imperfect world as it currently exists, rather than dealing in abstractions.

In sum, whether it is justified as an early warning system, a normative yardstick, or a foundational tenet, examining how organizational decisions affect people and the extent to which they can influence those decisions can help to advance four frontiers of democratic theory. First, what features of our social relationships should democratic arrangements *track*? Should democrats be principally concerned with power, domination, protection of fundamental interests, density of individual interactions, or some other characteristic? Second, how should democratic standards apply to decisions and actions that governments, corporations, and individuals take, when these have problematic *cross-border effects*? The AAP might help to account for the democratic inclusion and influence that migrants and other noncitizens ought to have, how border disputes can be settled democratically, and the influence that those who suffer the effects of decisions made in far-off places are entitled to have. Third, *economic power and concentration* of corporate wealth has swelled to mammoth proportions. Those corporations and their activities crisscross national boundaries and step footloose across the entire world. Governments often prove unwilling or unable to curb them. Can the AAP provide firmer ground to render such power accountable? Fourth, within and across the über-associations of nation-states are *many secondary associations*, including civic groups and ethnic and cultural communities, in addition to neighborhoods, towns, and cities, or private clubs or philanthropies. The operations and decisions of these associations not only affect one another but may also sometimes have consequences for those who are very distant – as happens, for example, when an international aid organization enlists wealthy donors to deliver services in another country. Can the AAP illuminate the obligations of these secondary associations or the rights of those whom they affect? To make progress, the chapters in this volume are organized along these four democratic frontiers.

TRACKING WHAT? SUBJECTION, INTERACTION, POWER, AND DOMINATION

Since Locke and Rousseau, legitimating the distinctive authority of government to coercively command its subjects has been a central justification for citizens' political rights.[11] This line of reasoning leads to the principle that all who are *subjected* to a government's authority should have influence over that government's decisions. And because national governments sit astride the apex of political hierarchies, citizens' political influence ought to track national governments' special power to make coercive decisions. The authors in the first part of this volume begin to explore the *All-Affected* Principle (in contrast to the *All-Subjected* Principle) by reconsidering this basic justification. In an increasingly globalized world, when so many of our vital interests depend upon decisions and actions outside of the governmental domain, why should democratic participation and influence be limited to tracking the exercise of government authority by territorial states?

In the first chapter of this volume, Robert Goodin continues the inquiry he began in his influential 2007 article "Enfranchising All-Affected Interests."[12] Goodin argues that both political authority and the franchise should track the thickness of the web of human interactions rather than geographic proximity or territorial boundaries. Once upon a time, the frequency, range, depth, and certainty of interactions between people may have correlated with territory and proximity. Under those circumstances, political authority could be plausibly organized geographically to regulate the densest interactions between people. In that old world, there was a convenient fit between democratic theories that prescribe political participation in national governments and patterns of human interaction. But in our contemporary world, webs of human interaction crisscross territories and localities in complex ways. It is time, Goodin argues, to bid the proximity principle "adieu," by reconfiguring political authority so that it tracks current densities of interaction and enfranchises individuals in those updated complexes of government.

Mark Warren (Chapter 2) and Sean Gray (Chapter 3) agree with Goodin and some other contributors to this volume that individuals should have influence and voice over decisions and collectivities well beyond territorial governments. But while Goodin focuses on the density of human interactions, Warren and Gray argue that influence and voice should track interests and interactions that are especially morally significant. Warren argues that two interests – self-development and self-determination – are especially important. When these interests are threatened decisions and actions beyond the reach of territorial states – as they are for many people with respect to climate change or global trade; or when they are jeopardized by decisions within territories – as with unresponsive or incompetent health and education authorities – Warren argues that the All-Affected Principle calls for the creation or empowerment of constituencies in ways that anticipate new demands for democratization.

Gray argues more generally that influence conferred by the AAP should track power in ways that enable people to defend vital interests in nondomination and against the usurpation of their own judgments. Instead of focusing on decisions or their effects, Gray argues that we should focus on the prior relationships that make problematic decisions (and effects) possible: "To call a decision-making process "undemocratic" is to signal that something is wrong with the relationships it presupposes."[13] The AAP can be deployed to confer influence to correct power imbalances in relationships that threaten domination or usurpation, while avoiding many of the charges of incoherency levelled by skeptics.

Melissa Williams (Chapter 4) is concerned with collective self-determination in a globalized age as well, but she argues that the AAP can only address part of the challenge. The AAP should be understood as a criterion of legitimate democracy: when people are importantly affected by decisions but lack influence, then democratic legitimacy is at stake. But, she argues, the AAP does not offer guidance on the prior problem of constructing a legitimate democratic order. Williams writes that:

democracy requires more than constraints on the exercise of political power [for which the AAP offers useful guidance]; it also requires the capacity to generate political power, that is, the capacity to produce binding (i.e. coercive) collective decisions aimed at advancing common interests [on which the AAP does not guide].[14]

On that second, prior, and perhaps more fundamental question, Williams argues that we should utilize a conception of constituent power that transcends territorial boundaries. Constituent power is constructed by people who "freely associate with the purpose of instituting an institutional order that is capable of generating binding collective decisions aimed at advancing common interests."[15] In the twenty-first century, this might be done by people living in many different countries who are, for example, vulnerable to the effects of climate change or members of communities that transcend state boundaries, as is the case with many Indigenous communities.

Anna Stilz provides an important counterpoint in Chapter 5 by developing several potent criticisms of the APP. Stilz acknowledges that those people affected by a decision may sometimes be entitled to a voice. But she argues that "affectedness" is not a strong basis for protecting important, justice-related interests. First, inclusive democratic procedures can be problematically fickle. In some cases, minorities (e.g. Indigenous Navaho people in the larger American polity) might simply lack the votes to defend their interests, while in other cases, especially those at the larger scale of including everyone at a continental or even global level, people might lack the information and media infrastructure necessary to know how to use their voice to defend their interests. Second, Stilz responds to some of the authors in this volume – Gray, Warren, and Gould – who claim that the AAP is important to achieving democratic *self-determination*. Against this claim, Stilz argues that AAP could jeopardize self-determination. Genuine self-determination begins with a group of people who share values and priorities – who share a "political will" – and govern themselves accordingly. The All-Affected Principle can undermine such a group's self-determination by granting those outside the group – who are affected but do not share their political will – influence over the self-determining group's decisions. Third and finally, Stilz questions the relationship between self-determination and influence within a community or group. Influence in the form of equal voting is not necessary for a group to be legitimately self-determining, Stilz argues. Many associations – churches, universities, corporations, and schools – are legitimately self-determining but not directly democratic, and this is perfectly compatible with the dictates of justice, even if it rubs some democrats the wrong way.

MEMBERSHIP WITHIN AND BEYOND BORDERS

Robert Dahl's quip that perhaps people in Latin America should be able to participate in elections in the United States remains resonant because it is paradoxical. On one hand, the proposal is absurd because, among other things, such expansion would add billions of people to the US electorate and severely dilute the franchise of US citizens. On the other hand, it seems undeniable that US military, economic, environmental, and immigration policy has affected adversely many people outside of US territorial borders and that those people have good cause for complaint. The authors in the second part of this collection explore the extent to which the All-Affected Principle can help to address some of the challenges that borders create for democratic theory. In different ways, each of the chapters illustrates how the AAP can contribute to – and in ways complicate – our understanding of membership and boundaries.

Revisiting his seminal work on immigration through the lens of affectedness, Joseph H. Carens (Chapter 6) argues that "the most important questions are not about who should participate in decisions but about what those decisions should be." When it comes to regulating migration and freedom of movement, there are "moral constraints on the acceptable range of decisions about immigration policies and immigration regimes" that have little to do with democratic inclusion.[16] Instead, Carens reasons that the primary issues in immigration policy concern human rights and justice rather than participation in decision making. If the AAP plays any role as a principle of democracy, it is as a limited trigger, supplement, or reinforcement of more fundamental principles of justice. For example, Carens believes that settled immigrants should be able to participate in the political decisions of the jurisdictions where they have migrated and now live. Not being able to do so would clearly violate the AAP. But Carens views that participation as a component of the citizenship to which long-term immigrants should have access. Similarly, Carens agrees with scholars like Arash Abidzadeh[17] that the AAP could be used to support the claims of *potential* migrants to having a voice in the border controls of receiving countries: "states are not morally entitled to decide unilaterally on immigration matters because border controls greatly affect the excluded."[18]

Analogously, Laura Valentini argues in Chapter 7 that while " "affected interests" should be taken into account in political decision making pretty much across the board," the AAP does not provide a general principle for boundary drawing. It can neither guide reasoning about what is most important in cross-boundary governance disputes nor ground the allocation of decision-making entitlements.[19] Rather than treating democracy – in the AAP or some other variant – as the ultimate value to be realized in devising governance institutions, we should instead ask what the most important values are in a particular context of governance. Drawing on her own personal experiences with the Brexit referendum in the United Kingdom in 2015, Valentini notes that she was greatly affected by this decision but as a noncitizen could not participate. Should she have been able to do so? Valentini concludes that she was entitled to some influence in the Brexit case, not because she was affected per se, but because she was a contributor (along with others in her position) to broader cooperative arrangements that sustain the UK, and participants to cooperative arrangements should have a right to determine changes to those arrangements. So, while Valentini should have been entitled to a voice, morally speaking, it wasn't because of her "affectedness" alone.

In Chapter 8, Tomer Perry deploys the AAP as a principle that calls for the periodic revision of boundary questions. The history of nations is replete with struggles to establish, abandon, or adjust boundaries. In the early twenty-first century, for example, such struggles appear in countries in the Middle East, regions of the UK, and Catalonia. Perry argues that contestation over borders should be normalized so that boundary adjustments are more regular, less turbulent, and governed by democratic considerations and perhaps even procedures. In this context, the AAP can provide a triggering standard for a boundary reconsideration. When a group of people cannot gain the influence necessary to defend their interests in the face of governmental decisions, it may be time for them – and their current compatriots – to consider whether they live in a democratically appropriate geography.

TAMING ECONOMIC POWER

One of the great insults to democracy in the late twentieth and early twenty-first centuries is the power of large economic organizations that escape meaningful control by territorial democracies and so, by extension, the citizens of those governments. J. K. Galbraith's early twentieth-century vision of government as a countervailing power that could discipline the concentrated economic might of corporations is, at best, a frustrated project.[20] That reality lies at enormous variance with a common ideal in democratic theory: that citizens operating through their constituted government make laws that regulate their interactions, including the complex nexus of economic and social interactions that produce multinational corporations. Instead, a decision taken in a boardroom in one country can reverberate across the globe. And some companies whose operations span many countries cannot be easily regulated by any government. As Elizabeth Anderson[21] and others have argued, companies can also exercise dictatorial powers over their employees that contravene democratic standards in the workplace. Within countries and across the boundaries that separate them, the AAP offers points of departure to examine how power stemming from economic conglomeration and interaction ought to be subjected to democratic control.

In Chapter 9, Carol Gould writes that "the main function of the All-Affected Principle is to address just these sorts of exogenous impacts of [corporate] decisions."[22] Specifically, the AAP justifies what Gould regards as a more ideal economic ordering: worker management of firms. Though in previous work, Gould favors a different grounding – her own shared activities principle – she argues that the AAP similarly supports economic democracy. When individuals are engaged in densely cooperative activities such as making things or providing services in firms, countless decisions about workplace organization, the division of labor, strategy, the distribution of gains and losses, and many other issues affect the interests of those working there. The logic of the AAP indicates that workers ought to be able to exercise influence over such decisions. Worker management is a direct way to confer such influence, but arguably workers might also exercise influence indirectly by advocating for protective laws and regulations. This use of the AAP does not merely indicate fundamental violations, but also points the way to an ambitious reconstruction of economic arrangements in a more democratic direction.

Like Gould, Terry Macdonald (Chapter 10) also argues that democratic voice and influence should track (among other vectors of power and interest) economic activities. However, Macdonald's realism requires democratic arrangements that are even more demanding than worker management of firms. The companies involved in global supply chains – think, for example, of extractive industries – take actions with profound consequences for people living in communities where they operate. Often, local and national governments are more beholden to those companies than they are to their own citizens. So, residents of affected communities are entitled to bypass their governments and should be directly included in corporate regulation. But on Macdonald's account, the locus of decision making around economic activities is broader than firms. Governance of multinational supply chains involves a complex of organizations that encompasses not just firms, but also governments, international multi-stakeholder nongovernmental organizations (INGOs), and an array of advocacy and community-based organizations. While there is no specific democratic blueprint for achieving appropriate voice and inclusion for such highly varied and complicated configurations of governance, Macdonald nevertheless suggests that a standard of democratic legitimacy ought to apply. The central question should be whether these arrangements "empower the exercise of collective political agency on terms that are inclusive of affected individuals."[23]

As evidenced by the discussion above, the AAP is usually applied to questions of collective decision making: who should be included in the decisions of a government or corporation, for example. Thomas Christiano and Melissa Lane depart from this path-more-travelled to generate normative insights about standards that ought to apply when individuals' important interests are affected in other ways.

In the marketplace, for example, most our vital interests are affected by the bargains and agreements that we strike with other individuals in decentralized transactions or with the bosses who hire us. In Chapter 11, Christiano explores the proposition that these bargains ought to be regulated by the AAP. An attractive standard is that an individual's bargaining power is proportionate to the extent to which their interests are affected in a particular bargain. The sad irony is that, as Karl Marx observed, in such transactions the party with more at stake typically has less bargaining power. This is *because*, often part of what it means to have more at stake is that one's alternatives to a negotiated outcome are worse than those of the counterparty. So, a low-income worker probably has much more at stake (putting food on the table, making rent) in getting hired than the restaurant franchiser has in hiring them. In part because of that vulnerability, the franchiser has more power (and influence) over the bargain and their interests are less affected (they typically have the option of hiring other workers, and even being down one worker is less important than missing meals or being evicted). Christiano surveys several ways to remedy this failure, including redistributing resources to increase the bargaining power of those who are economically disadvantaged, regulating employers directly, regulating bargaining process through (for example) laws governing collective bargaining, and collectivizing workplaces through the kinds of worker management initiatives that Gould recommends.

Many applications of the All-Affected Principle trace specific decisions, or the actions of decision-making bodies, to affected individuals. Melissa Lane offers climate change as a problem setting in which such causal attribution is inappropriate because the interactions are complicated, numerous, and stretch through centuries. With greenhouse gas (GHG) emissions, everyone in the world is both affecting (because we all conduct ourselves in ways that cause GHG emissions) and affected (because we're all subject to the effects of climate change). Nevertheless, Lane argues that the AAP demands that those who are most affected by climate change (and the GHG emissions that cause it) have a right to greater consideration and influence. One innovation in Lane's chapter is to present two distinct ways of reckoning climate change "affectedness." The first is to suppose that every individual on earth (and perhaps those in future generations) has a property right to an equal per-capita share of the common global carbon budget. Through this lens, the property rights of the peoples of poor countries in the global carbon budget have been violated – and so their interests have been importantly affected – by those living in wealthy countries through centuries of complex uneven economic development and current economic dynamics. Climate change also affects important interests by causing harm and creating risks of harm through severe weather, flooding, temperature rise, and other changes. Lane develops harm, and risk of harm, as a second way of determining who is most affected by climate change and greenhouse gas emissions. Following the logic of the AAP, those who are affected by having their property rights in the global carbon budget violated and those affected by suffering the harms of climate change (one tragedy of climate change is that these two groups overlap heavily) ought to be able to exercise influence to defend their interests by securing "compensation as well as mitigation and support for adaptation."[24]

AUTONOMY, AFFECTEDNESS, AND ASSOCIATIONS

In the final part of the volume, our authors consider the role of civil society organizations and their role as potential sites of governance and thus of democratization. Should private philanthropies, charities, and other civic groups be governed democratically? If so, why, and what are the appropriate standards and arrangements for democratic governance? One long line of thought stretching back to Alexis de Tocqueville emphasizes the benefits of democratic associations for democracy broadly.[25] But others have argued that democracy flourishes with associations that choose how to govern themselves in many different ways – including nondemocratically – so long as they do not violate duties of justice to their members.[26] The three chapters in this section investigate the application of the AAP to the problems of associative governance in the twenty-first century.

The contributions by Clarissa Hayward, Emma Saunders-Hastings and Rob Reich, and Jennifer Rubenstein operate squarely in the domain of nonideal theory. These three chapters are highly attentive to the ways in which associations operating against a background of unjust distribution of power and resources can reinforce or amplify injustice. Indeed, the existence of some associations – such as philanthropies dedicated to relieving deprivation in developing, often postcolonial, societies or antiracist social movement associations – practically presumes the existence of substantial background injustice (e.g. global economic injustice or structural racism). While the application of the AAP to associations might be superfluous or counterproductive under more just global or national conditions, it might be that the AAP can provide important ways to vindicate those who are negatively affected by associational activity under nonideal circumstances.

In Chapter 13, Clarissa Hayward takes on this challenge in the face of racial and economic injustice in public education in the United States. Local self-determination is a common justification for local control and financing of education in the United States. But against a backdrop in which some communities are very wealthy and others poor, and in which many school districts are de facto segregated by race, treating school districts as largely autonomous self-governing associations reinforces racial and economic injustice. This amplification of injustice occurs not through intentional and deliberate decisions of school boards and local communities, but rather through a complex nexus of some decisions, but also many nondecisions, taken by school boards, zoning commissions, transit authorities, real estate agents, banks, companies, and many others. While the AAP is most commonly deployed to analyze exclusion in decision making, Hayward argues that the "affecting" that results from this nexus of nondecisions, norms, and ongoing relations of domination is often far more important. So, like Gray earlier, Hayward argues that the AAP should track power – especially structural power – rather than decisions in order to accurately determine patterns of affectedness. Doing so in the case of educational inequality, Hayward suggests a range of reforms that would allow residents of disadvantaged school districts to exercise more influence over regional educational decisions such as regional governance and more fairly distributing resources to fund public education.

The contributions from Saunders-Hastings and Reich (Chapter 14) and from Jennifer Rubenstein (Chapter 15) examine the application of the AAP to altruistic associations that are intended to benefit others such as philanthropies and social justice groups that are led by advantaged people. One critical and novel observation, developed especially by Saunders-Hastings and Reich, is that the rationale for many such groups would disappear if ideal conditions of justice were somehow achieved, because many of these groups aim primarily to rectify injustice and its consequences. In the international development domain, aid organizations and philanthropies seek to address health, education, and other welfare challenges that result from global inequality and injustice. Within countries, many social justice organizations aim – as the category suggests – to rectify injustice. So, even if one thinks that the AAP should be limited to political institutions or that the AAP is superfluous once the ideal requirements of justice have been satisfied, the principle may nevertheless be important in establishing the standards and obligations of philanthropies and social justice organizations, which often presume quite nonideal conditions. Put another way, a philanthropy operating under circumstances of justice *might* be able to respond to a disadvantaged beneficiary that they need not exercise influence over the philanthropy's decisions because they have had the opportunity to exercise that influence by regulating how philanthropies operate, to whom they are held accountable, and how they protect beneficiaries' interests through the democratic political process. But many actually existing philanthropies – in both domestic and international contexts – operate to benefit people who cannot exercise such influence because unjust circumstances exclude them from political processes. Thus, neither philanthropists nor analysts of philanthropy can rely on the luxury of the political opportunities that would be provided under more circumstances to rebut the claims of affected beneficiaries that they should be able to exercise greater influence over their decisions. These claims are rooted in the AAP operating under nonideal conditions.

In their contribution, Saunders-Hastings and Reich argue that global philanthropies working in international development should subject themselves to the AAP by empowering affected beneficiaries to influence philanthropic decisions and policies. That voice would enable affected "beneficiaries" to defend themselves against harms wrought by wealthy and distant philanthropists. The chapter offers the striking example of giving by the Bill and Melinda Gates Foundation to address AIDS/HIV in Botswana. As a result of some $100 million to support treatment and care, deaths from AIDS fell significantly. But, at the same time, infant mortality grew and maternal mortality spiked. Some argue that Gates Foundation beneficence drew doctors and other healthcare workers away from primary care and towards AIDS/HIV treatment (AIDS work funded by the foundation paid far more than prevailing rates). Worse, the technocratic approach of the Gates Foundation afforded little opportunity for those in Botswana who suffered the consequences of these decisions to exercise influence.

Even if the decisions of the Gates Foundation and other philanthropists caused no harm and only increased welfare (which is clearly not the case), Saunders-Hastings and Reich argue that the Gates Foundation should still adhere to the AAP by affording influence to beneficiaries. Their *intrinsic* case for the AAP in the domain of philanthropy relies on the principle of anti-paternalism. When philanthropists make grants in order to advance the interests of beneficiaries, they disrespect those beneficiaries when they fail to include them in the determination of which interests should be advanced and how to do so. This sort of AAP disregarding philanthropy is a "failure to show respect for autonomous agents and a threat to relations of equality" and so "philanthropy is something that should be *done with* rather than *done to* the people who benefit from it," they write.[27]

Sharing this concern about paternalism and ways in which the AAP might respond, Jennifer Rubenstein explores the inverse of the AAP: those unaffected by a decision or action should not have influence over it. Rubenstein dubs this inverse the "exclusive face" of the AAP and argues that it has special bite in the case of altruistic organizations – those that seek to advance the interests of others – such as philanthropies and elite-led social justice organizations. Whereas most reflection on the AAP examines its "inclusive face," how individuals, such as philanthropy's beneficiaries, should have voice in organizational decisions, the "exclusive face has much more radical implications."[28] In some cases, it suggests that INGOs should simply not exist, at least not in anything like their current form. Insofar as they serve important functions, those should be taken over by local organizations, run by people who are significantly affected by the issues that INGOs address.

***

The circumstances of human association and the challenges we face in the early twenty-first century are far different from those of the eighteenth, nineteenth, and even mid-twentieth centuries. Many of the threats we face, such as pandemic viruses and climate destruction, are truly global in scope. They are global in part due to intensified economic, social, and political interconnectedness and interdependence. At the same time, it is clear that the hierarchical model of democratic governance – with states exercising supreme power to regulate the conduct, not only of individuals, but also corporations and nongovernmental associations – does not reflect a reality that is moving further from the image of nation-state supremacy. Instead, our present circumstances seem closer to a version of Robert Dahl's polyarchy. Power is exercised not just by states, but also irreducibly by firms, other organizations, and by governments of territories both larger and smaller than those of nations.

The authors of the chapters in this volume bring renewed attention to a principle of democratic governance that has been present since the dawn of democracy, but largely in the background of democratic theory and political philosophy. Rather than offering a single account or formulation of the AAP that displaces other conceptions or principles of democracy, the collective aim of the authors is more modest. These contributions develop several different variations of the AAP, explore whether the AAP can advance our democratic understandings and commitments across a wide range of social, economic, and political governance challenges, and seek to understand the AAP's limitations. We hope that these insights aid others in their efforts to understand and improve the theory and practice of democracy in many corners of public and private life. Only then will we be able to adequately respond to the many McHooligans of this world.

NOTES

1 Neal Stephenson, *Termination Shock: A Novel* (New York: Harper Collins, 2021). The billionaire's real name in the novel is T. R. Schmidt.
2 David Keith, "What's the Least Bad Way to Cool the Planet?" *New York Times*, October 1, 2021 (accessed March 3, 2022). www.nytimes.com/2021/10/01/opinion/climate-change-geoengineering.html.
3 This principle is elsewhere referred to as the "All Affected Interests Principle" or the "Principle of Affected Interests." In this book, we prefer the more compact "All-Affected Principle," since it doesn't smuggle in any controversial or contested claims that stand in need of argument (such as that having one's "interests" affected is the best formulation of the All-Affected Principle).
4 Robert A. Dahl, *After the Revolution? Authority in a Good Society* (New Haven: Yale University Press, 1970), p. 49.
5 Dahl, *After the Revolution?*, pp. 49–51.
6 Dahl, *After the Revolution?*, p. 51.
7 Robert E. Goodin, "Enfranchising All Affected Interests, and Its Alternatives," *Philosophy and Public Affairs* 35, no. 1 (2007): 40–68.
8 See, for example, Harry Brighouse and Marc Fleurbaey, "Democracy and Proportionality," *The Journal of Political Philosophy* 18, no. 2 (2010): 137–55.
9 Dahl, *After the Revolution?*, p. 50.
10 Gould, Chapter 9, p. 165.
11 John Locke, *Two Treatises of Government*, ed. Peter Laslett (New York: Cambridge University Press [1689] 2003); Jean-Jacques Rousseau, "The Social Contract," in

The Social Contract and Other Later Political Writings, ed. Victor Gourevitch (New York: Cambridge University Press, [1762] 2012).

12 Goodin, "Enfranchising All Affected Interests, and Its Alternatives."

13 Gray, Chapter 3, p. 61.

14 Williams, Chapter 4, p. 77.

15 Williams, Chapter 4, p. 85.

16 Carens, Chapter 6, p. 111.

17 See Arash Abizadeh, "Democratic Theory and Border Coercion: No Right to Unilaterally Control Your Own Borders," *Political Theory* 36, no. 1 (2008): 37–65.

18 Carens, Chapter 6, p. 123.

19 Valentini, Chapter 7, p. 136.

20 John Kenneth Galbraith, *American Capitalism: The Concept of Countervailing Power* (New York: Routledge, [1952] 2017).

21 See Elizabeth Anderson, *Private Government: How Employers Rule Our Lives (and Why We Don't Talk about It)* (Princeton, NJ: Princeton University Press, 2017).

22 Gould, Chapter 9, p. 165.

23 Macdonald, Chapter 10, p. 191.

24 Lane, Chapter 12, p. 216.

25 See, among others, Joshua Cohen and Joel Rogers, "Secondary Associations and Democratic Governance," in *Associations and Democracy*, ed. Eric Olin Wright (London: Verso, 1995); Robert Putnam, *Bowling Alone: The Collapse and Revival of American Community* (New York: Simone and Schuster, 2000); and Mark E. Warren, *Democracy and Association* (Princeton, NJ: Princeton University Press, 2001).

26 See, for example, Nancy Rosenblum, *Membership and Morals: The Personal Uses of Pluralism in America* (Princeton, NJ: Princeton University Press, 1998).

27 Saunders-Hastings and Reich, Chapter 14, p. 259.

28 Rubenstein, Chapter 15, p. 266.

PART I

SUBJECTION, INTERACTION, POWER, AND DOMINATION

I

Proximity Principle, Adieu[*]

Robert E. Goodin

Assuming the right to vote is of instrumental value to those possessing it, it is hardly surprising that those who already have it resist extending it to others. Doing so would simply water down the power of their own votes, after all. Such was the history of electoral reform in nineteenth-century Britain. In the run-up to the Great Reform Act of 1832, the *Poor Man's Guardian* editorialized, "We cannot think so ill of human nature as to think that those who will ... have gained their own freedom will not aid us to gain ours." But it was not to be. "Middle-class people, once given the vote, wanted to conserve institutions which they had formerly been inclined to attack."[1] Having secured voting rights for themselves, they were in no hurry to extend them to others.

Today, too, principled arguments for letting foreigners who are strongly affected by our elections have a say in them are met with something akin to slack-jawed incredulity.[2] People seem rigidly committed to keeping the franchise just as it is.[3] Pressed for a principled reason, they sometimes say that (all but only) those people who would be bound by a law should get a say in the making of it. But when shown that that principle too would imply a far more extensive franchise than at present,[4] people tend to back off that principle quick-smart. Even benighted ethno-nationalist rationales for expanding the demos meet with the same fate. In 1887, staunchly conservative A. V. Dicey (backed by James Bryce, H. G. Wells, and Andrew Carnegie) proposed a political union of white Anglo-American peoples worldwide. Dicey was dumbfounded when,[5] despite the celebrity of his recently published *Law of the Constitution*,[6] that proposal gained absolutely no traction. The bottom line seems to be this: Principles be damned; people insistently want to keep the electorate just as it is.

It is not unduly cynical to suspect that what's at work behind all those reactions is protection of existing privilege, just as it was in nineteenth-century Britain. But perhaps we can, and should, try to do better than that on behalf of those opposing our principled reasons for expanding the franchise. I think there *is* (or anyway once was) a respectable principled reason for a geographically delimited franchise of just the sort that presently prevails and people still seem to cherish. That is the Principle of Proximity.[7]

In the first three sections, I show why the Proximity Principle might once have appealed. But I conclude that proximity was only ever just a proxy for other things that morally matter. In earlier days, physical proximity was indeed a good proxy for those other things, and a geographically bounded franchise was morally broadly justified in consequence.[8] But nowadays physical proximity has ceased to be a particularly good proxy for those other things that morally matter, which now warrant extending the franchise beyond traditional territorial boundaries.

Like the Proximity Principle, its more apt modern rivals – the All-Affected and the All-Subjected Principles – pertain purely to the franchise. They tell us who should have a vote on matters that we should settle by a vote. What those things are, and indeed whether we should settle anything by democratic voting and if so with what structure, must be determined by altogether separate normative principles. Those are the subject of the fourth section.

THE STATUS QUO: GEOGRAPHICALLY DELIMITED ELECTORATES

When political theorists talk about who should properly be allowed to vote in a state's elections, they tellingly refer to that as "the boundary problem."[9] Boundaries are, first and foremost, lines on the map (and all too often fortifications on the ground). They demarcate, first and foremost, territory. They are, first and foremost, geographical concepts. To equate the issue of who should have a right to vote with the issue of where the geographical boundaries should be drawn is to suggest that, first and foremost (if not perhaps exclusively), locational considerations should determine who is included in and who is excluded from the self-governing demos.

Of course, not everyone inside a state's borders is necessarily entitled to vote. Children are not, for one reason; foreigners just passing through are not, for another; aliens who are permanent residents are typically not, for yet another. And, of course, some people outside the state's borders are entitled to vote in that state's elections (initially just the state's soldiers stationed abroad but subsequently extended to pretty much all citizens living abroad).[10] So there is no one-for-one matching of place of residence and right to vote.

Still, those are exceptions that prove the rule. Electorates are, for much the greatest part, geographically determined. Just as the state is defined territorially so too is the demos.[11] From a democratic perspective, the latter might seem to follow straightforwardly from the former. Democratic self-government requires that we have a say in how we are governed, and if the state that governs us is geographically delimited, then who has a democratic say in that government should be likewise. While that logic may have held good in previous times, it does no longer, I shall argue.

THE RATIONALE: THE PROXIMITY PRINCIPLE

By and large, the people around us are typically like us in various ways that may matter to us. We speak of "our nearest and dearest," as if the simple fact of "being near" makes them "dear" to us.[12] If that were all there was to the matter, the Proximity Principle would reduce without remainder to the Affinity Principle[13] – the reason we should make decisions by voting together with people near to us is that we like being together. Of course, that is not always true (recall that other old adage "good fences make good neighbors"). But maybe it's true often enough to explain away much of the Proximity Principle's apparent appeal.

But there is something else lying behind the Proximity Principle that is of much greater moral importance.[14] Living nearby to one another tends to have four salient consequences. Proximity is likely to increase:

- the *frequency* of your interactions;
- the *range* of your interactions;
- the *depth* of your interactions; and
- the *certainty* of your interacting.

Of course, once again there is no strict necessity in any of that. You might be relatively certain of having frequent, but not remotely deep, interactions with some near neighbors on a wide range of matters. (Relations with the people living next door are often like that.) You might be relatively certain of having only occasional but deep interactions on a narrow range of matters with other near neighbors (your family's mortician, for example). And there may be others who live nearby with whom your interactions have literally none of these features. Conversely, it's perfectly possible for you to be pretty certain of having frequent and deep interactions with distant others on a wide range of matters (your grown children living abroad, for example). So it is just contingently the case that these things are often (but not invariably) associated with, and indeed arise from, living in close proximity to one another. Still, the generalization may be true enough in a wide range of cases.

Each of those features is of consequentialist concern. Each taken separately (still more all of them taken together) is likely to make interactions with those living nearby generally more important to you in purely consequential terms.[15] Again, it's perfectly possible for a one-off, unlikely interaction on some narrow matter (with your oncologist, for example) to be much more important to you, both objectively and subjectively, than other interactions that are more frequent, certain, and wide-ranging. So, again, there is no strict necessity in it. Still, it's a relatively safe generalization that interactions displaying these features – which interactions with those living nearby ordinarily do – are ordinarily more important to us, for purely consequentialist reasons.

The "Mutual Interest in What One Another Does" Rationale

That, in turn, constitutes a prima facie case for us making decisions shaping the nature and content of those interactions jointly, in one way or another. That need not necessarily be through explicitly joint decision processes, still less by taking a vote. Nevertheless, if it matters a fair bit to me what you do, and it matters a fair bit to you what I do, then there is likely to be some considerable scope for each of us to improve the outcome from our own perspective by making our decisions at least partially in light of one another's preferences. It may be no more than a matter of realizing mutual benefits through simple coordination. Or it may be a matter of gains from trade where our preferences are more divergent.

The point is simply that where it matters to us what others do (as it typically does where people in close proximity are concerned), we are likely to want to make something more like a joint decision as to what each of us will do, in light of the preferences of each for what the others do. One way of accomplishing that is by sharing with one another decisional power (voting rights being one particularly salient form) over enforceable rules that shape the actions of all of us.[16]

That is the first broadly consequentialist argument for thinking that those in close proximity to one another should form a single decision-making body (at least for certain purposes) in which each has a say.[17]

The "Efficiency" Rationale

The second argument for that proposition builds on the efficiencies of having some regularized procedures for making decisions that are binding on a set of people who are relatively certain to be recurringly involved in relatively frequent, deep, and wide-ranging interactions with one another. The argument here is akin to Coase's theory of the firm and Simon's theory of the employment relationship.[18] The root idea in both cases is that instead of buying inputs into our production process (including workers) on a spot market, it can sometimes be more efficient to internalize the production of those inputs within our own firm. That provides a rational for "hiring rather than buying" in the case of Coase's firm, and for entering into a long-term employment contract with workers (rather than hiring day laborers at the employment exchange) in the case of Simon's employment relationship.

An analogous argument might apply to establishing relations of political authority among people who live in close proximity to one another and, because of that, are relatively certain to have frequent, deep, and wide-ranging interactions with one another. Such people could, of course, enter into bilateral negotiations with each of their neighbors on each occasion disputes or opportunities for mutually beneficial cooperative action arise. But if such occasions recur frequently, it is far more efficient to develop some standing rules that will be applied relatively automatically on each occasion as appropriate.[19]

The same efficiency argument also tells in favor of applying such rules to all those among whom such situations are likely to recur.

This is not yet an argument about whom to give a vote to. So far, it is merely an argument concerning the scope of political authority. It says merely that, purely for reasons of efficiency, people who live proximately to one another should be governed by the same political authority, insofar as their living proximately to one another gives rise to relatively certain, frequent, deep, and wide-ranging interactions recurring among them that it would be mutually advantageous for them to regulate through some system of rules that is common to all of them.[20]

But suppose we also think, for some other sorts of reasons,[21] that people should have a democratic say in the making of the rules governing them. Then that, combined with this argument about the scope of political authority, gives rise to the proposition that everyone governed by that authority should have a right to a vote on what laws are enacted by that authority. And insofar as the earlier argument justified extending the scope of that authority to people who live in relatively close proximity to one another, this argument provides justification for also giving a vote to people who live in relatively close proximity to one another.[22] That is the second broadly consequentialist argument for the Principle of Proximity.

What the Two Rationales Have in Common

Different though these rationales are in other respects, in both cases their justification for giving a right to vote to people who live geographically near to one another hinges on the contingent truth of an empirical proposition about the likely consequences of living in close proximity. Both rationales crucially assume that the interactions among people living in close proximity are empirically likely to be different (more frequent, more wide-ranging, deeper, more certain) than with others living at greater distances.

Where that empirical proposition holds true, those would indeed be good arguments for making decisions together with those living in close proximity to you. But everything depends crucially on whether, and to what extent, that empirical presupposition holds true. Once perhaps it did, but it largely does no longer.

THE WANING SIGNIFICANCE OF PROXIMITY

Imagine a world of closed communities hemmed in by imposing natural barriers that prevent individuals from interacting closely with anyone living more than 1,000 miles away. But suppose that they interact intensively with everyone within that distance. Suppose, too, that (either in consequence of that same natural necessity or as a matter of deliberate policy) the political authorities govern those communities in such a way that nothing they do affects or is affected by anyone else outside their territory. Think, perhaps, of Japan in the period just before Commodore Perry's arrival.[23]

In cases like that, the Principle of Proximity, the All-Affected Principle, and the All-Subjected Principle would all point in the same direction. As per the Principle of Proximity, people would interact in the requisite way only with people relatively near to them on the islands of the Japanese homeland. As per the All-Affected Principle, what happens in Japan affects only people in Japan. As per the All-Subjected Principle, the laws of Japan are applied only to people in Japan. So all three principles dictate that, insofar as Japan aspires to be a democracy (which, of course, it did not in that period), everyone in Japan should be entitled to vote in Japanese elections. But none of those principles would say that anyone outside of Japan should be so entitled.[24]

Globalization and Action at a Distance

Just how empirically realistic is that scenario, however? One might easily imagine it to have been true in some mythic past. One might – until one reflects upon all the great empires of antiquity. One might imagine that things were more like that in the Middle Ages.[25] But even then, there were clear exceptions. It's not just the Carolingian Empire and the Hanseatic League. Even the Vikings ranged from Greenland well into Asia Minor, not just as marauders but also as settlers governing their extended community according to shared ancestral traditions and norms.[26] In short, we are all too often tempted to think that "everything changed with globalization," and that that happened only within living memory. But globalization of a recognizably contemporary sort can clearly be found much earlier – certainly in the nineteenth century, if not before.[27]

In any case, globalization is now firmly upon us. In myriad ways, we have increasingly great capacity, increasingly utilized, to impact the lives of others far away.[28] Interdependence is the order of the day.[29] Action at a distance, which Einstein in another context dubbed "spooky," is now a fact of daily life.

The action at a distance that has come to characterize today's globalization may well be driven largely by socioeconomic actors. But states, even when they are not the prime movers, are often essential facilitators; and insofar as they are, what one state does affects a great many people outside its borders. Whenever that is the case, the All-Affected Principle would dictate that all those worldwide who are significantly affected by a state's policy should have a say in the making of that policy. Add to this all those who are directly affected by a state's policy in waging war, dumping agricultural surpluses, and so on. That is why scholars rightly suspect that, given the realities of the globalized world, the All-Affected Principle, systematically applied, would have seriously expansionary effects on the franchise, at least in all the major countries of the world.[30]

The increased capacity for action at a distance, both on the part of would-be perpetrators of offenses against a state and on the part of the state in resisting them, has also given rise to an increasing tendency for states to write their laws in such a way that they apply to people who are neither that state's citizens nor in that state's territory.[31] Details vary from state to state, of course. But most states claim at least some rights to criminalize, within their own legal code, actions of distant foreigners that would undermine the state's security. For a quaint example, states have conventionally claimed a right to prosecute anyone found counterfeiting their currency or their seal, wherever that counterfeiting occurs.[32] For a contemporary example, states often now claim a right to prosecute the planning, assisting, or carrying out of acts of terrorism by anyone anywhere in the world – generalizing the long-standing right that states claimed to prosecute people of whatever nationality engaging in piracy anywhere in the world.[33] Given those facts about state practice – the jurisdictional claims that they make, the range of people they purport to bind by their laws – a great many foreigners abroad should, under the All-Subjected Principle as well, have a right to vote in the making of such a state's laws (at least on *those* laws).

Implications for the Proximity Principle

What gives both the All-Affected and the All-Subjected Principles those expansionary implications for the franchise are new capacities for (and realities of) action at a distance. It simply is no longer necessarily the case, if ever it was, that we are only strongly affected by the actions of people geographically proximate to us. It is no longer necessarily the case, if ever it was, that we are subject exclusively to the laws of the state with authority over the physical space that we inhabit.

Those new realities mean that the empirical assumptions upon which the Proximity Principle rests can no longer be taken for granted. It is simply not necessarily true that we are most certain of being most frequently impacted in the deepest and most wide-ranging way by our interactions with those who are physically proximate to us.

Proximity was only ever a mere placeholder for those other features that are (or, rather, used to be) strongly but only contingently associated with it. Those features, and what follows from them, are what really matter morally. Physical proximity, as such, does not. Insofar as proximity has now become disassociated from those other features, and is no longer a good proxy for them, we no longer have any good reason to confine our political jurisdictions or our democratic electorates to people who live physically proximately to one another.

Abandoning proximity as a poor proxy, we are forced back to judging those matters in terms of the features that really matter – the frequency, depth, range, and certainty of interactions among people. If we systematically have interactions with distant others of requisite frequency, depth, range, and certainty (and if we think our collective affairs should be run in a democratic way at all), then we ought to extend a right to vote in our elections to those distant others for precisely the same reasons the Principle of Proximity used to tell us to extend such a right to our near neighbors.[34]

It is an empirical question to what extent distant others really are affected in these relevant respects by the laws enacted by any given state. Distant others will, of course, be more affected in these respects by some laws more than others. The same is, however, true of citizens in any existing state. They are more strongly affected by some laws than others, but we nonetheless think they should have a right to a vote, the *same one* vote, on all of their state's laws. Below I shall argue that we may want to apply the same principle within expanded jurisdictional authorities of the sort I propose.

Or, again, it may turn out that distant others are not affected in the relevant ways by a *large enough proportion* of a state's laws to justify giving them a right to vote on all the laws enacted by that state.[35] Even so, there may well be a case for giving the distant others a vote on specific sorts of laws that do systematically affect them in the relevant respects. Federal systems with devolved authority over some matters do that all the time. There may well be a good case for constructing any expanded jurisdictional authority on the same model, as I shall also argue below.

OTHER NORMATIVE PRINCIPLES AND THEIR NATURAL EXTENSIONS

The Proximity, All-Affected, and All-Subjected Principles all fundamentally serve to answer the same question: "*Who* should be governed together with one another, under a common body of laws?" *How* they are to be governed is a separate matter. That must typically be settled by *other* normative principles.[36]

When extending jurisdictional authority beyond tightly confined geographical spaces, as I have argued we must, we should presumably use the same normative principles for determining how that expanded polity is to be governed as we have traditionally used for governing the existing polity. There are three such principles of interest here. One is the principle that that authority should be exercised in a democratic manner. Another is the principle of "limited government," according to which there should be a private realm into which public decisions should not intrude. Third is the principle of decentralization, according to which decisions that can most effectively and efficiently be made and implemented locally should be made locally, and higher levels of government should do only what lower levels of government cannot (or perhaps will not).

Democratic Decision Making

Presumably the expanded polity should be democratic in just the same way and for just the same reasons that the current polity is or should be. Different political theorists specify those differently. Here there is no need to enter into those disputes. Choose whichever democratic theory you prefer. All I need to insist upon, for present purposes, is that you should apply those same democratic principles to the rules of governance for new, extended jurisdictional authority as apply to the current, more restricted jurisdictional authority.

If you opt for the All-Affected Principle or the All-Subjected Principle, those might give you an *extra* reason for deciding things democratically.[37] But it is an extra reason, over and above those reasons that we already have for making decisions democratically in polities presently organized around the Principle of Proximity. They may not be entirely superfluous, but neither are they remotely essential.

Under either of those two principles, it might seem natural to suppose that votes ought be apportioned according to the extent to which people are affected by or subject to the law that is being enacted.[38] If so, then insofar as people vary in either respect, their voting power ought to be proportional to their varying stakes in the issue.[39] Many contributors to this volume seem tempted by that thought.[40]

There are fancy ways in which that might be implemented. Various schemes for "point voting" have been devised.[41] The version most consonant with democratic equality would assign each person an identical number of points per year, which the person concerned can use to "weight" their vote on any given proposition.[42]

That is not what is done in any currently existing democracy. The rule is not "one interest one vote" but, rather, "one person one vote."[43] Here is a way to rationalize that practice, notwithstanding the obvious fact that people's interests vary across different issue areas.

In representative democracy, people vote on who is to represent them on a range of matters. Some people will have greater stakes in some of those matters, others in others. But everyone will, hopefully, have broadly the same stakes as everyone else across the full range of matters that will come before the representatives whom they elect. Insofar as that is the case, giving "one person one vote" for their representative would be vindicated.

That is essentially a "consolidation" strategy. It works because the representatives will be deciding a wide range of matters, some more important to some of their constituents and others more important to others in ways that roughly balance out. Were it a special-purpose jurisdiction (a school board or a water board, for example), that consolidation trick might well not work. There, perhaps, we really would have to figure out some way to apportion or weight votes proportionally to people's differing interests in the specific matters handled by that body. That is in some sense a violation of democratic equality (of "one person one vote" anyway).[44] And it is one that may well not be readily resolved by consolidating across merely a few such special-purpose jurisdictions, since some voters may have more at stake in the matters handled by *all* of those special-purpose bodies.

Hence we might be tempted to assign points in proportion to stakes. Before doing so, however, we had better find some good way of independently assessing how great people's stakes really are. Just asking people to say how great their stakes are would simply invite strategic misrepresentation, designed to get more points with which to (over)weight their votes.

From those reflections follows a clear design desideratum for the new extended polity that I am recommending. To avoid the latter difficulties, it would be better just to give every person one vote and leave it at that. But from the former observation, we know that we can justify doing that only if the new expanded polity has control over a *wide range of matters* across which people's stakes are likely to vary in a suitably counterbalancing way.

Limited Government

Whatever principle we adopt for democratically deciding those things that are to be decided by a vote, there are some things that should not be decided by a vote. Democratic authority is limited authority. Democratic majorities may be sovereign in the public sphere, but there is a private sphere upon which they may not properly intrude.

There are various ways of delimiting and defending that private sphere. Notions of individual rights and autonomy, privacy, and dignity typically come into play there. And some would extend those protections to (at least certain sorts of) associations as well as to natural individuals. Here I need take no stand on any of those issues.[45]

All that matters for present purposes is this. Insofar as we have good reasons for thinking that political authority should be limited in current polities, then those same limitations should continue to apply as we expand political authorities in light of the new realities of globalization and action at a distance.

Decentralization

A final normative desideratum, reflected in current practice virtually everywhere and commended by political theories of many stripes, is that government should be decentralized. That is to say, there should be various tiers of government, some more localized and others less so, standing in some ordered relation with one another; and matters that can efficiently and effectively be handled at the local level should be handled there, with higher-level jurisdictions being responsible only for matters that transcend local boundaries or cannot (or will not) be efficiently and effectively dealt with there.

This is, of course, just the principle of "subsidiarity" familiar from the writings of Althusius and the practice of the European Union.[46] But that makes the principle sound far more arcane than it actually is. Decentralization is the rule pretty much everywhere. Even in notionally unitary states, there is typically a tier of local government that enjoys considerable latitude in deciding matters pertaining to that locale alone.[47]

That is just to say that, over many matters, the Proximity Principle is still roughly right. In many respects, people are still frequently, certainly, and wide-rangingly affected by the activities of people physically proximate to them. Decisions governing those activities should still be made by that smaller, geographically delimited set of people in consequence.[48] With globalization and increasing action at a distance, however, people are in other respects frequently, certainly, and wide-rangingly affected by the activities of people at considerable physical distance from themselves. Decisions governing those activities should be made by the more widespread set of people involved.

We have already acknowledged that the Proximity Principle needs to be relaxed in some such way when consolidating and unifying smaller political units into much more extensive polities, sometimes straddling whole continents. As we created larger and larger political units, however, the smaller and more local units not only remain but also retain some considerable authority to manage their own affairs. We should follow the same practice as we move to expand jurisdictional authority yet further.

The Shape of an Extended Jurisdictional Authority

What would the new expanded polity look like, if designed to respect those same three normative requirements that we think rightly apply to current polities?

First, it will be a limited government. There will be some things that no government, at any level, will be permitted to do. Second, it will be decentralized government with a nested hierarchy of jurisdictional authorities. Higher levels will have authority over only those matters that cannot or will not be attended to effectively and efficiently by lower levels of government. Third, decisions all the way up and down that hierarchy of governments will be made democratically, with everyone within each jurisdictional authority having a right to vote on the decisions of that authority.

Hence, when we are expanding the jurisdictional authority and the democratic demos associated with it for some purposes, we would not be expanding it for all purposes. Matters that are genuinely of purely local concern will still be voted upon purely by members of that more local demos.

The only things that everyone in the extended demos would be voting on are matters that are, indeed, of concern to them all. My proposal for a new expanded polity merely prevents states from doing things that affect others outside their borders, or from subjecting them to their laws, without giving those outsiders a proper say in the making of those laws and policies.[49]

My preferred strategy for doing that, as I have said, is to create a higher tier of limited authority in which everyone extraterritorially affected or subjected has a vote. Assuming that there are sufficiently many and diverse matters with extraterritorial impact of that sort, everyone can just be given a single vote for representatives elected to make laws at that level, precisely as in current representative democracies.[50]

CONCLUSION

To recapitulate, I think the Proximity Principle constitutes the best principled defense that can be given to justify today's geographically delimited franchise. But proximity was only ever a proxy for what is truly of principled concern, and while it may once have been a good proxy, it is no longer. With globalization and the concomitant increase in the capacity for and reality of action at a distance, the same factors that used to tell so strongly in favor of people voting together with those living nearby now tell equally strongly in favor of extending the same rights to distant others who are now similarly affected by and subject to the laws being enacted. As we extend the polity beyond its traditional geographically delimited forms – extending the right to vote as we do, assuming these new polities, like the old, should operate democratically – we can nonetheless retain traditional constraints of limited and multilevel government.

NOTES

* This chapter benefited from discussions with Arash Abizadeh, Jeremy Waldron, and participants at the workshops that generated this book.
1 Michael Brock, *The Great Reform Act* (London: Hutchinson University Library, 1973), p. 319.
2 Robert A. Dahl, *After the Revolution? Authority in a Good Society* (New Haven, CT: Yale University Press, 1970), pp. 64, 68. Cf. Robert E. Goodin, "Enfranchising All Affected Interests, and Its Alternatives," *Philosophy and Public Affairs* 35, no. 1 (2007): 40–68.
3 Others simply deny there are any principled grounds for determining the demos. But then "however impeccable democratic decision-making may be within a given community, the outcomes are ... determined by the previous and inescapably undemocratic decisions that defined the community in the first place," as Frederick G. Whelan says in "Democratic Theory and the Boundary Problem," in *Nomos XXV: Liberal Democracy*, ed. J. R. Pennock and J. W. Chapman (New York: New York University Press, 1983), p. 41. The same is true in trumps of Anna Stilz's (see Stilz, this volume) self-determining peoples, insofar as the constitution of the people is (as she claims) endogenous to political institutions rather that prepolitically given.
4 Robert E. Goodin, "Enfranchising All Subjected, Worldwide," *International Theory* 8, no. 3 (2016): 365–89.

5 See A. V. Dicey, "England and America," *Atlantic Monthly* 82 (1898): 441–5. Quoted in Duncan Bell, "Beyond the Sovereign State: Isopolitan Citizenship, Race and Anglo-American Union," *Political Studies* 62, no. 2 (2014): 418–34, at 428.

6 A. V. Dicey, *The Law of the Constitution*, 8th ed. (London: Macmillan, 1915; originally published 1885).

7 Jeremy Waldron, "The Principle of Proximity," NYU *School of Law, Public Law & Legal Theory Research Paper Series*, Working Paper No. 11-08, 2011; available at https://papers.ssrn.com/sol3/papers.cfm?abstract_id=1742413. Cf. Waldron, "Kant's Legal Positivism," *Harvard Law Review* 109, no. 7 (1996): 1535–66, at 1555–6; Waldron, "Who Is My Neighbor? Humanity and Proximity," *Monist* 86, no. 3 (2003): 333–54, at 349. Waldron is building on a snippet from Immanuel Kant, *The Metaphysical Elements of Justice*, trans. John Ladd (Indianapolis, IN: Bobbs-Merrill, 1965; originally published in 1797), §42, 71.

8 I understand "proximity" as "being near or close by in space," which the *Oxford English Dictionary* says is "now the dominant sense." Cf. the distinctive sense of *"promimité"* in recent French politics, discussed in note 49. In Anglo-Australian tort jurisprudence, proximity is defined as the effects of one's acts (or omissions) being sufficiently direct upon someone else that you could and should reasonably have foreseen them, and you should be deemed negligent for not doing so. See William Dean, *Jaensch v. Coffey, 155 CLR 549* (1984); Desmond Manderson, *Proximity, Levinas and the Soul of Law* (Montreal: McGill-Queen's University Press, 2006); Linton A. Lewis, *The Theory of Proximity in International Law* (London: Gray's Inn, 2016). In the absence of an independent test of "directness," however, this analysis risks circularity: if we define "proximity" in terms of owing something (a duty of care, or a vote) to someone, then it would be circular to use the fact of proximity thus defined as an argument for why we owe such a duty. Adam Kramer, "Proximity as Principles: Directness, Community Norms and the Tort of Negligence," *Tort Law Review* 11 (2003): 70–103, at 75.

9 Whelan, "Democratic Theory and the Boundary Problem"; David Miller, "Democracy's Domain," *Philosophy and Public Affairs* 37, no. 3 (2009): 201–28.

10 In the UK, by the Representation of the People Act 1918 and the Representation of the People Act 1948 respectively.

11 According to the Montevideo Convention (1934, Article 1) a state must have "a) a permanent population; b) a defined territory; c) government; and d) capacity to enter into relations with the other states." Historically, of course, the territorial state was not the only model on offer, and there was no inevitably that it would eventually prevail; see Hedrick Spruyt, *The Sovereign State and Its Competitors* (Princeton, NJ: Princeton University Press, 1994).

12 Cf. Frank Jackson, "Decision-Theoretic Consequentialism and the Nearest and Dearest Objection," *Ethics* 10, no. 3 (1991): 461–82.

13 Waldron, "The Principle of Proximity."

14 How much moral importance ought we to attach to people's preferences over whom should have a say? The fact that the landed gentry preferred that their agricultural laborers not have a vote surely should carry no moral weight at all in determining who should have a say in affairs affecting both groups. Cf. Robert Nozick's "Utopia," in *Anarchy, State, and Utopia* (New York: Basic Books, 1974), Chapter 10 and Anna Stilz (this volume).

15 Some would say that they make the relations morally more important in other nonconsequentialist ways as well, giving rise for example to associative duties. Cf. Robert E. Goodin, "What Is So Special about Our Fellow Countrymen?" *Ethics* 98, no. 4 (1988): 663–86. Even those who think that that is true too have no reason to deny that there are also these consequentialist considerations at work here. See Samuel Scheffler, "Membership and Political Obligation," *Journal of Political Philosophy* 26 (2018): 3–23.

16 Markets are another way of accomplishing that without any formally joint decision making – although, of course, a fair bit of the latter is required to structure markets in the first place and to correct their subsequent failures.

17 Note that this is an argument *for* giving a say to those who have strong and recurring interactions with one another of the sort here in view. It does not necessarily give any reason *against* giving a say to people who do not – particularly if doing so would make no material difference to the outcome. On the latter point see Goodin, "Enfranchising All Affected Interests," pp. 58–9.

18 Ronald Coase, "The Nature of the Firm," *Economica* 4 (1937): 386–405; Herbert A. Simon, "A Formal Theory of the Employment Relationship," *Econometrica* 19 (1951): 293–305; Oliver Williamson. *The Economic Institutions of Capitalism: Firms, Markets and Relational Contracting* (New York: Free Press, 1985).

19 John Rawls, "Two Concepts of Rules," *Philosophical Review* 64 (1955): 3–32.

20 And since those local systems of rules will inevitably vary from one another, that gives rise to many of the place-specific rights and duties that Paulina Ochoa Espejo observes in "Taking Place Seriously: Territorial Presence and the Rights of Immigrants," *Journal of Political Philosophy* 24, no. 1 (2016): 67–87.

21 Or maybe the same reasons, since tallying votes is a good way of tapping preferences, whose maximally efficient satisfaction is (on this account) the point of setting up a proximity-based system of governance in the first place.

22 Once again, while this argument provides a reason for people who live proximately to one another having a vote in that place, it provides no argument *against* distant others having a vote there as well. This argument does not itself provide a positive reason for giving distant others a vote, but neither does it provide any negative reason *against* doing so.

23 Although even that is not a perfect case, since, of course, by cutting themselves off from others Japan probably affects those others.

24 Again, while none of them dictate that they *should* be, it's an open question whether any of them say they should *not* be.

25 Russell Hardin discusses what sorts of social norms would emerge, and why, in a place like eleventh-century St. Germaine, in that period "a rural parish distant enough from the center of Paris that many of its inhabitants may never have seen Paris. Virtually everything [someone living there] consumed was produced by about 80 people, all of whom he knew well. Indeed, most of what [he] consumed was produced by his own family. Perhaps no one other than these 80 people touched anything he consumed." Hardin, "The Priority of Social Order," *Rationality and Society* 25, no. 4 (2013): 407–21, at 411. See also Hardin, "From Bodo Ethics to Distributive Justice," *Ethical Theory and Moral Practice* 2 (1999): 399–413.

26 See the British Museum's 2014 exhibition "The Viking World"; available at www .britishmuseum.org/whats_on/exhibitions/vikings/vikings_live/the_viking_world.aspx.

27 For example, "with the laying of the trans-Atlantic telegraph line in 1866, communications between the major international financial centres became instantaneous. As a result of these linkages, the reliance on overseas investment of European countries and of the newly independent nations of Latin America was greater in 1914 than that of developing countries today." John Quiggin, "Globalization and Economic Sovereignty," *Journal of Political Philosophy* 9, no. 1 (2001): 56–80, at 58.

28 "Whether it is economic, political or cultural relations we have in mind … it cannot seriously be questioned that people belonging to different states frequently have more intense contact than citizens of the same state" as Hans Kelsen wrote at the end of the Second World War; see his *General Theory of Law and State* (Cambridge, MA: Harvard University Press, 1945), p. 183.

29 Robert O. Keohane and Joseph S. Nye, Jr., *Power and Interdependence* (Boston: Little, Brown and Company, 1977); Keohane and Nye, "Power and Interdependence Revisited," *International Organization* 41 (1987): 725–53.

30 Goodin, "Enfranchising All Affected Interests."

31 Insofar as the All-Subjected Principle is supposed to be different from the All-Affected Principle, a person is subject to the law of a state purely insofar as that law purports to bind him – insofar as he could in principle (however unlikely it may be in practice) be prosecuted in that state's courts for violation of that law. Goodin, "Enfranchising All Subjected Worldwide"; Robert E. Goodin and Gustaf Arrhenius, "Enfranchising All Subjected: A Reconstruction and Problematization," *Politics, Philosophy and Economics*, in press.

32 William Blackstone, *Commentaries on the Laws of England* (Oxford: Clarendon Press, 1765), Book 4, Chapter 6, pp. 83–4.

33 See, for example, the USA Patriot Act, 18 US Code §2339(B)(d)(2). Blackstone, *Commentaries*, Book 4, Chapter 5, pp. 71–3. See further: Sarah Song, "The Boundary Problem in Democratic Theory: Why the Demos Should Be Bounded by the State," *International Theory* 4, no. 1 (2012): 39–68; Goodin, "Enfranchising All Subjected Worldwide."

34 What counts as meeting each of those criteria to a "requisite" degree is a matter for judgment: that requires further discussion; there is almost certainly no "bright line" in any of those matters. How those four dimensions interact, and to what extent shortfalls in one dimension can be compensated by overachievement in others, is another matter requiring further discussion.

35 For problems with that proposal, however, see Goodin and Arrhenius, "Enfranchising All Subjected."

36 There is a tendency across some the other chapters of this book to treat the All-Affected Principle as if it were attempting to answer several or indeed all of these other questions, rather than being confined to this one. But that, in my view, is making the poor little principle bear far more weight than can reasonably be expected (cf. Stilz, Valentini, this volume).

37 Anyway, those principles argue for giving people who are affected by or subject to the laws a "say" in the making of those laws. Whether they can be given a "say" in ways that would not qualify as fully "democratic" just depends on how you interpret each of those terms (cf. Gray, Stilz, Macdonald, Lane, Rubenstein, this volume).

38 Cf. Goodin and Arrhenius, "Enfranchising All Subjected."

39 Harry Brighouse and Marc Fleurbaey, "Democracy and Proportionality," *Journal of Political Philosophy* 18, no. 2 (2010): 137–55.

40 Including Warren, Gray, and Christiano (this volume).

41 Dennis C. Mueller, *Public Choice III* (New York: Cambridge University Press, 2003), pp. 169–74; Aanund Hylland and Richard Zeckhauser, "A Mechanism for Selecting Public Goods When Preferences Must Be Elicited," *KSG Discussion Paper 70D*, Harvard University, August 1979; available at http://home.uchicago.edu/~weyl/hyllandzeckhauser.pdf.

42 A more radical version would give people with more interests more votes altogether. Welfare economists may see advantages in that. See, for example, Mueller, *Public Choice III*, p. 174. Democratic theorists would not. See Robert E. Goodin and Ana Tanasoca, "Double Voting," *Australasian Journal of Philosophy* 92, no. 4 (2014): 743–58.

43 Historically, under British electoral law persisting into the early twentieth century, someone who owned estates in two different constituencies could cast votes for the member of Parliament for each constituency – giving them in effect two votes in deciding what party would form the national government. Over 6 percent of people on the UK electoral register in 1911, for example, were plural voters of that sort. Neal Blewett, "The Franchise in the United Kingdom 1885–1918," *Past & Present* no. 32 (1965): 27–56, at 31, 44–8.

44 Albeit in favor of what Warren (this volume) terms "democratic equity."

45 Beyond noting that there *are* all these principled reasons for excluding some matters from being decided by voting, even if others are affected by those decisions. Stilz (this volume) sees such exclusions as "ad hoc," thinking only in terms of the All-Affected Principle. But they are the very opposite, once we see that principle as being supplemented by these other normative principles.

46 Johannes Althusius, *Politics [Politica Methodice Digesta]*, trans. Frederick S. Carney (Boston: Beacon Press, 1964; originally published in 1603); Andreas Føllesdal, "Subsidiarity," *Journal of Political Philosophy* 6, no. 2 (1998): 190–218; Kees van Kersbergen and Bertjan Verbeek, "Subsidiarity as a Principle of Governance in the European Union," *Comparative European Politics* 2, no. 2 (2004): 142–62.

47 Robert E. Goodin, "World Government Is Here!" in *Varieties of Sovereignty and Citizenship*, ed. Sigal R. Ben-Porath and Rogers M. Smith (Philadelphia: University of Pennsylvania Press, 2013), pp. 149–65, 293–300, at pp. 155ff.

48 There is also, of course, a good argument for politicians to get "closer" to the people, listening to their concerns, rather than remaining aloof from them. In part that is a matter of political style; in part it is an argument for devolution of decisions to lower levels of government where possible. Both figured in the rallying cry of "*promimité*" in recent French political debates. Pierre Rosanvallon, *Democratic Legitimacy: Impartiality, Reflexivity, Proximity*, trans. Arthur Goldhammer (Princeton, NJ: Princeton University Press, 2011; originally published 2008), p. 169 and pt. IV passim; Bernard Pudal, "La 'Proximité' avec 'la France d'en bas'," *Bulletin des Bibliotéques de France* 49, no. 2 (2004): 5–7; available at http://bbf.enssib.fr/consulter/bbf-2004-02-0005-001; Rémi Lefebvre, "Rhétorique de la proximité et 'crise de la représentation'," *Cashiers Lillois d'Économie et de Sociologie* 35–6 (2000): 111–32.

49 Climate change being a paradigm case; see Lane (this volume).

50 Various other second-best alternatives might be contemplated, should such arrangements prove infeasible. Goodin, "Enfranchising All Affected Interests," pp. 65–7;
Goodin, "Enfranchising All Subjected Worldwide," pp. 385–6. But I assume that
most of those alternatives would probably prove even more unpalatable to those
who find themselves aghast at my primary proposal.

2

Equity, Social Justice, and the All-Affected Principle[*]

Mark E. Warren

The principle that all those affected by a collective decision should be included in the decision is long-standing, dating at least back to the Justinian Code in Roman private law: "what touches all must be approved by all" (*Quod omnes tangit debet ab omnibus approbari*; see Lane, this volume).[1] Over the last several decades, the idea has migrated into democratic theory.[2] The reason is the principle expresses a very basic intuition about what democracy is good for: I should want to have a say in decisions that significantly affect my life. With say, I am part of networks of codependents who can collectively self-determine and provide opportunities for self-development. Without it, I am likely to be subject to forces over which I have little or no control.

The implications following from the All-Affected Principle (AAP) are, however, often in conflict with the standard view of political inclusion dating back to the democratization of modern nation-states. On the standard view, entitlements to a say over collective matters should follow membership, formalized as citizenship. The powers and limitations of citizenship are tied to residence in organized political jurisdictions: nation-states, states, provinces, municipalities, and so on. They are made effective through voting, electoral representation, and rights-based protections for speech, organization, and advocacy. Indeed, in Europe, the Americas, and a few other places, the most important democratic project from the mid-eighteenth century until recently was the democratization of the nation-states that began to consolidate in the early modern period.

Yet justifications for democratic inclusion based on membership are increasingly undermined by the changing circumstances of politics. From the standpoint of social and political development, the impacts of collective decisions reverberate across jurisdictions. Governments, organizations, firms, and citizens of countries, states, counties, and cities make decisions that produce effects borne by people in other jurisdictions. Often these effects deeply affect people's lives, through problems of security and war, economic development, trade and markets, and environmental externalities including climate change. A decision taken "democratically" in one polity – inclusive of its members – can be experienced as oppression, domination, or tyranny in another. No justification of exclusions based on membership can make such effects democratically acceptable. Indeed, such arguments are central to anti-globalization and populist demands for recentering power in nation-states by hardening borders to trade and migration. Even if democratic theorists are not using the AAP, large numbers of people already do so intuitively, although too often with reactive framing. Yet despite the recent surges in reactive nationalism in most of the developed democracies, increasing numbers of people understand our obligations to others as those of social justice that should extend to every human being, uncontained by the boundaries of political membership.[3]

These are not new problems or insights. What is new, emerging over the last decade or so, is a discussion of whether membership-based principles of democratic inclusion might be either supplemented or even replaced by the AAP. Just as new is the pushback: those who defend membership-based entitlements for inclusion commonly note that the AAP is unworkable or unorganizable owing to its expansiveness; or that membership trumps weaker or more extensive externalities owing to thicker ethical obligations among co-nationals; or that being affected in itself does not justify claims for inclusion. For the most part, those of us who have been using the AAP have not developed a fully adequate account that responds to these questions.

Here I sketch an approach to the AAP that begins to respond to both the normative claims inherent in democratic ideals, as well as to the issues of organizing these ideals into institutions and practices beyond state-based constituencies. I do so by making the following arguments.

First, I interpret the AAP as a normative specification of social justice as it relates to democratic inclusion. It is a claim about who should, normatively speaking, be entitled to inclusion in political constituencies – existing or latent – based on how their essential interests in self-development and self-determination are affected by others. That is, it is not a theory of political organization, nor is it a replacement for the ties of memberships. But it is a way of specifying normatively the reach of democracy under conditions of extensive interdependency. It captures the common-sense normative core of democracy as self-government and challenges us to imagine institutions and practices that might respond. Second, I comment on the three most common objections to the AAP – all species of the objection that the AAP is unworkable as a principle of democratic inclusion. While these objections are compelling in their own terms, they suffer increasing irrelevance to the changing circumstances of politics. Third, I comment on the All-Subjected Principle (ASP), an important alternative account of entitlements to democratic inclusions. While the ASP captures one important kind of affectedness, it remains tied to the project of democratizing consolidated nation-states, and so fails to respond to evolving patterns of interdependency. Fourth, I suggest that the normative force of the AAP should be derived primarily from social justice, specified as obligations that follow social relationships that support self-determination and self-development under conditions of extensive interdependency.[4] Fifth, specifying the AAP in this way produces a distinction between democratic *equalities* and democratic *equities*. Whereas democratic equalities are empowerments that are equally distributed and empowered by states or state-like entities (rights to vote, speak, organize, etc.), equities are about essential interests related to self-determination and self-development. When the AAP is interpreted as a principle of equity as it relates to inclusions, the claims that follow should be *proportional* to these essential interests. This interpretation helps to specify the scope of the AAP to those effects that are most important for individuals: those affecting self-determination and self-development. Sixth, this approach to the AAP helps to identify *constituencies* – actual or latent – relative to essential interests. Because such constituencies will not necessarily match the territorial organization of jurisdictions, the AAP challenges us to find new ways and means of democratic inclusion for essential interests. Finally, I look at the question as to whether the AAP is workable in practice. I note the principle is far from unknown within existing democratic polities: we have many institutions and principles of responsiveness that are proportional and equity-based, such as entitlements for schooling limited to school-age children, cancer treatments for those who have cancer, administrative directives for "stakeholder" or "community" engagement in policy development, and so on. These proportional, equity-based entitlements work in parallel with democratic equalities, which provide the empowerments that citizens may differentially activate, depending upon their essential interests. Thus, we already use the AAP extensively if unevenly. We now need to theorize the principle so we can figure out what it requires of democratic political organization.

INTERPRETING THE ALL-AFFECTED PRINCIPLE

The All-Affected Principle, as I shall conceptualize the idea here, is a principle of inclusion relative to problems of democratic self-government. The relevant *interests* are those related to the goods of self-development and self-determination. Following Iris Marion Young[5] and others, *self-development* refers the development of capabilities necessary for individuals to actualize their potentials, while *self-determination* refers to opportunities to self-govern together with others, and to participate with others in determining the conditions of self-determination (see also Gray, this volume, and Gould, this volume). The relevant *affected* interests are those that significantly impact chances and opportunities for self-development and self-determination through (a) relationships of codependence and co-vulnerability, and (b) externalities of organized collective entities or structural phenomena such as markets. The status of the AAP as a normative claim turns on affectedness in these senses: *negatively,* when effects undermine self-determination or self-development (that is, effects that amount to domination or oppression), and *positively* as conditions for self-determination or self-development. *All* is a marker of inclusion that I will interpret as relative to "affected interests." From a democratic perspective, the ethics behind the "all" is relatively simple and uncontroversial: each individual is morally equal with respect to self-development and self-determination. No individual should be merely an instrument of the interests of others, nor beyond the consideration of others with respect to support for self-determination and self-development, nor denied self-determination and self-development through domination or oppression. That is, each individual holds equal moral entitlement to develop the life they have and to govern that life – both through individual choices, and through others in those matters related to codependence and co-vulnerability.

Two important features of the AAP follow. First, the *scope* of the principle is relative to effects that impact individuals' capacities for self-determination and self-development. That is, the AAP should identify just those effects that matter to these fundamental interests. Second, the normative claims for inclusion increase *proportionally* to the extent fundamental interests are affected. So "all" does not mean everyone who is potentially affected in any way, but rather with respect to one's fundamental interests in self-development and self-determination.[6] Thus, although everyone is potentially affected by almost everything in a world of thick interdependencies, some are deeply important for self-determination and self-development (food, clothing, shelter, education, security, etc.), while others are relatively trivial and/or have little or no bearing on social justice (e.g. being crowded out of seeing a new movie release).

Since the AAP is a principle of inclusion, we also need to ask: Included in *what*? The most immediate implication is that it tracks effects that mark out potential *demoi* or *constituencies* (a point to which I return below), for which there should be corresponding empowerments and sites of collective action. Framing this question is one of the most productive features of the AAP – and it is a question that is framed out of the membership-based model of democracy, which assumes inclusions must refer to states or state-like entities. In contrast, the AAP expands entitlements for inclusion into complexes of effects for which collective agency is much less clear, particularly beyond nation-states, or within polities with complex jurisdictions that do not map onto the patterns of affectedness, or as consequences of structural forces such as markets that do not seem to have any particular responsible collectivity.[7] These kinds of situations are not an argument against the AAP, but rather an argument for using the principle as a way of identifying normatively important patterns of effects that amount to constituencies for which there is no responsible collective entity. In such cases, collective agents should be invented and created just so collective responses can exist. In the case of global climate change, for example, the Paris Accords counted as a step toward creating a collectivity that can coordinate and distributing responsibilities. In other cases, such as global trade, treaties among states can bring into existence multilateral bodies and procedures that can, at least in principle, begin to scale collective agency to market externalities, which can, at least in principle, be pushed in democratic directions. In this way, the AAP highlights those areas in which collective agents should exist to address effects, or (alternatively) where they do exist but do not function democratically.

Finally, there is the question of how inclusions in effect-based *demoi* or constituencies should be democratically *empowered* within potential or actual sites of collective action. Standard democratic theory simplifies the question by assuming that these sites are state-based jurisdictions, and the key empowerments are rights to votes in competitive elections, structured to form governments and hold them to account (see e.g. Goodin, this volume; Stilz, this volume). Although voting rights are basic and crucial democratic empowerments, they are not the only kind – a point that is important if we are to conceive of empowerments that are sufficiently flexible to map onto effect-based constituencies. Democratic polities include (and depend upon) a variety of other empowerments that (a) are enabled and protected by liberal-democratic constitutional states, but which (b) can be deployed by individuals and groups selectively, and (c) can function across organized jurisdictions. These include public argument and deliberation, association for a purpose, protest and resistance, legal standing with respect to claims or entitlements, representation by advocacy groups, capacities to exit, and so on.[8] As I shall argue below, ideally each individual should have empowerments appropriate to the ways in which their essential interests are affected, and the kind of collectivity (existing or latent) that might respond to these effects.

THREE OBJECTIONS

Objections to the AAP are primarily that (1) the principle comes with unacceptable costs to workable units of self-government, and/or (2) that it is so expansive as to threaten other goods, and/or (3) that it is too expansive to be feasible.

The first objection, that the AAP would undermine workable units of self-government, challenges its most basic conceptual purpose: identifying *demoi* by focusing on affected interests. As complexes of affectedness become more extensive, *demoi* should also expand. As *demoi* expand, democratic self-government becomes more difficult in two ways. First, expanded *demoi* thin out the ties of obligation and community that are a consequence of individuals living in proximity to one another. As ties weaken, so do the social and moral requisites of democratic self-government.[9] Second, and closely related, as *demoi* expand, the say that any individual might have within a collectivity shrinks, up to the point that it becomes infinitesimally small, effectively depriving "democracy" of any practical meaning.

While these problems are challenging, they are less so if we interpret the AAP as tracking important kinds of embeddedness in complexes of effects. When we do so, the AAP identifies *demoi* that will differ in nature and extent depending upon kinds of embeddedness and their impact upon essential interests in self-development and self-determination. We should thus imagine expansive *demoi* as addressing issues in ways that underwrite (rather than undermine) self-determination and self-development, including (say) bonds of place-based community, or protecting locales from (say) externalities of trade or the consequences of climate change. What these kinds of *demoi* might require would be disaggregated and overlapping political regimes that map onto complexes of effects. Most such regimes would focus on single issues or complexes of related issues, such as trade, migration, food security, climate change, and so on (e.g. Young 2000, Chapter 7). These kinds of *demoi* and related regimes are not only imaginable, but many already exist in UN agencies, INGOs, and treaty organizations. The AAP helps to theorize the *demoi* that correspond to and justify these regimes, and to identify their (usually latent) democratic potentials. For regimes at large scale, empowerments might be realized through advocacy representation and issue-focused publics in ways that build upon state-based rights and protections.

A second kind of objection is that empowerments that follow the AAP would actually threaten other important goods. This point is often made by citing Nozick's story about several individuals' desire to marry someone who loves someone else. They do not gain the entitlement to decide whom the loved one will marry by virtue of being affected, as such an entitlement would undermine the goods of liberty and autonomy.[10] While it is always important to be attentive to trade-offs among goods, this objection loses its force when we specify the interests at stake as those of social justice: self-determination and self-development. Clearly "having a say" should not justify a situation in which the essential interests in self-determination and self-development are overridden by the preferences of others. It is *not* that "democracy" and "liberty" conflict, but rather that the *basic point* of democracy, self-government based on equal moral worth, is violated by a decision by some to impose an essential life choice on another.[11] For the same reason, Nozick's generalization of autonomy rights from the private realm to the self-determination of states – setting up a conflict between the autonomy rights of members and nonmembers – also fails. The relevant moral units of a democracy are individuals, not states.[12] States (or any other kind of political regime) should be justified as providing essential conditions of self-development and self-determination, not as means for members to exercise autonomy rights at the expense of nonmembers.[13]

A third kind of objection amounts to a *reductio ad absurdum*. As Goodin has argued,[14] if the most basic right of inclusion, voting, were to be distributed through the AAP, everyone would have a right to vote on almost everything, or for representatives who decide on almost everything (see also Stilz, this volume). At best, we would have to imagine a world government; at worst, we should imagine a situation in which a global *demos* somehow decides on every collective decision, externality, or structural effect that makes a difference for anyone.[15] Even if desirable (it would not be), such a situation would clearly be infeasible, defeated by sheer scale and complexity. Yet this kind of reduction depends upon imagining that every effect produces equal entitlements, particularly voting rights. But if we conceive entitlements as relative to essential interests, *and* recognize that entitlements can be empowered by many other forms of democratic influence, the *reductio ad absurdum* goes away. The resulting picture is complex and institutionally demanding – as are the circumstances of politics today – but it is not absurd.

THE ALL-SUBJECTED INTERESTS PRINCIPLE?

A combination of these concerns and objections are behind the main conceptual competitor to the AAP: the principle that "all those subjected" to the powers of a state should have a say in state-based collective decision making (ASP). The ASP stipulates that the only collective effects that generate democratic entitlements are those that follow from the coercive implementation of law or policy. Democratic entitlements follow from the circumstances of legal subjection to decisions, either actual or potential.[16] While the ASP has the advantage of narrowing the scope of democratic entitlements, it does so at a high cost to our ability to think about democracy under conditions of extensive interdependency.

First, it assumes that the key problem for democratic theory going forward remains the democratization of states. While this project remains crucially important and is very far from complete, we now live in a world in which even most high-capacity states do not control all those effects important for the self-government of their own citizens. Because the targets of democratization are evolving, the relative cleanliness of the ASP is bought at the expense of relevance. By stipulation, the ASP excludes problems of self-government that follow from extensive interdependencies (both across borders and within borders) that generate problems of self-government – and, thus, problems of democracy.

Second, the ASP backs democratic entitlements out of the circumstance of subjection. Legitimate subjection to laws and policies are part of democracy, as they make possible collective responses to problems of collective action.[17] But treating subjection as the basis for democratic entitlements fails to provide a positive normative argument for democracy. It is a reactive grounding focused on a harm to be avoided – illegitimate subjection – rather than goods to be achieved. The democratic project, however, has always been about more than subjection, actual or potential. It is about collective organizing and acting in ways that underwrite self-determination and self-development.

SOCIAL JUSTICE AND ETHICS

The AAP, I am suggesting, should be about those effects that are important for social justice, interpreted, following Iris Young and Onora O'Neil,[18] as entitlements and obligations that follow from those interdependencies necessary for self-development and self-determination.[19] While self-development and self-determination are activities of individuals with the support of others, from a political perspective we should be thinking about the general conditions that make these activities possible. Self-development depends upon standard welfare supports, including those that expand capacities and mitigate life risks: education, healthcare, housing, basic income, and so on. Self-determination depends upon rights that provide political standing, such as rights to vote, due process, etc., and freedoms that protect against oppression and domination, while enabling association, speech, and advocacy.[20] "Democracy" is (always) a complex combination of these supports and protections that, together, enable individuals to collectively self-govern. Democracy has value just because it provides individuals with influence over those collective interdependencies necessary to underwrite self-determination and self-development. Stated in this way, social justice is a description of the goods that justify democracy. It follows that we should conceive of the relevant collectivities as those configured to address effects relevant to social justice.

The case that democracy and social justice are intrinsically related has long been part of the traditions that have underwritten contemporary democratic theory, from the emphasis on self-determination (especially through reasoning together with others) in Aristotle, to a focus on the development of democratic capacities in Jefferson, Tocqueville, Mill, and Dewey. Less noticed, however, is the close relationship between Kantian ethics and the AAP – and this relationship also helps to justify the AAP (see Gray, this volume). The relationship can be built out of the categorical imperative and its related political formulations: "Act only according to that maxim whereby you can, at the same time, will that it should become a universal law." With respect to legislation and law, Kant developed a parallel formula: "Every action which by itself or by its maxim enables the freedom of each to co-exist with the freedom of everyone in accordance with a universal law is *right*."[21] These formulations have, of course, been hugely influential in ethics, liberal-democratic constitutionalism, and human rights discourse. Less remarked is their close relationship with the AAP, even though they have been effectively incorporated into some influential formulations.[22] The categorical imperative and the theory of right ask individuals to imagine themselves as members of universal communities, where those communities are populated with other individuals, each of whom has a life to live, interdependent with others. Each has the capacity, by virtue of being human, to be self-governing, and each is entitled to equal moral respect. While the categorical imperative is most often interpreted as a reason-based ethics of duty (as in deontological ethics), we should notice that it also directs us to imagine how our actions might *affect others' capacities for self-governance* – leading us to consider those chains of effects, potential and actual, that link our actions to those of others, considered as moral equals.[23] The AAP can thus be viewed as an elaboration of this kind of moral imperative, such that we arrive at a proto-democratic view of what social justice requires. All other things being equal, inclusions should follow patterns of effects that rise to the level of importance for social justice.[24]

THE AAP AS A PRINCIPLE OF EQUITY

If these intuitions into social justice within contexts of extensive interdependencies justify the AAP, what are the implications for *political* equalities? In particular, how does the AAP fare from the perspective of democratic equality? As noted above, if we interpret the AAP as requiring equal votes or voice over all the interdependencies that affect us, the principle collapses. If we narrow the scope to *essential* interests, as does Fung,[25] the AAP captures the intuition that we should care about those inclusions in collectivities that are most important for individuals. And if we follow this logic, we could end up with the somewhat surprising position that democratic inclusions should be *proportional* to the nature and extent of affectedness for these essential interests. Following roughly this argument, Brighouse and Fleurbaey propose that democratic entitlements such as voting should *not* be distributed equally, but rather proportionally, relative to individuals' stakes in their essential interests.[26] They argue that a (social justice) principle of *equal moral worth* incorporated into all democratic theory requires proportional empowerments, distributed according to differential individual circumstances and capacities.

The social justice logic of this argument is compelling. But it is hard to see how this kind of proposal could ever be legitimate. Publics, especially in democracies, view equal political entitlements, such as the right to vote, as public recognitions of equal moral worth. Indeed, in the very unlikely event that such a system were to be proposed within a political arena, most would view it as denoting differing kinds and classes of citizenship, and a clear violation of moral equality. Moreover, it would almost certainly undermine the reciprocity necessary for public attention to considerations of social justice. Social justice rights (e.g. to education and healthcare) can only be effective if matched to duties and responsibilities (e.g. supporting public education and universal healthcare). Adding empowerments to the *rights* side of the equation at the expense of the *duties and responsibilities* side of the equation would undermine general commitments to welfare policies by (relatively) misrecognizing and disempowering those very people upon whom the burdens of duties fall. Indeed, this logic is what the All-Subjected Principle gets right: entitlements to voice and votes are at least partly justified by the burdens of citizenship, including paying for (say) state-based welfare entitlements. In short, it is hard to imagine a proposal that would more quickly and completely undermine public commitments to social justice.

But we can still retain Brighouse and Fleurbaey's argument that higher stakes, or greater impacts on social justice-based interests, should scale proportionally onto importance of inclusions, as the AAP would suggest. We can do so in a way that is both morally robust and politically viable by distinguishing *equality* from *equity*. The intuitions captured by the AAP are best conceived as a democratic way of thinking about equity – in particular, the proportionality inherent in equitable social relationships. Thus, democratic *equality* is justified by equal moral worth and a default competence assumption that individuals are capable of collective self-government.[27] *Democratic* equality cashes out in equal distributions of political entitlements (or empowerments) necessary to exercise influence over collectivities. These include protective rights to liberty and autonomy, positive rights to vote, speak, and organize, welfare rights such as rights to education, a basic income, etc., as well as rights of exit from social and economic relationships. Democratic equalities provide *recognitions* among co-equals of their moral worth, and *political standing* to individuals so they might act as democratic citizens. These rights are necessary to exercise democratic agency, and they should be organized into collectivities.[28] States or state-like entities (such as the EU or the International Criminal Court) are the key distributors and guarantors, and it is difficult to imagine a future in which this would not be the case. Constitutional liberal-democratic states provide platforms, as it were, for individuals to act within, between, and beyond jurisdictions.

Equities, however, are by their very nature proportional to affectedness, and thus require differing kinds of collective attentiveness. Elaborated through the lens of social justice, equity is what we owe to one another by virtue of those co-dependencies and externalities that affect our abilities to self-develop and self-determine. Ideally, equitable inclusions are scaled proportionally to basic needs, so that individuals approach equality in their capacities. As Young quite sensibly puts it, because "of their differing attributes or situations, some people need more or different to enable equal levels of capability with others."[29] Thus, in higher-functioning welfare states, citizens are *equally* and universally entitled to receive state services. What we expect, however, is that services are delivered and used *equitably*, in accordance with the AAP – what Rosanvallon has perceptively called "the legitimacy of proximity."[30] Every citizen has an equal right to schooling for their children, but it is primarily school-aged children and their parents that have directly affected interests (including interests as taxpayers, interests in a productive economy, etc., but less directly). Schooling is thus distributed not in accordance with the principle of equality, but rather equity. Entitlements to voice are magnified for those most directly affected through institutions like Parent-Teacher Associations. In Canada, to take another example, entitlement to medical treatment is equal and universal, but, ideally, it is delivered equitability (and unequally) according to specific health needs. This kind of equity tracks the kinds of responsiveness from collectivities that people tend to want in democracies – a kind that Rosanvallon perceptively calls the "democratic legitimacy of particularity."[31]

This relationship between equalities and the proportional qualities of affectedness helps to make sense of patterns of political activity we might ideally expect in a democracy. Even when they are robustly guaranteed, people tend to activate their (ideally equal) rights when their essential interests are at stake. Even though democratic rights are equally distributed, they are not equally used. Most use their voice and votes quite selectively, according to the issues they prioritize. They speak and organize on issues they consider urgent, they activate entitlements to medical care when ill or injured, and so on. So, ideally, democratic equalities make possible vectors of inclusion that respond (proportionally and differentially) to equities.

On this view of the complementary relationship between equalities and equities, it is important to think about political arrangements that are sensitive to individual circumstance, and which can be used by individuals according to their needs. While the examples I have used lean toward collective attentiveness, we should also be thinking about arrangements that enable and empower voluntary transactions that respond immediately and directly to needs – particularly associative and market-like transactions. Thomas Christiano (this volume) experiments with the idea that, under fair conditions, decentralized voluntary transactions (including associative and market transactions as well as self-selected political forums) might be viewed as means of realizing the AAP; when people can choose their relationships (through joining and exiting, or buying and selling), they can choose the ones that are more likely to serve their more important interests.[32]

Of course, as Christiano argues, these kinds of voluntary ways of realizing the AAP will work *democratically* not just when people have democratic equalities, but also relatively equal capacities to engage, bargain, and transact. Inequalities of circumstance undermine capacities to use equally distributed democratic empowerments,[33] and unequal bargaining power within markets undermine the fairness of transactions. Owing to these well-known defects of self-selected organization, democratic theorists have perhaps overlooked the importance of voluntarily-exercised citizen powers that can reflect the relative importance of interests. Yet because of the importance of voluntary political activity as a vector for the AAP, we should attend more closely to the conditions that square its patterns with democracy. And because it is difficult to imagine a democracy within which voluntary transactions are not an important vector of self-government, proportionally supplied equities (consistent with the AAP) that underwrite relatively equal capacities to choose, transact, vote, and so on are all the more important.

In an ideal democracy, then, equality and equity would be complementary, with equal powers of citizenship underwriting proportional social justice claims, while proportional social justice underwrites relatively equal capacities of citizenship. The AAP gives such proportionality its democratic substance by relating it back to self-government.

CONSTITUENCY

We can elaborate the AAP still further through the more obviously political concept of constituency. *Constituency* defines units of membership identified in relation to representatives who stand for, speak for, or act for its members. In standard democratic theory, constituencies are determined (typically) by states and their subunits of government, divided into electoral districts, usually based on residence.[34] In federal systems, constituencies will differ by level of government and are layered, so that individuals are members of multiple constituencies. The standard theory assumes that individuals' essential interests are encompassed by residence-based constituencies, and that their essential interests can be empowered through elections.[35]

Interpreted through the AAP, however, the question of constituency becomes more interesting and productive. On the one hand, the principle suggests that for some kinds of issues – particularly those important for social justice – democratic self-government should be sorted by issues representing essential interests, with each issue (or set of related issues) identifying a constituency. Interpreted through the AAP, individuals are no longer conceived as residence-based packages of essential interests, but rather as plural packages of interests connected to others who share similar interests (challenges, injustices, etc.). Considered politically, each such package can count as a constituency – either one that is organized and active with representatives, or an unorganized, *latent constituency*. Individuals can have (and often do have) multiple memberships in many constituencies, linked by common interests or shared struggles. On the other hand, when we think of constituencies as identified by the AAP, we can also identify *democratic deficits*: issues related to essential interests for which there is no representative locus of organization.[36] The AAP helps us to think about where there are needs for political organization that do not correspond to residency-based constituencies, including (most obviously) issues that flow across borders such as climate change, trade, and migration.

THE AAP IN PRACTICE

This interpretation of the AAP is still challenging, but in a way that matches the evolving circumstances of politics to empowered inclusions that are important for self-determination and self-development. A key piece of the challenge is to imagine forms and powers of citizenship with corresponding sites of collective action that would underwrite the proportional, equity-based demands of the AAP. In this final section, I address the question of how the AAP might be organized into political practices and institutions. I do so from two perspectives: that of the powers individual/citizen might employ for inclusion, and that of institutions and organizations that might respond (or be created to respond). I illustrate the analysis with examples that are familiar and even mundane. I do so not to undermine the progressive implications of the AAP, but rather to show we already know something about its nature and demands. The AAP is a challenge to extend and deepen democracy, but it is not utopian.

CITIZEN POWERS AS VECTORS OF THE AAP

A key to thinking about how the AAP might be instantiated is to identify the kinds of empowerments individuals might have to organize or pressure sites of collective action. In almost all cases, empowerments require functioning liberal-democratic constitutional states with the capacities to distribute and enforce politically important rights, both protective and positive, as suggested above. Rights provide citizens with some kinds of direct empowerments, such as voting governments in and out of office. But they provide many more *indirect* empowerments that they can use in graduated and proportional ways, depending upon how individuals rank and prioritize issues and preferences. Where people have rights to speak and organize, they can also resist, advocate, pressure, organize for common purposes, and exit.[37] Importantly, these powers might be directed at governments, but they can also cross boundaries and jurisdictions, as well as focus on other kinds of collective actors such as IGOs, INGOs, and corporations, potentially tracking the demands of the AAP.

These kinds of powers scale onto proportional affectedness more easily than, say, voting in competitive elections. It is true that every election prioritizes some issues over others, and that voters can decide which candidates or parties rank issues as they would. But voters are also locked into multi-issue, programmatic agendas set by parties or candidates. Indeed, some kinds of issues almost never make it into elections, such as endemic political corruption in places where every politician or party is corrupt. But it is possible to speak, organize, protest, strike, and sue. In the United States, civil rights were not addressed by the elected branches of government for a full century after the adoption of the Thirteenth, Fourteenth, and Fifteenth Amendments, and almost a century after the end of Reconstruction. Progress, when it came, was the result of determined activists using powers of organization to shape public discourse and voting, and to achieve standing in the court system to leverage constitutional standards against unconstitutional statutory law as well as illegal practices.

As I have been arguing, liberal-democratic constitutional states remain essential to realizing the AAP, not because they instantiate the principle directly, but because rights provide *citizenship standing*, which in turn empowers individuals to work below, across, above, and outside of state-based jurisdictions and constituencies.[38] It is not accidental that most transnational and international organizations use liberal-democratic states as their locations, as they provide the freedoms and protections necessary for activism. We should also notice that many such organizations and networks help to provide little bits of citizen powers even where states are authoritarian, arbitrary, kleptocratic, or failed. When international organizations focus on basic social justice issues such as refugee status, genocide, hunger, the treatment of women and minorities, they are often reaching across borders to provide some of the most basic elements of citizenship standing where states do not.[39] Of course, such empowerments are highly imperfect and uneven in their effects. But they are also relatively recent developments, and count as projects in the making. We should also pay close attention to international regimes created without any human rights or democratic pretensions, such as trade agreements. Once in place, they can become sites of leverage for democracy-related goods – sometimes formally and extensively, as exemplified by the development of the trade and economic development-focused European Commission into the European Union.

With the powers of citizenship, individuals can self-select into organizations in ways that reflect their own views of their essential interests. They can bring latent constituencies to the fore; they can precisely calibrate their advocacy; they can even organize to provide collective goods that governments neglect, as in the case of early social insurance associations.[40] What Laura Montanaro calls "self-appointed representatives" (advocacy entrepreneurs) or what Michael Saward calls "representative claim-makers" can transform latent constituencies into active ones.[41]

The ways these kinds of powers are actually deployed, of course, will not necessarily serve everyone's essential interests. Any kind of power that remains latent until activated through individual choices will be sensitive to differences in economic security and bargaining power, social standing and status, and education. Organizing for public, diffuse, or long-term goods – those for which high individual efforts result in only incremental payoffs – will be relatively more challenging than organizing for goods with focused and timely payouts.

TRANSFORMATIONS OF GOVERNANCE REFLECTING THE AAP

If we look at these same kinds of relationships from the side of governance, we can see that the AAP, interpreted as an equity-based principle of democracy, is already part of the current and emerging patterns, even if we have not theorized them as such. Consider the following kinds of examples.

Stakeholder and Community Engagement

These terms are commonly used in enabling legislation for agencies and ministries, and date back to the post–Second World War era in the United States and many other countries. The intent was to provide standing to those "stakeholders" or "communities" that are directly, differentially, or disproportionally affected by legislation, particularly in the development of policies and administrative rule making. These directives define relevant publics as those with "stakes" – in effect, instantiating a version of the AAP. In most cases, these kinds of "engagement" and "consultation" rely on individuals or representatives of groups self-selecting into these processes. Depending upon the issue, the results may not be especially favorable to democracy, as they will skew toward well-organized groups and (often) permanent lobbyists for well-resourced groups or business interests. But for some issues, especially those related to social justice and often at the local level, we now see more proactive targeting of affected publics – a process I have elsewhere called *governance-driven democratization*.[42] These democratic innovations may be instigated by professionals who are genuinely interested in inclusions, but they are often reactions to advocacy, particularly the kinds that can disrupt governance.[43] This kind of development is thus often functionally related to the kinds of citizen powers I underscored in the previous section. In still other cases, agencies or ministries may use near-random or stratified sampling selection to populate a citizen group (or *deliberative minipublic*[44]) to better represent an affected public – a tactic that is especially important when the advocacy landscape around an issue poorly reflects those who are affected or potentially affected, or when powerful groups threaten to co-op a process.

Single-Issue Jurisdictions

More mundanely, governments in the liberal democracies have long formed single-issue jurisdictions to manage specific tasks or problems, effectively institutionalizing other forms of the AAP. Examples include school districts, transportation authorities, health authorities, and soil conservation and irrigation districts. In many cases, the units of government proactively engage with those drawn into these jurisdictions. Vancouver Coastal Health (a government agency responsible for delivering health to a region of British Columbia), for example, creates a variety of user groups, such as those with complex diabetes management problems, in order to define and refine their missions. School districts in the United States and Canada institutionalized Parent-Teacher Associations long ago. Transportation districts seeking to develop (say) a subway extension will often seek input from potential riders and property owners, as well as from broader constituencies of those affected by congestion, taxes, and climate change.

Single-Issue Cross-Jurisdiction Governance

Similarly, especially in transnational and international contexts, problems that affect people across borders can result in governance regimes that implicitly reflect the AAP. As I suggested above, some of these regimes are constructed specifically for social justice issues, such as human rights, food security, and displacement of persons. But they also include many kinds of joint problem-focused regimes, such as the International Joint Commission on the Great Lakes boundary waters, the Montreal Protocols on chlorofluorocarbons, or the United States–Mexico–Canada Agreement (USMCA) with its labor and environmental conditions and riders.

The point of these examples is not to deflate the demanding character of the AAP, but rather to underscore the fact that the intuitions it expresses are quite common, and that we have, in fact, created institutions in response. We use the AAP all the time, in ways that combine political equalities with attentiveness to differential equities. Our problem is to extract the principles from these practices, examine their normative force, and then figure out what they demand of us.

CONCLUSION

While "democracy" involves a number of principles, the AAP is one that will help us to conceive of where democratic inclusions should exist in a world with denser interdependencies and co-vulnerabilities, and where existing units of collective action or market-like structures produce extensive externalities. But because of the density of embedded effects, we shall need to prioritize, focusing on the inclusions that are most important for people's lives. This is why I am arguing for specifying the AAP through social justice, in this way focusing on those effects that impact individuals' capacities and opportunities for self-determination and self-development.

There is a new urgency to retooling democratic theory to reflect the changing circumstances of politics. Reactive movements in the United States, UK, and much of Europe use a state-centric view of democracy – popular sovereignty focused on state powers – to justify withdrawing from global interdependencies and responsibilities. These may be politics of the past, but they remain attractive to large sectors of populations that feel their collective control slipping away into interdependencies that do not benefit them. Recentering politics on state-controlled boundaries seems compelling to people not just because of its simplicity, but also because there have not been good institutional responses for many kinds of cross-jurisdictional affectedness that threaten to downgrade lives and livelihoods. We democratic theorists need to show that we can think about democracy in this kind of post-sovereign world. The AAP will help us to extend and deepen the kind of democratic imagination that might respond.

NOTES

* For their very helpful suggestions, thank you to Annette Zimmerman, Sean Gray, and participants in the Harvard Kennedy School workshops on "Democratic Inclusion in a Globalized World – Debating the All Affected Principle."

1 Bruce Frier, ed., *The Codex of Justinian: A New Annotated Translation* (New York: Cambridge University Press, 2016), vol. 2, pp. 1358–9.

2 Iris M. Young, *Inclusion and Democracy* (New York: Oxford University Press, 2000), Chapters 1–2; Jürgen Habermas, *Between Facts and Norms: Contributions to a Discourse Theory of Democracy*, trans. William Rehg (Cambridge, MA: MIT Press, 1996), pp. 105, 11; Robert A. Dahl, *After the Revolution? Authority in a Good Society* (New Haven: Yale University Press, 1970), pp. 49–63; Seyla Benhabib, *The Rights of Others: Aliens, Residents, and Citizens* (New York: Cambridge University Press, 2004); Cf. Archon Fung, "The Principle of Affected Interests: An Interpretation and Defense," in *Representation: Elections and Beyond*, ed. Rogers M. Smith and Jack H. Nagel (Philadelphia: University of Pennsylvania Press, 2013); Robert E. Goodin, "Enfranchising All Affected Interests, and Its Alternatives," *Philosophy and Public Affairs* 35, no. 1 (2007): 40–68; Sofia Näsström, "The Challenge of the All-Affected Principle," *Political Studies* 59, no. 1 (2011): 116–34; Ian Shapiro, *The State of Democratic Theory* (Princeton, NJ: Princeton University Press, 2003), Chapter 1.

3 Benhabib, *The Rights of Others*.
4 Following Young, *Inclusion and Democracy*; see also Gould (this volume).
5 Young, *Inclusion and Democracy*, pp. 31–3.
6 See, for example, Fung "The Principle of Affected Interests."
7 Mathias Keonig-Archibuigi, "How to Diagnose Democratic Deficits in Global Politics: The Use of the "All-Affected Principle," *International Theory* 9, no. 2 (2017): 171–202.
8 Mark E. Warren, "A Problem-Based Approach to Democratic Theory," *The American Political Science Review* 111, no. 1 (2017): 39–53.
9 David Miller, "Democracy's Domain," *Philosophy and Public Affairs* 37, no. 3 (2009): 201–28.
10 Robert Nozick, *Anarchy, State, and Utopia* (New York: Basic Books, 1974), p. 269; Niko Kolodny, "Rule Over None I: What Justifies Democracy?" *Philosophy and Public Affairs* 42, no. 3 (2014): 195–229, at pp. 222–3.
11 Laura Valentini, "No Global Demos, No Global Democracy? A Systemization and Critique," *Perspectives on Politics* 12, no. 4 (2014): 789–807.
12 Robert A. Dahl, *On Democracy* (New Haven: Yale University Press, 1998), Chapters 6–7.
13 Thank you to Annette Zimmerman for adding this point.
14 Goodin, "Enfranchising All Affected Interests."
15 Goodin, "Enfranchising All Affected Interests"; Robert E. Goodin, "Enfranchising All Subjected, Worldwide," *International Theory* 8, no. 3 (2016): 365–89.
16 Arash Abizadeh, "On the Demos and Its Kin: Nationalism, Democracy, and the Boundary Problem," *The American Political Science Review* 106, no. 4 (2012): 867–82; Näsström, "The Challenge of the All-Affected Principle"; David Owen, "Constituting the Polity, Constituting the Demos: On the Place of the All Affected Interests Principle in Democratic Theory and in Resolving the Democratic Boundary Problem," *Ethics and Global Politics* 5, no. 3 (2012): 129–52; Sarah Song, "The Boundary Problem in Democratic Theory: Why the Demos Should Be Bounded by the State," *International Theory* 4, no. 1 (2012): 39–68; cf. Goodin, "Enfranchising All Subjected."
17 Jane Mansbridge, "On the Importance of Getting Things Done," *PS: Political Science and Politics* 45, no. 1 (2012): 1–8.
18 Young, *Inclusion and Democracy*, chaps. 1–2; Onora O'Neill. *Toward Justice and Virtue* (New York: Cambridge University Press), Chapter 3.
19 For similar claims, see Harry Brighouse and Marc Fleurbaey, "Democracy and Proportionality," *The Journal of Political Philosophy* 18, no. 2 (2010): 137–55; James Bohman, *Democracy across Borders: From Demos to Demoi* (Cambridge, MA: MIT Press, 2007); and Gould (this volume).
20 Young, *Inclusion and Democracy*, Chapter 1; Bohman, *Democracy across Borders*; see also Philip Pettit, *On the People's Terms: A Republican Theory and Model of Democracy* (New York: Cambridge University Press, 2012).
21 Immanuel Kant, *Political Writings*, ed. Hans Reiss, trans. H. B. Nisbet (New York: Cambridge University Press, 1991), p. 133.
22 For example, Habermas, *Between Facts and Norms*, Chapter 3; Benhabib, *The Rights of Others*, Chapters 1–2.
23 Cf. Hannah Arendt, *Lectures on Kant's Political Philosophy*, ed. Ronald Beiner (Chicago, IL: University of Chicago Press. 1982), pp. 75–6.
24 Young, *Inclusion and Democracy*, pp. 223–4.

25 Fung, "The Principle of Affected Interests."

26 Brighouse and Fleurbaey, "Democracy and Proportionality."

27 Robert A. Dahl, *Democracy and Its Critics* (New Haven: Yale University Press, 1989); Dahl, *On Democracy*.

28 Habermas, *Between Facts and Norms*, Chapter 4; John Rawls, *Political Liberalism* (New York: Columbia University Press, 1993).

29 Young, *Inclusion and Democracy*, p. 32.

30 Pierre Rosanvallon, *Democratic Legitimacy: Impartiality, Reflexivity, Proximity*, trans. Arthur Goldhammer (Princeton, NJ: Princeton University Press, 2011).

31 Rosanvallon, *Democratic Legitimacy*, Part IV.

32 Mark E. Warren, *Democracy and Association* (Princeton, NJ: Princeton University Press, 2001); Mark E. Warren, "Voting with Your Feet: Exit-Based Empowerment in Democratic Theory," *The American Political Science Review* 105, no. 04 (2011): 683–701.

33 See, for example, Martin Gilens, *Affluence and Influence: Economic Inequality and Political Power in America* (Princeton, NJ: Princeton University Press, 2012).

34 Nadia Urbinati and Mark E. Warren, "The Concept of Representation in Contemporary Democratic Theory," *The Annual Review of Political Science* 11 (2008): 387–412.

35 Andrew Rehfeld, *The Concept of Constituency: Political Representation, Democratic Legitimacy, and Institutional Design* (New York: Cambridge University Press, 2005); cf., Jane Mansbridge, "Rethinking Representation," *American Political Science Review* 97, no. 4 (2003): 515–28.

36 Keonig-Archibuigi, "How to Diagnose Democratic Deficits."

37 Warren, "A Problem-Based Approach to Democratic Theory."

38 Melissa S. Williams, "Nonterritorial Boundaries of Citizenship," in *Identities, Affiliations, and Allegiances*, ed. Seyla Benhabib, Ian Shapiro, and Danilo Petranovich (New York: Cambridge University Press, 2007).

39 Christopher Tenove, *Justice and Inclusion in Global Politics: Representing and Advocating for Victims of International Crimes*. Doctoral Dissertation (University of British Columbia, Vancouver, 2015).

40 Warren, *Democracy and Association*; Lisa Jane Disch, *Making Constituencies: Representation as Mobilization in Mass Democracy* (Chicago: University of Chicago Press, 2021).

41 Laura Montanaro, "The Democratic Legitimacy of Self-Appointed Representatives," *The Journal of Politics* 74, no. 4 (2012): 1094–107; Michael Saward, *The Representative Claim* (New York: Oxford University Press, 2010); see also, Urbinati and Warren, "The Concept of Representation"; Disch, *Making Constituencies*.

42 Mark E. Warren, "Governance-Driven Democratization," in *Practices of Freedom: Democracy, Conflict and Participation in Decentred Governance*, ed. Steven Griggs, Aletta Norval, and Hendrik Wagenaar (New York: Cambridge University Press, 2014).

43 Edana Beauvais and Mark E. Warren, "What Can Deliberative Minipublics Contribute to Democratic Systems?" *European Journal of Political Research* 58, no. 3 (2019): 893–914.

44 Maija Setälä and Graham Smith, "Mini-Publics and Deliberative Democracy," in *The Oxford Handbook of Deliberative Democracy*, ed. André Bächtiger, John S. Dryzek, Jane Mansbridge, and Mark E. Warren (Oxford: Oxford University Press, 2018).

3

Two Complaints about Undemocratic Exclusion

Domination and Usurpation[*]

Sean W. D. Gray

The goal of democratic inclusion is to equalize power. To demand inclusion on "democratic" grounds is to demand not to be under the arbitrary and one-sided power of others. Nobody should be able to rule us but ourselves. The value of democratic inclusion isn't reducible to any one set of political institutions or decision-making procedures, such as equal rights of participation or competitive elections. Nor is it based on knowing who counts as a citizen or member, or what the boundaries between two communities should properly be. From the perspective of those who have been undemocratically excluded, there exists a more fundamental source of complaint. It's about the character of a relationship that makes self-rule impossible.

In opening my argument this way, I've perhaps left out some of the nuance. The reality is that governments are in desperate need of principled guidance on how to deal with the growing number of demands for inclusion from outside their borders. Globalization and the many issues that it raises – about migration, trade, human rights, climate change – has undermined the ability of states to draw clear lines, especially as the world becomes evermore connected and interdependent. Today, a decision made in one place can impact people in countless others. And, increasingly, the decisions with the most impact on people's lives aren't being made by states at all, but by private corporations, nongovernmental organizations, international governance institutions, and the like. These challenges can make an appeal to democratic ideals seem misguided, even quaint. What need do we have for abstract appeals to the value of democratic inclusion? How does this address the urgent practical questions of who is entitled to inclusion, to what degree, and on what basis?

I work out an answer roughly as follows. I start by considering two candidate principles that seek to put our normative ideals of democracy into practice. According to proponents of the All-Affected Principle (AAP), we should be looking to distribute participatory rights and empowerments to those whose interests a given decision-making process most significantly affects. A competing proposal is the All-Subjected Principle (ASP), which would have us settle questions of inclusion by determining who is subjected to a decision's terms. Both principles share a similar concern for ensuring that the boundaries of democratic inclusion track the outcomes of decision making. But both principles also miss something important, I argue. People do not see themselves as wrongfully excluded from a decision-making process just because of its outcome. What about the underlying relationships of power and circumstance that render people vulnerable to a decision's consequences to begin with? To make progress, what's required is an understanding of undemocratic exclusion that avoids reducing our concerns to the possible effects of a decision. What is the underlying wrong to which complaints about undemocratic exclusion are typically directed? One complaint is about *domination* – the exposure to arbitrary interference. Another complaint is about *usurpation* – having decisions made for you, without your involvement. In the final third of the chapter, I use these two complaints as a guide to sketching out an alternative formula for democratic inclusion – one that, I believe, can do a much better job of explaining why democratic inclusion is justified in some cases, but not others, and to what degree. My argument speaks to the relational value of democratic inclusion. It offers a more grounded understanding of our democratic obligations to one another, sensitive to our equal moral claims consideration, but tailored for a globalized world.

A NORMATIVE DEFINITION OF DEMOCRACY

The standard picture that we paint of democracy is in one sense too familiar. It's tempting to leave out the core principles and cut straight to institutional questions about implementation. Still, I think it's worth periodically revisiting the specific values that are appealed to when we speak of "democracy," separate from the institutions and practices with which it is usually associated. Democracy as an ideal is compatible with any number of institutional configurations and isn't reducible to any single activity. So, if we want to know what democracy *is* and what it *asks* of us, it simply won't do to read off a definition secondhand.

At the highest level of abstraction, democracy means – and, I believe, is most often taken to mean – *collective self-rule* under conditions that afford everyone political standing and consideration in matters of common concern. I won't defend this working definition here, but I take some version of it to be implicit in most theories of democracy today. When John Rawls outlines his vision of a "well-ordered constitutional democracy" in which citizens "exercise ultimate political power as a collective body," he is embracing this conception of self-rule.[1] Robert Dahl expresses this conception with even greater clarity: "[A] democratic order is above all the freedom of self-determination in making collective and binding decisions: the self-determination of citizens entitled to participate as political equals in making the laws under which they live together as citizens."[2] This emphasis on the fundamental equality of individuals is important. In Niko Kolodny's words, it "is rooted in a concern not to have anyone else "above"—or, for that matter, "below"—us," such that "none rules over any other."[3]

I want to suggest that this definition of democratic self-rule provides an entry point for thinking about diverse demands for inclusion, especially in a globalized world. It spells out for us what democracy requires *in normative terms*, separate from the specific institutions and practices through which it may be realized, such as elections, or representation, or citizenship. My central claim is that what democracy implies, at bottom, is a commitment to fostering the conditions under which individuals can be said to rule themselves as equals. This requires, first, that we are in fact able to make choices *as individuals*, to think for ourselves, and to craft plans that are personally meaningful and not the result of arbitrary interference or manipulation. It also requires that we enjoy equal rights and protections, including an equal say in the duties and obligations that collective life imposes. As individuals, we must be willing to share our thoughts and judgments with others. And, as a group, we must agree to fair procedures that allow us to consider what each of us wants in order to arrive at a collective decision that everyone can endorse – through voting or deliberating, for example. It follows that *the possibility of democracy* depends on the character of our relationship to collective decisions. This is true in a negative sense, insofar as being excluded from collective decision making, when we're owed consideration, does damage to our autonomy. This is also true in a positive sense, insofar as having sufficient capacities and opportunities to influence collective decision making is a basic condition for democratic self-rule.

Now, none of this should be new or surprising to democratic theorists. But it bears repeating precisely because of what's still up for grabs. Our working ideal of democracy doesn't come prepackaged with a means of marking out democracy's boundaries.[4] There is no rule-set for determining *who* is entitled to be included in any given decision-making process, and on what basis. If we are committed to the ideal of democratic self-rule, then what grounds do we have for including some people and excluding others? There is a diversity of ways to formulate such criteria, from shared identity, to territorial residence, to tracing the effects of a decision on those it impacts. In what follows, I explore the two most prominent proposals found in the literature to address this so-called "boundary problem."

THE ALL-AFFECTED PRINCIPLE

Suppose that we determine who is included in decision making based on whom it might affect. This strategy seems fairly straightforward. Take a given decision, trace its possible consequences, note all of the constituencies that are impacted by each possibility, and then empower them in the decision-making process. What emerges is the All-Affected Principle: "very likely the best general principle of inclusion that you are likely to find."[5] A rough formulation of the principle states that anyone potentially affected by a collective decision should be included in the making of that decision. As a rule of inclusion, it's fundamentally outcome based. The motivating concern is to ensure that decision making is responsive and accountable when people's vital interests are at stake, such as their human rights, or their freedom, or their basic well-being. Early proponents of the All-Affected Principle saw it as a means of shifting boundaries: enfranchising citizens from *one* country by giving them a vote in the domestic laws and policies of *another* country, on issues that affect them. It seemed obvious that extending voting rights beyond state borders was the surest approach to protecting "communities whose actions, policies, and laws are interrelated and intertwined."[6] Recent advocates for the All-Affected Principle have doubled down on its radically expansive implications. Robert Goodin argues that a consistent application of the principle means that "we should give virtually everyone a vote on virtually everything virtually everywhere in the world."[7] Since we cannot know in advance who is *going* to be affected by a decision, it is impossible to settle the question of who should be included without including everyone, as a precaution – either that, or we must be prepared to cough up and provide considerable financial compensation to those who are wrongfully excluded. This leads to a controversial conclusion. On this *classic interpretation* of the All-Affected Principle, we appear committed to expanding the state by endorsing some form of world government.

The classic interpretation of the All-Affected Principle is criticized for taking an unrealistic, overly broad approach to inclusion. But if we want to be more targeted, then we need to specify what exactly is owed to different constituencies, depending on the degree to which a decision affects them. And, we also need to define the ranges of relevant effects for which different degrees of inclusion is justified. Say there was a way of calibrating the All-Affected Principle to distinguish those that a decision-making process *regularly* or *deeply* affects from those that it does not. This would be a substantial improvement, many think.[8] It would allow us to widen the All-Affected Principle's scope so that it is no longer tracking the consequences of just a single decision point. Instead, we would be able to identify the aggregate effects of multiple related decisions on a given constituency within a given domain. We could then distribute people's participatory entitlements accordingly, *in proportion* to how persistent or pervasive the effects of particular decisions happen to be. One advantage is being able to adopt a more nuanced approach to distributing democratic empowerments, such as voting rights, to "nations, regions, towns, and other geographical areas" according to what is at stake.[9] People's standing to influence collective decision making should vary depending on its relative significance to their lives. Some should be entitled to a full vote, others to fair representation or deliberation, while others still might be correct to demand to at least be consulted, or to have sufficient standing to ensure their interests are legally protected. The All-Affected Principle, on this *pluralist interpretation*, is now a principle of proportionality, allowing for multiple "circles of inclusion and participation" within and across existing borders and different levels of government.[10]

I find this pluralist understanding of the All-Affected Principle to be far more attractive than its classic predecessor. It pushes our thinking about democratic inclusion beyond state-based voting rights, by emphasizing the number and variety of rights and empowerments that self-rule requires. Still, I think the pluralist view leaves far too much undefined, since the idea of proportional inclusion is possible only if we have adequate conceptions of "affectedness" in hand. How can we determine the thresholds at which affectedness warrants a specific type of inclusion? And to whom are these thresholds applicable? The problem is that assigning appropriate weightings based on different degrees of affectedness involves a substantial amount of contextual judgment. The best we can do, on the pluralist account, is to try to work out where the boundaries of democratic inclusion lie on an ad hoc, case-by-case basis.[11] So, as a strategy for inclusion, I think we're better off looking elsewhere.

THE ALL-SUBJECTED PRINCIPLE

If interpretations of the All-Affected Principle leave too much on the table, then it is necessary to search for narrower criteria. A proposed alternative is the so-called "All-Subjected Principle."[12] As a rule of inclusion, it states that all of those subjected to a collective decision have the right to a say in that decision. Proponents of this view make their case by emphasizing that the most basic presumptive wrong that could occur is when someone is unjustly excluded from collective decision making, but has to abide by its terms. What explains the wrong of denying people rights to inclusion to which they're entitled?

From the perspective of those who have been wronged, the complaint is *illegitimate coercion*: "the view that political power is legitimate only insofar as its exercise is mutually justified by and to those subject to it."[13] If adopted, the All-Subjected Principle would supposedly have the benefit of shrinking democracy's domain down to a more appropriate size. "[I]t explains the widely held view that [only] people who live in a country and are routinely subject to its legal system are entitled to be admitted." This eliminates any need to expand the electorate much beyond established borders, since other complaints about being affected "can often be dealt with in ways other than by widening the *demos*."[14]

Once we distinguish being subjected to coercion from other kinds of affectedness, then people's various demands for inclusion seem directly answerable. I admit that this prospect initially sounds quite appealing, since it seems to do away with the need for any complicated weightings. But notice, first, that simply replacing "affectedness" with "coercion" doesn't necessarily limit democracy's boundaries in the way that some might hope. For, surely it is a mistake to think that autonomy-impairing coercion is something that inheres *only* in the collective decisions and actions of states or state-like entities with a global reach. Many other important social and political relationships where people's autonomy is at stake – in the workplace, in the university, in the church, in the family – can be objectionably coercive in ways that trigger legitimate demands for more democracy. This makes it look like we would require a method for distinguishing different forms of coercion that warrant different kinds of protection in different domains. Otherwise, this principle would become just as radically expansive as its rival.[15] But wait. Wasn't the appeal of the All-Subjected Principle precisely that it could do away with the need for such complicated weightings? Posing this question is revealing in itself. We seem to be circling back to where we left off with the All-Affected Principle.

It's time to take stock. I have examined two candidate principles that can be used to determine democracy's boundaries. Both begin with the premise that who is included in collective decision making should be based on a decision's consequences. This follows from their shared view of inclusion as something that is instrumental to protecting people's equal claims to autonomy – the normative meaning of democratic self-rule. Defenders of the All-Affected Principle focus on the various impacts that decisions can have on people's basic interests. They argue that rights and opportunities to influence decision making should be distributed in proportion to people's relative stakes in the process. Defenders of the All-Subjected Principle adopt a similar strategy, but use a different threshold for inclusion. Their criterion is subjection to unjustified coercion by the law or other means. My review suggests that neither principle entirely satisfies. The problem is that both principles are too backwards-looking, making determinations about participatory rights and entitlements solely on the basis of a decision's outcome. From this after-the-fact point of view, there's little room left to consider the background conditions against which a decision takes place.[16] Missing is any accounting of the relationships of power and circumstance that render someone vulnerable to a decision's consequences to begin with. What about the power relationship in a decision-making process can lead to someone being impacted in an undemocratic way? The two principles we have so far considered make it tempting to focus on only the right-hand side of the equation. While the outcome of a collective decision surely matters, equally important is *how* that decision gets made.

TRACK POWER, NOT JUST ITS EFFECTS

How, then, should we proceed? What we need, I argue, is a way of characterizing the democratic complaints that different constituencies could have about a decision-making process that avoids reducing their concerns to the possible effects of the decision. My suggestion is that, from a democratic perspective, we care about how we *relate* to collective decision making, in addition to its consequences. To call a decision-making process "undemocratic" is to signal that something is wrong with the relationships it presupposes. This foregrounding of the relational value of democracy is not novel.[17] But if we build from the idea that democratic self-rule inheres in the structure of relations between persons, then I believe that we can reframe current debates about democratic inclusion in a new and illuminating way.

To set up this argument, I want to highlight how this shift in emphasis – from decisions to relationships – can change our view of people's participatory entitlements. To see this, start with a hypothetical. Two countries share a border. One of them, perhaps it's the United States, decides to pass a law that would allow for heavy amounts of pollution to be pumped into the other, Canada. Based on our discussion so far, we want to say that there are *democratic* grounds for including Canadians in the United States' decision making in this instance. It's their health that will be grossly affected, after all. This seems plausible enough. But now suppose the United States government reconsiders, and decides *not* to implement this controversial law. Now no Canadians are affected, and their demands for inclusion seem less justified. Of course, it remains within the power of the United States to still pass its polluting law at any time of its choosing, and thus to bring about an outcome that would burden the lives of millions across the border. Isn't there still something wrong with this scenario? What is objectionable, I submit, is not whether a given decision has or hasn't affected a constituency's important interests in a particular case. Rather, it is that an agent is *in a position* to arbitrarily make decisions that would significantly impact that constituency's interests in the first place.

These observations tell us something important about the true source of democratic demands for inclusion. We do not see ourselves as having been wrongfully excluded from collective decision making *just* because of the outcome. The basis of our objections, I argue, lies in the one-sided way that an agent relates to us in making decisions that affect us. Complaints about undemocratic decision making always reference an asymmetrical power relationship that enables one side to unilaterally and arbitrarily impose terms on the other. They tap deep intuitions that most of us share about what democracy *is*, and *why* we value it.[18] What makes democratic practices worthwhile is that they underwrite and protect the fundamental moral equality of our most important social and political relationships. They secure the conditions under which we could be said to rule ourselves as free equals.

One implication of this view, I suggest, is that democratic inclusion isn't really about defining boundaries at all. Rather, it's about *redressing* imbalances of power *within* social and political relationships. It propels us towards *equalizing* asymmetrical relationships of domination and dependency, by identifying areas of our collective lives where more democracy is needed. This is why, according to Ian Shapiro, "the principle of affected interests suggests [that] the structure of decision rules should follow contours of power relationships, not that of memberships, or citizenships."[19] Though he doesn't explicitly link the source of people's complaints to the underlying relational structure of decision making, we can draw a general rule of thumb from Shapiro's remarks: *track power, not just its effects.*

My contention is that we have in these reflections the beginnings of an alternative formula for democratic inclusion – one that can operate in the same spirit as the All-Affected and All-Subjected Principles but avoid their blind spots. It starts by picking out the complaints that may arise when people's autonomy is undermined by an asymmetric power relationship. After all, a useful rule for inclusion must be intelligible from the standpoint of those who invoke it. So, what is the underlying wrong to which complaints about undemocratic exclusion are seeking to draw our attention? The first complaint is about *domination*. People are dominated when exposed to arbitrary interference. There is also an important second complaint about *usurpation*. People are usurped when their judgments are displaced without their consent. Importantly, both of these complaints reference more than outcomes. How might these complaints, democratically made, do a better job of indicating the degree to which people are owed inclusion in collective decision making? Let's turn to an examination of each.

DOMINATION: COMPLAINTS ABOUT CONTROL

We know what it looks like when domination is the reason for undemocratic exclusions. A dominant agent – a person, a group, a state – occupies a position of power over us, and is able to interfere in our choices with impunity – for example, by threatening us, or by implementing rules and policies that limit the options available to us. When we complain about domination, I argue, we are objecting to a relationship upon which our basic interests and well-being are dependent, but that we are incapable of controlling.[20] Such domination represents an arbitrary restriction of our equal freedom, under conditions where we ought to have that freedom. Here, interference is an ever-present danger, even if it never actually occurs.

Suffering domination, so understood, *isn't* about being subject to coercion, as some have claimed.[21] It is about the exclusionary character of a relationship that leaves us unprotected from the whims of the more powerful. There's a strong whiff of arbitrariness about it that admits in intensities and degrees. A relationship is arbitrary to the extent that it exists only at the will or pleasure of another agent, without sufficient constraints.[22] In practice, the most visible forms of such wrongful arbitrariness occur when actors with an advantage of resources in society – for example, governments, international trade and financial organizations, corporations – possess the unconstrained capacity to shape people's choices. Less visible forms of domination may also exist in private, in the arbitrariness in relationships between bosses and workers, husbands and wives, or parents and children, among others. The remedy to these injustices, and others like them, is for people to somehow wrest back control over their own circumstances.

To achieve control in one's important social and political relationships is a convincing rationale for demanding democratic inclusion, I argue. As a criterion within our theory, it is clarifying in two key ways. First, it invites us to focus on how undemocratic exclusions are experienced from the standpoint of the wrongfully excluded. Set aside the All-Affected and All-Subjected Principles' earlier focus on the consequences of decision making. The fact that you are somehow affected or coerced by a decision isn't the most basic wrong that's being picked out when one complains about being dominated. Instead, the complaint is that a more powerful agent is depriving you of necessary conditions for self-determination. The location of this wrong is in the asymmetric relationship between you and this agent. The democratic ideal that everyone be treated as free and equal – as "self-ruling" – affords you some form of protection from domination. No one else should be able to arbitrarily interfere in the decisions that determine your life. You're in control only to the extent that your preferences and judgments are decisive in shaping your life's central features – compatible with same for others.[23] This in turn requires that your most important relationships – including the laws and powers to which you are exposed – are clear, predictable, legitimate, and (in the case of relations between free equals) symmetric. Put this way, the connection between domination and democratic inclusion is clearer. Demands for inclusion are in many cases demands for sufficient remedies such that nobody can arbitrarily dictate the terms of a relationship, and everybody can rule themselves equally.

But using nondomination as a metric for inclusion also offers a second advantage, I think. In particular, it can help us to navigate some of the complexities that plague other approaches. How do we sort out complaints that warrant inclusion from those that do not? You can fail to get the job you wanted, have your marriage proposal refused, be denied entrance to that fancy private school, and, in general, have your life goals and plans "affected" – all in ways that are, in a relational sense, perfectly nondominating, and thus perfectly consistent with the ideal of democratic self-rule.[24] Even if your plans are frustrated, you can still retain *the capacity* to rule yourself. Insofar as life's frustrations do not touch the underlying relationships that enable you to continue to freely make choices, inclusion isn't an issue.[25] So, there's no great mystery as to why we sometimes don't feel the need to include people in decision making, even if the outcome affects them in significant ways. To know when democratic inclusion is justified, we need only see undemocratic exclusion for what it is – irreducibly about one's mistreatment within relations of asymmetric power with others.

If we take complaints about domination to only be about undemocratic exclusion, are we committing a category mistake? The approach for which I am advocating helps us to see that many demands for inclusion are best understood as complaints about domination. It makes clear just how difficult it is to achieve nondomination without extending the basic rights and empowerments that are constitutive of democratic self-rule. Note that this does not necessarily require the equal extension of the full voting rights to all affected parties, but it *does* require that a decision-making process ensures that everyone is afforded sufficient rights and standings to be secure from domination, and thus capable of self-rule. People are entitled to varying degrees of inclusion in collective decision making, not because some should have equal standing and others shouldn't. Rather, it is because to count as democratic, a decision-making process must extend to everyone the degree of consideration that is warranted by the circumstances. It is therefore a mistake, I think, to suggest that "moral right[s] to due consideration (e.g., to harms avoided or compensated)" are not "*constitutive* requirements of democratic legitimacy."[26] The error is in deriving democratic inclusion solely from the consequences of a given decision. Missing is inclusion's relational component.

USURPATION: COMPLAINTS ABOUT INVOLVEMENT

We've established one sufficient condition for being included in collective decision making. Whatever else democratic self-rule requires, our decision making must be structured in such a way as to avoid dominating one another. But if, as I suggest, minimizing domination needn't always warrant one's *full* inclusion in a decision-making process, then what does? Can we identify a complaint about exclusion that could *only* be remedied through the extension of equal voting rights and opportunities for participation?

I think we can, but it will require elaboration of a residual complaint that the concept of domination fails to capture. Another agent can be perfectly responsive to our interests, and make only non-arbitrary decisions in relation to us, and yet *still* wrong us by failing to involve us. In such cases, the wrong isn't that you condition your judgments within an asymmetric power relationship in anticipation of the whims of the dominating agent. Rather, it's the separate but related wrong of having your judgment *displaced* entirely on a matter that is either solely or equally yours to decide. There is a compelling objection, I argue, to being forced to sustain collective decisions or policies that you had no hand in shaping. Following Patchen Markell, I call this uniquely democratic complaint *usurpation*: "whatever it is that's happening, and however it's being controlled, to what extent is it happening *through you*, through your activity?"[27]

Complaints about usurpation shed light on the important moral difference between making a decision yourself and having that same decision made for you, without your permission. Here, the democratic nerve struck by this complaint is easily identified. Our collective lives together must instantiate relationships that respect our equal freedom, including our freedom to judge for ourselves what we should do, both individually and collectively. Any relationship that would sideline your input and authority while undertaking obligations on your behalf should be seen as nothing more than undemocratic imposition.[28]

To see the force of this complaint, consider the example of the benevolent technocrat. They follow established rules and procedures perfectly, and track their constituents' interests impeccably. Their decisions are never arbitrary, and will clearly foster conditions that are better for everyone. We – the technocrat's constituents – may have no complaints about domination, and would likely defer to her judgment if given the chance. Yet it is the fact that we aren't given the chance that is democratically troubling. She's unilaterally imposing "her judgement with respect to a matter in which her judgement is not supposed to be authoritative."[29] Nobody should have the authority to speak and act in our name if this excludes us. Put in terms of our theory, such disregard isn't just insulting, it's *usurping* – a displacement of our judgment entirely.

Of course, theorizing usurpation as a distinct kind of democratic complaint is relatively easy. But what more can it actually give us? It's true that the traditional (liberal) view of individual rights already holds that there are certain decisions – over one's body, one's occupation, one's partner – that no one else may decide for you. But usurpation is not a problem of overstepping such (negative) personal boundaries, but rather of implicating us in collective ones. In actual politics, we are routinely faced with organizations and collectivities that make decisions for us, without involving us, on nontrivial matters that are of great significance to the duties and obligations we are (rightly or wrongly) responsible for upholding and that cannot be shirked or escaped. When private corporations ignore the concerns of stakeholder communities, when international organizations step in to manage a country's fiscal policy (think of the International Monetary Fund), or when a municipal government quietly greenlights a development project without any public participation – these "usurpations" implicate people's agency, without involving their judgments, to sustain cooperative schemes. It is the importance of barring asymmetries of this type from altering the structure of relationships that ultimately makes usurpation such an important complaint in its own right. It explains the intuition, reported by Anna Stilz, that people feel alienated when they cannot see themselves as "authors (or "makers") of the institutions to which they are subject."[30]

Should people be entitled to demand an unqualified right to equal participation in organizations or institutions that operate through their agency? Focusing on the underlying structure of relationships, I am arguing, can help us make a determination on this point. Warranted charges of usurpation provide far weightier reasons for demanding rights and standings than do other complaints about exclusion. They are made when individuals find themselves trapped as unwilling cooperators within relationships that are insufficiently democratic. Whereas domination admits in degrees, it is not obvious how complaints about usurpation could be answerable but through full and equal inclusion in decision making. If a relationship imposes collective decisions on an individual's behalf, then, to my mind, there is an unqualified right to an equal say in those decisions – double, if there is no realistic possibility of exit.

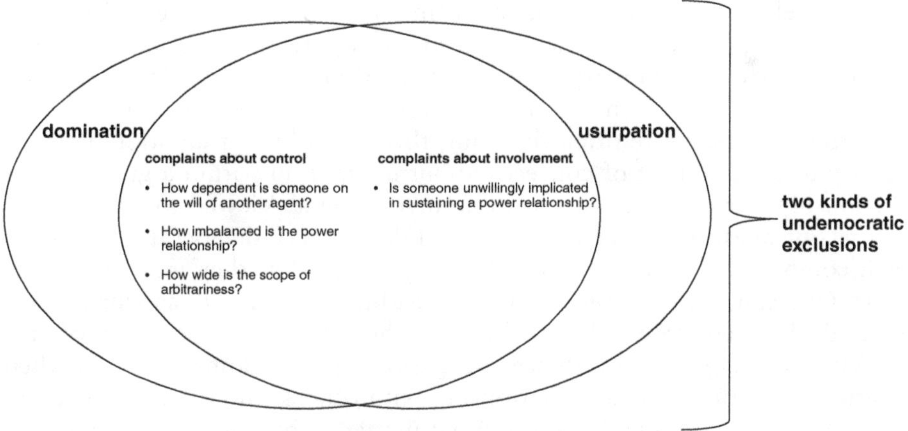

FIGURE 3.1 Two complaints about exclusion

A PEACEMAKING PROPOSAL

If the distinctions that I've drawn are sound, then I think we have in our possession the rough outlines of an alternative principle for democratic inclusion. Having laid out the pieces, all that's required is some assembly. It's common to think we are owed inclusion in collective decision making when the outcome affects us. But when it comes to making good on this intuition, one can quickly become overwhelmed by the complexities involved. In order to move forward, I suggested taking up the following challenge. Without appealing to a decision's outcome, is it possible to specify the different kinds of complaints about exclusion for which different degrees of inclusion is the response? I claimed that an answer comes into focus once we pause and reflect on the norms of democracy. Its value is found in the *relationships* of equal standing between self-ruling persons. It follows that people's complaints about undemocratic exclusion are fundamentally relational in orientation. From the point of view of the complainant, undemocratic exclusion is dominating, usurping, or both. These complaints pick out relational features that are constitutive of, and logically prior to, decision outcomes and effects. So, if we take these two complaints as a guide, then we can get a built-in metric for distinguishing the different degrees of inclusion that are warranted under different circumstances. Call the resulting formula for inclusion the *relational interpretation* of the All-Affected Principle. Or, if that's too partisan a label, call it the "All-Considered Principle." Whatever it's called, I believe that it does a much better job of explaining why democratic inclusion is justified in some cases but not others, and to what degree.

What can this alternative formula tell us about what we owe one another in a globalized world? Even if my argument in this chapter is just a sketch, it suggests a method of determining the appropriate response to people's diverse complaints about exclusion (see Figure 3.1). We ask first: In any pairwise relationship, do people stand in rough relations of equal power? If the answer is "no," we then proceed to inquire into the nature of the underlying power asymmetry. One set of questions identifies relational structures that amount to domination: questions about dependency, imbalance, and arbitrariness. More often than not, this initial line of questioning leads directly to a second set of concerns about usurpation within a given power relationship: concerns about unwilling involvement. Viewed together, these two sets of questions make clear the dual demands of democratic inclusion. Such complaints often travel together in practice, but they may also come apart. One can, for example, be dominated but not usurped, as when a person finds themself wrongfully conditioning their choices on the whims of others. Likewise, one can experience usurpation without domination, as when a person finds themself in a relationship with others who predictably act in their name while leaving them out. What matters, I have argued, is that both of these wrongs reflect relational asymmetries that are best remedied through inclusions to equalize them.

CONCLUSION

A final thought: I won't pretend that the approach to democratic inclusion for which I've advocated was built through conceptual analysis alone. It's normative, all the way down. It explicitly derives its force from a substantive appeal to what lies at the core of our ideal of democracy. I recognize, of course, that there will always be difficult tradeoffs between the realization of this democratic ideal and other important values, such as shared identity, culture, membership, or history. I also recognize that, even in our global era, there are practical constraints on the institutional forms that democracy may take, absent the protections and supports that sovereign states provide. What I am arguing, simply, is that insofar as collective decision making instantiates relationships of domination and usurpation – within and across existing borders – then those affected have solid *democratic* grounds to demand to be included. This, I hope, is something that everyone can agree upon.

NOTES

* Earlier versions of this chapter were presented at the joint Harvard workshops, "Democratic Inclusion in a Globalized World – Debating the All-Affected Principle," held in December 2016 and June 2017. A version was also presented at the 2017 Annual Meeting of the American Political Science Association (APSA). For helpful comments and suggestions, I wish to thank Arthur Applbaum, Lisa Gilson, Lucas Stanczyk, Mark Warren, and especially Eric Beerbohm, as well as participants at the two Harvard workshops and audience members at the 2017 APSA panel.

1 John Rawls, *Political Liberalism*, Expanded Edition (New York: Columbia University Press, 2005), p. 445.

2 Robert A. Dahl, *Democracy and Its Critics* (New Haven: Yale University Press, 1989), p. 326.

3 Niko Kolodny, "Rule Over None I: What Justifies Democracy?" *Philosophy and Public Affairs* 42, no. 3 (2014): 196.

4 Indeed, Rawls goes so far as to bracket the inclusion question entirely, by stipulating "that a democratic society, like any political society, is to be viewed as a complete and closed social system … entry into it is only by birth and exit from it is only by death." See Rawls, *Political Liberalism*, pp. 40–1.

5 Robert A. Dahl, *After the Revolution? Authority in a Good Society* (New Haven: Yale University Press, 1970), p. 64. For an excellent overview of the All-Affected Principle and the debates surrounding it, see Sofia Näsström, "The Challenge of the All-Affected Principle," *Political Studies* 59, no. 1 (2011): 116–34.

6 David Held, *Democracy and the Global Order: From the Modern State to Cosmopolitan Governance* (Stanford: Stanford University Press, 1995), p. 232.

7 Robert E. Goodin, "Enfranchising All Affected Interests, and Its Alternatives," *Philosophy and Public Affairs* 35, no. 1 (2007): 64.

8 For pluralist interpretations of the All-Affected Principle see, for example, Archon Fung, "The Principle of Affected Interests: An Interpretation and Defense," in *Representation: Elections and Beyond*, ed. Rogers M. Smith and Jack H. Nagel (Philadelphia: University of Pennsylvania Press, 2013); Mathias Koenig-Archibugi, "How to Diagnose Democratic Deficits in Global Politics: The Use of the "All-Affected Principle," *International Theory* 9, no. 2: 171–202; and Terry Macdonald, *Global Stakeholder Democracy: Power and Representation beyond Liberal States* (New York: Oxford University Press, 2008).

9 Harry Brighouse and Marc Fleurbaey, "Democracy and Proportionality," *The Journal of Political Philosophy* 18, no. 2 (2010): 139.

10 Fung, "The Principle of Affected Interests," p. 252.

11 For an illustration of what a pluralist account of the All-Affected Principle might entail, institutionally speaking, see Macdonald (this volume).

12 Nancy Fraser, *Scales of Justice: Reimagining Political Space in a Globalizing World* (New York: Columbia University Press, 2009), pp. 64–5.

13 Arash Abizadeh, "Democratic Theory and Border Coercion: No Right to Unilaterally Control Your Own Borders," *Political Theory* 36, no. 1 (2008): 47. A variant of the All-Subjected Principle specifies that the triggering condition is being subjected to authoritative legal or moral obligations, rather than just being subject to wrongful coercion. But for my purposes here, this is a distinction without a difference. Insofar as both are tracking the outcomes of decisions, the problem is the same.

14 David Miller, "Democracy's Domain," *Philosophy and Public Affairs* 37, no. 3 (2009): 225. Italics original. On this point see also, Sarah Song, "The Boundary Problem in Democratic Theory: Why the Demos Should Be Bounded by the State," *International Theory* 4, no. 1 (2012): 39–68.

15 For a more full-throated criticism of the All-Subjected Principle along these lines, see Robert E. Goodin, "Enfranchising All Subjected, Worldwide," *International Theory* 8, no. 3 (2016): 365–89.

16 To be fair, Fung acknowledges this point explicitly, writing that, "decisions [can be] affected by factors that include not just formal provisions for voice, but also indirect laws and regulatory mechanisms, social structures of power, and the collective creation of culture and habit." Fung, "The Principle of Affected Interests," p. 258.

See also, Carol C. Gould, *Globalizing Democracy and Human Rights* (New York: Cambridge University Press, 2004), chap. 7.

17 Here I'm drawing inspiration from Iris Marion Young's "relational approach" to theorizing problems of exclusion. See Young, *Inclusion and Democracy* (New York: Oxford University Press, 2000), chaps. 1 and 7.

18 For an elaboration and defense of this view, see Niko Kolodny, "Rule Over None II: Social Equality and the Justification of Democracy," *Philosophy and Public Affairs* 42, no. 4 (2014): 287–336.

19 Ian Shapiro, *The Moral Foundations of Politics* (New Haven: Yale University Press, 2003), p. 220. For a discussion of structural power, see Hayward (this volume).

20 I follow the Kantian definition of domination of Arthur Ripstein, *Force and Freedom: Kant's Legal and Political Philosophy* (Cambridge, MA: Harvard University Press, 2009), chap. 2. For an opposing, consequentialist view on domination, see Frank Lovett, *A General Theory of Domination and Justice* (New York: Oxford University Press, 2010), pp. 119–23; Philip Pettit, *On the People's Terms: A Republican Theory and Model of Democracy* (New York: Cambridge University Press, 2012), chap. 1.

21 Cf. David Owen, "Constituting the Polity, Constituting the Demos: On the Place of the All Affected Interests Principle in Democratic Theory and in Resolving the Democratic Boundary Problem," *Ethics and Global Politics* 5, no. 3 (2012): 140–3.

22 Thus, I can accept the thrust of Philip Pettit's influential argument that achieving democratic self-rule (in part) "presupposes relationships with others and consists in relating to them on a pattern that rules out domination" – so long as domination here is understood in broadly deontological, and not consequentialist, terms. Pettit, *On the People's Terms*, 91.

23 Says Kant: "*Freedom* (independence from being constrained by another's choice), insofar as it can coexist with the freedom of every other in accordance with a universal law, is the only original right belonging to every man.... [It] involves the following authorizations ... innate *equality*, that is, independence from being bound by others to more than one can in turn bind them; hence a human being's quality of being *his own master* (*sui iuris*) ... and finally, his being authorized to do to others anything that does not in itself diminish what is theirs." Immanuel Kant, *The Metaphysics of Morals*, trans. Mary Gregor (New York: Cambridge University Press, [1797] 1996), p. 30. Italics original.

24 Cf. Robert Nozick, *Anarchy, State, and Utopia* (New York: Basic Books, 1974), pp. 268–271. For a different take on Nozick's marriage proposal example, see Stilz (this volume). While Stilz presents Nozick's argument as fatal to the AAP (and others like the university admissions case), I think the challenge is easily answerable on a relational construal of the AAP that centers domination and usurpation.

25 See Ripstein, *Force and Freedom*, pp. 15–16.

26 Arash Abizadeh, "On the Demos and Its Kin: Nationalism, Democracy, and the Boundary Problem," *The American Political Science Review* 106, no. 4 (2012): 878. Italics original. I single out Abizadeh's important article here because of its influence. In my view, being afforded the standing needed to have "harms avoided or compensated" is a necessary (but not always sufficient) condition for any genuinely democratic relationship, and thus a constitutive requirement for democratic legitimacy.

27 Patchen Markell, "The Insufficiency of Non-Domination," *Political Theory* 36, no. 1 (2008): 12. Italics original. For a useful extension of Markell's view, see Sharon R. Krause, *Freedom Beyond Sovereignty: Reconstructing Liberal Individualism* (Chicago: University of Chicago Press, 2015), pp. 22–8.

28 My use of usurpation here calls to mind an older distinction drawn by Benjamin Constant between "the despot" and "the usurper." A despot, Constant writes, "rules by means of silence, and leaves man the right to be silent." Whereas a usurper "deprives the oppressed of his last remaining consolation" by forcing "him to speak" through acts wrongly portrayed as exercises of popular sovereignty. Constant, *"The Spirit of Conquest and Usurpation and their Relation to European Civilization,"* in *Political Writings*, trans. Biancamaria Fontana (New York: Cambridge University Press, [1814] 1988), pp. 96–7. Bryan Garsten convincingly argues that, despite Constant's well-known liberal sympathies, his concern about despotism is best read as a democratic one. See Garsten, "Representative Government and Popular Sovereignty," in *Political Representation*, ed. Ian Shapiro, Susan C. Stokes, Elisabeth Jean Wood, and Alexander S. Kirshner (New York: Cambridge University Press, 2009).

29 Seana V. Shiffrin, "Paternalism, Unconscionability Doctrine, and Accommodation," *Philosophy and Public Affairs* 29, no. 3 (2000): 226. On paternalism and the usurpation complaint, see also Saunders-Hastings and Reich (this volume).

30 Anna Stilz, "Decolonization and Self-Determination," *Social Philosophy and Policy* 32, no. 1 (2015): 12. That said, in her contribution to this volume, Stilz rejects the approach that I set out here.

4

Deterritorializing Democratic Legitimacy[*]

Melissa S. Williams

A key task of democratic theory in an age of global interdependence is to retrieve and reconstruct core concepts and normative principles from the long history of democratic thought and practice. The need for reconstruction arises from the fact that democratic theory in the modern period developed primarily as an account of the political legitimacy of territorially bounded sovereign states. Many of the defining principles of democratic legitimacy, such as the consent of the governed and equal rights under law, have long carried unquestioned presuppositions about the territorial boundedness of democratic political orders. Although these principles provide potent standards for evaluating the legitimacy of political orders, their built-in presupposition that the principles can only be realized within territorially bounded states makes them less useful for criticizing, resisting, and transforming forms of political and economic power that exceed the boundaries of states.

Recent work in democratic theory has made significant progress in returning to central concepts in the history of democratic thought, reconstructing them so as to free them from their territorial presuppositions, and using them to gain critical purchase on the question of what it would mean to render existing global power relations more legitimate from a democratic point of view. Two principles of democratic legitimacy – the All-Affected Principle and the All-Subjected Principle (hereafter AAP and ASP) – stand out as especially important contributions to democratic theory in a global age. Both principles have deep roots in the history of Western political thought generally, and in the history of democratic thought in particular.

In this chapter, I argue that we can fruitfully *historicize* recent work on the AAP and the ASP as reconstructions of two distinct traditions in the history of democratic thought. The AAP, I suggest, reconstructs the intuition that legitimate government requires the rational consent of the governed, an idea that lies at the heart of the liberal tradition of democratic thought. The ASP, by contrast, is better understood as a reconstruction of the republican ideal of equal freedom under and through law. And yet useful as these concepts are for criticizing and reforming already constituted structures of power beyond the state, such as supranational institutions and transnational corporations, they fall short as criteria of *democratic* legitimacy because they lack a normative account of democratic agency. This shortcoming is twofold. First, the two principles become effective as instruments of democratic legitimacy only when they are taken up by democratic collective agents as principled grounds for resisting or overturning unjust or illegitimate sites of decision-making power. Advocacy for affected interests or subjected persons may produce more egalitarian outcomes, but it is not democratic unless advocates are accountable to those they claim to represent.[1] Second, and more fundamentally for my purposes in this chapter, the democratic legitimacy failures of our age go well beyond the undemocratic character of existing institutional orders. The problem is not only that already constituted orders are undemocratic, but that in many key domains we lack *any* institutionalized capacity to address the urgent collective action problems we face as a consequence of globalization, such as climate change and rampant inequality. Addressing the democratic legitimacy failures of our age requires an account of how new political orders can be constituted in a democratically legitimate way.

Turning back to the history of democratic thought, we find that the doctrine of popular sovereignty was an important device by which to explain how democratically legitimate powers of binding collective decision can come into being. Popular sovereignty, however, is a doctrine tied at a deep conceptual level to the form of the territorially bounded modern state, and hence not useful for making sense of the possibility of democratic collective agency across borders. I turn to a different concept, that of constituent power, as an alternative resource for rethinking democratic agency in a way that liberates it from the territorial presuppositions embedded in the concept of popular sovereignty. Although constituent power and popular sovereignty are often linked tightly to one another in the history of democratic thought, I argue that this link is not unbreakable, drawing evidence from the history of the idea of constituent power from the medieval and early modern periods and from the thought of the French revolutionary thinker, Emmanuel Sieyès. Having reconstructed the idea of constituent power as a "deterritorialized" way of understanding democratic collective agency, in the chapter's conclusion I reflect briefly on the relationship between the AAP, the ASP, and constituent power as jointly necessary principles of democratic legitimacy.

DETERRITORIALIZING CONSENT: THE ALL-AFFECTED PRINCIPLE

The AAP expresses the common intuition that "individuals should be able to influence decisions that affect them."[2] Stated in such an abstract and general way, the principle is insufficient as a standard for evaluating decisions, since virtually every action has some effect on others, and it would be an unreasonable constraint on individual autonomy if we had to woo the consent of every actually and potentially affected other before acting.[3] Democratic theorists have been refining the principle so that it can serve as a defensible standard for establishing and evaluating mechanisms for holding a wide variety of *collective agents* (state and nonstate, public and private) responsible for the significant and enduring effects of their decisions on others.[4] Taken together, these arguments constitute an advance in democratic theory in an age of heightened global interdependence because they let go of the assumptions embedded in earlier formulations of the principle: that territorial states were the appropriate context for its application, and citizens of such states were the appropriate bearers of entitlements to have their interests taken into account in decision-making processes. As Ian Shapiro argues, "[t]he causal principle of affected interest suggests that ideally the structure of decision rules should follow the contours of power relationships, not that of memberships or citizenships: if you are affected by the results, you are presumptively entitled to a say."[5]

To my knowledge, no one has yet written a conceptual history of the AAP. Nonetheless, some scholars have marked out some of the starting points and pivotal moments in the history of this idea. As Melissa Lane notes in her chapter for this volume, it makes sense to trace the idea back to a Roman law precept compiled as part of the Justinian civil code: *quod omnes similiter tangit, ab omnibus comprobetur*, "What touches all similarly must be approved by all."[6] Gaines Post has chronicled the evolution of *quod omnes tangit* from a principle of private law to a procedural principle of public law in the medieval period, showing that it gradually became a procedural principle of consent and a secular source of legitimate political authority.[7] By the fourteenth century the principle was explicitly linked to the legitimacy of taxation and to the claims for representation in conciliar, administrative, and judicial proceedings.[8] It became a key tenet of reform in the age of democratic revolutions, as in the American revolutionary slogan, "No taxation without representation." And from there, it is not difficult to see the connection to interest-group pluralist theories of democracy, in which the equitable representation of potentially conflicting interests becomes a defining criterion of democratic legitimacy.[9]

Read in this way, the AAP captures the normative core of the liberal tradition of democratic thought, in which democratic institutions, together with basic civil and political rights, are seen as *instrumentally* valuable for the protection of fundamental interests (rather than as intrinsically valuable). Scholars have recently adapted and amended the principle so that it can function as an instrument for evaluating, criticizing, and reforming governance institutions in the global age. As Sofia Näsström has argued, the AAP "has done much work to detach the ideal of democracy from its conceptual reliance on the nation state."[10]

DETERRITORIALIZING EQUAL FREEDOM UNDER
THE LAW: THE ALL-SUBJECTED PRINCIPLE

Some democratic theorists have argued that the ASP is a better way to conceptualize democratic legitimacy in the global age than the AAP, and we can trace a similar project of retrieval and reconstruction in their work. Arguing that the AAP is too indeterminate to serve as a stand-alone criterion of democratically legitimate governance,[11] these theorists turn to the ASP for greater specificity in identifying the group of persons who should be empowered with civil and/or political rights in relation to an order of rule.

The normative core of the ASP is that a coercive order of rule is legitimate only if it recognizes and secures the status of all subject to it as free and equal persons.[12] As Nancy Fraser states,

What turns a collection of people into fellow subjects of justice is neither shared citizenship or nationality, nor common possession of abstract personhood, nor the sheer fact of causal interdependence, but rather their joint subjection to a structure of governance that sets the ground rules that govern their interaction. For any such governance structure, the all subjected principle matches the scope of moral concern to that of subjection.[13]

Because there are cross-border, suprastate and transnational configurations of political power, the *demos*, read as the people subject to coercive power, can also be understood to exceed the boundaries of citizenship within a territorial state. On one side, the ASP prescribes that non-citizens subject to the coercive authority of states also be recognized as bearers of basic rights against domination that states have a duty to realize and protect.[14] From another angle, the ASP seeks to recognize non-state forms of institutionalized power as bearing a duty to recognize and protect the rights against domination of those who are subject to them.[15]

As with the AAP, different contemporary theorists have offered different interpretations of the ASP. Here, I highlight two, one wide and one narrow, to suggest that while they have in common a reconstruction of the normative core of the republican tradition of democratic thought, each retrieves a different strand of republicanism in order to render it usable for thinking about democracy in an era of globalization. On the wide reading of the ASP, it retrieves the idea of democratic freedom as collective self-legislation. On the narrow reading, the ASP reconstructs the republican ideal of freedom as nondomination, an idea that underwrites but does not entail the wider view. On the wider view, democracy is intrinsically valuable because participation in the exercise of collective autonomy is constitutive of the individual autonomy of those subject to binding law. On the narrower view, democracy is instrumentally valuable because it empowers individuals to contest both public and private forms of domination.[16]

My purpose here is not to try to adjudicate between different interpretations of the ASP, but to suggest that it is illuminating to read the contrasting

interpretations of the ASP as reworkings of different strands within republican traditions of thought that loosen them from their territorial presuppositions. Following Philip Pettit's distinction between the "Italian-Atlantic"
and "Franco-German" traditions of republicanism,[17] we can read the narrow
interpretation of the ASP as the retrieval of an element common to both traditions, whereas the wide interpretation retrieves an idea that is distinctive
to the Franco-German tradition of republicanism. The core of the narrow
interpretation of the ASP can be summed up as the principle of freedom as
nondomination. The second can be summed up as the principle of freedom
as self-legislation (*auto-nomia*) that underwrites the Rousseauean/Kantian tradition of popular sovereignty.

As Pettit has argued throughout the development of his neo-republican
project, the origins of the idea of freedom as nondomination lie in Roman
republican thought, and in particular the distinction between the free person
(*liber*) and the slave (*servus*). To be a slave is to live according to the arbitrary
will of a master, that is, under another's rule or *dominium*; to be a free person
is to be publicly recognized as an equal under law, that is, a citizen, and not
subject to another's will (*civis*).[18] The purpose of republican legal order is to
secure each citizen's nondominated status. Law is not a will that stands over
and against individuals' wills as a master, but secures the equal freedom of
all citizens through a mixed constitution and by protecting the contestatory
powers of citizens so that they can defend themselves against both private and
public domination.[19] The narrow reading of the ASP, in which subjection to
coercion generates a right to contest the order of law to which one is subject,
loosens this tradition of freedom as nondomination from its longstanding presupposition that legal citizenship within a polity is what gives a person standing to contest the coercive power of its laws. Instead, buttressed by the idea of
human rights, which recognizes all human beings as persons with standing to
claim equality under the laws to which they are subject, the ASP extends the
principle of freedom as nondomination to anyone who is subject to any coercive order. This expansion does not entail that all who are subjected to a legal
order in any respect have a right to participate in the lawmaking process, but
that they have a claim to contest any coercive law that unjustifiably restricts
their freedom.

The wide interpretation of the ASP, in which being subject to coercive law
generates a right to participate in the making of law as its equal co-author,
ties back into a different tradition of republican thought in which Rousseau
and Kant are key figures. In that tradition, freedom as nondomination is reinterpreted not only as independence from the arbitrary will of another, but as
autonomy, that is, being the self-originating source of the law by which one is
bound. Its *locus classicus* is Rousseau's idea of moral freedom as stated in the
Social Contract: "obedience to a law one prescribes to oneself."[20] This reflexive understanding of freedom-as-independence is read into the civic realm as
the idea of collective autonomy, in which individuals' obligation to obey law

can be reconciled with individual autonomy just insofar as they participate as co-equal members of the self-legislating community. Law is not the imposition of an alien will, but a self-imposed restriction on individuals' own arbitrary wills, aimed at securing the possibility of realizing collective goods that would be impossible to realize if individuals pursued only their separate interests. In Abizadeh's reconstruction of the ASP as a principle of collective self-legislation, he strips away the deeply rooted presupposition that the self-governing *demos* must be bounded by common culture, nationhood, or historically settled territorial borders, arguing that since borders themselves are coercively enforced, those excluded by them are subject to the coercive power of the states concerned and of the state system as a whole. This idea transforms the ASP into a regulative ideal that can never be fully met in practice, but which is nonetheless analytically clear as a standard for evaluating any actually existing coercive order, including territorial borders.[21]

DETERRITORIALIZING DEMOCRATIC AGENCY: CONSTITUENT POWER

My purpose thus far has been to make explicit what contemporary theorists are doing when they debate and refine theoretical articulations of the AAP and the ASP as resources for rethinking the possibilities and criteria for democratic legitimacy under conditions of globalization. I have argued that we can understand their inquiries as efforts to rework familiar ideas from the long history of democratic thought in order to make them usable for analyzing and criticizing existing structures of political power, and for generating normative insights into how these structures might be rendered more legitimate from a democratic point of view. As the contributors to this volume demonstrate, the AAP and the ASP provide rich argumentative resources for identifying the democratic deficits of a wide range of contemporary global structures: immigration regimes,[22] global governance institutions,[23] international trade and its impact on labor,[24] international philanthropy,[25] climate change,[26] and so on.

Taken together, these arguments make a strong case that the AAP and the ASP are valuable (and perhaps necessary) criteria of democratic legitimacy. It also makes sense, as several theorists have argued, to view them as complementary to one another rather than as rivals.[27] But the question remains whether they are sufficient to ground a full or adequate account of what democratic legitimacy entails. I believe they are not. The AAP and the ASP provide valuable insights into the normative constraints that must be placed on the exercise of power in order for it to count as legitimate. But democracy requires more than constraints on the exercise of political power; it also requires the capacity to *generate* political power, that is, the capacity to produce binding (i.e. coercive) collective decisions aimed at advancing common interests. As Jane Mansbridge has argued, democratic theory and activism have long been preoccupied with the important task of *resisting* illegitimate forms of coercive power. Invaluable as this "resistance tradition" has been for making political power more legitimate by rendering it more democratically accountable, an almost exclusive emphasis on resistance has led to the underdevelopment of theories of democratically legitimate collective action.[28] This neglect takes on a particular urgency under circumstances of globalization, when domestic and international or transnational capacities for collective action are less and less of a match for the complex problems that arise from increasing global interdependence and mutual affectedness.

Viewed from this angle, the AAP and the ASP are valuable reworkings of elements in the venerable resistance tradition of democratic theory, but offer limited resources for understanding the character and origins of democratically legitimate collective action. If the democratic deficits of a globalized world arise not only from the illegitimate *use* of coercive power, but also from the *lack* of collective agency, then the AAP and the ASP are not adequate for a thorough-going diagnosis of the demands of democratic legitimacy under circumstances of globalization.

In the history of democratic thought, the concept of popular sovereignty has performed important work as an account of democratically legitimate collective agency. It is perhaps for this reason that several contemporary theorists have characterized popular sovereignty as a principle of democratic legitimacy that stands in a complementary relationship to the AAP and/or the ASP.[29] Yet in an age of globalization, where the cross-border effects of state decisions are increasingly visible, it is clear that the principle of popular sovereignty as a form of democratic agency at the scale of the state is not adequate to secure the democratic legitimacy of the state system as a whole. The AAP and the ASP offer criteria by which to clarify the external legitimacy constraints on the democratic agency that is realized through states whose internal legitimacy is grounded in the idea of popular sovereignty.

The idea of popular sovereignty, however, like the idea of democratic self-determination to which it bears close kinship,[30] may be impossible to extricate from the presupposition that democratic collective agency can only be realized within territorially bounded political communities – if not states, then state-like jurisdictions that enjoy considerable autonomy in relation to other polities.[31] It is for this reason that some theorists have argued against the idea that democracy is possible, or even conceivable, beyond the scale of the territorial state.[32] Others have argued that if democracy is realizable beyond the scale of the state, it will be through a divided or multilevel form of popular sovereignty institutionalized through nested territorial jurisdictions, as may eventually be possible in the European Union.[33] These reconstructions of popular sovereignty as a way of reconceiving democratic collective agency beyond the state remain tied to the presupposition that democratic agency can only be exercised by territorially bounded *demoi*. This supposition is based, in turn, on the idea that only a collectivity whose members see themselves as participants in a common, stable, durable, and substantial system of cooperation is capable of sustaining a project of collective self-legislation, and hence of democracy properly so-called.[34]

The idea that collective political agency in the form of self-legislation is possible only among people who see themselves as bound to one another in relations of interdependence or mutual affectedness into the foreseeable future carries a great deal of intuitive good sense. The question I wish to explore in the remainder of this chapter is whether it is possible to extricate this idea from the presupposition that shared occupancy of a determinate territory is a necessary presupposition of democratic collective agency. In other words, is the concept of popular sovereignty, read as the power of collective self-legislation of a territorially bounded *demos*, the only imaginable form of meaningfully democratic agency? Or is there a normative core to the idea of democratic agency expressed by the concept of popular sovereignty that it is possible to extricate and reconstruct in a manner that liberates it from its territorial presuppositions, much as the AAP reconstructs the normative core of *quod omnes tangit* and the ASP reconstructs the normative core of equal freedom under law?

I believe that there is in fact a normative core to the idea of popular sovereignty that can be retrieved and reconstructed in this way: the idea of *constituent power*, that is, the rightful authority that people have to freely associate with one another in jointly establishing the law-governed order that will regulate their relations with one another and through which they will generate binding collective decisions aimed at serving their common interests. Through much of the history of modern Western thought, the concept of popular sovereignty and that of constituent power have been read as nearly synonymous terms. Constituent power – the power to constitute an order of government, to create a constitution – is often read as the power that properly belongs to the popular sovereign as the ultimate authority on which legitimate order is based.

It would take a far more detailed historical treatment than is possible in a brief essay to trace the concepts of constituent power and popular sovereignty through the history of Western thought, let alone the complex relationship between them. Other scholars have done this work far more thoroughly than I can hope to do here.[35] Instead, I will briefly sketch two moments in the history of the concept of constituent power to show that it is unquestionably possible to read it as independent of the concept of sovereignty, and hence of the concept of popular sovereignty. First, the concept of constituent power long *antedated* the concept of popular sovereignty, and indeed the concept of the sovereign state. Second, the modern thinker most strongly associated with the concept of constituent power, Emmanuel Sieyès, embraced it at the same time that he rejected the concept of sovereignty as having a proper place in his theory of political legitimacy.

Although the concept of constituent power is usually associated with the age of democratic revolutions, Daniel Lee has recently shown that the idea has much older roots in the history of European thought.[36] Lee traces the evolution of the concept of constituent power from sixteenth-century figures such as

Donellus and Brutus (who used the concept to ground a claim of the people's authority over the king) back to the much older doctrine of *lex regia*, which dates back to late Roman thinkers. The fiction at the core of the *lex regia* was that the people of the Roman republic had transferred their legislative authority to the emperor;[37] in the medieval period, the doctrine was mobilized again to make sense of the (de facto) authority of free cities to establish their own orders, free from interference from the Holy Roman Empire, kings, or lords. Here, the doctrine combined with the concept of a "free people" (*populus liber*) within Roman *ius gentium*, in which allies of the Roman empire were treated as having the right to govern themselves according to their own laws. Medieval jurists used these concepts to extend the logic of *lex regia* to *all* free peoples.[38]

For the purpose of retrieving and reconstructing the idea of constituent power as a way of conceptualizing democratic agency, it is worth highlighting two points from this quick sketch of a long history. First, the idea of constituent power as the foundation of democratic authority is not inextricably tied to the idea of the territorially bounded sovereign state. This is clear from the simple fact that the normative core of constituent power was expressed well before the emergence of the idea of the sovereign state, in the form of arguments on behalf of the right of free cities to govern themselves. Second, the history shows that the idea of "the people" that possesses the right of self-legislation is indeterminate; the concept of a *populus liber* was variously used to denote the people of the Roman republic, the free peoples in the Roman law of *ius gentium*, the citizens of medieval city-states, and, eventually, the people of the territorially bounded modern state.[39] The character and composition of "the people" on whose behalf this potent idea has been mobilized across the centuries is not singularly identifiable with the people of the modern territorial state, and there is no reason in principle why the idea cannot be mobilized for new constructions of "peoplehood" in the twenty-first century. Although the concept of popular sovereignty is inextricably linked to the concept of the sovereign territorial state, the concept of constituent power is not.

The separability of the concept of constituent power from that of popular sovereignty is also evident from the thought of Sieyès, the person most often credited with distinguishing the constituent power of the people from the constituted authority of the state. According to Sieyès, the legitimacy of ordinary positive law rests on its having been promulgated in accordance with constitutional laws fixing the organization and powers of legislative and executive governance bodies. The legitimate authority of the constitution, in turn, issues from its consonance with the will of the people (or, in Sieyès' term, "the nation"). Constitutional laws, he wrote, "are said to be *fundamental*, not in the sense that they can be independent of the national will, but because bodies that can exist and can act only by way of these laws cannot touch them. In each of its parts a constitution is not the work of a *constituted power* but a *constituent power*."[40] Sieyès' theory of constituent power has a number of features that are problematic from the standpoint of a democratic theory committed to egalitarian inclusion.[41] Nonetheless, two features of his argument stand out as useful resources for a contemporary reconstruction of constituent power as democratic agency. The first is that Sieyès explicitly distances the concept of constituent power from the concept of sovereignty, including popular sovereignty. The second is that although at points he does describe "the nation" as a quasi-natural and pre-political subject, a more nuanced reading of his text shows that what makes the *demos* as a potential collective agent is not a common history, culture, or language but a dense network of social and material interdependence that is the *objective* condition of possibility for the formation of a *subjective* sense of collective purpose and agency. For Sieyès, what transforms a latent or potential "nation" or "people" into a political agent is an *act of representation* through which a plurality of individuals can be reimagined as a unified collectivity capable of acting jointly toward their common good.

On the first point, Sieyès explicitly criticizes the concept of sovereignty because he regards it as tied to absolutism. The decision to form a constitutional order was a choice to live under a system of law that would secure the freedom of each, which on his view (as in the Roman republican tradition) depended upon a mixed constitution in which no element reigns supreme. "It is a mistake," he argued, "to talk of the sovereignty of the people as if it had no bounds."[42] In a later writing, *pace* Schmitt's interpretation, he rejects the political theology with which the concept of sovereignty is bound.[43] As Lucia Rubinelli has recently argued, Sieyès "never relied on the notion of sovereignty to describe the principle of the people's power," and instead *substituted* the concept of constituent power for that of sovereignty.[44]

The significance of Sieyès' rejection of sovereignty for this chapter's project of retrieval and reconstruction is straightforward. These passages demonstrate that one can embrace the concept of constituent power while rejecting the absolutism and decisionism that is constitutive of many theories of sovereignty, including the most common readings of Hobbes and Rousseau and, certainly, Schmitt's politico-theological account of popular sovereignty. These passages show clearly that for Sieyès the constituent power of "the people" did not entail that the will of the people was self-validating. Rather, a legitimate political order is always constrained by principles respecting the equal freedom of its individual members.

The second key point I wish to retrieve from Sieyès' theory of constituent power is that his conception of the people as a collective agent is not best understood as pre-political. In the opening chapter of "What is the Third Estate?"[45] Sieyès defines a nation not as a people defined by shared history, language, or culture but as "a body of associates living under a *common* law, represented by the same *legislature*, etc." In other words, the people as a collective agent is itself constituted by its members' joint decision to live together under a common order of law which they share a role in making. Sieyès' description of the activities that make a society are explicitly materialist and based on his analysis of the social division of labor. The heart of Sieyès' critique of the existing order is that the very people whose productive activities and relationships jointly create the conditions for a flourishing social life are excluded from a role in the political order under which they live.

Yet the objective reality of the interdependence and cooperative activities of individual members of society is not in itself sufficient to make them a political agent. Sieyès invites his readers to imagine a three-stage process by which the multitudinous participants in these common social and economic activities become a political unity capable of collective action. The first stage is simply the emergence of a will among "a more or less substantial number of isolated individuals seeking to unite." "This fact alone," he writes, "makes them a nation." At this stage, it is the convergent wills of individuals who see the advantage of acting together that constitutes a collectivity who make their association itself the object of their work.[46]

The second stage is one of deliberation through which associates' several individual wills are forged into a "*common* will."[47] Here Sieyès explicitly introduces the concept of power as something that is generated only through a process of common will formation:

[P]ower belongs to the public. Individual wills still lie at its origin and still make up its essential underlying elements. But taken separately, their power would be null. Power resides solely in the whole…. Without this unity of will, it would not be able to make itself a willing and acting whole. It is also certain that this whole has no rights that are not connected to the common will.[48]

The third stage in Sieyès' account of the formation of collective agency is *representation*. For Sieyès, the formation of political agency should be understood as a part of the larger social division of labor. The inconvenience, inefficiency and, in a society with large numbers of people, the impracticability of assembling to form a common will through deliberation generates the need to "entrust" the common will "to the exercise of some of their number."[49] This trust, he emphasizes, does not mean that the community "divest[s] itself of the right to will," and the appointed delegate has no authority to "alter the limits of the power with which it has been entrusted." Yet the character of the common will is transformed by the shift from deliberation to representation: "it is no longer a *real* common will that acts, but a *representative* common will," which can only ever be an incomplete and limited expression of the common will.[50] In other words, the authority of the representative to act on behalf of the community is always qualified by the fact that there is a gap between what the members of the association truly want and the representation of their common will by their delegates. Because of this gap, the possibility remains open that the community, whose constituent power has set up the system of representation, may reclaim its authority if its current delegates have misinterpreted its will.

We find, then, in the *locus classicus* of the concept of constituent power, the basic elements of a methodologically and normatively individualist theory of group agency[51] for a particular kind of group – one that seeks to bring into being, where it did not exist before, a law governed order that treats all who live under it as free and equal persons, over the *longue durée*.[52] Sieyès' theory provides the basic conceptual resources for separating democratic collective agency both from the concept of sovereignty and from the supposition that territory provides the relevant material underpinnings for the formation of a democratic collective agent.[53] Rather, it is the coming-into-consciousness of ongoing relations of material interdependence that generates the first movement toward the formation of joint intentions to identify common interests and, through deliberation, forge a common will. This *common* will is not a *general* will in Rousseau's sense, as it acknowledges the ongoing plurality of its constituent members. Sieyès' theory also recognizes that in the moment of transition between the constituent power and the constituted power – the moment of representation – there is always some violence done to this plurality. The representation of the collective agent as a unity always leaves a remainder, which is why the constituent power is not extinguished by the creation of the constituted power, and why claims to represent "the people" must always remain open to contestation.[54]

CONCLUSION

I have argued that recent works aimed at specifying the AAP and the ASP as criteria of democratic legitimacy for a global age can be understood as endeavors to retrieve and reconstruct much older ideas in the history of democratic thought, liberating these ideas from democratic theory's long-standing entanglement with the usually unexamined presupposition that democracy is possible only within territorially bounded forms of political community. The AAP and the ASP are potent rearticulations of normative principles that *all* forms of political power, and not only those centered in territorially bounded states, must meet if they are to claim even a modicum of democratic legitimacy. Any structure of power that does not satisfy these criteria fails to treat as equals those human beings who are affected by its decisions or subject to its coercive power. Since the equal moral worth of all persons as such is the *sine qua non* of any conception of democracy, no political order that fails these tests can validly claim to be legitimate from a democratic point of view.

Yet both the AAP and the ASP fall short of a thoroughgoing account of democratic legitimacy because both are focused on appropriate normative constraints on political power, and not on the democratically legitimate conditions under which power, understood as a capacity for binding collective decision, can emerge. I have suggested that both are reconstructions for a global age of elements in the long-standing resistance tradition of democratic theory, where the principal concern is to restrain the illegitimate exercise of political power. In the era of globalization, there has been a proliferation of forms of political and economic power that is not constrained to track all affected

interests or the equal rights under law of all subjected. The AAP and the ASP
provide useful analytical toolkits by which to diagnose these normative deficiencies of the current global order. They track the *objective* facts of the matter about whose interests are adversely affected and whose equal standing as
a subject of lawful or unlawful subjection is being violated by contemporary
arrangements of political power. But these principles operate, more or less,
from a *juridical* point of view. They are addressed to the normative strengths
or weaknesses of already constituted powers, but offer little insight into the
injustices that result from the absence of collective decision-making capacity
in those domains where a power vacuum not only reproduces an unjust status
quo but, as Mansbridge emphasizes, amplifies the *drift* of the complex global
system toward outcomes that are unquestionably disadvantageous for the vast
majority of human (and non-human) beings.[55] In order to understand the
potentials for democratic legitimacy under conditions of globalization, we
need, as well, a better understanding of the possibility of democratic agency
which, like the AAP and the ASP, is unmoored from the presupposition that
democracy is possible only within territorially bounded political communities. We need to understand how democratically legitimate forms of binding
collective decision-making capacity can be generated in domains where it does
not already exist.

Through this chapter's provisional reconstruction of the idea of constituent
power as democratic agency, I have sought to show that we need not hold onto
the supposition that the powers of collective self-legislation are available only
to territorially bounded political peoples. The democratic peoplehood of territorial states will undoubtedly be an important resource for democratic agency
for some time to come, as the institutionalization of collective agency through
elections, projects of constitution making, and the like is still concentrated at
the level of the territorial state. Moreover, the citizen empowerments that are
crucial to democratic mobilization and will formation – rights of expression,
association, and participation – are now institutionalized only at the scale of
the state, and these are crucial instruments for leveraging political influence at
other scales of politics.

The link between democratic collective agency and the powers of territorial
states is a historically contingent phenomenon, not written into the concept
of democracy as the self-rule of the people. In principle, there are only two
constraints on the formation of democratic collective agency. The first is that
there are enduring objective conditions of social and material interdependence
among the people. In the absence of lasting social and material conditions of
interdependence, which Sieyès characterized in terms of a social division of
labor, there is no clear reason why individuals should strive to forge an association united around common interests over a sufficiently long term to warrant
the establishment of a durable order of democratic self-rule. In addition, there
must be a *subjective* consciousness of the fact of interdependence potent enough
to motivate diverse and dispersed individuals to form an association around

their common interests and make these common interests a site of collective self-legislation. They must discursively represent, first to themselves as consociates in a shared process of material and social production, and later to others who are also implicated in this process, their character as participants in a common social project. This moment of discursive representation, the articulation of an imagined political relationship between a multitude of individual actors as parts of a larger social whole that can and should be made democratically legitimate, is a condition of possibility for the political representation of common interests and the constitution of new powers of binding collective decision.

The boundaries of "the people" as the collective subject of constituent power, then, are constrained but not determined by either territorial boundaries or the facticity of material relations of social interdependence. Objective conditions of interdependence form one limit of the possibility of constituent power as democratic agency. The history of the post-Westphalian system of territorially bounded states carries the consequence that material relations of interdependence are especially strong at the scale of the state. Legal regimes of property, labor, taxation, and redistribution remain concentrated at the scale of the state, and state policies around economic development continue to exert enormous influence over the future prospects of individuals within state jurisdictions. But the fact of globalization has generated material and social relations of interdependence that cross state boundaries, much as the colonial policies of European states historically crossed the boundaries of ethno-cultural peoplehood to generate global divisions of labor in which some classes but not others were represented in the decisions by which the benefits of economic codependence were distributed.

Historically, the idea of constituent power has commonly been associated with revolutionary moments and moments of constitutional founding. This is a mistake; such moments are important instances of constituent power, but they do not exhaust the category. Democratic agency as constituent power is much more common than revolutionary moments. It exists wherever individuals freely associate with the purpose of instituting an institutional order that is capable of generating binding collective decisions aimed at advancing common interests. Whether or not it succeeds in instituting a new order or reconstituting an existing one, the essence of constituent power is contained in the joint intention to form a democratically legitimate order.

In concluding, let me briefly return to the proposition, noted earlier, that we should understand basic principles of democratic legitimacy as complementary to one another rather than as rivals. Whereas other theorists have suggested that the AAP and/or the ASP should be understood as complementary to the principle of popular sovereignty, I want to suggest that we should read them as complementary to the principle of constituent power. Indeed, the AAP, ASP, and constituent power can be understood as *jointly necessary* and *mutually constraining* principles of democratic legitimacy. An element of constituent power is internal to the democratic bona fides of the AAP and the ASP.

A decision-making process cannot take affected interests into account or preserve the equal freedom of those subject to its decisions unless those interests and persons are *represented* as having a valid claim within the process. The representation of interests and persons, in turn, is not *democratic* unless it reflects the self-understanding of the represented as to the interests they have at stake in a given process. If the interests of the affected or subjected are represented from a juridical point of view, based on an analysis of the objective facts in a given context of decision making, the resulting decision may be just but it cannot properly be called democratic. Conversely, an exercise of constituent power, aimed at creating institutions capable of generating binding collective decisions, is democratic to the extent that it treats as equals all persons who are included in the collectivity. However, democratic constituent power is not legitimate if it does not take into account the interests that are significantly affected by its exercise, or the claim to equal freedom of those who fall subject to the institutions it establishes, even if those interests or persons fall outside the boundaries of the collective agent. In other words, the AAP and the ASP can be read as side constraints on the legitimate exercise of constituent power.

The argument advanced in this chapter proceeds at a regrettable level of abstraction. Ideally, I would turn to some illustrative cases to show how this retrieval and reconstruction of the idea of constituent power enables us to see, *as forms of democratic agency*, political formations that have arisen across borders in the global era. The climate change movement is one instructive example: the cross-border mobilization of diverse people who understand themselves as bound to one another by the shared human condition of vulnerability to climate change, and act jointly toward the goal of instituting a global order of binding rules that would limit climate change and address its effects.[56] Other examples include the transnational movement of Indigenous peoples and the United Nations Declaration on the Rights of Indigenous Peoples that their mobilization generated, and the transnational peasants' movement, La Vía Campesina, which is organized democratically at local, state, regional, and global levels and has made significant progress toward the goal of ratifying a UN Declaration on the Rights of Peasants and Other People Working in Rural Areas. For the moment, my hope is to have contributed to the larger project of reworking democratic theory for a global era through the retrieval and reconstruction of old ideas in the history of democratic thought.

NOTES

* Earlier versions of this chapter were presented in 2017 at the Annual Meeting of the American Political Science Association and the Toronto Chapter of the Conference for the Study of Political Thought. I am grateful to participants in those discussions, and to participants in the 2016–17 Harvard workshops on the "Democratic Inclusion in a Globalized World – Debating the All-Affected Principle" for the conversations that prompted me to write this chapter. In particular, I wish to thank

Sean Gray, Tomer Perry, Yann Allard-Tremblay, Carol Gould, Archon Fung, Stefan Macleod, Lucia Rubinelli, Daniel Lee, Annabelle Lever, Mark Warren, and Joseph Carens for critical feedback and helpful discussions.

1 Laura Montanaro, "The Democratic Legitimacy of Self-Appointed Representatives," *The Journal of Politics* 74, no. 4 (2012): 1094–107; Michael Saward, *The Representative Claim* (New York: Oxford University Press, 2010).

2 Archon Fung, "The Principle of Affected Interests: An Interpretation and Defense," in *Representation: Elections and Beyond*, ed. Rogers M. Smith and Jack H. Nagel (Philadelphia: University of Pennsylvania Press, 2013), p. 237.

3 As captured by Robert Nozick's (in)famous example of the effect of a woman's decision to marry one of her four suitors has on the lives of the rejected candidates. Nozick, *Anarchy, State, and Utopia* (New York: Basic Books, 1974), pp. 268–71. For critical discussions of Nozick's argument, see Fung, "The Principle of Affected Interests," p. 246; and Carens (this volume).

4 See e.g. David Owen, "Constituting the Polity, Constituting the Demos: On the Place of the All Affected Interests Principle in Democratic Theory and in Resolving the Democratic Boundary Problem," *Ethics and Global Politics* 5, no. 3 (2012): 148; Fung, "The Principle of Affected Interests," p. 247 ("An individual should be able to influence an organization if and only if that organization makes decisions that regularly and deeply affect that individual's important interests"); Carol C. Gould, *Interactive Democracy: The Social Roots of Global Justice* (New York: Cambridge University Press, 2014), p. 89 ("[I]t is possible to demarcate those who are *importantly affected* in terms of a notion of the *fulfillment of basic human rights*, and to propose that when people are thus affected in their ability to realize these basic rights, they should have significant input into the decision or policy in question, though not necessarily fully equal rights of participation").

5 Ian Shapiro, *The Moral Foundations of Politics* (New Haven: Yale University Press, 2003), p. 219. For further discussion, see Gray and Hayward (this volume).

6 Lane (this volume).

7 Gaines Post, "A Romano-Canonical Maxim, '*Quod Omnes Tangit*,' in Bracton," *Traditio* 4 (1946): 197–251.

8 Post, "A Romano-Canonical Maxim," pp. 49–50.

9 Robert Dahl, the preeminent theorist of pluralist democracy, declared the AAP to be "very likely the best general principle of inclusion you are likely to find," even though, he quickly added, "it turns out to be a good deal less compelling than it looks." Although the principle is too indeterminate to provide a complete account of legitimate government, it is "not such a bad principle to start with" because "[i]t gives people who believe themselves to be seriously affected by decisions at least a prima facie case for participating in those decisions and puts the burden of exclusion" on those who argue that considerations of competence or efficiency outweigh claims for inclusion. Robert A. Dahl, *After the Revolution? Authority in a Good Society* (New Haven: Yale University Press, 1970), pp. 49, 51.

10 Sofia Näsström, "The Challenge of the All-Affected Principle," *Political Studies* 59, no. 1 (2011): 123.

11 These theorists offer two main arguments concerning the indeterminacy of the AAP. First, since the composition of the group affected by a decision changes with each decision, the AAP cannot generate relationship between decision-making institutions and those to whom they can and should be held accountable. Second, since

virtually every decision affects virtually everyone in some respect, the logical conclusion of the AAP is that there should be a single global decision-making authority
in which all persons are enfranchised. Some proponents of the AAP, such as Robert
Goodin, do not flinch from this conclusion as a judgment in ideal theory; but others
regard it as a *reductio ad absurdum* showing that because the AAP can offer no
clear criteria for specifying morally and politically relevant social relations, "it has
trouble resisting the one-size-fits-all globalism it sought to avoid." Nancy Fraser,
Scales of Justice: Reimagining Political Space in a Globalizing World (New York:
Columbia University Press, 2009), p. 64.

12 For alternate formulations of the ASP, see e.g. Owen, "Constituting the Polity,"
p. 148 ("*any* person subject to autonomy-violating forms of political power, whether
coercive or not, by a polity in respect of a given domain of law is entitled to inclusion within the demos of that polity with respect to the relevant domain of law");
Näsström, "The Challenge of the All-Affected Principle," p. 120 ("those *subject* to
a rule should also be its *authors*").

13 Fraser, *Scales of Justice*, p. 65. Arash Abizadeh adds precision to the concept by
emphasizing that being subject to *coercive* power always compromises individual
autonomy in the form of freedom from the imposition of another's will, and hence
always stands in need of justification. See Arash Abizadeh, "Democratic Theory and
Border Coercion: No Right to Unilaterally Control Your Own Borders," *Political
Theory* 36, no. 1 (2008): 40.

14 Abizadeh, "Democratic Theory and Border Coercion"; James Bohman,
"Domination, Global Harms, and the Priority of Injustice: Expanding Transnational
Republicanism," in *Domination and Global Political Justice: Conceptual, Historical,
and Institutional Perspectives*, ed. Barbara Buckinx, Jonathan Trejo-Mathys, and
Timothy Waligore (New York: Routledge, 2015), p. 78 ("[A]n increasing number of
people, such as undocumented and illegal noncitizens, lack … basic statuses even in
democratic societies, with the consequence that they are exposed to domination and
injustice meted out by a variety of actors, including citizens, without the protections
of non-domination that republics seem to be able to offer").

15 Thus the ASP has "a broader scope than previously thought, since people can be
subjected to a variety of non-state actors (such as private corporations). Under current circumstances of injustice, … powers of subjection are dispersed across various institutions and various units." Bohman, "Domination, Global Harms, and the
Priority of Injustice," p. 79.

16 Arash Abizadeh and Sofia Näsström are exemplars of the wide interpretation of
the ASP, based on the idea of democratic freedom as collective self-legislation. On
this view, the ASP expresses the idea that the legitimacy of a coercive order of law
depends upon the law's co-authorship by those who are subject to it. See Arash
Abizadeh, "On the Demos and Its Kin: Nationalism, Democracy, and the Boundary
Problem," *The American Political Science Review* 106, no. 4 (2012): 867–82;
Näsström, "The Challenge of the All-Affected Principle," p. 120. For these authors,
in contrast to the AAP, the ASP expresses a principle of democratic self-rule as an
intrinsic and not merely an instrumental good. In contrast, Rainer Bauböck argues
that the wide interpretation of the ASP expands its scope of democratic inclusion
too broadly by construing as full members of a polity those who are subject only to
a limited domain of its coercive power or (as in the case of transients) are subject
to its power for only a limited period of time. On his reading of the ASP does not

generate rights of full membership in a self-legislating *demos* for all who are subject to a polity's coercive decisions, but rather a right to participate as equals in the contestation of the decisions to which they are subject. Bauböck, *Democratic Inclusion* (Manchester: Manchester University Press, 2017), 31, 28.

17 Philip Pettit, *On the People's Terms: A Republican Theory and Model of Democracy* (New York: Cambridge University Press, 2012).

18 See e.g. Philip Pettit, *Republicanism: A Theory of Freedom and Government* (New York: Oxford University Press, 1997), 32.

19 See e.g. Pettit, *On the People's Terms,* 170–171.

20 Jean-Jacques Rousseau, "The Social Contract," in *The Social Contract and Other Later Political Writings,* ed. Victor Gourevitch (New York: Cambridge University Press, 2003), p. II.8.

21 For Abizadeh, the answer to "the normative question of which collection of individuals, given the existing structures of power, should receive democratic institutional articulation … is directly political: everyone subject to the exercise of political power." Abizadeh, "The Demos and its Kin," p. 881.

22 Abizadeh, "Democratic Theory and Border Coercion"; Carens (this volume) (though Carens does not believe that the AAP provides better ideational resources than other theoretical approaches to immigration).

23 Macdonald (this volume).

24 Gould (this volume).

25 Saunders-Hastings and Reich (this volume).

26 Lane (this volume).

27 E.g. Fung, "The Principle of Affected Interests"; Bauböck, *Democratic Inclusion.*

28 Jane Mansbridge, "On the Importance of Getting Things Done," *PS: Political Science and Politics* 45, no. 1 (2012): 3–4.

29 Archon Fung states the link between the idea of popular sovereignty and that of democratically legitimate collective agency succinctly: "Effective organization requires authority. Authority resides in the territorial state and takes the form of laws that impose obligations of obedience upon citizens. To be acceptable to the citizens whom they obligate, laws must be made democratically: by citizens themselves as political equals. From the principle of popular sovereignty, a legitimate order is a 'self-legislating demos…'". Fung, "The Principle of Affected Interests," p. 237. See also David Owen, "Refugees and Responsibilities of Justice," *Global Justice: Theory Practice Rhetoric* 11, no.1 (2018): 23–44.

30 See e.g. Joeseph H. Carens, *The Ethics of Immigration* (New York: Oxford University Press, 2013), pp. 6–9; Daniel Lee, *Popular Sovereignty in Early Modern Constitutional Thought* (New York: Oxford University Press, 2016), p. 320.

31 E.g. Bauböck, *Democratic Inclusion.*

32 E.g. David Miller, "Why Immigration Controls Are Not Coercive: A Reply to Arash Abizadeh," *Political Theory* 38, no. 1 (2010): 111–20; Will Kymlicka, *Politics in the Vernacular: Nationalism, Multiculturalism, and Citizenship* (New York: Oxford University Press, 2001).

33 E.g. Jürgen Habermas, "Why Europe Needs a Constitution," in *Constitutionalism and Democracy,* ed. Richard Bellamy (New York: Routledge, 2016).

34 E.g. Bauböck, *Democratic Inclusion,* p. 46.

35 On popular sovereignty, see especially Lee, *Popular Sovereignty* and Richard Tuck, *The Sleeping Sovereign: The Invention of Modern Democracy* (New

York: Cambridge University Press, 2016); on constituent power, see especially Andreas Kalyvas, "Popular Sovereignty, Democracy, and the Constituent Power," *Constellations* 12, no. 2 (2005): 223–244, Martin Loughlin, "The Concept of Constituent Power," *European Journal of Political Theory* 13, no. 2 (2014): 218–237, and Andrew Arato, *Post Sovereign Constitutional Making: Learning and Legitimacy* (New York: Oxford University Press, 2016). Lee and Tuck do trace some of the history of the relationship between constituent power and popular sovereignty, on which I draw here – a history that I believe sharply undercuts Carl Schmitt's reading of both concepts in *Dictatorship. From the Origin of the Modern Concept of Sovereignty to Proletarian Class Struggle* (1921), trans. M. Hoelzl and G. Ward (Cambridge: Polity Press, [1921] 2014) and *Constitutional Theory*, trans. J. Seitzer (Durham: Duke University Press, [1928] 2008).

36 "The intellectual history of constituent power … must be rewritten," Lee argues. "It does not begin, as in the conventional wisdom, in the thought of the French Revolution. Sieyès is but the tail end of a long intellectual trajectory that begins in early modern legal thought." Lee, *Popular Sovereignty*, p. 143, n. 100.

37 Lee, *Popular Sovereignty*, Chapter 1.

38 Lee, *Popular Sovereignty*, Chapter 2. Of particular interest here is the theory of Baldus de Ubaldis (1327–1400), who linked the self-legislating capacity of a *populus liber* to the Roman private law theory of corporations, through which an association of free persons can constitute themselves as a unitary "corporate person" with authority to act on behalf of its members. Through this device, Baldus argued that the *populus* of a city can constitute itself as a "unitary juridical entity" with the power to legislate through itself, whether through the delegation of its authority to appointed magistrates or directly through the assembly of the entire people.

39 As Lee concludes, the thinkers who contributed to the long history of ideas of popular sovereignty "have given us no shortage of possible images of peoplehood." Lee, *Popular Sovereignty*, p. 319.

40 Emmanuel Joseph Sieyès, *Political Writings*, trans by Michael Sonenscher (Indianapolis: Hackett, [1789] 2003), p. 136.

41 For an example of such critiques, see e.g. Bernard Yack, "Popular Sovereignty and Nationalism," *Political Theory* 29, no. 4: 517–536. First, his conception of "the nation" is vulnerable to the charge that it rests on a pre-political conception of the *demos* and hence risks the unitary, exclusionary, decisionistic, and populist variants of democracy that are inimical to principles of individual freedom, equality, and plurality. Statements such as this make Sieyès vulnerable to this line of critique: "The nation exists prior to everything; it is the origin of everything. Its will is always legal. It is the law itself. Prior to the nation and above the nation there is only natural law." Sieyès, *Political Writings*, p. 136. Sieyès' view has certainly been put to use by proponents of decisionistic variants of popular sovereignty, notably Carl Schmitt. However, note that Sieyès' reference to natural law clearly contradicts the decisionistic view that the popular will has absolute and unlimited authority. Although is beyond the scope of this chapter to argue in detail against reading Sieyès in this way, I will argue briefly as to why I think his conception of constituent power is instructive for a project of retrieving and reconstructing the idea of constituent power as a way of thinking about democratic agency, notwithstanding the passages in which he seems to characterize "the nation" as a pre-political subject. Second, although Sieyès' account of the people as the bearer of constituent power is quite

radically egalitarian, the constitutional structure that he builds on this foundation is unabashedly hierarchical and hence indefensible from a democratic point of view.

42 I am relying here on Richard Tuck, who is in turn indebted to Pasquale Pasquino, for this passage. Tuck, *The Sleeping Sovereign*, pp. 175–76.

43 "The word [sovereignty] only looms so large in our imagination because the spirit of the French, full of royal superstitions, felt under an obligation to endow it with all the heritage of pomp and absolute power which made the usurped sovereignties shine…. [P]eople seem to say, with a kind of patriotic pride, that is the sovereignty of great kings is so powerful and so terrible, the sovereignty of a great people ought to surpass it." Again, I rely here on Tuck's reading of Pasquino and of Sieyès. Tuck, *The Sleeping Sovereign*, pp. 176–77.

44 Lucia Rubinelli, "How to Think Beyond Sovereignty: On Sieyès and Constituent Power," *European Journal of Political Theory* 18, no. 1 (2019): 51.

45 Sieyès, *Political Writings*, p. 97. There are interesting parallels between Sieyès' principle of democratic inclusion and Carol Gould's "common activities" model. See Gould (this volume).

46 Sieyès, *Political Writings*, p. 134.

47 Note that Sieyès resists the Rousseauean language of a "general will" in favor of that of a "*common* will," whose content is discovered not through silent internal reflection, as for Rousseau's general will, but through communication and deliberation.

48 Sieyès, *Political Writings*, p. 134.

49 Sieyès, *Political Writings*, p. 134.

50 Sieyès, *Political Writings*, pp. 134–135.

51 Although space constraints do not permit me to make the argument here, I see Sieyès' account of constituent power as broadly compatible with List and Pettit's account of group agency; indeed, in subsequent work, Pettit invokes Sieyès in his "dual aspect" model of democracy, in which "the people" has both a constituting and a constituted dimension. See Christian List and Philip Pettit, *Group Agency: The Possibility, Design, and Status of Corporate Agents* (New York: Oxford University Press, 2011); and, Pettit, *On the People's Terms*, pp. 286–87.

52 On this temporal dimension of the collective imagination necessary for the formation and maintenance of democratic orders, see especially Paulina Ochoa Espejo, *The Time of Popular Sovereignty: Process and the Democratic State* (University Park: Penn State University Press, 2011). See also, e.g. Bauböck, *Democratic Inclusion* (on the demos as intergenerational community).

53 On the declining salience of territory, or geographic proximity, as a proxy for the mutual affectedness of interests, see Goodin (this volume).

54 As Pettit stresses in *On the People's Terms*.

55 Mansbridge, "On the Importance of Getting Things Done."

56 See e.g. John Dryzek, "The Forum, the System, and the Polity: Three Varieties of Democratic Theory," *Political Theory* 45, no. 5 (2017): 610–636.

5

Self-Determination and the All-Affected Principle[*]

Anna Stilz

This chapter explores what I see as some problems with the All-Affected Principle (AAP), and with the proposals for redrawing political boundaries that have been made on its basis. I define the AAP as holding that everyone affected by a decision should have a right to participate (e.g. through voting, or some other form of direct influence) in a procedure governing that decision. My construal is neutral as to how votes should be weighted, whether equally or proportionally to the degree to which the decision affects individuals' interests. My definition of the AAP is narrower than some, yet I believe this narrowness is necessary to capture the putative connection between the AAP and *democracy*. While a broader reading of the AAP might suggest that all those affected should have their interests considered, be represented by an advocate, or have a chance to plead their case, those broader principles are not obviously democratic. A benevolent monarch might well consider his subjects' interests, allow them advocates, or grant them opportunities to make a case. Still, the monarch's subjects would be deprived of all power in the monarch's political decision making. I therefore opt for the narrower construal.

The first part of the chapter asks whether there is a convincing philosophical justification for the AAP. The second part asks whether it is best understood as a substantive or procedural principle. The third investigates whether the AAP provides a useful way to approach boundary questions. Unlike the AAP's defenders, I argue that the principle does little to realize individual or collective self-determination. Whatever one thinks of the AAP, it is important to acknowledge that it has significant costs for self-determination as a moral ideal.

I should say at the outset that I agree with the AAP's defenders that salient issues facing the world today cry out for global regulation: climate change and refugee crises are two obvious examples. But I worry that the AAP provides an overly blunt and simple approach to these problems. To see why, we need a better grasp of the principle.

JUSTIFYING THE AAP

Let me start by asking: What does it mean to be "affected?" I propose that one is affected by a decision if it has a causal impact (or perhaps a sufficiently important causal impact) on one's interests (or perhaps sufficiently important interests). Yet it is often counterintuitive to include everyone whose interests are affected in making a decision.[1] Consider Robert Nozick's famous counterexample:

If four men propose marriage to a woman, her decision about whom, if any of them, to marry importantly affects each of the lives of those four persons, her own life, and the lives of any other persons wishing to marry one of these four men, and so on. Would anyone propose, even limiting the group to include only the primary parties, that all five persons vote to decide whom she should marry?[2]

Proponents of the AAP have tried various strategies to deal with this "overinclusiveness" worry. Yet limiting relevant "affected interests" to self-determination and self-development (as does Warren, this volume) does not seem to avoid Nozick's critique: surely one has a self-development interest in being able to marry one's beloved. Nor does it help to adopt the proportionality interpretation of the AAP (favored by Gray and Warren, this volume).[3] Since my marriage has a greater impact on my interests than those of others, perhaps we could give me the greatest say over this decision, and a lesser say to other interested parties, such as my suitors, parents, and friends. But is it really plausible that these others should have any say at all?[4] To be sure, even if the decision is mine to make, I have a moral obligation to consider my suitors' interests, and not to gratuitously harm them – e.g. I should express my decision in a way that is sensitive to their feelings. But I need not grant them any say in my decision making.

The lesson of Nozick's example is that sometimes "ways of importantly affecting the lives of others are within the rights of the affecter."[5] Most of us believe that an individual's personal autonomy rights grant them an important domain of choice regarding their own life, including – besides their right to decide whom to marry – rights of free expression, freedom of religion, and free choice of occupation. People are owed some range of options within which to make choices that realize their own personal self-determination, even when these choices affect others. Self-determination is not infinite, of course; it is limited by duties of justice. But within the limits of my self-determination rights, once those are properly specified, it is I, and not anyone else, who has a claim to decide.

In response to this concern, one might exclude personal autonomy rights from the domain of the AAP. When some individual has a personal autonomy right over a choice, on this view, the fact that outsiders' interests might be affected does not entitle them to any say. Notice, however, that Nozick's worry seems to extend beyond individuals to associations and organizations. For example, in 2016, Harvard University rejected 35,315 applicants. This decision certainly affected their important interests. Should these applicants have a say in Harvard's admissions policies? It seems to me – by analogy to the personal autonomy case – that this is a choice Harvard alone has a right to make, *in spite of* its effects on outsiders' interests. Since the number of rejected applicants is larger than the number of current Harvard University students and faculty, were they to be included in Harvard's decisional processes, then, given their strong preferences to attend the university, they would likely have to be admitted. And were that to happen, Harvard's educational purposes would become very difficult to attain.

Of course, like personal autonomy rights, the shape and scope of organizations' decisional rights are limited by duties of justice. That is the reason why Harvard cannot deny admission to (among others) African American, Jewish, or female applicants on grounds of race, religion, or sex. All citizens have an important claim of justice to a fair opportunity for higher education, and excluding them on discriminatory grounds is not essential to the university's attainment of its educational purposes. But though its decisional rights are limited by constraints of justice, within its rights, Harvard has a claim to determine which applicants to take, without granting them a say, even when the decision importantly affects their interests.

One might respond here by further limiting the AAP, holding that when *either* an individual *or* an organization has an autonomy right to make a decision, affected nonmembers lack any claim to participate in making *that* decision. It is worth noting that some adherents of the AAP reject this response. They argue that firms, universities, and churches ought to be democratically organized and to include all those whose interests they affect (see Gould, this volume).[6] On this interpretation, the AAP becomes a radical principle. Most people do not think there is any nonnegotiable demand for democratic inclusion and decision making in all associational contexts.

I believe we should reject this radical interpretation. A just society should leave appropriate space for associations to have "a free and flourishing internal life."[7] Consider a limit case: should the nuclear family be democratically organized and include all those whose interests it affects? State pensioners and recipients of welfare benefits have an interest in my child's future earnings. Must I grant them a say on whether they should take after-school piano lessons or learn computer programming? To require all affected outsiders to be included in the family's decisions would undermine the goods the family makes possible for its members. This is not to say that outsiders' interests are irrelevant. Yet the right way to respect these interests is to place justice-based limits on the family's *decisional power*, drawing the boundaries of its autonomy rights in the appropriate way. Thus, the choice not to educate one's child, or to bequeath them one's large estate free from tax, is not one any family should have the right to make.

Suppose, then, that one accepts this further suggested limit to the AAP: *both* individuals *and* associations/organizations can have (limited) autonomy rights to make decisions without granting outsiders a say. The question then becomes: How much is left of the principle? Some authors postulate a category of "decisions in principle open to democratic adjudication," exogenously defined, and hold that when it comes to *those* decisions, one has a claim to inclusion insofar as one's interests are affected.[8] But in light of our discussion, this response seems ad hoc. If a nonpolitical organization can have rights to make autonomous decisions when those decisions affect others' interests, then why can't a political organization have such rights as well? Suppose the Navajo Nation is considering whether to opt for English-only or Navajo language instruction in its elementary schools. Various nonmembers' interests are at stake: the profits of textbook salesmen, the employment opportunities of English teachers. But I believe this decision is one for the Navajo Nation alone to make. If this is correct, then the work of determining who should be included in the *demos* is done not by the AAP, but rather by an independent account of individual and collective autonomy rights and the constraints that justice imposes on the shape and scope of those rights. A just institution should "build in" decisional permissions to facilitate individual and associational pursuits, "while defining their boundaries by general standards."[9] This is as true of a well-ordered global framework as it is of a domestic one.

One might object here that my argument merely shows that certain decisional permissions ought to be granted as a matter of *substantive justice*, if we are to secure important individual and associational interests at tolerable cost to other values. But who should have the *authority* to decide which permissions our basic structure should recognize? Perhaps everyone affected – not a bureau of technocrats, or some unelected judge – ought to decide. Someone could hold that the all-affected possess legitimate authority to determine the shape of the global basic structure, while simultaneously holding that they ought to recognize personal and collective autonomy rights. Some theorists have argued, for example, that a global democratic institution is required in order to legitimately demarcate the boundaries of the world's constituent political units.[10] On this view, as Abizadeh puts it, "the self-determination of differentiated democratic polities" should be viewed as "*derivative* of the self-determination of the 'global demos' as a whole"[11] (italics in original).

It is true that the AAP might plausibly be construed as offering a theory of legitimate authority rather than a theory of substantive justice. Still, a convincing theory of legitimate authority needs to be constrained by some "core" elements of substantive justice, including basic autonomy rights. Legitimate authority cannot take a *purely procedural* form: decisions at odds with "core" justice requirements can undermine the authority of a democratic procedure altogether.[12] These core requirements, in my view, include not only rights integral to the proper functioning of a democratic procedure itself – like freedom of political speech and association – but also other rights, like freedom of conscience, personal privacy, and the freedom to choose one's occupation. Were a democracy to fail to recognize these autonomy rights, its citizens would have no reason to consider its verdicts binding.

Further, I believe the preconditions of democratic legitimacy extend to collective autonomy rights as well as personal ones. Were a higher-level *demos* (i.e. the US federal government, or a possible future global democracy of the all-affected) to decide that the Navajo Nation was not entitled to self-governance, forcibly merging its members into a wider polity against their will, I believe this decision would undercut the legitimacy of that higher-level *demos*. Members of the Navajo Nation would have no reason to see that verdict as binding on them. So even if the AAP is construed as a theory of legitimate authority, personal and collective autonomy rights may still constrain it.

FOUR DISTINCTIONS

The AAP is often invoked to support the view that we should aim for global democracy. The idea is that in the contemporary era the domain of affectedness has expanded, through global trade, investment, communication, and cross-border environmental impacts. These developments have displaced a prior equivalence between territorially based populations and the effects of political decisions that is often (in my view dubiously, given the history of global trade and colonialism) presumed to have obtained in earlier eras. To comply with the AAP, we must extend the reach of democracy over time and as circumstances allow, ultimately to the global level. Does global democratic enfranchisement indeed follow from the AAP?

It is helpful here to distinguish between two different construals of the AAP:

(1) *Substantive Justification*: when someone's justice-related interests are affected by a decision, decision makers are required to take that interest into account (along with other affected interests), aiming for a fair balance of fulfillment of justice-related interests among all affected parties; and

(2) *Procedural Justification*: when someone's justice-related interests are affected by a decision, that person should be provided with institutional influence (e.g. through a voting procedure) over that decision.

International interdependence clearly changes the scope of substantive justification, and this may give rise to justice constraints that should limit states' decisions. I absolutely agree that when individuals and collectives exercise their autonomy rights, they are morally bound to consider the interests of those affected. Yet just about every moral view endorses (1), including those theories that limit themselves to negative duties not to violate others' rights or to harm them in significant ways. Construed this way, the AAP does not say anything particularly novel. Most defenders of the AAP instead take it to imply (2): we have a duty to include the affected in an authoritative decision-making procedure. All affected interests should enjoy a *say* over the outcome.[13]

Why is procedural justification necessary? One thought is that a democracy of the all-affected is the institutional setup most likely to lead to a substantively justified outcome. (This is the traditional instrumentalist defense of democracy.) When individuals whose justice-related interests are affected by a decision are provided with mechanisms to represent and advocate for those interests, this is likely to promote a fairer balance of interest fulfillment. On this view, "making decisions democratically … is the best way to protect and promote people's interests."[14]

This is often a plausible view, but it is subject to important empirical preconditions. Democratic decision making only reliably leads to a substantively justified outcome when voters are able to gain good information about others' interests, and when they are disposed to take those interests into account in voting. Suppose that factories in Peru emit pollutants blown downwind to Bolivia, affecting the well-being of people there.[15] Many advocates of the AAP suggest that in situations like this, we ought to establish a democratic institution that can promulgate environmental policies binding both Peru and Bolivia, and that citizens of both countries should be given a vote in determining these policies. But is this the best way to promote a fair balance of interest fulfillment? It depends.

Ideally, the 30 million Peruvians would be informed about the impact of their downwind emissions on their 10 million Bolivian neighbors, and ideally they would care about these effects, voting for emissions limits even at some cost to their own prosperity. Suppose, however, that nearly all the Peruvians favor allowing their factories to pollute, at whatever cost to their neighbors, since the emitting industry is a "national" champion on which many jobs depend. In these circumstances, justification through a democratic procedure is unlikely to lead to a substantively justified outcome. A fairer balance of interest fulfillment might instead be secured by an institution (say, an international regulatory commission) that allowed for representation of affected interests and gave them a chance to contest or appeal its verdicts, but did not give them direct influence over the decision. Of course, it may well be possible to design a democratic mechanism that would do better than a simple majority vote. But the point is that whether democratic participation promotes a fair balance of substantive interest fulfillment in a given scenario is contingent. Where it does not, then from the point of view of substantive justification, we should prefer a procedure that does not grant the all-affected any say over the outcome.

Were we to institute a global democracy at present, I think the trade-off between substantive and procedural justification would be huge.[16] In a domestic context, we rely on the media, personal, associational, and social ties, and shared educational institutions to gain some (imperfect) understanding of our compatriots' interests. Of course, there is a global media and, increasingly, a global network of social and associational ties. But these networks are fragmented: they unify mainly elites, and they exclude large parts of the world entirely. Cultures, economic circumstances, and political values still vary much more widely across countries than within them. This means that it is hard for ordinary citizens of the Netherlands, say, to get a good grasp on the interests of people in the Central African Republic, and vice versa. Without denying that some subnetworks have established dense global ties, when we look at the world as a whole, diversity and lack of connectedness remain great, and our resources for bridging these gaps are not well developed. Similar worries could be raised about political motivation. Even where individuals have an understanding of distant others, they are likely to prioritize their own and their compatriots' interests. So in the near term, we face contexts where, as Valentini puts it, "the preconditions for democracy to be successfully established at the global level are ... missing."[17] Presently, a global democracy is not likely to lead to substantively justified outcomes.

Is that a reason not to aim for global democracy? One could argue that someday a reasonably just global democracy might become feasible, and it is worth putting into place the preconditions for that scenario by gradual steps.[18] Perhaps global social movements should educate people around the world to develop solidarity with distant others and to establish better links across societies, which would unify masses as well as elites. I leave it open whether an instrumentally justified global democracy might become feasible in the future, and I do not rule out social movements that attempt to establish the preconditions for it. However, at any given moment, to make the instrumental case for global democracy, one must argue that it would produce more substantively justified outcomes than a nondemocratic institution would. In current circumstances, I doubt that this case can be made. I want to stress that I fully agree that global decision makers ought to be externally constrained to take into account the interests of those affected by transnational processes, e.g. not to impose significant harms on them. But I doubt that global democracy would be better at providing these constraints than would alternative, nondemocratic institutions, like international courts or regulatory bodies.

Are there other, noninstrumental reasons to work towards global democracy? Here we need some understanding of why democratic influence might be intrinsically important, apart from its effects on substantively justified outcomes. Of course, many people believe that even if a benevolent dictator or bureau of technocrats were to make substantively well-justified decisions in our behalf, there would still be an important objection to their rule. But what exactly is the nature of this objection, and does it apply to global decision making as strongly as it does in the domestic context?

Here there are two prominent arguments for democracy's intrinsic value. The first – which I mention only to set aside – invokes *public equality*. It holds that to respect people as equals, it is not enough to merely to take their substantive interests into account. Instead, some institutional *recognition* of their equal status is required, and (at least in certain circumstances) this recognition should take the form of democratic enfranchisement. Disenfranchising people brands those excluded as inferior, fails to extend equal respect to their judgments amid disagreement, or fails to treat them as social equals.[19] Whether the public equality argument would prescribe global democracy depends importantly on the nature of status inequalities at the global level, whether these inequalities are perceived as rendering some people publicly inferior to others, and finally whether granting all persons an equal say in a global democratic procedure is the best way of affirming their equal moral status. Though the public equality argument raises many interesting issues, I lack space to examine it here. For that reason, this chapter should not be seen as articulating an all-things-considered case against global democracy. I leave it open whether the demands of public equality might extend beyond the nation-state, in a way that demands the institution of global democratic procedures.

Instead, I take up a second argument for democracy's intrinsic value: that granting people democratic influence over what affects them helps to realize a moral ideal of self-determination.[20] I scrutinize the self-determination argument here because the AAP's defenders often invoke it (for examples, see Gray, Warren, and Gould, this volume), and also because I myself believe that self-determination has considerable value. But I believe democratic voting procedures are neither necessary nor sufficient to realize self-determination. So the self-determination argument cannot support a clear obligation to pursue, over time, equal political influence at the global level. Instead, I will suggest that once we better understand the ideal of self-determination, we will see that global democracy is in significant tension with it.

SELF-DETERMINATION, DEMOCRACY, BOUNDARIES

The self-determination argument for democracy begins from the idea that each person has a fundamental interest in being the author of their own life. This interest is commonly thought to ground individual liberties, like freedom of expression, freedom of religion, and the freedom to marry and form personal relationships. These liberties allow a person to express their evaluative judgments in their life-commitments. But government decisions also have an impact on the shape of a person's life, profoundly affecting their natural and social environment in ways that pose a prima facie threat of domination. (Here I gloss over an important debate over *what exactly* it is about government decisions that threatens individuals' autonomy. Is it the imposition of authoritative legal obligations? The state's enforcement of directives, through threats or coercive sanctions? Or simply the causal impact that these decisions have on an individual's ability to lead their life as they see fit? While this debate is important – and it is not clear to me that the AAP gets the best of it – for the purposes of this chapter, I shall assume that the AAP correctly describes the prima facie concern about domination.)

The self-determination argument then suggests that if a political subject is to be fully autonomous, the prima facie threat of domination from political decisions must be overcome. How is this to be accomplished? The answer is that, just like their life-commitments, the political decisions applied to an individual should somehow reflect their own judgments and choices. The final premise is that by granting people a right to participate in a democratic process, we enable them to be "authors" of the decisions under which they must live.[21] In affording each citizen an opportunity to influence the state's decisions, democracy neutralizes the threat that political rule poses to their autonomy, turning *alien rule* into *self-rule*. The argument can be extended to global democracy: since the decisions made by foreign states, corporations, and international organizations have consequential effects on people's lives, to be fully autonomous, they must be given a right to participate in these decisions.

I agree with proponents of the self-determination argument that political decisions often pose a prima facie threat of domination. Yet while I agree that self-determination is an important value, I believe democratic voting procedures are neither necessary nor sufficient to secure it. Note here that I adopt a narrow definition of "democracy," which refers to a procedure granting each person equal opportunity for influence: a procedure such as majority rule, or perhaps a lottery system.[22] I argue that a shared commitment to collective political action is crucial to enabling self-determination: in the absence of shared commitment, democratic procedures have little significance; in its presence, they are not required.

Let me first explain why voting procedures are *insufficient* for self-determination. Recall the worry that individuals are not fully autonomous when they are substantially affected by decisions beyond their control. Yet it is not clear how global democratic procedures will solve this worry, since these procedures *also* would not afford individuals meaningful control over life-affecting decisions. Since 7 billion other citizens share voting power in a global democracy, whether or not decisions reflect *my* priorities and judgments will always be partly up to *them*. Indeed, they may impose their alien views on me, as happens whenever I am in the dissenting minority on some serious political question. Here, it seems, we are ruled by the global majority, "subject to the collective will of multiple others"; we do not rule ourselves.[23]

Thus, it seems impossible for global democracy to extend an autonomous individual control over decisions that affect them. Global citizens have only a minuscule, utterly negligible political influence, and this influence will not afford them the power to ensure that political decisions reflect their own judgments and choices. Further, in any global democracy, large numbers of people will still be outvoted, as the worry about tyranny of the majority illustrates, and these individuals will certainly see central features of their lives shaped by decisions they reject, including the possible overriding of local interests they regard as important. Given all this, in what sense does global democracy enable autonomous self-rule?

In general, individual autonomy is furthered by *personal control* over decisions, not by an infinitesimal share of collective control. Suppose you are out to dinner with a large group of friends. Are you more autonomous if the group takes a majority vote to decide what you will order, or if you get to choose your meal for yourself? It seems that you are autonomous only in the second case.[24] Only then can you ensure that the meal you will eat will robustly reflect your own judgments about what meal would be best.

Given this line of thought, one might be tempted to conclude that self-determination is simply an illusory political ideal: political decisions cannot be authored by the entire group of people subject to them. I do not accept this conclusion. Instead, I believe self-determination is a realistic and valuable ideal. But I do think these reflections show that democratic voting plays little role in safeguarding self-determination.

In response, I propose to conceive self-determination somewhat differently. I hold that an individual is self-determining when they are governed on the basis of values and priorities that they in some way share. Of course, no individual's personal priorities can be mirrored in each and every political decision, but there is a second-order sense in which an individual's priorities *are* often reflected in group decisions – namely, when they share a commitment to a valued political enterprise and to certain shared policies by which they believe that enterprise should be structured. A commitment to participating in collective political action, on this view, is very important in enabling self-determination.

Consider a small-scale example, say, a partnership running a joint venture together. Often, in the context of such cooperative activities, a group develops shared commitments about how their enterprise should go. This does not mean that the participants converge in all their first-order judgments. Still, even when they do not converge, partners are often able to generate shared commitments – not reducible to their own judgments – about how their joint venture should be run. These commitments frequently emerge as compromises in the face of disagreement or bargaining about how the group should structure their enterprise. For example, a group might form a shared commitment to certain methods of making decisions, such as majority voting after public discussion, or to certain higher-order ideals or values.[25]

Participants can freely accept their group's commitments, and the outcomes that result, even when these outcomes diverge from their first-order judgments. Here, the participant is perfectly autonomous when they comply with the group's decisions. To take an example: while I often disagree with my colleagues about whom to hire, I prefer that we make our own hiring decisions together, according to our accepted consultation procedures, even though that means accepting some decisions with which I disagree. Indeed, I would consider myself disrespected if the dean overruled our collective decision, even when the result was to impose my preferred candidate. Though my colleagues' decisions do not always correspond to my first-order preferences, there is still an important, second-order sense in which *my* priorities are reflected in these decisions. I share a commitment to a valued cooperative enterprise together with these colleagues, and to certain shared policies by which I believe our enterprise should be governed. If this is correct, then my interest in self-determination can be fulfilled even when I am subjected to decisions that I do not personally control and with which I may disagree, so long as I value my participation in the collective venture and endorse the group's higher-order values and procedures. Though I may not endorse every outcome, I am governed by institutions that I view as appropriate.

When a group of citizens share commitments of this kind, I will say that they *share a political will*. A shared political will is an interlocking structure of joint intentions among individuals to cooperate together in a political enterprise and to endorse higher-order policies as to how their enterprise should run. Collective self-determination, as I understand it, requires a (robust) *correspondence* between citizens' *shared political will* and their *institutions*, under conditions that enable their free deliberative reasoning.

On my view, it is a shared political will – not the existence of democratic voting procedures – that is essential for self-determination. Note that voting procedures say nothing about the composition of the *demos* ruled by those procedures, including whether it contains subordinated minorities. But the ideal of collective self-determination is not indifferent to the *demos*'s composition. Consider the following case:

Political Incorporation. In 1945, the Allies occupied Germany through a just use of force. Suppose that instead of restoring the territory to the German people, the US had annexed their zone of occupation, turning it into an additional state of the union. To legitimize this, US authorities conducted a referendum in the combined territory, in which Germans and Americans had equal votes, and a majority (composed almost entirely of Americans), voted in favor of annexation. Would this annexation have been legitimate?

I suggest that this annexation would not be legitimate. Majority voting procedures are not naturally authoritative independent of considerations about the constitution of the group ruled by those procedures, including whether that group contains unwillingly subjected minorities.[26] Self-determination is not a purely procedural ideal, it is a normative theory of the conditions under which political power is consistent with the autonomy of those subject to it. These conditions are substantive, not just procedural; they include certain basic rights, as well as the institution of appropriate boundaries between political groups.

More controversially, I also hold that democratic voting procedures are not *necessary* for collective self-determination. Recall that I am adopting a narrow definition of "democracy" as a procedure that grants each person equal opportunity for influence. A broader definition of "democracy" refers to any system that ties legitimate political power to a process of shared deliberation among free and equal citizens.[27] There is significant overlap between my account of self-determination and this broader democratic ideal. Since correspondence between a group's shared will and their institutions is valuable only where citizens' judgments are freely formed, my view stresses the protection of basic liberties of conscience, free expression, and free association, and the importance of deliberative public opinion.

While my account might be said to rest on broadly democratic values, I doubt that democracy in the *narrow, procedural* sense is necessary for self-determination. A particular group's policy for self-governance might involve equal votes and majority rule, but it also might not. Participants may agree, under authentic deliberative conditions, that a particular individual – say, their *monarch* – is especially wise, virtuous, and good at interpreting the group's shared commitments, and defer to their judgments day-to-day. So long as participants share commitments about how their joint venture should go, and so long as the monarch's decisions count as reasonable elaborations of those commitments, then participants will be as self-determining under their monarch as they would be in a democracy. If this seems far-fetched, consider that many nonpolitical associations do exactly this. Many churches, schools, and businesses are governed by nondemocratic norms that their participants genuinely accept, and which protect their fundamental interests.

One might object here that to be self-determining, it is not enough for political institutions to reflect the authentic shared will of the population. Instead, that group must have the ability to *control* their institutions to serve their commitments, should they change their minds as to how they wish to be ruled. Voting procedures, it might be argued, are necessary to ensure this. I agree that there must be some way for the people to revoke authorization of their regime. But a range of different mechanisms might serve this purpose. Lockean rebellion seems antiquated and unreliable, but it might be sufficient in a society where the power of leaders depends heavily on the cooperation of the people and technologies of social coercion are undeveloped. Even under contemporary conditions, in states that possess armies and secret police, I believe it is possible for citizens to authorize a government that is not democratic – say, a constitutional monarchy – so long as there is some mechanism by which to initiate a process of constitutional reform, e.g. an amendment procedure.[28] If this is so, elections and voting are not *necessary* to self-determination.

One might also wonder whether my argument implies that democratic voting is not a requirement of justice. I think the *public equality* argument explains why justice often demands democratic procedures: formally equal votes reinforce citizens' equal social status. While I hold that voting procedures are insufficient to ensure self-rule, I agree that they enable a valuable recognition of citizens' equal status, and this is an important reason for preferring them (see also Gray, Gould, and Warren, this volume). Still, a nondemocratic state can be legitimate – with a right to rule its population free from interference – even when its institutions are not fully just (say, because they fail to fully enable equal moral recognition). On my view, a state is legitimate if it protects its citizens' basic rights and provides for their self-determination, even if this occurs through nondemocratic institutions. Such a state has a right not to be forced to become a democracy.

Thus, the ideal of self-determination, as I understand it, holds that it is important that political subjects see their *demos* as a cooperative enterprise that they value, and that they generally endorse its institutions, even when they disagree with particular decisions. This facilitates their political freedom; it gives them the ability to appropriately see themselves as governed in a way that reflects their own values and priorities, rather than being subjected, against their will, to hostile or dominating powers. So unlike the AAP, the ideal of collective self-determination suggests that political boundaries should be drawn so as to enable people to *affirm* their inclusion in a particular *demos* and to endorse the institutions that structure it.

It is natural to object here that however desirable shared political commitment may be, it is unachievable among territorially defined populations; there are always dissenters among us. While there is much to be said about this issue, I do not believe that self-determination requires that collective commitment be *unanimous*. Sometimes it is permissible to coerce dissenters who fail to share the commitments underwriting political institutions. One such case is where dissenters are alienated only because they hold gravely unjust political values. I believe these dissenters lack a claim to self-determination, because self-determination is conditioned upon a commitment to the principle of equal autonomy from which its value is derived. A second case is where there is no feasible institutional configuration that could accommodate dissenters' priorities and still carry out morally mandatory state functions at reasonable cost. Here I appeal to the importantly *territorial* nature of our duties of justice; we cannot establish property and contractual rights, enforce those rights, and punish violators unless people who live in proximity and interact regularly are subject to common institutions. Lone dissenters therefore have a duty to accommodate to *some* feasible political scheme, and to compromise with their neighbors in order to do so. To claim self-determination, then, a group must be territorially organized and possess broadly representative practices.

Still, I believe the ideal of self-determination will often support (re)drawing political boundaries to allow groups to be governed by institutions that reflect their shared commitments. Here I have in mind groups (a) who have political commitments that are consistent with basic justice for others, (b) who possess or can create a territorially organized structure of representation, and (c) whose dissent can be feasibly addressed, at reasonable cost, by granting them separate institutions. Thus, self-determination favors decolonization over a wider metropole in the case of former subject peoples. It also grounds a preference for independent political institutions for Indigenous groups incorporated into settler states, and greater autonomy for persistently alienated minorities in e.g. Scotland, Catalonia, or Quebec.

The ideal of self-determination need not be predicated on the existence of prepolitical "peoples" marked out by characteristics – like language, shared culture, or common interests – that specially suit them for self-rule. I doubt that there is any such Archimedean point of view from which to delineate political peoples. Instead, on my view, a people is born only when its members engage in institutionalized political cooperation, and come to value that cooperation. Some structure of institutional representation is necessary to create groups with sufficient corporate agency to act as peoples. But this "people-forging" process can succeed or fail. Sometimes political institutions generate "uptake" among their constituents, who come to value their joint enterprise and to willingly support the institutions that govern it. But in other cases such "uptake" fails to occur, and subgroups remain persistently alienated, either because of a historical legacy of conflict or oppression, or because they share many distinctive political priorities, which go unrecognized by the majority. In this case, the ideal of self-determination may call on us to reconfigure political boundaries, to enable persistently alienated groups to be governed by institutions that better reflect their shared commitments.

CONCLUSION

Thus, the ideal of self-determination has implications for boundary drawing that are rather different from those suggested by defenders of the AAP; it suggests the continuing possibility of fission, rather than pressure toward global fusion. Because individuals have an important interest in seeing themselves as willing coauthors of the institutions that govern their lives, we ought to draw political boundaries, to the extent possible, to enable people to participate in cooperative enterprises that they identify with. In defining the people, we look to the patterns of affirmation and alienation that emerge as artifacts of our currently existing institutions. We then ask: Are there feasible institutional alternatives – consistent with maintaining a stable, minimally just structure of political authority – that would better realize self-determination for those who currently lack it? We delineate a new "people" – when we do – not because we are recognizing something that already independently exists, but because we have some reason to hope that a new institutional configuration will lessen alienation at reasonable cost. On this approach, the process of constituting the people is never finished, once and for all. The "people" is a mutable entity, and negotiating and renegotiating political boundaries is a process that we can expect to be ongoing.

I should stress here that self-determination is not an absolute right, but rather a moral claim that must be applied with due regard for circumstances, and it can be outweighed by competing concerns. In concrete cases, we will need to weigh the grievances of the persistently alienated against the countervailing risks to just institutions, including the potential for civil unrest, instability, ethnic conflict, or rights violations. I also do not hold that self-determination necessarily implies a right to a sovereign state; federalism, devolution, or internal autonomy may be appropriate vehicles for self-determination in many circumstances.

Yet if it is to avoid engendering pernicious alienation, a just global frame-work needs to make space for collective self-determination. We should extend groups the permission to form separate institutions and to order their affairs in accordance with their shared priorities, because this facilitates a valuable form of political freedom. As with the autonomy rights of individuals and associations, there are justice-based limits to self-determination: a *demos* is not entitled to make decisions that significantly harm others or threaten their essential rights. Transnational decisions that have these effects must be reg-ulated. Yet global democracy is not the only – or the best – way to address these problems; international courts or oversight bodies – perhaps requiring proportionate representation from non-Western states – are another option. Self-determining peoples can also be required to form global institutions where their cooperation is essential to sustaining basic justice, e.g. by com-batting climate change and ensuring that refugees receive a new home and protection for their human rights. These and other justice-duties will place limits on the *demos*'s autonomous decision-making power.

Still, securing basic justice for others is the only reason why a self-determining people ought to be forced to submit to the rule of global institutions. Since it is especially valuable for people to be ruled in a way that reflects their own priori-ties, global justice should "build in" permissions for collective self-determination, allowing groups to establish separate jurisdictions and granting them autonomy rights to make their own decisions, even where those decisions affect others' interests (so long as they thereby violate no duties of justice). If this is correct, then it is not clear that the moral ideal of self-determination supports an obliga-tion to pursue global democracy.

NOTES

* Thanks to Lucas Stanczyk, the editors of this volume, and participants at the All-Affected-Interests Principle Workshop at Harvard for helpful comments.
1 Niko Kolodny, "Rule Over None I: What Justifies Democracy?" *Philosophy and Public Affairs*, 42, no. 3 (2014): 195–229, at pp. 222–3.
2 Robert Nozick, *Anarchy, State, and Utopia* (New York: Basic Books, 1974), pp. 268–9.
3 Harry Brighouse and Marc Fleurbaey, "Democracy and Proportionality," *The Journal of Political Philosophy* 18, no. 2 (2010): 137–55.
4 Kolodny, "Rule Over None I."
5 Nozick, *Anarchy, State, and Utopia*, p. 269.
6 See also Brighouse and Fleurbaey, "Democracy and Proportionality," p. 154; Archon Fung, "The Principle of Affected Interests: An Interpretation and Defense," in *Representation: Elections and Beyond*, ed. Rogers M. Smith and Jack H. Nagel (Philadelphia: University of Pennsylvania Press, 2013), p. 237; Carol C. Gould, *Globalizing Democracy and Human Rights* (New York: Cambridge University Press, 2004), pp. 219–34; and Iris Marion Young, *Inclusion and Democracy* (New York: Oxford University Press, 2000), p. 27.

7 John Rawls, *Justice as Fairness: A Restatement* (Cambridge, MA: Harvard University Press, 2001), p. 165.

8 Laura Valentini, "No Global Demos, No Global Democracy? A Systemization and Critique," *Perspectives on Politics* 12, no. 4 (2014): 789–807, at p. 793.

9 Thomas Nagel, *Equality and Partiality* (New York: Oxford University Press, 1991), p. 25.

10 Arash Abizadeh, "Democratic Theory and Border Coercion: No Right to Unilaterally Control Your Own Borders," *Political Theory* 36, no. 1 (2008): 37–65; Arash Abizadeh, "On the Demos and Its Kin: Nationalism, Democracy, and the Boundary Problem," *The American Political Science Review* 106, no. 4 (2012): 867–82; Daniele Archibugi, *The Global Commonwealth of Citizens* (Princeton, NJ: Princeton University Press, 2008), p. 173; Raffaele Marchetti, *Global Democracy: For and Against* (New York: Routledge, 2008), p. 81.

11 Abizadeh, "Democratic Theory and Border Coercion," p. 49.

12 Thomas Christiano, "The Authority of Democracy," *Journal of Political Philosophy*, 12, no. 3 (2004): 266–90.

13 See Young, *Inclusion and Democracy*; Robert E. Goodin, "Enfranchising All Affected Interests, and Its Alternatives," *Philosophy and Public Affairs* 35, no. 1 (2007): 40–68; Brighouse and Fleurbaey, "Democracy and Proportionality"; though an exception is Fung, "The Principle of Affected Interests," who argues for a broader sense of "passive influence."

14 Goodin, "Enfranchising All Affected Interests," p. 50.

15 Goodin, "Enfranchising All Affected Interests," p. 49.

16 David Miller, "Democracy's Domain," *Philosophy and Public Affairs* 37, no. 3 (2009): 201–28.

17 Valentini, "No Global Demos, No Global Democracy?" p. 790.

18 Valentini, "No Global Demos, No Global Democracy?" p. 790.

19 Charles Beitz, *Political Equality* (Princeton: Princeton University Press, 1989); Thomas Christiano, *The Constitution of Equality: Democratic Authority and Its Limits* (New York: Oxford University Press, 2008); Kolodny, "Rule Over None I"; and Daniel Viehoff, "Democratic Equality and Political Authority," *Philosophy and Public Affairs* 42, no. 4 (2014): 337–75; see also Gray (this volume).

20 Abizadeh, "On the Demos and Its Kin"; Brighouse and Fleurbaey, "Democracy and Proportionality"; Eva Erman, "The Boundary Problem and the Ideal of Democracy," *Constellations* 21, no. 4 (2014): 535–546; Sofia Näsström, "The Challenge of the All-Affected Principle," *Political Studies* 59, no. 1 (2011): 116–34.

21 Thomas Christiano, *The Rule of the Many: Fundamental Issues in Democratic Theory* (Boulder, CO: Westview Press, 1996), pp. 18–19.

22 Kolodny, "Rule Over None I"; Christiano, "Legitimacy and the International Trade Regime," *San Diego Law Review* 52, no. 5 (2015): 981–1013.

23 Assaf Sharon, "Domination and the Rule of Law," in *Oxford Studies in Political Philosophy*, vol. 2, ed. David Sobel, Peter Vallentyne, and Steven Wall (New York: Oxford University Press, 2016).

24 For similar arguments, see Christiano, *The Rule of Many*, p. 267; Allen Buchanan, "Democracy and Secession," in *National Self-Determination and Secession*, ed. Margaret Moore (Oxford: Oxford University Press, 1998), pp. 16–21; Andrew Altman and Christopher Wellman, *A Liberal Theory of International Justice* (Oxford: Oxford University Press, 2009), pp. 18–20.

25 Michael Bratman, *Shared Agency: A Planning Theory of Acting Together* (New York: Oxford University Press, 2014).
26 A. John Simmons, *Boundaries of Authority* (Oxford: Oxford University Press, 2016).
27 Joshua Cohen, "Reflections on Deliberative Democracy," in *Contemporary Debates in Political Philosophy*, ed. Thomas Christiano and John Christman (New York: Blackwell, 2009).
28 For a similar argument, see Altman and Wellman, *A Liberal Theory of International Justice*, pp. 27–9.

PART II

MEMBERSHIP WITHIN AND BEYOND BORDERS

6

The All-Affected Principle and Immigration

Joseph H. Carens

Migrants and potential migrants are often affected by decisions in which they have not participated. For that reason, and because of my previous work on immigration, the editors of this book asked me to think about whether the All-Affected Principle might provide a useful perspective on immigration. I have concluded that, with a few important exceptions, the All-Affected Principle does not help very much to reflect more deeply about immigration.

This does not mean that I reject the All-Affected Principle. On the contrary, as the other chapters in this book make clear, this principle can be a valuable theoretical tool for identifying and exploring a wide range of questions about democratic inclusion. But like all tools, it is best used only on certain objects. The All-Affected Principle does help us to think about who should be included in decision making, but, in my view, in the case of immigration, the important questions are not about who should participate in decisions but about what those decisions should be, or more precisely, the moral constraints on the acceptable range of decisions about immigration policies and immigration regimes. Moral principles, especially democratic principles other than the All-Affected Principle, greatly constrain morally permissible collective choices about immigration. There is much less room for discretionary democratic self-determination in this area than is commonly assumed. Thus, the question of who should participate in decision making is correspondingly less urgent.

So, think of this chapter as a cautionary tale. Exploring some of the limitations of the All-Affected Principle with respect to the topic of immigration can serve as a reminder of the ways in which the All-Affected Principle needs to be supplemented by other principles and other perspectives when we engage in normative reflection.

In what follows I will identify what I see as the most important normative questions about immigration. I will then sketch briefly my answers to those questions, drawing primarily – and occasionally explicitly, though without formal citations – upon a recent book.[1] I hope that the importance of the questions I am asking will be self-evident, even to those who disagree with my answers. I will consider whether the All-Affected Principle helps to answer those questions or to identify important related issues that have been neglected.

NOTES ON METHOD

Every inquiry takes place against a background of presuppositions: normative, empirical, intellectual, linguistic, etc. There is no Cartesian starting point in political philosophy. We have to bracket some questions so that we can focus on others. There are often good reasons for adopting one set of presuppositions rather than another, given a particular intellectual goal, but we should never imagine that the intellectual goal we are pursuing is the only possible one. It is common to adopt a presupposition for one question that we subject to critical scrutiny for another. In what follows, I will try to be explicit about my key presuppositions, and I will change one important presupposition as I go along to illustrate both methodologically and substantively why it is so important to pay attention to presuppositions.

One of my key presuppositions is that it is possible to distinguish between the question of who has the right to make a decision and the question of whether that decision is morally acceptable. More specifically, I assume that it is possible for a political community to include everyone who ought to be included in a decision-making process and to include them in appropriate ways, and for the decision that the community makes to be morally wrong. To put it in a slightly different way, democracies sometimes act unjustly, not because there was a problem with who was included in the democratic process but because the outcome of that process was substantively unjust. I do not think of this as a particularly controversial presupposition, although, like every moral claim, it could be challenged. It is an important presupposition for this inquiry, however, because it draws attention to one of the limits of the All-Affected Principle.

Another key presupposition is that it is possible to assert that an agent, whether individual or collective, has the moral right to make a particular choice and yet to criticize the moral limitations of the options from which the agent is choosing. Everyone recognizes that the robber who says "Your money or your life" is not enhancing the victim's autonomy by presenting the victim with this choice. But we sometimes do not notice the ways in which other choices are problematically constrained by entrenched institutions and norms so that who has a say in a particular decision may not get at the most important moral issues in a case.

Consider, for example, a famous passage from Robert Nozick that is often used, including by authors in this volume, to illustrate the limits of the All-Affected Principle. In this passage, Nozick says that if four men want to marry a particular woman, the fact that they (and others) will be greatly affected by her decision does not matter. Only the woman herself has a right to make that decision. She has a right to act autonomously.

Nozick is right, of course, that respect for autonomy precludes the men from having a claim to participate in the woman's decision and so calls into question incautious, general formulations of the All-Affected Principle, but his construction of the example also obscures the important ways in which her choice is constrained and her autonomy restricted.

Nozick's book appeared in the early 1970s. If Nozick had said then that two women and two men wanted to marry the woman in question and it was up to her to decide which if any of them to marry, the example would not have done the work he wanted in illustrating a widely accepted commitment to individual autonomy and limits on collective choice. At the time, same-sex marriage was not legally permitted. The democratic process had excluded that option. Moreover, same-sex marriage was not thought by most Americans to be morally permissible, whatever their general views on the importance of individual freedom. So, a woman's autonomy with respect to her ability to make her own decision about which willing potential marriage partner to accept was constrained by democratic laws and by the public norms of a democratic society. Indeed, one might argue that because marriage itself was a patriarchal, heteronormative institution, both legally and socially, in the 1970s and because being unmarried in a patriarchal, heteronormative society entailed its own severe legal and social restrictions, to say that a woman facing such constraints was autonomous because she was free to decide whether or not to marry a man who wanted to marry her would be deeply misleading.[2] In what follows, I will draw attention at times to the ways in which questions about immigration look different depending on what one assumes about the moral legitimacy of the background conditions.

ACCESS TO CITIZENSHIP

I begin with the issue of access to citizenship. The central question is this: On what terms should lawfully admitted immigrants and their children (and subsequent descendants) become citizens of the state in which the immigrants have settled?

Notice two of the presuppositions of this question. First, it simply assumes as a background the moral legitimacy of the division of the world into states, each of which has its own political process through which it exercises authority over immigration admissions and over access to its citizenship. The question here is about access to citizenship for immigrants whom the state has chosen to admit as permanent residents, not about access to citizenship for anyone who wants to live in a state. Second, it assumes implicitly that we know what citizenship means, and, in particular, what it entails as a legal status, at least within certain parameters. If we did not have some sense of that, how could we talk about who was or was not entitled to citizenship? For example, in democratic states in the modern world, citizenship is normally treated as a fundamental status that entitles one to equal rights with other citizens, with minor qualifications such as age restrictions on the right to vote. Moreover, under national and international law, citizens normally have some rights that noncitizens do not have, such as the right to vote in national elections, and the right to reside in a state whose citizenship one possesses and to enter that state if one is outside it. If citizenship did not have these familiar features, the question of who is entitled to be a citizen might appear quite different.

It would certainly be possible to challenge these presuppositions, either from the perspective of the All-Affected Principle or from some other perspective. Later I will explore one way of doing so. But doing that would make it impossible to explore the particular question that I want to ask, because that question arises precisely in the context of these two assumptions and others, including those previously identified. As I noted above, to explore one question, one must bracket others, at least temporarily.

Note that the question I have posed is *not* a question about whether immigrants themselves should be able to participate in a state's decisions about the terms under which immigrants will be given access to citizenship. There are ways in which the All-Affected Principle could be used to raise that sort of question, as we will see at the end of this chapter. At this point, however, that question is simply precluded by my first assumption. My question is not "who should participate in deciding the terms under which immigrants gain access to citizenship?" but rather "what are the moral constraints upon that decision?" or, to put it another way, "what access to citizenship must a democratic state grant to immigrants and their descendants, if the state is not to violate basic democratic principles?"

How should we answer this question? Let's start with access to citizenship for adults who have arrived as immigrants. My view is that settled immigrants should have relatively easy access to citizenship, in part because people have a right to participate in collective decisions that affect their lives on an ongoing basis and the right to participate fully is normally attached to the legal status of citizenship. Obviously, I am appealing here to a version of the All-Affected Principle. This is one of those cases in which I think the All-Affected Principle is highly relevant to a question about immigration, but it plays that role because citizenship is so deeply connected (in most states) to the right to participate in collective decision making.

Participation in collective decision making is not the only reason why immigrants should have easy access to citizenship, however. As I noted previously, citizenship status carries with it certain important rights under international law, a contingent fact but one important to the moral argument. Citizenship is also the way that we recognize people as full members of a political community in the modern world. In my view, simply living in a democratic society over time normally entitles one to that sort of recognition.

I do not think that the All-Affected Principle, understood as a principle focused on claims to participate in decision-making processes, encourages attention to this concern with the normative importance of social membership. I am not saying that the All-Affected Principle conflicts with the claim that social membership matters morally. The participation and social membership arguments for access to citizenship are complementary. The point is rather that the All-Affected Principle does not include all of the considerations that are morally relevant to this issue.

It is worth noting the indeterminacy of the phrase "easy access to citizenship." There can be reasonable disagreements about what counts as easy access, and that sort of reasonable disagreement is the kind of thing best settled by democratic processes. So, different states might have somewhat different rules regulating access to citizenship, without violating the principle of easy access.

Turn now to the question of who should gain citizenship at birth. Birthright citizenship poses a puzzle. Why make infants into citizens? Infants are not agents. They are not capable of participating in collective decision making. So, the All-Affected Principle does not seem to apply to them, at least not directly, in the way it does to adults. Part of the answer as to why we make infants into citizens lies in the way the world is organized overall. It is divided into separate states and every human being is supposed to be attached to one state (at least) as a citizen. No one should be stateless. And, as I have noted, we assume that there are important rights that go along with this sort of attachment, even for infants, such as the right to enter and reside. But the requirement that everyone be attached to some state does not in and of itself provide any guidance as to what state anyone should be attached to. Moreover, I think that birthright citizenship has a deeper connection to our understanding of what a democratic political community is. We expect a child born to resident citizens to be an ongoing member of the political community and we grant citizenship at birth as a way of recognizing that belonging from the outset. But if that is indeed the rationale for birthright citizenship, then the same rationale applies to a child born to settled immigrants within the state where they have settled. So, the child of settled immigrants should also be recognized as a member of the community from the outset and should gain citizenship at birth. Again, what I am presenting is a certain kind of social membership argument.

It is probably possible to construct a complementary argument for birthright citizenship from the perspective of the All-Affected Principle, if we interpret the practice of birthright citizenship as a way to securing children's right to participate in democratic decision making when they reach maturity. I don't think that this way of defending birthright citizenship would be in conflict with my account, but I'm not sure about its adequacy, and, in any event, I don't see what it really adds to the social membership argument.

INCLUDING IMMIGRANTS AS FULL MEMBERS

Full membership in a political community involves much more than having the legal status of citizenship. If immigrants or their descendants possess citizenship status but are excluded from the economic and educational opportunities that others enjoy, if they are expected to conceal things related to their immigrant origins in order to fit in, if they are viewed with suspicion and hostility by others, if their concerns are ignored and their voices not heard in political life, then they are not really included in the political community, even if they are citizens in a formal, legal sense. They are not likely to see themselves or to be seen by others as genuine members of the community. In many important ways, they will not belong. So, what is required for the full democratic inclusion of immigrants and their children besides granting them citizenship status?

Promoting the full inclusion of citizens of immigrant origin might include duties as well as rights for both the immigrants and the nonimmigrant population, and it may involve not only formal rules but also things like informal norms, incentives, practices of recognition, and conceptions of national identity. This question about inclusion requires us to explore issues relating to economic opportunity, multiculturalism, social interaction, and many other matters. For reasons of space, I will not spend any time spelling out the details of my analysis here. My main concern is to contrast this way of framing the problem of democratic inclusion with the one that arises from the All-Affected Principle, which is itself often presented as a (the?) principle of democratic inclusion, as the title of this volume illustrates. The All-Affected Principle is usually understood as a principle concerned with the question of who is entitled to participate in decision making, and as such, it does not invite attention to the kinds of concerns I am trying to explore in raising the question of full inclusion. Again, I am not saying that the All-Affected Principle contradicts the idea that these issues matter or precludes concern with them, but only that they are not the sorts of issues that the principle either naturally brings into view or offers much help in addressing once they have been raised.

LEGAL RIGHTS OF LEGALLY ADMITTED NONCITIZENS

Some immigrants are not citizens, at least not yet. How should their legal rights resemble or differ from the legal rights of citizens? Again, this question is posed within the constraints of the presuppositions noted above, and again the question is not the procedural one of who should participate in deciding what these rights should be, but the substantive one of what those rights should be and why.

Let's start with noncitizens who are permanent residents and with the actual practices of democratic states. The striking fact is that permanent residents now enjoy almost all of the legal rights that resident citizens enjoy except for some political rights (voting, running for office) and a few other relatively minor matters. We tend to think of citizen/noncitizen as the key dividing line when it comes to legal rights, but in reality, the key dividing line is resident/nonresident.[3] The current practice of granting extensive legal rights to permanent residents is a major change from the practices in most democratic states in the late nineteenth and early twentieth centuries when there were sharp differences between the rights of resident citizens and resident noncitizens. In my view, this change was something that was morally required because moral claims to many legal rights, especially social and economic rights, derive from membership in society, which derives in turn simply from living in the society over time. (I do not claim that moral reasoning caused the change, however.)

Would the All-Affected Principle help us to see why residents ought to enjoy the same rights as citizens for the most part? Not if the primary focus is on participation in collective decision making. That's the one area where resident noncitizens do *not* enjoy the same rights as citizens, which is why it is important for immigrants to have easy access to citizenship. But many permanent residents choose not to become citizens even when they can do so easily, in part because they enjoy almost all of the legal rights that citizens enjoy except the right to participate fully in the political process.

Immigrants are often admitted on a temporary basis at first and sometimes they are required to leave after a certain period of time. That is, they are not ever on a path to permanent residence. One could ask whether it is morally permissible to admit people with such restrictions on their ability to remain, but I want to bracket that question at this stage of the discussion, simply assuming (as most people do) that states are morally entitled to admit people on a temporary basis.

Assuming that temporary admissions are morally permissible does not mean that states are morally free to treat temporary residents any way they choose. Even with that assumption, we can and should ask, "What legal rights should temporary residents have?" In my view, temporary admissions must be truly limited in time or the state forfeits the (presupposed) right to require the immigrants to leave, and temporary immigrants are morally entitled to a wide range of legal rights, including many but not all of the legal rights that permanent residents enjoy.

I don't pretend that my position is obviously correct or that there is no reasonable basis for disputing it. For example, some have argued that it would be morally preferable to grant temporary workers fewer legal rights because rich democratic states would then be willing to admit many more temporary workers.[4] I do not have the space to explore the arguments for and against these different positions here. My main point is simply that the All-Affected Principle does not help us address this question.

Some might object that it could. The argument goes like this: Potential temporary workers have important interests both with regard to the terms of their admission and with regard to the numbers admitted. Therefore, the

All-Affected Principle implies that these potential temporary workers should have a say in the tradeoff between these competing concerns.

From my perspective, this sort of argument illustrates the dangers more than the virtues of the All-Affected Principle when one applies it on an ad hoc basis. The All-Affected Principle works best, it seems to me, in contexts in which there are relatively clear parameters for the morally permissible options in some collective decision-making situation (or at least in which one assumes this to be the case for purposes of immediate analysis) and the question is who should be able to participate in identifying those options and choosing among them.

It is not enough to ask who should have a say. Some options should be off the table. If my argument that temporary workers are morally entitled to certain rights is correct, then depriving workers of those rights is not a morally permissible option for a democratic state, even if workers agree to their removal. The fact that some or even most potential temporary workers might consent to forego those rights in order to increase their chances of getting in does not, by itself, establish this as a morally permissible option. Desperate people will agree to almost anything.

Even most advocates of reducing rights for temporary migrants do not go so far as to argue that the bundle of rights possessed by temporary migrants should depend simply on what the receiving state and the migrants would agree upon. They criticize actual policies, like those of the Gulf States, which admit large numbers of migrants with only a temporary permit to stay, no matter how long they remain, and with very limited rights. The fact that no one forces migrants to go to these states does not make that package of policies morally permissible for any state, much less one committed to democratic principles. The All-Affected Principle is a principle to guide our thinking about democratic decision making in contexts of collective action, and it has a valuable role to play in that context. It should not be reinterpreted either as a version of utilitarianism or as a version of libertarianism.

IRREGULAR MIGRANTS

Turn now to the issue of irregular migrants (i.e. people who have entered and/or settled without the state's permission). What legal rights should they have? Again, the background presuppositions of this question are crucial. I have been assuming that states are morally entitled to control immigration, at least for the most part, because that is the conventional view of the matter. So, it is useful to examine the claims of irregular migrants within the constraints of that view, even if one might want to challenge that presupposition in another context (as indeed I do).

Even if one accepts the conventional view, irregular migrants are morally entitled to a range of legal rights. I think that many of these legal rights should be protected by a firewall between those responsible for protecting these rights and those responsible for enforcing immigration rules. I also think that irregular migrants acquire a moral claim to legal status over time simply by living within a society.

My views on this issue have not gone uncontested, to put it mildly, but the important question for this chapter is not what position is correct but whether the All-Affected Principle helps us to think about this topic of irregular migration. So far as I can see, the answer to that question is "no."

Neither my own arguments on this issue, nor the counterarguments that I have seen, appeal explicitly to the All-Affected Principle, and the arguments on both sides do not seem to me to flow from or to fit well with a concern for the question of who should participate in collective decisions on this issue. So, I do not see how the All-Affected Principle advances our thinking about irregular migration. Indeed, I worry that the discussion of the issue of irregular migration would be impoverished rather than enriched if one used the All-Affected Principle as a primary lens through which to view the issue.

ADMISSIONS

Turn now to questions about criteria of selection and exclusion of potential immigrants. The conventional view is that states are normally free, not only legally but also morally, to admit as many or as few immigrants as they choose and to decide what selection criteria to use with respect to admissions (e.g. education, skills, age, more distant family ties, etc.). But wide discretion is not absolutely unfettered choice. Even people who endorse the conventional view normally recognize that there are some immigration policies that would be morally wrong. So, what are the moral constraints on admissions policies within the conventional view? (Notice again how this question deliberately accepts the conventional view as a presupposition for certain analytical purposes.)

Set aside for the moment the issue of refugees, which will receive separate treatment below. One important negative constraint on admissions policies is nondiscrimination. At a minimum, most people who see themselves as committed to democratic principles think that democratic states ought not to exclude potential immigrants on the basis of race or religion. It is true that democratic states openly discriminated in the past and sometimes try to discriminate today without acknowledging that they are doing so (as with Donald Trump's efforts, while he was President, to exclude Muslim immigrants). It is also true that this norm against discrimination is increasingly being subjected to overt challenges in ways that would have been unthinkable in the previous twenty or thirty years. Even so, the norm persists, and this constraint is reflected in various ways in national laws and international conventions, including the need to try to conceal the fact that one is discriminating when one does so.

On the positive side, most people recognize that the immediate family members of citizens and permanent residents have particularly strong moral claims to admission if they are not yet present. There are some qualifications to this duty and states do not always fulfill it, but, again, the principle is widely accepted, and it is widely reflected in laws and policies.

As always, this brief summary ignores many complications and complexities. But the question for this chapter is whether the All-Affected Principle helps in thinking about the normative limits on admissions policies within the constraints of the conventional view or whether it draws our attention to related but neglected questions. Again, I think the answer is no. The limited constraints on state discretion that I have identified (nondiscrimination and family reunification) flow not from the nature of the decision-making processes but from independent moral values that are supposed to constrain decision-making processes in this area. So, I don't think the All-Affected Principle would affect the debate on the question I have posed.

Does the principle pose new and neglected questions that we ought to consider, perhaps about the ways in which current immigration policies fail to take into account the interests of citizens affected by immigration? I cannot rule out that possibility, but I have to say that I am skeptical that the All-Affected Principle will help to provide much moral guidance. The priority given to family reunification is clearly a response to affected interests, but it protects those interests by trying to remove them, at least to some extent, from the conventional calculations about interest that normally drive immigration policy. The same might be said of nondiscrimination rules.

Set aside these sorts of moral constraints. Some current citizens are undoubtedly more affected by immigration than others, but there are often disputes about what the effects of immigration are and about which effects are legitimately a subject of collective concern. The important general point is that in this respect – i.e. that a particular policy has a differential and contested impact on the interests of citizens – immigration policy is no different from most public policies. If we find a better way than the one provided by existing institutions to create more effective links between the nature and extent of a citizen's ability to influence a public policy and the ways and extent to which that citizen's interests are affected by the policy in question, and if we think that is desirable, as the All-Affected Principle might seem to prescribe, this is likely to require a wide transformation of the overall processes of democratic decision making within the state. In that sort of enterprise, the specific features of immigration policy are likely to seem relatively unimportant.

Perhaps someone will object that focusing only on the ways in which the interests of *citizens* are taken into account is a mistake. What the All-Affected Principle does is to draw our attention to the interests of those who are not citizens but who are affected by this policy. After all, those seeking to migrate clearly have an important interest in whether or not they will be admitted, and those who stay behind also have important interests at stake because they may be benefitted by the emigrants' departure (e.g. through money sent home) or harmed by their departure (the brain drain). Wouldn't the All-Affected Principle require that these people have a say in immigration policies as well?

This question just illustrates why it is so important to be clear about the presuppositions of one's inquiry. Remember that the question I am asking here simply presupposes the moral validity of the conventional view in order to make it possible to see that the conventional view does contain certain (modest) moral limits on what states may do with respect to immigration. But the wide latitude provided to the state by the conventional view can exist only if a state has no moral duty to consider the interests of people outside its own population in constructing its immigration policy. The state is morally entitled to be self-interested (however that self-interest is defined) in what it does with regard to immigration so long as it respects the sorts of constraints I have identified. A state can choose to be generous if it wishes and take the interests of some external group into account, but it is under no moral obligation to do so. Of course, as I have noted before, we can refuse to adopt this presupposition and challenge the conventional view. The All-Affected Principle provides one way to do that, though there are other ways as well, as we shall see. But it is important not to introduce this sort of challenge in an ad hoc way, rejecting the conventional view for some purposes in a given argument but implicitly relying upon it for others in the same argument.

REFUGEES

Before turning to the challenge to the conventional view, I want to mention one other way in which the conventional view is constrained, even on its own terms. Most democrats think that refugees have a special moral claim to admission. Again, that is a view that has been under much sharper challenge in recent years than it was for most of the post–Second World War period, but, as with nondiscrimination, all democratic states have signed international conventions and passed domestic laws recognizing the special claims of refugees to some extent. My own view is that even within the constraints of the conventional view, democratic states have much stronger duties in this area than they have recognized. As always, I do not have the space to spell out those arguments here. Rather, I want to draw attention to one way in which I think the All-Affected Principle can be helpful in identifying an important and understudied question about refugees, namely, the question of who should decide where refugees are to settle when they need a new home.

The All-Affected Principle says that people (significantly) affected by a decision should have a say in that decision. Where one lives is something that has a major impact on most people's lives. The existing refugee regime organizes decisions about where refugees will live in two, very different ways: asylum and resettlement.

Under the asylum regime, which all democratic states have accepted legally, where refugees will live depends primarily on the place where they first ask for protections, which in turn depends upon their ability to travel. So, it is a system that gives almost no voice (in principle) to the receiving state on the question of how many refugees will be admitted and which ones (though, of course, many states take various steps to prevent refugees from arriving on their territory). How much say the refugees themselves have in this matter depends very heavily on their economic and other resources.

In contrast to granting asylum, admitting refugees for resettlement is an entirely voluntary practice, in which only a few states participate, which involves admitting people who have been recognized elsewhere as refugees and providing them with a new home. This is a process in which the refugees themselves have almost no say about where they will go. Of course, they do have to agree to go to whatever state is offering resettlement, but when the alternative is remaining in a refugee camp, this is often not much of a choice.

A just refugee regime (if I may use that oxymoron) would clearly distribute the responsibility for refugees much more widely. One of the questions one would have to address in thinking about a just refugee regime is how much choice such a regime would provide to the refugees themselves in deciding where they would ultimately live and how much choice it would provide to states in deciding how many and which refugees to admit. Although the prospects for creating anything remotely resembling a just refugee regime seem quite remote at the moment, it can be helpful, nevertheless, to reflect upon these sorts of fundamental questions, if only as a way of providing clearer critiques of some of the efforts to defend existing arrangements. In pursuing such reflections, I think that the All-Affected Principle would provide a valuable reminder of the need to think about who ought to have a say about where refugees would go under a just refugee regime.

OPEN BORDERS

Consider now the possibility of challenging the conventional view in a more fundamental way. Suppose we stop treating the idea that states are generally entitled to control immigration as a presupposition and ask instead: "Is it true that states are morally entitled to wide discretion with respect to who enters and lives within their territory?" If one accepts some basic moral assumptions, such as the idea that all human beings are of equal moral worth and that social institutions must be compatible with that moral equality in order to be justifiable, one might well conclude that the current global order is not morally acceptable. The way the world is currently organized serves the interests of the few (i.e. those living in rich democratic states) much more than the interests of the many (i.e. most of those living elsewhere in the world), and giving states discretionary control over immigration is a crucial factor in maintaining this (unjust) order. From this perspective, asking questions (as I was doing earlier) about what morality requires with respect to immigration while simply assuming the contemporary world as the background context is like asking what autonomy for women requires while simply assuming a heteronormative, patriarchal society as the background context.

In my view, a just world would be one in which the economic and other differences between political jurisdictions would be greatly reduced. In such a world, people should and would also be largely free to move across jurisdictional boundaries and settle where they chose, and this sort of freedom would not generate huge problems.

This brief summary leaves out lots of nuances and qualifications and does not consider the many important objections to the position I have just outlined. Nevertheless, I hope that it is sufficient to highlight a few points for the purposes of this chapter. First, it illustrates the ways in which one can adopt presuppositions for certain analytical purposes and then move beyond them for other purposes. Second, it illustrates the point that even fundamental critiques of the status quo do not proceed without presuppositions. My open borders position presupposes the moral equality of humans and that social institutions serve certain purposes and require certain sorts of justifications. Third, and most importantly for this chapter, my claim proceeds without appealing to the All-Affected Principle. The argument for a just world with open borders that I have outlined is an argument about what substantive arrangements are compatible with justice, not an argument about who ought to participate in decisions.

Of course, if one probed further, one would quickly have to recognize that there would inevitably be many important areas of indeterminacy, even in a just world, and so questions would then arise as to how collective decision making should be organized to deal with such issues. And in that discussion, the All-Affected Principle would certainly have a place (though it might not be the only principle one would want to consider). For my immediate purposes, however, the important point is that one can construct a fundamental inquiry into, and even a fundamental challenge to, the idea of discretionary control over immigration without relying upon the All-Affected Principle.

There is, however, another way in which the All-Affected Principle can be brought to bear on the open borders debate which does focus on participation in a decision-making process. This is what Arash Abizadeh does in his well-known article on the unbounded *demos*, in which he argues that from the perspective of democratic theory, states are not morally entitled to decide unilaterally on immigration matters because border controls greatly affect the excluded, and so those entitled to participate in decisions about closure include, in principle, anyone who might want to move from one state to another.[5] This then is another important exception to my claim that the All-Affected Principle does not help much in thinking about immigration.

Abizadeh actually constructs his argument on the basis of a more restricted principle of democratic theory, namely that all those subjected to coercion are entitled to participate in the decisions that coerce them, but he notes that the more expansive All-Affected Principle leads to the same conclusion.[6] Abizadeh's approach differs from my own, and I think that it adds something valuable to normative discussions of immigration through its strong link to claims to participation. As he makes clear, however, this participation-focused account leaves open to some extent the outcome of such a democratic process.

He contends that democratic principles will almost certainly lead to porous borders but that they might not require open borders in my sense of the term.

As I read Abizadeh, he simply leaves open the question of whether there are reasons independent of democratic theory for requiring borders to be open. So, I don't think that his democratic theory argument conflicts with the reasons I have offered for thinking that open borders are required as a matter of substantive justice. Our arguments are complementary rather than in conflict. On the other hand, from my perspective, the fact that an analysis that starts from a version of the All-Affected Principle leaves open the question of whether or not borders would be open illustrates again the potential dangers in relying only on procedural principles in normative discussions.

This is not a critique of Abizadeh's analysis, which is very explicit about its goals and presuppositions and about the limits of his claims. As I noted at the outset, everyone has to bracket some questions in order to explore others. It is simply a cautionary note again about the importance of substantive claims about justice and the related limitations of the All-Affected Principle, even when that principle advances our understanding in some important respects.

NOTES

1 Joseph H. Carens, *The Ethics of Immigration* (New York: Oxford University Press, 2013).

2 Some would argue that marriage has the same characteristics today. See Clare Chambers, *Against Marriage: An Egalitarian Defense of the Marriage-Free State* (Oxford: Oxford University Press, 2017).

3 Citizens who are not residing in the state in which they hold citizenship typically enjoy many fewer legal rights in relation to that state than residents of the state who are not citizens. Indeed, contrary to what might seem implied by the familiar claim that citizenship is the right to have rights, even nonresident noncitizens who are present in a state (say, as tourists) enjoy some important legal rights, such as basic civil rights, and the security of those rights has much more to do with the regime within which they find themselves than with the state in which they hold citizenship.

4 See, among others, Martin Ruhs and Philip Martin, "Numbers vs. Rights: Trade-offs and Guest Worker Programs," *International Migration Review* 42, no. 1 (2008): 249–65.

5 I have greatly oversimplified Abizadeh's complex and subtle argument. See "Democratic Theory and Border Coercion: No Right to Unilaterally Control Your Own Borders," *Political Theory* 36, no. 1 (2008): 37–65.

6 Abizadeh, "Democratic Theory and Border Coercion," p. 45.

7

Who Should Decide? Beyond the Democratic Boundary Problem[*]

Laura Valentini

Who should have a say in a given decision for it to count as democratic? This is the question with which the *democratic boundary problem* is concerned. Three main "solutions" have emerged in the literature: the All-Affected Principle (AAP), the All-Subjected Principle (ASP), and the Affinity Principle (AP).[1] These principles respectively hold that, from a democratic point of view, a say should be given to all and only those affected by a decision, all and only those subjected to a decision, and all and only those who share national, social, or cultural affinities.[2]

As things stand, the AAP and ASP are the "front-runners" in the race for the best solution to the boundary problem, with the AP lagging somewhat behind. And as several scholars have observed, both the AAP and the ASP come with radically expansive implications as far as the scope of the franchise is concerned.[3] Subscribing to either of them implies that democracy should go – to a greater or lesser degree – global.

This is, in a nutshell, the state of the debate on the boundary problem.[4] My aim in this chapter is to question the presuppositions underpinning this debate. Scholars have proceeded by taking *democracy* for granted, treating it as an ultimate value. Consequently, the best solution to the boundary problem has been framed as the one that most loyally reflects the value of democracy. But it is not at all obvious that democracy is best conceptualized as an ultimate value. Arguably, democracy marks out a family of decision-making systems – characterized, at a minimum, by universal suffrage, free and fair elections, and broadly majoritarian voting procedures – that are themselves justified by appeal to how they reflect and promote important values in particular circumstances.[5] The values in question range from equality and self-determination to peace, security, and respect for fundamental rights. In other words, what we call "democracy" is *itself* one of several possible solutions to the boundary problem (i.e. the problem of *who* should take part in a given decision) – a solution that is contingently justified by appeal to a variety of different values. Or so I shall argue.

The chapter proceeds as follows. First, I explore different moral dimensions of decision making – the "who," "how," and "what" dimensions – and locate the boundary problem in relation to them. Next, I explain that democracy is one possible and contingently justified answer to the "who" question. In the third part, I revisit the most popular purported solutions to the boundary problem: the AAP, ASP, and AP. I show that all of them fail to offer general principles for allocating decision-making entitlements. Instead, they often pick out features that matter to *how* decisions should be made. Overall, this leads me to conclude that the search for a "general democratic principle" to answer the boundary problem is misguided.[6] Finally, I support this conclusion by looking at two real-world cases: the US presidential election and the Brexit referendum. I argue that neither the AAP nor the ASP nor the AP makes sense of the wrong involved in disenfranchising those who, intuitively, ought to have been given a say in these decisions. By contrast, taking into account a broader set of considerations that bear on the distribution of decision-making entitlements sheds light on this wrong.

THREE DIMENSIONS OF DECISION MAKING

Whenever a decision has to be made, there are at least three questions we may ask in relation to it: the "who," "how," and "what" questions.

- *Who* should make the decision? Who should have the moral power to issue authoritative pronouncements about the matter at hand? (This is the question the boundary problem is concerned with.)
- *How* should the decision be made? Through what process (e.g. reasoning, data gathering, consultation, etc.) should the decision makers make the decision? What considerations should they take into account?
- *What* should the content of the decision be? What is the right answer to the question at hand?

To illustrate the difference between these dimensions of decision making, consider the following three issues, which we assume are up for decision.

- Issue A: To which charity should Marc's money go?
- Issue B: Which questions should feature in the exam for the undergraduate module "Contemporary Political Theory" (CPT)?
- Issue C: Who should receive an offer for an assistant professorship in politics at University College London (or any other university)?

In relation to issue A, if it is Marc's money we are talking about, then presumably it is *up to Marc* to pick the relevant charity: this is our answer to the *who* question. Furthermore, in deciding which charity should receive his beneficence, Marc should consider the importance of the goals promoted by different charities, and the effectiveness and dedication with which each pursues them. This appears to be the most natural answer to the *how* question. Regarding the *what* question, probably several charities are worthy recipients of Marc's generosity, and several are not, due to corruption or inefficiency.

Turning to issue B, intuitively, whoever is in charge of CPT – i.e. whoever teaches it – ought to determine the structure and content of the relevant exam. Or, at least, this is how most universities operate. In setting the exam (the *how* question), the course convenor should consider the material covered and what students may be reasonably expected to know. Finally, with respect to the *what* question, the exam should be neither too easy nor too difficult, and allow markers to differentiate between well prepared and poorly prepared students. Here too several possible exam papers would presumably count as fair tests of the candidates' knowledge.

While, with regard to issues A and B, answers to the *who* question are intuitively straightforward, issue C is a little more complicated. I would imagine that most would fall back on whatever departmental practice is adopted in the institution(s) where they currently work, or for which they have worked in the past. (Yes, I suspect my readers are academics.) Some would likely answer that the entire department should decide whom to hire, through a majority vote after deliberation. Others might insist that a committee of department members, appointed by the head of department, should make the decision. Others still might suggest that the committee should include members of the hiring department, members of other departments, as well as external experts.

This variation has some significance, and I will come back to it shortly. For now, it suffices to note that plausible answers to the *who* question will typically involve some combination of members of the university advertising the position and, possibly, third-party experts. Regarding the *how* question, decision makers should go about deciding whom to hire by carefully considering the candidates' strengths and weaknesses as researchers, teachers, and prospective colleagues, with sensitivity to considerations of inclusion and diversity. Finally, the answer to the *what* question should be: "the best candidate." Of course, there is likely to be reasonable disagreement about who that is. But even in those rare cases where a candidate is ranked top by every decision maker, they may turn out to be a disappointment. Giving right answers to the *who* and *how* questions does not guarantee the right decision outcome.

I have offered these three examples to illustrate the differences between the *who*, *how*, and *what* questions.[7] Let us now zoom in on the *who* question in particular, and ask what reasons support our intuitive answers in each of the cases discussed. Regarding choosing a charity (issue A), the reason why Marc should be ultimately in charge is that it is his money at stake. It would be a violation of his autonomy if he were forced to donate to one charity or the other, contrary to his will. Furthermore, the very point of the practice of charitable donation – as opposed to, say, taxation – involves voluntary transfers from donors to recipients. To the extent that this voluntariness strikes us as valuable – say, because it expresses a sincere willingness to help others – that value can only be preserved by letting each individual decide where their donation should go.

Moving on to setting exam questions (issue B), here the justification for letting each course convenor be in charge probably appeals to values other than autonomy, e.g. education, fairness, etc. On the whole, assigning decision-making authority such that each course convenor sets the relevant exam papers is likely to ensure the best results – fairest, best-designed exams – overall. Since this distribution of decision-making authority typically promotes the values behind the practice of a university, it is, all things considered, justified.

Finally, as we have seen, when it comes to procedures for appointing a new assistant professor, a variety of possibilities appear intuitively plausible. Each of them has its advantages and disadvantages. The more-inclusive procedures give more people a sense of ownership over the new hire, but in sufficiently large and internally divided departments, they might exacerbate conflicts and result in stalemates. The less-inclusive ones are more agile and efficient, but may not be as accurate or as conducive to building a strong sense of joint ownership within a department. Which procedure is best, it seems to me, will depend on local factors, including the relevant departmental culture, composition of the department, and so forth. But once again, how decision-making power ought to be distributed rests on what best furthers the point and purpose of the practice of a university (within the constraints of fundamental rights): high-quality teaching and research.

In sum, depending on the particular practice and context at hand, different values and considerations will bear on our answer to the *who* question. With this general theoretical background in place, we can now turn to one particular answer to the *who* question, and its relevant context of application: democracy within political communities.

DEMOCRACY AS A RULE OF REGULATION

The term "democracy" refers to a family of decision-making procedures, which we perceive to exhibit several moral virtues. Disagreement immediately arises, however, whenever we ask for a precise definition of democracy.[8] This, I suggest, following Arrhenius, is because the term "democracy" is associated with *both* a particular set of institutions – involving free and fair elections, universal suffrage, and broadly majoritarian voting procedures – *and* the values that justify those institutions, such as procedural equality, substantively correct outcomes, stability, solidarity, security, inclusion, non-domination and so on.[9]

I suggest that, for clarity's sake, we should use the term democracy to refer to a set of (contingently justified) institutions, rather than to the value or set of values those institutions are supposed to embody.[10] To put the point in a language familiar from contemporary debates about justice, it may be best to think of democracy as a particular family of "rules of regulation," the justification of which goes back to some fundamental values in conjunction with a variety of empirical facts.[11] This terminological recommendation is well motivated. After all, if we ask ourselves why, within a given political community, decision-making power should lie with all citizens, via their elected representatives, our answer won't itself appeal to "the value of democracy." Such an answer would be uninformative. Instead, the answer will point to how allocating decision-making power in this way favours stability, respect for fundamental rights, expresses citizens' equality in the circumstances at hand, and so on.

Furthermore, understanding democracy to designate rules of regulation is consistent with the widespread conviction that democracy cannot be the correct way of allocating decision-making power no matter which polity one is looking at. Polities characterized by considerable internal divisions, instability, and lack of mutual trust cannot be easily governed democratically. Instituting a democratic decision-making system when the conditions for its institution are not ripe can be inimical to the very values that justify democracy under the right circumstances.[12]

The foregoing observations, I should emphasize, are not dependent on a purely instrumental account of the value of democracy. They also hold for views that regard democracy as intrinsically valuable because it expresses a certain kind of respect for persons.[13] After all, whether universal suffrage, free and fair elections, and broadly majoritarian decision procedures express that kind of respect depends on the background circumstances at hand. It is hard to see how a democratic institutional setup could be said to embody a commitment to equal respect if, when implemented in certain settings, it would foreseeably lead to chaos and instability.[14] Similarly, the equal right to vote has now acquired a certain symbolic meaning, but this meaning is likely to be the result of a contingent historical process.

The unhelpfulness of treating democracy as an ultimate, context-independent value can be observed in debates about the justification of judicial review of legislation. By judicial review, I mean the practice – most typically exemplified by the US Supreme Court – of suspending the application of, or striking down, legislation approved by elected representatives. A good portion of the scholarly debate about judicial review concerns its democratic credentials (or lack thereof). Theorists such as Jeremy Waldron regard it as undemocratic, since it gives ultimate decision-making power to unelected judges, who are not representatives of the people.[15] Theorists such as Ronald Dworkin, by contrast, argue that judicial review can be democratic, provided judicial decisions promote the egalitarian values at the justificatory heart of democracy.[16] Others still, such as Corey Brettschneider, see judicial review as always "suboptimally democratic," though itself contingently justified by appeal to democratic values.[17]

The use of the language of democracy, which dominates this debate, obscures rather than clarifies matters, precisely because "democracy" is sometimes used to refer to specific decision-making procedures and sometimes to

the values that justify them. The debate on judicial review would be more fruitfully conducted if it were couched in terms of judicial review's overall *justification*. This will likely appeal to the values that also justify democracy, including
stability, procedural and substantive equality, respect for human rights, and
much else. Whether judicial review is justified or not will depend on whether
it facilitates or hinders expression and protection of these values, compared to
feasible alternatives.[18] These values, however, *are not* the same as democracy,
even if several of them may contingently justify what we routinely describe as
democratic decision procedures.

These considerations, about how best to understand the conceptual domain
of democracy, support the hypothesis that there is something wrong-headed in
framing the boundary problem as essentially democratic. This framing treats
democracy as an ultimate value, and then proceeds to ask which distribution
of decision-making power is most responsive to it. But, as I have suggested,
democracy is best understood as designating a particular institutional distribution of decision-making power, the justification of which refers back to several values. The question we should be asking, then, is: Which distribution of
decision-making power is justified in any given context, in light of the values that
bear on the relevant practice and feasibility constraints? We should not be debating about which distribution of decision-making power is most democratic.

THE BOUNDARY PROBLEM REASSESSED:
THE NO-GENERAL-SOLUTION THESIS

The previous two sections have offered arguments in defence of the following
theses:

a) the question "who should be given a say" ought to be answered in rela-
    tion to each given practice – and, specifically, its underlying values – in
    light of the constraints imposed by the context in which the practice
    operates (first section);
b) "democracy" is a contingently justified answer to the *who* question, one
    that itself appeals to a variety of different values (second section).

Theses (a) and (b) should make us sceptical about the possibility of identifying a one-size-fits-all solution to the boundary problem: a *general principle*
determining the scope of the franchise. And, as anticipated, they should also
make us suspicious of the assumption that the relevant solution should always
be democratic. Yet, the most prominent answers to the boundary problem – the
AAP, ASP, and AP – have tried to do just that: articulate a *general* answer to the
question of what makes a certain distribution of decision-making power *democratic*. To further support my theses, I critically discuss the AAP, ASP, and AP
in turn. Doing so will reveal that each principle *either* captures considerations
relevant to answering the *how* and *what* questions, *or correlates with* – but does
not embody – considerations relevant to answering the *who* question.

Examining the AAP

The AAP cannot provide a general answer to the "who should decide" question. As Robert Nozick famously put it, the decision to marry someone is for each person to make. Potentially rejected suitors, albeit deeply affected, should have no say in it.[19] Similarly, although candidates for an assistant professorship are highly affected by hiring decisions, it would be absurd to include them in the decision-making process.[20]

Proponents of the AAP might reply – as they typically do – that the scope of the AAP is restricted.[21] The AAP is meant to operate within the constraints of individual rights (e.g. the right to choose a romantic partner) and of group rights (e.g. the right of a university to hire its employees). Even with this scope restriction, the success of the AAP as a principle addressing the boundary problem remains doubtful. Recall how, in the university hire example discussed above, even once we have ruled out candidates taking part in a decision, a number of different possibilities remain on the table as to who should be included. These range from all faculty in the department, to a committee of department members, to a committee of both department members and external assessors.[22] While the first of these possibilities may be "rationalized" by appeal to the AAP, the other two cannot (or at least not straightforwardly).[23] But it seems mistaken to suggest that only the first one ought to be adopted by any department or university.

As I mentioned earlier, each procedure has its virtues and vices. Which is best depends on the circumstances. And when circumstances take a certain shape, then some scope-restricted version of the AAP will correspond to the "right answer" to the boundary problem. Note, however, that the AAP won't be what *justifies* the ascription of certain decision-making entitlements in that case. Instead, the AAP will just happen to *match* the ascription of decision-making entitlements recommended by underlying considerations about values and feasibility constraints.

Where the AAP seems to have greater – though still less than perfect – purchase is in relation to the *how* dimension of decision making. As other scholars have already pointed out, while it is doubtful that all those affected by a decision ought to participate in its making, it seems plausible that when a decision needs to be made, decision makers should take the interests of those affected into account.[24] So, when deciding whom to marry, I should be sensitive to the feelings of the potential suitors I reject. Equally, when a small committee decides whom to hire, they should be sensitive to the interests of all department members.

Even with respect to the *how* dimension of decision making, though, the AAP fails to qualify as a fully general principle. Consider, again, the simple case of an academic hire. Even though those most affected are, arguably, the candidates themselves, taking *their* interests into account – beyond treating them professionally and fairly – is not what selectors ought to do. Doing so would be contrary to the purpose of the practice of hiring.

In sum, the AAP appears to be neither a general principle for addressing the boundary problem, nor a general principle articulating how decisions should be made. Although it may, on occasion, match our considered judgements about who should participate in a given decision, it does not offer a plausible explanation of those judgements, which are ultimately traceable to our assessment of (i) the values at stake and (ii) which allocation of decision-making entitlements best honours and realizes those values in the circumstances at hand.

Examining the ASP

The ASP states that all and only those who are subjected to a decision ought to have a say in it. This formulation is ambiguous between at least two interpretations of subjection. The first sees subjects as the targets of coercion. A, in this case, is subjected to B, if and only if B coerces A (i.e. if B forces A to perform certain actions by threatening sanctions). The second focuses on someone's being the addressee of certain de facto authoritative commands. A, in this case, is subjected to B, if and only if B issues authoritative commands directed at A. Everyone falling within a state's jurisdiction counts as subjected to the state's commands in both senses.[25]

The ASP too, in both formulations, is not a plausible general principle for the allocation of decision-making entitlements. Consider, for instance, the coercion interpretation of the principle. If you insist on entering my apartment, I (or the police) may well permissibly coerce you to prevent you from getting in. It would seem absurd to suggest that such coercion could only be justified if you had participated in my decision to keep you out. While, to be sure, the use of coercion is subject to strict normative standards, those standards are typically *not* participatory. Coercion may be legitimately employed to protect people's rights, and what people's rights are is, at least to some extent, independent of the outcomes of collective decision-making procedures. Instead, those outcomes can be valid only if they respect the relevant rights.

It might be objected that although some rights are independent of collective decision making, others are not. The latter are rights on which there is reasonable disagreement, but whose content needs to be settled. This means that respect for everyone who will be subjected to coercion in the name of those rights requires them to contribute to deciding what the boundaries of those rights are.[26]

The difficulty with this argument is twofold. First, it is unclear why *only coercion* in the name of certain (potentially controversial) rights is disrespectful towards the prospective coercees, if they have not themselves taken part in the decision-making process determining the contours of those rights. What is so special about coercion as compared to, for example, affectedness more generally? After all, on the face of it, both can be inimical to individual autonomy, though in different ways: coercion through will bending, affectedness through reducing one's options, sometimes quite dramatically.[27] But if the rationale for focusing on coercion collapses into affectedness, then we already know, as stated earlier, why it fails to offer a general account of how entitlements to participation should be allocated.

Second, even if we just focus on coercion narrowly construed (i.e. as involving the threat of sanctions), it is unclear why participation is necessary to make such coercion in the name of reasonably contested rights justified. The argument here often refers back to how participation preserves individuals' autonomy. But this argument is known to be mostly metaphorical. It is unclear how an outvoted minority coerced in the name of what it regards as a mistaken understanding of rights preserves its *autonomy* through having participated. More likely, participation in such cases contributes to conveying, symbolically, the equal status of those coerced and to fostering a sense of ownership over the relevant decision and broader political institutions. These are, of course, important values, but they are, as we have seen, not the only ones that matter when it comes to allocating decision-making entitlements. Stability, respect for fundamental rights, and much else matter too – at least in contexts we regard as paradigmatically "political." So, while there may be contingent reasons in favour of some form of participation in decisions that coerce one, those reasons don't add up to vindicating *a general principle*.

Let us now turn to the second meaning of subjection, concerning one's claim to authority over others. Here, too, reflection makes it apparent that the ASP could not serve as a general basis for distributing decision-making entitlements. Consider a teacher and her pupils. She clearly claims authority over them, in certain domains. For instance, she claims authority over the content of the exams she will set, she claims authority to release students from the obligation to remain seated during her lecture, and so forth. It would appear absurd to suggest that her claim to authority is invalid unless students also contribute to making the relevant decisions. Such a principle would be contrary to the purpose of educating children.

Even once we move to broader contexts – including entire political communities – the validity of claims to authority does not seem systematically dependent on participatory entitlements being granted to those who are subjected to the relevant authority. To be sure, participation may (again) contribute to generating a sense of ownership over a given decision, and to conveying a special type of respect towards the subjects of authority. But it is unlikely to be sufficient (or necessary) for a claim to authority to be justified.

This can be easily seen by considering a scenario inspired by similar ones famously proposed by Robert Nozick and John Simmons.[28] Assume that I, and some others in my neighbourhood, want to set up a street-beautifying scheme. You're also a resident in the neighbourhood, but are not particularly interested in making our streets prettier or cleaner. The neighbourhood holds a referendum on whether to institute this scheme. You, qua resident, are given a right to vote. However, you don't exercise that right. The majority of voters select a fairly expensive street-beautifying scheme. This results in a decision to implement the scheme that is presumptively binding on you. Does the fact that you were given a say *validate* the claim to authority made by the neighbourhood and place you under an obligation to contribute? The intuitive answer appears to be "no," which suggests that entitlements to participate in a decision – even assuming its content is fully morally acceptable – are insufficient for claims to authority to be justified. In sum, the ASP too – in its different interpretations – does not offer a general answer to the boundary problem.

Examining the AP

Finally, I very briefly turn to the Affinity Principle (AP). This holds that, when it comes to political decisions, those who belong to the same nation or people should be given a say. I won't dwell much on the AP, since it has already been successfully challenged by others. I just limit myself to noting that one's cultural, social, or national affinities appear irrelevant to the issue of whether one should be given a say in certain decisions as a matter of principle. What the AP, however, seems to point to are the *empirical conditions under which* institutions we would most readily define as democratic can function reasonably well.[29] These are conditions characterized by sufficient mutual trust, commonality of interests, and mutual understanding. If so, the AP may be *a proxy* for one or more of the de facto conditions under which a democratic distribution of decision-making power, within a certain context, is justified.[30]

We have seen that the AAP, ASP, and AP do not offer general principles justifying the allocation of decision-making power. This further corroborates my hypothesis, namely that there is no single solution to the boundary problem: different assignments of decision-making power are justified in different circumstances.

IMPLICATIONS

To complete my discussion, I now wish to focus on two recent political events that raise the "who should decide" question quite prominently: the 2016 referendum on the UK's membership of the European Union (EU), and the 2016 US presidential election. Let me give you a bit of context for my choice of focus. I am an Italian citizen, and until December 2020 I was a resident in the UK, where I had lived, with short interruptions, for several years. Like any other non-British European citizen, I had no say in the decision about whether the UK should remain in the EU. And like any other non-US citizen, I had no say over whether Hillary Clinton or Donald Trump should be the next US president. I have found both forms of disenfranchisement somewhat troubling, but the former considerably more than the latter. What could explain these feelings?

I know I am not alone in having felt like this – at least within the relevant demographic – so I hope that taking my intuitions as provisional "data points" to be explained is not too idiosyncratic. I will attempt to show that, while neither the AAP, nor the ASP, nor the AP can make sense of how I have felt in relation to the Brexit vote and US presidential election, looking at the plurality of factors that bear on the *who* question can.

Consider the AAP first. It is far from clear that my stakes in the Brexit decision were greater than my stakes in the US presidential election. Arguably, the reverse was the case. To be sure, I had lived in the UK for many years, I identified with the UK a lot more than I did with the United States (for that very reason), so my immediate moral intuitions may have been clouded by a sense of disappointment, rejection, and alienation. But the truth is, there is only so much damage that Brexit could do to someone in my position. If things took a turn for the worse, I told myself, moving back to the European continent, for instance, would be a feasible alternative – as it turns out, an alternative I eventually took, as I am now residing in Germany. And even a significant downturn in the British economy wouldn't have had deleterious consequences for someone in a fairly privileged position, like myself.

Who becomes US president is, bluntly put, a much bigger deal. I can (and did) escape Brexit, but I doubt anyone could escape the Trump presidency, no matter their location in the world. Just consider Trump's statements about climate change, his lack of diplomatic skills, his "America first" mantra, and his war-mongering tendencies. I was and still am upset about Brexit, but I was a lot more *anxious* about Trump (and still am, although he is no longer president). This alone suggests that when it comes to stakes, at least in my perception, the much more consequential decision was taken in the United States. If the AAP were the correct principle for defining the *demos*, then I should feel a lot more aggrieved for not having been given a say in the Clinton-vs-Trump race than for my lack of participatory entitlements in the Brexit referendum. Or, at the very least, I should feel equally aggrieved in the two cases. Yet my intuitions go in the exact opposite direction.

Now consider the ASP. Might it be that, because my degree of subjection to UK law – whether in terms of coercion or in terms of being the addressee of obligations – was much greater than my subjection to US law, this explains my intuitions? I doubt it. People like me are obviously subjected to several pieces of US law – e.g. US immigration law as well as law for which the United States claims extra-territorial jurisdiction – both in the sense of being coerced by it and in the sense of being addressees of presumptively binding commands.[31]

Still, one could insist that the *degree* to which I was subjected to UK rule while still a resident in the UK was much greater than the degree to which I was and still am subjected to US rule. But is this really so? For what does subjection amount to? In the eyes of proponents of the subjection argument, it involves the issuing of commands (backed by the threat of sanctions). But consider the following commands: "Don't steal on US territory, otherwise you shall be punished in accordance with US law" and "Don't steal on UK territory, otherwise you shall be punished in accordance with UK law." Someone like me is subjected to both of them, simultaneously, all the time. It just so happens that, since until December 2020 I was physically present in the UK a lot more than in the United States, the latter command was arguably more likely to have an impact on me than the former. But in both cases, the commands take the form: "Don't perform action X, otherwise you'll face consequence Y." It seems that *how likely* I am to perform action X is irrelevant to my degree of subjection to the corresponding commands. After all, I was and am supremely unlikely to commit theft in the UK (or anywhere else), yet, as a UK resident, I was most definitely subjected to UK criminal law – both in the sense of being coerced by it and in the sense of being presumptively bound by it.[32]

So, even as far as subjection is concerned, it is not clear that there was much of a difference between my relation to the United States and to the UK, even though I was a resident of the latter. And if there was one, this appears to reduce to a matter of affectedness: UK subjection was more likely to affect me than US subjection, for the reasons just mentioned. But as we have seen, overall, the Brexit vote arguably affected my interests *less* than the US presidential vote.

Finally, regarding affinity, I think it is fair to say that I had (and possibly still have) greater "affinity" to the UK, rather than to the United States, for the simple fact that I had lived there for many years. My sense of identification with the British polity, both cultural and political, was certainly greater than my sense of identification with the United States. But while this affinity might explain why being disenfranchised from the Brexit vote was somewhat upsetting to me, it does not explain why I ought to have been included in it. To begin with, as I have already argued, it is not clear why identification and affinity are in principle relevant considerations when it comes to assigning participatory entitlements. Moreover, I am not aggrieved about the fact that I am not a British citizen and that I was not allowed to vote in UK national elections, despite residing in Britain. Yet exclusion from the Brexit vote had a very different effect on me. Mere affinity cannot explain this disanalogy. I thus conjecture that something to do with the *nature of the question being decided on*, in the Brexit case, may do part of the explanatory work.

What explains my intuitions here – i.e. that EU citizens' exclusion from the Brexit referendum was problematic in a way that their exclusion from the US presidential election was not – is a combination of factors, which cannot be captured by a single, overarching principle. First, while I think "affected interests" should be taken into account in political decision making pretty much across the board, *how* they should be taken into account – e.g. whether via enfranchisement or some other mechanism – is a contingent matter. A rule of regulation that required all those affected by the US election to have a say in it would be utterly impracticable in the world in which we live, incompatible with the state system as we know it. Trying to implement it would be disastrous. By contrast, allowing long-term EU residents to vote in the Brexit referendum would have been entirely feasible. The different *feasibility* of including someone like me in the relevant *demoi* for these two decisions has certainly influenced my intuitive judgements. If ought implies can, as a matter of principle, the United States cannot have "wronged me" by not including me. The same is not true of the UK.

Second, I had moved to the UK on the bona fide assumption that this came with the guarantees of EU citizenship and, quite suddenly, those guarantees may be unilaterally revoked. It is, therefore, as if an implicit "social contract" had been breached. By analogy, when the terms of a contract are changed, either all parties to the contract get to participate in the change in terms and conditions, or at least changes in the contract should *not* alter the rights and duties of the parties excluded from the amendment process. Such exclusion, then, appears particularly problematic in the Brexit case, for reasons that do not equally apply to the United States.

It might be tempting to add to these two reasons – one pragmatic (feasibility), the other principled (unilateral change in terms and conditions) – that EU residents in the UK had acquired a sort of "moral citizenship," by virtue of their long-standing cooperation within British society. Such cooperation, in turn, would entitle them to becoming co-authors of the relevant terms of cooperation, including in the case of Brexit.

These considerations about moral membership, however, would do little to explain the sense of unfairness felt by EU residents in the UK for being excluded from the Brexit vote. Typically, long-term residents would have qualified for citizenship. Had they taken up citizenship – which, admittedly, involves a number of hurdles – they would have been automatically included in the franchise. The option of becoming a UK citizen was available. To that extent, long-term EU residents who chose to exclude themselves from the franchise have little to complain about, or so it could be argued.[33]

This response has some merit, but it ignores the fact that, for many, the choice not to take up citizenship was made *under the assumption* that their rights would be guaranteed by virtue of the UK's membership of the EU. Those were the terms and conditions under which many EU citizens moved to the UK in the first place. This is why the sense of unfairness for being excluded from the Brexit *demos* is best explained by appeal to a perceived "unilateral change in terms and conditions," rather than by a failure to acknowledge long-term residents' moral entitlement to citizenship.

An objector might counter that, in fact, "terms and conditions" were not changed. After all, at least as a matter of principle, each EU country retains a right to leave the Union. This raises interesting questions about how to *ascertain* the terms of an implicit contract, such as the contract that arguably exists between a legal immigrant and their host state. Depending on our answer, the "unilateral change in terms and conditions" argument for the unfairness of excluding permanent EU residents from the Brexit vote will either stand or fall.

The point to be emphasized in this context, though, is that the peculiar sense of unfairness felt by EU residents in the UK excluded from the Brexit vote cannot be explained *solely* by reference to the AAP, the ASP, or AP. Rather, it likely also hinges on feasibility considerations as well as on the impression – the validity of which, I have suggested, is arguable – that an implicit "deal" has been *unilaterally* broken by one of the parties.

CONCLUSION

In this chapter, I have tried to cast doubt on the framing of the boundary problem. Instead of asking who should be given a say for a decision to count as democratic, we should focus on the question of what distribution of decision-making power is justified in any given circumstance. Democracy is itself a *contingently justified* answer to this broader question. To call the boundary problem "democratic" from the start is to put the cart before the horse, to prejudge our answer to the "who should decide" question. In any given circumstance, how decision-making power should be distributed depends on the values underpinning the practice within which the decision has to be made, broader applicable moral principles (e.g. concerning legitimate expectations, implicit contract making, and so forth) in conjunction with feasibility constraints. This means that our answer will sometimes look like democracy and sometimes not, and that the search for a general one-size-fits-all principle for answering the boundary problem is, ultimately, misguided.[34]

A final objection is worth considering. This is that, even though decisions shouldn't always be made democratically, there is always some value in the democratic pedigree of a given decision. So it may still be useful to ask "who should be given a say for a decision to instantiate democratic value?" If my argument is correct, however, there is no such thing as "democratic value" per se. Instead, there are several values that contingently justify our attachment to democracy. Of course, one might concentrate on one such value in particular – say, autonomy, or political equality, or non-domination – and call it "democratic." But it is unclear what the advantage is, other than rhetorical, of using language in this way. It would be better to instead say that a commitment to autonomy, or political equality, or some other value gives us a pro tanto reason to confer decision-making power on some people rather than others. This, however, falls short of a conclusive answer to the "who should decide" question. And to the extent that reference to democracy is often seen to point to a particular set of concrete decision-making mechanisms, labelling particular values "democratic" obscures the pro tanto nature of such determinations. Moving away from a democratic framing of the boundary problem, then, still allows us to capture all that democrats find valuable in substance, without becoming blind to the full range of morally relevant considerations that bear on the "who should decide" question.

NOTES

* I am grateful to Lucas Stanczyk and Jane Mansbridge for their insightful written comments, and to Christian List as well as the participants in the AAP workshops (Harvard, December 2016, June 2017) for their questions and suggestions. I would also like to express my gratitude to audiences at the DEMOS 21 convocation, organized by the American University of Paris, and at the Cosmopolitanism and Global Justice in Practical Contexts conference (LMU Munich) for their questions and comments. Special thanks go to the Editors of this volume for their advice and engagement with the chapter.

1 There is also a fourth contender, namely the "Proximity Principle" (PP). I omit to discuss it here since, as Robert Goodin shows in his contribution to this volume, proximity is just a proxy for other morally salient factors, and comes close to affectedness.

2 Frederick G. Whelan, "Prologue: Democratic Theory and the Boundary Problem," in *Liberal Democracy: NOMOS XXV*, ed. James R. Pennock and John W. Chapman (New York: New York University Press, 1983); Gustaf Arrenhius, "The Boundary Problem in Democratic Theory," in *Democracy Unbound: Basic Explorations I*, ed. Folke Tersman (Stockholm: Filosofiska institutionen, 2005); Robert E. Goodin, "Enfranchising All Affected Interests, and Its Alternatives," *Philosophy and Public Affairs* 35, no. 1 (2007): 40–68; Arash Abizadeh, "On the Demos and Its Kin: Nationalism, Democracy, and the Boundary Problem," *The American Political Science Review* 106, no. 4 (2012): 867–82; Sofia Näsström, "The Challenge of the All-Affected Principle," *Political Studies* 59, no. 1 (2011): 116–34; David Owen, "Constituting the Polity, Constituting the Demos: On the Place of the All Affected Interests Principle in Democratic Theory and in Resolving the Democratic Boundary Problem," *Ethics and Global Politics* 5, no. 3 (2012): 129–52.

3 For example, Goodin, "Enfranchising All Affected Interests"; Robert E. Goodin, "Enfranchising All Subjected, Worldwide," *International Theory* 8, no. 3 (2016): 365–89; Arash Abizadeh, "Democratic Theory and Border Coercion: No Right to Unilaterally Control Your Own Borders," *Political Theory* 36, no. 1 (2008): 37–65.

4 For further details, see the Introduction to this volume.

5 For discussion see, for example, Richard J. Arneson, "Democracy Is Not Intrinsically Just," in *Justice and Democracy*, ed. Keith Dowding, Robert E. Goodin, and Carole Pateman (New York: Cambridge University Press, 2004); David Estlund, *Democratic Authority: A Philosophical Framework* (Princeton, NJ: Princeton University Press, 2008); Thomas Christiano, *The Constitution of Equality* (New York: Oxford University Press, 2008); Laura Valentini, "Justice, Disagreement and Democracy," *British Journal of Political Science* 43, no. 1 (2013): 177–99; Robert A. Dahl, *Democracy and Its Critics* (New Haven, CT: Yale University Press, 1989).

6 A pluralistic picture of (democratic) inclusion has recently been offered by Rainer Bauböck, who accepts the AAP, ASP and the "all citizenship stakeholder" principles as each relevant to determining who should be included within democratic boundaries in different contexts. The principles should thus not be conceived of as competing, but as working in concert. See Rainer Bauböck, *Democratic Inclusion* (Manchester: Manchester University Press, 2018).

7 I am assuming that, in cases of collective decision making, someone is included in the answer to the "*who* question" only if their will is given more than zero weight

in determining the outcome. (This is to exclude limiting cases in which everyone votes, but the procedure for aggregating votes takes a particular person's vote – i.e. the dictator's – to be always decisive.)

8 W. B. Gallie, "Essentially Contested Concepts," *Proceedings of the Aristotelian Society* 56 (1956): 167–98; Christian List, "The Logical Space of Democracy," *Philosophy & Public Affairs* 39, no. 3 (2011): 262–297.

9 Arrhenius, "The Boundary Problem in Democratic Theory."

10 For views that instead see democracy as itself a value, see Gray and Warren (this volume).

11 G. A. Cohen, "Facts and Principles," *Philosophy & Public Affairs* 31, no. 3 (2003): 211–45.

12 David Miller, "Democracy's Domain," *Philosophy and Public Affairs* 37, no. 3 (2009): 201–28; David Miller, "Against Global Democracy," in *After the Nation: Critical Reflections on Post-Nationalism*, ed. Kaith Breen and Shane O'Neill (Basingstoke: Palgrave Macmillan, 2010); Sarah Song, "The Boundary Problem in Democratic Theory: Why the Demos Should Be Bounded by the State," *International Theory* 4, no. 1 (2012): 39–68; Laura Valentini, "No Global Demos, No Global Democracy? A Systemization and Critique," *Perspectives on Politics* 12, no. 4 (2014): 789–807.

13 For example, Christiano, *The Constitution of Equality*; Christopher G. Griffin, "Democracy as a Non–Instrumentally Just Procedure," *Journal of Political Philosophy* 11, no. 1 (2003): 111–21.

14 Arneson, "Democracy Is Not Intrinsically Just."

15 Jeremy Waldron, "The Core of the Case Against Judicial Review," *Yale Law Journal* 115 (2006): 1346–406.

16 Ronald Dworkin, *Law's Empire* (Cambridge, MA: Harvard University Press, 1986); Ronald Dworkin, *Freedom's Law* (Cambridge, MA: Harvard University Press, 1996).

17 Corey Brettschneider, "Balancing Procedures and Outcomes within Democratic Theory: Core Values and Judicial Review," *Political Studies* 53, no. 2 (2005): 423–41.

18 Brettschneider, "Balancing Procedures and Outcomes Within Democratic Theory."

19 Robert Nozick, *Anarchy, State, and Utopia* (New York: Basic Books, 1974).

20 See the example offered in Stilz (this volume).

21 Owen, "Constituting the Polity, Constituting the Demos"; Valentini, "No Global Demos, No Global Democracy?"

22 I am here assuming that votes would be aggregated via majority rule. But of course one could think of more creative aggregation procedures, e.g. where votes by different individuals are given different weights. Cf. Mathias Koenig-Archibugi, "Fuzzy Citizenship in Global Society," *The Journal of Political Philosophy* 20, no. 4 (2012): 456–80; Harry Brighouse and Marc Fleurbaey, "Democracy and Proportionality," *The Journal of Political Philosophy* 18, no. 2 (2010): 137–55.

23 One could argue that any hire in department X affects the relevant university and/or the relevant discipline as a whole. Even if true, it remains the case that the hiring department is orders of magnitude more affected.

24 This corresponds to what Stilz (this volume) calls the "substantive" as opposed to "procedural" reading of the All-Affected-Interests Principle. See also Rainer Bauböck, "Global Justice, Freedom of Movement and Democratic Citizenship,"

European Journal of Sociology / Archives Européennes de Sociologie 50, no. 1 (2009): 1–31; Owen, "Constituting the Polity, Constituting the Demos"; Charles Beitz, "Global Political Justice and the 'Democratic Deficit'," in *Reasons and Recognition: Essays on the Philosophy of T. M. Scanlon*, ed. R. Jay Wallace, Rahul Kumar, and Samuel Freeman (New York: Oxford University Press, 2011), p. 235.

25 See, respectively, Abizadeh, "Democratic Theory and Border Coercion"; Miller, "Democracy's Domain"; John Rawls, *A Theory of Justice* (Cambridge, MA: Harvard University Press, 1971), p. 194; cf. Goodin, "Enfranchising All Subjected," p. 9.

26 Cf. the arguments in Anna Stilz, *Liberal Loyalty: Freedom, Obligation, and the State* (Princeton, NJ: Princeton University Press, 2009).

27 Laura Valentini, "Coercion and (Global) Justice," *American Political Science Review* 105, no. 1 (2011): 205–20; Laura Valentini, "No Global Demos, No Democracy?"

28 A. John Simmons, *Moral Principles and Political Obligations* (Princeton, NJ: Princeton University Press), p. 133; Nozick, *Anarchy, State, and Utopia*, p. 94.

29 Miller, "Against Global Democracy"; Christian List and Mathias Koenig-Archibugi, "Can There Be a Global Demos? An Agency-Based Approach," *Philosophy & Public Affairs* 38, no. 1 (2010): 76–110; Song, "The Boundary Problem in Democratic Theory."

30 Cf. the structure of Goodin's argument about the proximity principle (this volume).

31 Abizadeh, "Democratic Theory and Border Coercion"; Goodin, "Enfranchising All Subjected."

32 Cf. Goodin, "Enfranchising All Subjected."

33 In fact, for some, long-term residents should be obliged to take up citizenship. See Helder De Schutter and Lea Ypi, "Mandatory Citizenship for Immigrants," *British Journal of Political Science* 45, no. 2 (2015): 235–51.

34 Arthur Applbaum expressed a similar concern in discussion.

8

Boundaries of Political Communities and the All-Affected Principle

Tomer J. Perry

What procedures should be used to determine the boundaries of political communities? What principles should govern the structure of these procedures? This chapter sketches an answer to these questions rooted in democratic thought and based on the idea of the All-Affected Principle (AAP) – the idea that people who are affected by a decision should have a voice in it.

I start with a commitment to democracy as a foundational normative theory, in the sense that "no prior or more basic institutional commitment rightly commands our allegiance."[1] The plausibility of this position hinges in part on democracy's ability to address fundamental questions of political morality. The challenge of delineating the boundaries of political communities is one such question. The AAP, though not without its difficulties as a principle to guide our thinking about boundaries, is a promising starting point for this exploration.

Yet the AAP on its own is ambiguous. What does it mean to be affected? And what does it mean to have influence over decisions that affect oneself? Though often it is lauded for its intuitive appeal, there is much disagreement surrounding the appropriate interpretation of the AAP. The AAP offers a simple and powerful idea, which seems to track core democratic intuitions. And yet, this simple version of the principle has attracted serious and valid criticisms that require addressing. In my account, I aim to salvage the core idea of the principle. To do so, this chapter provides a pluralistic interpretation of the AAP, joining other scholars who move away from identifying one simple principle to determine boundaries of membership.[2]

THREE DIMENSIONS OF DECISION MAKING

What are the boundaries we seek to determine? Two kinds of boundaries are often mentioned in the literature: *boundaries of membership*, delineating a set of people who comprise the community, and *scope of jurisdiction*, delineating the affairs a community has authority over. Typically, considering the question of inclusion (or the problem of the *demos*, as Robert Dahl calls it) turns our attention to criteria for membership and away from questions of jurisdiction.[3] While the abstract question is sometimes phrased as "Who should be included in the *demos*?", the discussion often concerns a specific (though not typically specified) context of assumed institutional jurisdictions, such as "Who should get to vote in the elections of representatives who rule state institutions that have ultimate authority and de-facto control in a given territory?"

Compounding the confusion between membership and jurisdiction, political and ethical disagreements on questions of immigration focus on power over *territorial borders* – the right of a state to exercise control over a clearly defined territory, including movement of people (and sometimes goods) across territorial lines. These discussions, however, make assumptions on, or else implicate, a host of issues regarding the rights associated with membership as well as the jurisdiction of the states involved. Whether a state should be permitted to bar nonmembers from entering a given territory depends on the plausibility of assumptions regarding the state's right to grant or deny membership status to these particular individuals, as well as its impact on the circumstances that led them to want to move.[4]

The point is that the plausibility of an ethical judgment passed over a policy which concerns boundaries, for example in the discussion of naturalization laws, hinges on background assumptions regarding jurisdiction and border control. Therefore, I argue that questions of membership, jurisdictions, and borders should be examined, and answered, together. How we should do this will, I hope, become clear as we discuss the AAP, but we can already see what we are aiming at: a judgment regarding the relationship between membership, territory, and jurisdiction.

Before proceeding, I should note that the three dimensions of democratic decision making I am concerned with – membership (who can take part in decisions), jurisdiction (what the decisions should be about), and territory (where do they apply) – are substantively connected. In other words, it is not unusual for people to make assumptions that connect these topics, because judgments about one ordinarily come with the other. Thus, arguments about movement often assume that members cannot be barred from movement or that people who inhabit a territory have a right to membership in whatever political association governs that territory.[5]

I should also note at the outset that in discussing political communities, I am thinking of a wide array of social institutions and not just about states, especially not the misleading conceptions of the state as either a Hobbesian ultimate (as in unlimited and undivided) authority or the Weberian centralized monopoly on legitimate power in a territory.[6] Not only do these notions of statehood measure poorly when examined in light of the rich variety of political orders that exist in the world today, they also restrict democratic theory without good reason. If we examine the theoretical foundations of democratic theory, we find that the *reasons* for inclusion and membership in the state apply to other political structures, including local authorities and global governance bodies. The boundary problem of democratic theory is much more prevalent than has been appreciated, and it is interesting to note that the philosophical debates about democratic boundaries more often engage the case of citizenship than disagreements regarding the proper jurisdiction of political power, of the kind that is typical in the literature on (say) federalism.[7] Yet the disputes that arise around boundaries of local communities are of the same kind as the controversies surrounding borders of states. A principled democratic response is needed in all these contexts, at least for those of us committed to democracy as a foundational normative commitment.

To see the force of the last point, I briefly present my approach to democratic theory and sketch the considerations that lead us to be concerned about boundaries. The discussion lays the foundation for a presentation of the AAP in the following section.

SOCIAL POWER AND POLITICAL COMMUNITIES

Political Justice and Social Power

On my account, democracy is a demand of justice. Democratic theory *is* a theory of political justice, as distinguished from a distributive conception of justice.[8] This view is contrasted with much of the literature that sees democracy as a standard of legitimacy, often leaving ambiguous its relationship to justice. Nonetheless, several democratic theorists have advanced views that locate democracy's value in its contribution to a just society. My view aligns with those that are also tied to a "relational" view of justice or equality.[9]

Political justice concerns the structure of society and the way people relate to one another. In particular, political justice is concerned with the regulation of *social power*.[10] This position resonates with central concerns of deliberative democracy, even if much of the theory aims to provide a standard of legitimacy because "the point of deliberative democracy is to subject *the exercise of power* to reason's discipline, to what Habermas famously described as 'the force of the better argument.'"[11] Given the centrality of this idea to deliberative democracy, we can see why it makes sense to see it as a theory of political justice.

What is social power? Humans form relations that give rise to social facts that are "intersubjective" – they are true in virtue of the fact that people believe that they are true, yet they are not a matter of personal preference or opinion. Some such social facts concern the ability of some people to make others do things they would not do otherwise. In other words, some social facts are about *power*. Shared beliefs bestow power on some people and it is that power that I call, following Miranda Fricker, *social power*.[12] Social power is the ability to make others do as they would not otherwise *in virtue* of the shared beliefs that people have.

This analysis points us towards formal institutions and decisions that take place within them, but the focus is not exclusive. Democratic theory focuses on regulating the exercise of social power, and so follows social power where it appears. The proliferation of sites of power is reason to look beyond state institutions.[13]

Social power is rooted in shared perceptions that form among groups of people. Relationships change over time, but shared perceptions typically arise in the context of relatively stable relationships, which together comprise *social orders*. The hallmarks and delineators of social orders are *norms* – social rules that dictate behavior in particular situations, due to a formal role or specific relationship; they are "a standard of appropriate behavior for actors with a given identity."[14] Norms are enforced and circulated through a variety of social mechanisms such as social pressures and sanctions, ostracism, imitation, and internalization.

Norms are often contrasted with laws, because norms are weakly enforced by social pressures while laws are backed by coercion or the threat of it. The distinction is important, as coercion plays a fundamental role in various normative theories and is often said to require a special justification.[15] Yet the fundamental concern of democratic theory, on my account, is with social power and not coercion, and therefore the distinction obfuscates the important similarity between norms and laws as exercises of social power that require justification.

I should add that my expansive operationalization of social power aims to include subtle or invisible forms of social power like what Stephen Lukes calls the "third dimension" of power,[16] which manifests in latent, rather than actual, conflicts. Lukes maintains that the exercise of power need not be conscious or intentional but rather can be the product of "socially structured and culturally patterned behaviour of groups, and practices of institutions, which may indeed be manifested by individuals' inaction."[17] The first two dimensions, Lukes argues, cannot account for the way in which power is exercised to shape individuals' preferences such that they become unaware of their *real* interests. Absence of conflict, or even consensus, may not reflect an authentic agreement but be the result of manipulation or thoughtless acceptance of cultural norms.[18] This aspect of power illuminates how interests of certain people are ignored or undermined by prevalent beliefs, cultural norms, and the status quo without any observable conflict. And yet, a focus on state institutions or legal enforcement completely misses this form of social power.

Exercises of power along any of these dimensions can take various forms. Democracy, as a theory of political justice, concerns itself with relatively stable patterns of interactions that I will refer to as *social orders*.[19] A focus on stable patterns is implicit in the analysis of both the first and second dimensions of power, where the discussion referred not to ephemeral observable conflict but to the social structures where such conflict tends to arise, and these are commonly accepted as the subjects of democratic principles, being the central venues of decision making.[20]

However, I argue that democratic theory also aims to regulate the third dimension of power. Cultural and social norms are not the product of decision making in a straightforward sense, but they are "decisions by accretion" since "widespread societal conclusion[s] ... [are] reasonably described as ... collective decision[s]."[21] In other words, *cultural norms allocate social power*. To say that they are on par with decisions of the kind made in more formal institutions is to treat them as exercises of power. When I accept and uphold a norm that also serves my interests, I am exercising power over someone even though I may not intend it. This interpretation of norms dovetails with Lukes' analysis of power, as he notes that the third dimension of power reflects the fact that "the bias of the system can be mobilized, recreated and reinforced in ways that are neither consciously chosen nor the intended result of particular individuals' choices."[22] The power of norms is real; as John Stuart Mill noticed, "social tyranny" can be "more formidable than many kinds of political tyranny" and the use of social sanctions "leaves fewer means of escape, penetrating much more deeply into the details of life, and enslaving the soul itself."[23]

To recap briefly: political justice concerns the regulation of social power. To locate social power, we examine stable patterns of interactions, social orders, which form informal arrangements as well as formal institutions and organizations. The delineators of social worlds are norms, which I consider "decisions by accretion" for the purposes of democratization. These social worlds are the contexts within which we should allocate participation and voice.[24]

Political Communities

The picture we have is one of multiple overlapping social worlds that are diverse and slowly evolving, as "norm entrepreneurs" challenge entrenched norms, others push back, and various other factors (demography, technology, etc.) interact to shape the social world.[25] Social norms are powerful but not irresistible. Prevalent norms are followed by most members of a social world because people accept that "this is how they should behave" (prevalent and uncontested norms may be accepted somewhat thoughtlessly). In addition, violations lead to social pressures, including shaming and ostracism, that are often enough to deter people from breaking these norms.

Yet there are always people who, for various reasons, do break norms. The stigma rightfully attached to murder, with the accompanied threat of social shaming and ostracism, act as important deterrence to prevent murder, but as a society we do not accept that as a sufficient means for ensuring certain important norms are adhered to.[26] Societies have therefore developed all sorts of social technologies to strengthen the enforcement of certain important rules: codification in written documents, threat of punishment, processes of reputation, and so forth. Legal systems are a particularly relevant social technology; they typically aim at enforcement of norms as well as adjudication of conflicting claims regarding norm breaking. What makes legal systems complicated in this regard is that they both enforce norms but also are upheld, to an extent, by norms. Following the law becomes a norm on its own and in turn the legal system also functions to enforce it, typically by using the threat of punishment.

These various social technologies used to enforce norms are what we call *political institutions*, and the people who find themselves within the same political structure form a political community. I use the term *political* here because political institutions reflect the attempt to create a community and manage the way it operates. Sometimes political institutions are conscious and intentional, other times they are implicit in the practice of social norms. *Political institutions are those social institutions that exercise the social power embedded in the social world*; if there are norms, there are consequences to violating them, and the political institutions are those rules and norms that govern those consequences.

In other words, political institutions are the subset of social institutions that attempt to institute a *common good*. We often focus on the fact that political institutions establish a "good" and argue about the permissible limits of such a practice, but political institutions also establish the community for which that good is common. Political institutions create boundaries. Sometimes, political institutions trace existing patterns of norms, defining the boundaries of the target population as close as possible to existing social patterns. In other words, sometimes the institutions that police enforcement of rules are applied mostly to people who already accept, perhaps reluctantly or thoughtlessly, the set of norms that the political institutions enforce. Yet the opposite is also true, as social patterns form around existing institutions. Being subjected to a system of social rules may give rise to a shared identity and the creation of a social world.[27]

In discussing political communities, we tend to think mostly about states, but that tendency is misleading – first, because states are not the only political communities. Cities, for example, also "express and prioritize different social and political values" and are "sites of collective self-determination" whose boundaries matter for the same reasons.[28] Political communities overlap and reside within each other as people, members of various social worlds, create, reform, and inhabit institutions. But more importantly, the term state is not particularly useful because it lumps together political orders that are relevantly distinct. The most problematic assumption is that states are unitary actors that enjoy ultimate authority over a territory, associated with the idea of sovereignty. In fact, many states do not enjoy ultimate authority as various internal and external actors restrict their effective power or their perceived legitimacy, yet these instances are dismissed as exceptions.[29] Furthermore, even assuming states as unified ultimate authority over a territory, the institutions we call states are different in relevant ways. Some states are federative systems with robust substate structures that exercise a certain measure of autonomy. Some are part of regional organizations that have a great deal of influence over their internal affairs, while others depend on market forces, donations, or other states in order to provide basic functions from security to economics. Some share power with a variety of non-state organizations in and outside of their territory. Some states control disputed areas whose inhabitants have strong affinities to other states, who in turn contest and challenge that control.

Lastly, many states are not actually unitary agents. While it makes sense to look at them as such for the analysis of certain situations, they are in fact collections of agents and institutions that are intermingled together in a variety of complicated relations. For example, it is typical to consider states as sole actors that can deploy coercive force to back their demands. Yet if we look closer at the state, there are various agencies and organizations with capacity to use violence in various situations. The executive branch may need approval from the legislative branch to deploy military force, but actually does so on its own in an unauthorized way, sometimes; or it may be that state leaders have a legal authority to use military force, but they are limited because they believe the military will refuse to obey certain commands; or there is a civilian authority that technically rules over the military commander but in fact is restricted by it. In addition, there are often various domestic actors with varying degrees of coercive power or coercive threat: courts, police forces of different levels, intelligence organizations, bureaucrats, civil society, illegal organizations, and so forth.

Therefore, in thinking of political communities we shouldn't restrict ourselves to thinking about states. Instead of assuming the power of coercive threat is concentrated in one entity, we should inquire into who can authorize coercion and under what circumstances. It is an open question whether any political institution should have any given set of powers. The idealized version of a system of states is not our point of departure.[30] In absence of such point of departure, what should guide us as we consider the boundaries of various political communities? In the next section, I defend the AAP as a better normative starting point for thinking through these issues.

THE ALL-AFFECTED PRINCIPLE

The All-Affected Principle is the simple and intuitively appealing idea that those who are affected by a decision should have a voice in it. Scholars who support the AAP treat it as a freestanding principle central to democratic theory. Archon Fung describes the All-Affected Principle as a "starting point" of democratic theory, "perhaps the most basic of democratic intuitions," while Mark Warren calls it a "defining norm of democracy."[31] I start by examining a simple and clearly stated idea of the AAP:

- *AAP: The people that are relevantly affected by a decision ought to have, in some sense, influence over it.*[32]

Despite its commonsensical appeal, the AAP is quite revolutionary; existing decision-making structures rarely follow power rather than membership, especially when considering the boundaries of political communities.[33] The most obvious context where our institutions do not even attempt to track power is the system of states in the global (or "international") realm, where the legal norm is to exclude noncitizens and completely ignore the voices of nonresidents. However, the AAP also offers a critical perch in many contexts of asymmetrical power including racial and socioeconomic inequalities within states, where those arise out historical or circumstantial factors that never did, and still do not, give voice to the people on the weaker side of the asymmetry.

That said, even a simple version of the AAP suffers from conceptual challenges that threaten its plausibility. The rest of this section outlines these challenges and offers revisions to the principle that aim to salvage its core appeal. First, critics argue (rightly) that the AAP's focus on decisions is misguided and conjures an image of a single set of choices among a clear set of options, one after another. To reform the AAP, we therefore need to start by turning away from thinking about decisions and towards thinking about *decision-making structures*. My earlier concern with social power led us to look at stable patterns of interactions, social institutions, through which social power is typically exercised. Decision-making structures are a subset of these social institutions that explicitly involve transforming a group of people into a collective agent by instituting procedures that create a unified collective perspective to guide action. Decision-making structures create collective agency.[34]

The more important conceptual difficulty that plagues the literature on the AAP is an ambiguity regarding the conditions of affectedness that trigger the principle and the content of the influence that it grants. Many criticisms of the principle stem from the implausible mismatch between a weak affectedness condition, such as being "merely" affected, and a strong conception of influence, such as being entitled to full voting rights.[35]

The first step to dispel this ambiguity is to accept a *pluralistic* account of the AAP, according to which people who are affected in different ways are granted different forms of influence over decisions. The main benefit of a pluralistic account is that it abandons binary conceptualization of affectedness and influence. Once we clear up the ambiguity, we can see that a binary version of affectedness and influence is the main grounds for criticizing the AAP. For example, Dahl criticizes the AAP based on the observation that "the logic of the Principle of Affected Interests is that for every different set of persons affected there [will] be a different association or decision-making unit."[36] This kind of criticism hinges on a conception of influence that is conceived only in terms of *direct* participation in decision making.

For Dahl, it is other democratic requirements, the criteria of economy and competence, that "argue strongly against this degree of direct participation; they argue instead in favor of indirect participation."[37] Yet the AAP is not committed to direct participation as the unique mode of influence. Advocates have no reason to ignore the fact, pointed by Dahl earlier in the same passage, that "people affected by a decision are by no means affected *equally*."[38] Sometimes affected people have the right to participate directly, but the principle allows, indeed requires, that some of the people affected by decisions will only be granted indirect influence. Thus, the AAP does not require a different association for every different set of people affected, but rather that every association provides a variety of avenues for influence, both direct and indirect.[39]

The preceding discussion suggests that the AAP is actually a scalar or proportional principle, granting more influence to individuals who are more affected. The proportional logic fits with the intuitive appeal of the AAP. If the reason people deserve a voice is that they are affected, shouldn't they be granted more voice if they are affected more?

Yes and no. In fact, I think the temptation to interpret the AAP in a *strictly* proportional manner should be resisted. The main reason is related to the way we conceptualize affectedness. The relevant effect that triggers demand for voice, on my account, is being subjected to social power. Yet social power operates in a variety of different ways, from soft pressures to conform, to punitive sanctions, to internalizing self-depreciating stereotypes – and none of these easily fall along a scalar continuum. Proportionality may play a role in interpreting the AAP as we consider clusters of cases as having a greater or more serious effect on people's lives, but the pluralistic framework allows for more differentiation in form rather than scale.

In the same manner, there are many possible avenues of voice that do not fit easily into categories of voice. An important avenue of voice is voting rights. Binary accounts of the AAP often take voting rights as synonymous with being granted a voice. Proponents of the AAP typically think that anyone that is affected (in whatever way that is conceptualized) deserves to be included in the sense that they deserve full voting rights. The problem with this view is that it both over- and underemphasizes the role of voting in granting voice to people. On the one hand, voting is only one of the ways in which political institutions allow individuals to participate in, and shape, the way norms are enforced. A democratic society is one where members are active and participate regularly, beyond voting, in public discussion, protests, public meetings, hearings, and so forth. On the other hand, voting rights are rightly tied to an ongoing relationship with a particular political community. Granting voting rights to everyone in the world, as in Goodin's account, or to other people whose relationship to the community is only temporary, risks making the act of voting even less influential than it is today.[40] A pluralistic perspective avoids these problems by locating voting rights within the context of other avenues of voice.

Thus, the pluralistic account of the AAP presents a picture where decision-making structures allow multiple channels of influence, each open to a group of individuals affected in a manner that fits that kind of influence, and individuals find themselves in many such groups. In short, the AAP requires that, in creating decision-making structures, we make sure to match scope and domain – that is, match the people participating in the decision with the array of matters that they have power over. It requires that *decision-making structures bring together power with constituency.* This is what makes the AAP a foundational democratic principle – it is concerned with empowering the people who are subjected to social control.

My account departs from the AAP as it is often understood. To clarify these differences, I offer this reformulation of the principle:

- *Decision-making structures rightly wield social power as long as the people that are subjected to it have sufficient influence over it.*

This formulation is still abstract, as it does not specify what influence is sufficient for any particular case. But it contributes to addressing the question of boundaries by providing a criterion for evaluating the justifications of political structures. The premise behind the concern for political justice is that social power requires justification. The AAP, as a democratic principle, addresses this concern by specifying the form of justification required, namely that decision-making structures must demonstrate that they provide avenues of influence to the people subjected to their social power, and explain why such influence is adequate. This may seem like a weak conclusion to be drawn from the principle, especially given the promise that it would resolve the question of what makes the boundaries between two or more communities legitimate. However weak this conclusion may be, I contend that it has sufficient implications to merit our attention. To conclude, the next section explores one such implication: the need for democratic decision making surrounding the establishment of boundaries.

PROCEDURES FOR DETERMINING BOUNDARIES OF POLITICAL COMMUNITIES

What does adopting the AAP as I have defined it entail for the institutionalization of boundaries? What are the implications of embracing my pluralistic interpretation for the resolution of boundary-disputes? The first answer is that we ought to have democratic procedures for determining the boundaries of political communities. Since the question of inclusion, of boundaries, of the *demos*, is a fundamental determinant of the character of the power wielded by a social structure, there is no way in which people have sufficient influence over the systems that wield power around them if they do not, among other things, have a voice in the question of boundaries. Even if they have a voice in the *substantive* decisions made by the structure, they ought to have a voice in the *procedural* question of who gets to have a voice. Most importantly, the AAP suggests that the group of people entitled to be involved in boundary-drawing procedures may be different than the groups that we normally think of as entitled. It cannot be the case, for instance, that "current voters" have the power to decide whether nonvoters have the right to vote because the latter group is obviously implicated by that decision. Thus, the pluralistic account of the AAP points to the need for having a separate and special procedure for determining boundaries of political communities.

As trivial as it sounds, this is a controversial position. The commonplace assumption, in political life as well as political theory, is that the way political communities have formed is less important than the way they are managed. The atrocities of the past may give rise to claims of historical justice, the view goes, but they do not undermine the legitimacy (or justice) of existing political structures so long as those are governed according to democratic principles such as majority rule and rule by representatives.[41] We have come to think of political communities as if they are born in one constituent moment, out of thin air, and from then onward there exists a political community where before there wasn't one. Democracy, we've been led to believe, is what happens in between such "constituent moments" where ordinary politics is suspended, and "the people" comes into being momentarily as people step forward to change the existing definition.[42] Each such change is thought to be permanent as the boundaries are presumed to be, at least in principle, stable.

This position is untenable. Political structures create boundaries by organizing the way social power enforces norms and rules. This practice must be justified not only in principle but also in practice. This idea is central to deliberative democracy, which centers around a "reason-giving requirement."[43] The reason-giving requirement restricts the kinds of reasons that can justify policies but also requires establishing procedures that facilitate participation and provide opportunity for political influence. Reason is not alone required; for a system to be democratic there must be actual reason-giving. Likewise, the AAP requires that political communities provide an account of the ways in which they empower the people subjected to their power. The only way to do that is to institute procedures whereby such arguments can be articulated, contested, defended, and ultimately decided in some manner that reflects a collective judgment. In other words, it requires a democratic procedure. Despite the violent and dark history surrounding the formation and delineation of many political communities, the practice of democracy is ahead of the theory when it comes to procedures for setting boundaries.

Consider referendums. In recent years, we have seen referendums used to determine the boundaries of political communities. Referendums raise many complicated questions and there is no doubt that the practice of referendums is far from ideal. Yet at least in some cases they are unique as examples of boundary setting procedures that are intentionally designed to reflect democratic values.[44] For example, two recent UK referendums focused on questions of boundaries: the 2014 vote on Scottish independence, and the United Kingdom European Union Membership Referendum (a.k.a. the Brexit vote).[45] Both were touted for their democratic credentials even though they also raised serious concerns from a democratic perspective. Even if these referendums failed to live up to the democratic ideal, they represent the potential for democratic procedures to determine borders on an ongoing, and forward-looking basis. Theory can learn from these practices and offer revisions that address the challenges they bring up. One of the challenges raised by the Scottish independence and Brexit votes was the arbitrariness of the timing of such votes, and the way voting eligibility was manipulated to try to achieve particular results. Many of the people who voted against Scottish independence argued, reasonably, that they would have voted differently if the results of the Brexit referendum were taken into consideration, especially its economic implications for the UK as a whole. The problem is that many intended their vote to be a protest that initiated a further process of reason-giving. Instead, these referenda were presented as "once in a lifetime" opportunities to determine boundaries "once and for all," reflecting the same position that democratic systems need to assume boundaries in the background rather than subject them to continual examination.[46]

The concern that a constant reexamination of boundaries may interrupt effective operation of the political community is understandable. Brexit discussions dominated British politics for a long while and many other policies and issues had to be put on hold until the question of membership in the EU was settled. Yet the conclusion cannot be that questions of boundaries need to be determined "once and for all" without any additional opportunity for revision and reexamination, but rather that they cannot be too frequent. Just like ordinary election of representative cannot occur too frequently, or constitutional amendments require supermajorities or other exacting constraints, referenda on boundaries cannot be frequent or commonplace. Yet there must be in place a principled procedure that can trigger them. That is, I argue, an implication of the AAP.

For an illustration of how this balancing act might be accomplished, Stuart White suggests a system he calls PAR, which stands for petition, assembly, referendum.[47] According to this scheme, when enough citizens sign a petition in favor of a bill (for White, this is limited to constitutional amendments), the communities affected are required to set up a citizens' assembly to look at the proposal and decide what, if anything, should be put out to a referendum. Thus, there is an institutionalized deliberative process, which relies on popular participation, that shapes the agenda of any such referendum. I cannot here provide a full account of such procedure for boundaries referenda, but the proposal serves as a fruitful starting point for developing democratic procedures for setting the boundaries between political communities in a way that is, in principle, revisable and open-ended.

CONCLUSION

In this chapter, I have argued that the AAP urges us to think about instituting processes that open the question of the *demos* for periodic contestation and allow revision of the boundaries of the *demos*. Democratic rule is temporary and elected representatives must periodically submit themselves to the judgment of the people. In the same vein, the people itself must be periodically reexamined and constituted. This periodic rebirth need not only be the result of a revolution or moments of rapture, it can also be incorporated into the structure of democratic institutions. If these kinds of procedures were integrated into our political structures, we would have a more expansive view of what kinds of decisions ought to be made democratically – not just how we rule, but also who.

NOTES

1 Ian Shapiro, *Democratic Justice* (New Haven: Yale University Press), p. 21. For an elaboration of this view, see Gray and Warren (this volume). I agree with these authors that democracy is best seen as a theory of political justice and not as a theory of legitimacy, but defending this position is beyond the scope of this chapter.

2 For examples, see David Owen, "Constituting the Polity, Constituting the Demos: On the Place of the All Affected Interests Principle in Democratic Theory and in Resolving the Democratic Boundary Problem," *Ethics and Global Politics* 5, no. 3 (2012): 129–52, and Rainer Bauböck, *Democratic Inclusion* (Manchester: Manchester University Press, 2017). Some earlier pieces have also advanced somewhat pluralistic positions even if they nominally accept a single principle. See, among others, Arash Abizadeh, "Democratic Theory and Border Coercion: No Right to Unilaterally Control Your Own Borders," *Political Theory* 36, no. 1 (2008): 37–65; David Miller, "Democracy's Domain," *Philosophy and Public Affairs* 37, no. 3 (2009): 201–28; Archon Fung, "The Principle of Affected Interests: An Interpretation and Defense," in *Representation: Elections and Beyond*, ed. Rogers M. Smith and Jack H. Nagel (Philadelphia: University of Pennsylvania Press, 2013). For further discussions of applying a pluralistic understanding to the All Affected Principle to the boundary problem, see also Carens, Valentini, and Macdonald (this volume).

3 See Robert Dahl, *Democracy and Its Critics* (New Haven: Yale University Press), pp. 121, 207. Schumpeter (1950) and Whelan (1983, 40, 42) note something similar: "democratic theory cannot itself provide any solution to disputes that may – and historically do – arise concerning boundaries." Joseph A. Schumpeter, *Capitalism, Socialism, and Democracy* (New York: Routledge, [1950] 2003); Frederick G. Whelan, "Prologue: Democratic Theory and the Boundary Problem," in *Liberal Democracy*, ed. James R. Pennock and John W. Chapman (New York: New York University Press, 1983).

4 For example, it is often argued that a state has an obligation to accept immigrants if it is partially responsible for the political turmoil or economic difficulty that is relevant for understanding the immigrants' motivation to leave their country of origin.

5 At least if they have been living there for a prolonged period. See, for instance, Joseph H. Carens, *The Ethics of Immigration* (New York: Oxford University Press, 2013).

6 In this, I follow the insightful analysis provided in William E. Scheuerman, "Realism and the Kantian Tradition: A Revisionist Account," *International Relations* 26, no. 4 (2012): 453–77. Though Scheuerman's criticisms are addressed to cosmopolitans who reject the need of a state because of their mistaken view of what a state is, his diagnosis applies with equal force to statists who favor states on the basis of the exact same mistaken view.

7 The chapter by Clarissa Hayward in this volume is a much welcome exception.

8 On the recent interest in political justice, also referred to as 'relational' justice, see Terry Macdonald and Miriam Ronzoni, "The Idea of Global Political Justice,"

Critical Review of Social and Political Philosophy 15, no. 5 (2012): 521–33. These more recent defenders of political justice owe a debt to earlier critiques of egalitarianism in liberal theory offered by, among others, Elizabeth S. Anderson, "What's the Point of Equality?" *Ethics* 109, no. 2 (1999): 287–337.

9 There is a long tradition of democratic theorists who have articulated a "relational" conception of democracy (a view represented by Gray, this volume), in contrast to a view of democracy defined in terms of decision-making procedures (a view represented by Valentini, this volume).

10 The focus on power is shared by other authors; see Gray, Hayward, Williams, Macdonald (this volume).

11 Joshua Cohen, *Philosophy, Politics, Democracy* (Cambridge, MA: Harvard University Press, 2009), p. 330. Emphasis added.

12 For Miranda Fricker, *Epistemic Injustice: Power and the Ethics of Knowing* (New York: Oxford University Press, 2007), p. 4, power is a "social situated capacity to control others' actions."

13 Fung, "The Principle of Affected Interests," p. 238. Fung turns his attention to organizations, which are "entities that collectively control resources, advance purposes, and make decisions whose effects are moderately consistent over time." (pp. 249–50). Yet, Fung's definition is ambiguous, and it's not clear whether it covers social institutions such as social norms. In addition, his reasons for focusing on organizations include that they are relatively stable and "are typically the object of demands for inclusion," which strikes me as an insufficient reason to exclude other social institutions (if indeed it is meant to exclude informal social institutions).

14 Martha Finnemore and Kathryn Sikkink, "International Norm Dynamics and Political Change," *International Organization* 52, no. 4 (1998): 891.

15 See for example Abizadeh, "Democratic Theory and Border Coercion," pp. 37–65; and Laura Valentini, *Justice in a Globalized World: A Normative Framework* (New York: Oxford University Press, 2011).

16 See Steven Lukes, *Power: A Radical View*, 2nd ed. (London: Palgrave Macmillan, 2005).

17 Lukes, *Power*, p. 26.

18 This dimension of power mirrors what Iris Marion Young calls 'hegemonic discourse,' under which "people may come to an agreement that is nevertheless at least partly conditioned by unjust power relations and for that reason should not be considered a genuinely free consent." Iris M. Young, "Activist Challenges to Deliberative Democracy," *Political Theory* 29, no. 5 (2001): 685.

19 In some literatures, this is called 'institutions' though I find that confusing as institutions sometimes are only formal but other times are relatively stable social structures that can be either formal or informal, for example: "[Institutions are] the humanly devised constraints that structure political, economic and social interactions. They consist of both informal constraints (sanctions, taboos, customs, traditions, and codes of conduct), and formal rules (constitutions, laws, property rights)" Douglass C. North, *Institutions, Institutional Change, and Economic Performance* (New York: Cambridge University Press, 1990), p. 97.

20 Formal decisions and conflicts (the first dimension) receive by far a lot more attention by democratic theorists than nondecisions (the second dimension) but discussion of agenda-setting aren't unusual and see also the important works of Hayward, Macdonald, and Rubenstein (this volume), who draw attention to the importance of nondecisions.

21 Jane Mansbridge et al., "A Systemic Approach to Deliberative Democracy," in *Deliberative Systems: Deliberative Democracy at the Large Scale*, ed. John Parkinson and Jane Mansbridge (New York: Cambridge University Press, 2012), p. 8.

22 Lukes, *Power*, p. 25.

23 John Stuart Mill, *On Liberty and Other Essays* (New York: Oxford University Press, [1859] 1991), pp. 8–9.

24 For a similar point, see Carol Gould's related account of "common activities" (this volume).

25 Martha Finnemore and Kathryn Sikkink, "International Norm Dynamics and Political Change," *International Organization* 52, no. 4 (1998): 891.

26 An important example of the insufficient strength of norms is the case of human rights. A growing literature documents the rise of human rights as international norms that affect state policies as well as involves a wide array of non-state actors. Human rights are not merely norms but are also institutionalized in several treaties and conventions, yet there is no doubt that in world society, there has not been sufficient institutionalization to ensure enforcement of such an important norm.

27 Benedict Anderson's famous comparison of national identity to an 'imagined community' is a relevant example. See Anderson, *Imagined Communities: Reflections on the Origin and Spread of Nationalism* (London: Verso, 1991).

28 Daniel Bell and Avenir de Shalit, *The Spirit of Cities: Why the Identity of a City Matters in a Global Age* (Princeton, NJ: Princeton University Press, 2011), pp. 2–4. Bell and de-Shalit advance the radical thesis that so long as cities' set of values are not in conflict with basic human rights and are not self-defeating, cities should be allowed to express whatever values are 'prevalent' among their community. I say this is a radical thesis because adopting it entails reducing greatly the authority states have over a variety of important issues, including, for example, taxation and economic distribution.

29 For a discussion of the ways in which practice of international affairs does not match the ideals of sovereignty, see Stephen D. Krasner, *Sovereignty: Organized Hypocrisy* (Princeton, NJ: Princeton University Press, 1999).

30 Separate from the various defenses of the states as normatively important, several theories defend the status-quo as a starting point for normative inquiry from which we should offer reform and see for example Michael Blake, "Distributive Justice, State Coercion, and Autonomy," *Philosophy and Public Affairs* 30, no. 3 (2001): 257–96.

31 Fung, "The Principle of Affected Interests," p. 237; Mark E. Warren, "What Does Corruption Mean in a Democracy?" *American Journal of Political Science* 48, no. 2 (2004): 333.

32 Gustaf Arrenhius, "The Boundary Problem in Democratic Theory," in *Democracy Unbound: Basic Explorations I*, ed. Folke Tersman (Stockholm: Stockholm : Filosofiska institutionen, Stockholms Universitet, 2005), p. 20.

33 A similar point is made by Gray and Hayward who endorse the slogan "track power, not just its effects." I agree though prefer the phrase "social power" for the reasons laid out earlier in my chapter.

34 For an insightful discussion of the connection between decision making and collective agency, see Christian List and Philip Pettit, *Group Agency: The Possibility, Design, and Status of Corporate Agents* (New York: Oxford University Press).

35 For example, Goodin's influential account grants full participation rights to anyone who is "possibly affected', which leads to the implausible conclusion that "virtually everyone a vote on virtually everything virtually everywhere in the world." See Goodin, "Enfranchising All Affected Interests, and Its Alternatives," *Philosophy and Public Affairs* 35, no. 1 (2007): 40–68.

36 Robert A. Dahl, *After the Revolution? Authority in a Good Society* (New Haven: Yale University Press, 1990), p. 51.

37 Dahl, *After the Revolution?*, p. 50

38 Dahl, *After the Revolution?*, p. 50

39 This is a feature of governance that already exists within territorial democracies, as Warren notes (this volume).

40 Goodin, "Enfranchising All Affected Interests."

41 That is the argument made by Whelan: "democratic theory cannot itself provide any solution to disputes that may – and historically do – arise concerning boundaries... before democratic procedures can begin to operate, boundaries must be established in one fashion or another... thus it must be a matter of concern to all democrats – both the citizens of an existing democratic system and well-wishers of democracy in general – that boundaries of democratic communities be generally acknowledge as fair and appropriate." *Prologue*, pp. 40–2.

42 I borrow the term from Jason Frank, *Constituent Moments: Enacting the People in Postrevolutionary America* (Durham: Duke University Press, 2010).

43 Amy Gutmann and Dennis F. Thompson, *Why Deliberative Democracy?* (Princeton, NJ: Princeton University Press, 2004), p. 3.

44 For debates within democratic theory about the purpose, value, and dangers of referendums as boundary-drawing mechanisms see David Altman, *Direct Democracy Worldwide* (New York: Cambridge University Press, 2011); and Lawrence LeDuc, "Referendums and Deliberative Democracy," *Electoral Studies* 38 (2015): 139–48.

45 Other examples include Quebec, which voted on succession twice, and Catalonia, where efforts to create a referendum for succession have so far failed.

46 In the archives of the Scottish government, there are copies of the website scotreferendum.com that was set up to support its independence referendum. Under the heading of 'Questions & Answers,' the Scottish government states: "It is the view of the current Scottish Government that a referendum is a once-in-a-generation opportunity. This means that only a majority vote for Yes in 2014 would give certainty that Scotland will be independent." www.webarchive.org.uk/wayback/archive/20150119120852/www.scotreferendum.com/questions/ifscotland-votes-no-will-there-be-another-referendum-on-independence-at-a-later-date/.

47 See Stuart White, "Parliaments, Constitutional Conventions, and Popular Sovereignty," *British Journal of Politics and International Relations* 19, no. 2 (2017): 320–35.

PART III

TAMING ECONOMIC POWER

9

The All-Affected Principle and Labor Rights[*]

Carol C. Gould

Economic globalization, characterized by the spread of capital and the emergence of a world market, has transformed both production and consumption. It has brought ever more global supply chains, the outsourcing of labor to low-wage countries, increasingly free trade, and the proliferation of marketing and advertising across borders. We have witnessed growing power on the side of capital coupled with a diminishing power of labor, as evidenced in part in widening inequalities in income and wealth both within national states and more globally (despite a decrease in absolute poverty). Forms of labor exploitation persist and are widespread, whether as child labor, sweatshop labor, forced labor and trafficking, or the use and abuse of undocumented laborers and guest workers. At the same time, important institutions of global governance have come to prominence, providing loans to governments and facilitating and regulating trade, especially the International Monetary Fund (IMF), the World Bank, and the World Trade Organization (WTO). These institutions, which were initially set up by developed countries and most often act in their interest, establish policies and make decisions with wide impacts. However, those affected by their functioning, especially developing countries and the global poor, as well as labor more generally, most often lack the right to participate in their decisions or even in the deliberative processes that lead up to them.

If we believe that democracy signifies at its root the right to share in determining the direction of the communities of which one is a part or in institutions that deeply affect one's life chances, then we need to address the democratic deficit in these communities and organizations, whether they be at the national or transnational level. We have noted the deficit in global governance institutions, but I suggest that similar problems of lack of access to decision making apply within political communities and, I will argue, within a range of economic organizations, including corporate firms. The All-Affected Principle (AAP) is particularly well suited to address the democratic deficits arising from globalization, inasmuch as the laws, rules, and policies of powerful actors – whether they be governments or other institutions – have profound effects on distantly situated people or groups, beyond their import for their members alone. Thus traditional democratic understandings of citizens or members as those who have an exclusive right to participate in decision making or to be represented do not give sufficient weight to the rights and needs of others who may be deeply affected by their decisions. The All-Affected Principle calls on us to structure democratic decision making such that all those who are affected by a collective decision, policy, or law in institutional or communal contexts of political, economic, or social life should have a say in making it. In this chapter, I will briefly lay out my understanding of this principle and its scope, as well as of the original criterion for the scope democracy, which I have denominated the Common Activities Principle. I believe that both principles have important implications for dealing with contemporary forms of the democratic deficit. I will then sketch some of the applications to the case of labor, developing the import for management in firms, and finally for a broader range of labor rights under capitalism.

TWO CRITERIA FOR DEMOCRATIC PARTICIPATION AND INPUT

In previous work, I have proposed two criteria for determining the appropriate scope for democratic decision making, that is, where it ought to pertain and who should have rights to take part and be represented.[1] Each applies to many existing contexts but both also have some radical implications for democratic transformation. Briefly, the first criterion poses a requirement for democratic decision making about what can be called common (or joint) activities, where these refer broadly to institutions or communities organized around shared goals. In such contexts, we can normally identify members, and indeed, equal members of the institution or community in question. The main exemplar has been taken to be citizens of states (or more local communities), but I argue that similar considerations apply to a host of other self-understood communities or institutions, including cross-border ones, regional associations of states, and economic institutions like corporate firms, as well as social organizations like voluntary associations. The argument for democratic rights of participation and deliberation in such contexts does not depend on the coerciveness of law, as in many theoretical approaches, and it proposes an alternative to standard autonomy views as well.

Without going into it at length, I have argued that democratic rights of participation follow from the recognition that opportunities to engage in common activities are important conditions for people as social beings, and that if one is not to dominate others within these contexts, all should have equal rights to codetermine these activities. In my elaborated view, I appeal to what I call a principle of *equal positive freedom* (as a principle of justice), which presupposes opportunities for the exercise of free choice but goes beyond these to require (prima facie) equal rights of access to a fuller set of conditions for self-transformation over time, or for self-development (of individuals or groups). These necessary conditions involve freedom from constraining ones like domination or exploitation and access to a range of enabling conditions so that choices can be effective, including material means of life activity, security, and forms of social recognition. In my view, these conditions are specified in human rights, including both civil and political ones, and economic and social rights, and these rights themselves can be distinguished into basic and nonbasic (though still essential) ones, where the basic are conditions for any human life activity whatever and the nonbasic are conditions for its further flourishing over time.[2]

This common activities criterion calls for extending democracy beyond national states to a wide range of other communal or institutional contexts defined by shared goals, whether they be subnational or across borders, and political or economic or social. Thus, I do not take the basic justification for democracy in this sense to involve an appeal to the All-Affected Principle or even to the All-Subjected Principle (ASP), since in my view the crucial factor involves institutions oriented to shared goals. An important dimension of these institutional contexts is that we can identify members, and indeed, something like an equality of membership. The importance of this equal membership has been recognized in the case of political equality, but I argue that it should be extended more broadly to relevantly similar economic and social institutions as well. The All-Affected Principle unfortunately lacks a notion of equality, except if it were to extend globally as in Robert Goodin's interpretation where it requires enfranchising all-affected interests.[3] However, although this latter approach might apply to truly global concerns like climate change, if applied to all issues it would pose new problems, including insufficient attention to local communities and their specific concerns, along with permitting only the most minuscule contribution on the part of any given individual to a decision when taken at this global scale, with billions of potential participants.

The All-Affected Principle has other drawbacks if employed as a general argument for democracy. The list of those affected, including through the unintended consequences of decisions, is vast and cannot be fully known in advance, and it extends to indeterminate numbers of future generations. Moreover, inevitably people are differentially affected by policies and decisions, which would yield not only unequal rights of participation, but also shifting communities or other groupings for the purpose of making various decisions, as is explicitly proposed by Archon Fung.[4] However, determining in advance the relevant set of those specifically affected so as to authorize their participation in the decision making would be cumbersome, if possible at all, and would seem to require a constant reconstitution of the relevant set of deciders in order to match those potentially affected. This raises the question of who would decide on those affected in each case, with the theoretical possibility of an infinite regress of decisions about who makes the decisions and how they are to be made, and in practice presenting an opening for the replication of existing power relationships, as well as for deep disagreements. Moreover, not only would this method eliminate the equality of citizenship (or other memberships), but it would likely undermine people's equality across the various groups in which they could conceivably be a part.

Despite these drawbacks if taken as the sole principle for justifying democracy and determining its scope, we can observe that in a sense the All-Affected Principle is implicated in the Common Activities Principle as well. If the latter proposes that members of an existing community or institution should have rights of codetermination about its direction, that is, something like self-rule, then it is also the case that they, being primarily affected by the ongoing processes of that community, are the ones who should determine it, or democratically decide about those plans and processes. From this perspective, the common activities criterion can be viewed as a specification of the All-Affected Principle to contexts of communities of fundamentally equal members (e.g. those recognized as citizens or members of nation-states). This may also explain the appeal that the principle has for us in which it seems to serve as a general justification for democracy and its scope.

However, appealing to the All-Affected idea as the main justification for democracy in such contexts would diminish the role of collective agency that I believe is most characteristic of them – that is, in ongoing communities or institutions, it is the process of projecting shared goals and planning ways of meeting them that is decisive. Of course, we are indeed setting these goals for ourselves – that is, those who will be affected by the decisions. There is here a commensurability between the "we" who decide (either directly or through representatives) and the "us" who will be affected. Insofar as we recognize each other, however tacitly, as equal members in this community with overlapping shared goals and who depend on each other for their realization, we do not have to determine specifically who would be affected each time, and we regard ourselves as equally so, even though the specific decisions in fact may impact us somewhat differently. To use the All-Affected Principle as the essential one would also give our common activities an excessively individualistic reading, deriving as it does largely from consequentialist accounts in ethics, and would call on us to aggregate those specifically affected into a group with rights to participate in the decision. I believe that conceiving matters this way would lose the primary sense of our comembership in an ongoing collective activity, in which we jointly construct our ways of being together, and do so (normatively at least) through democratic procedures. Of course, since our being together also means that we are affected by each other and by the decisions we make, we would certainly do well to attend to how our choices will impact or affect us, avoiding those that diminish the life chances of some of our members. But our projecting goals for future activity and making decisions about this activity is what is most decisive in these communal or institutional contexts, and is also responsive to our own individual functioning as intentional and goal-projecting agents.

Although it is thus not a first principle for democracy in my view, the All-Affected Principle does have a crucial place in democratic theory and necessarily supplements the common activities criterion. It does so in several ways. For one thing, the principle serves as a heuristic by which to evaluate the democratic adequacy of the scope of existing communities and institutions and can in turn serve as a corrective, by pointing toward more inclusive understandings of the communal or institutional bodies that ought to have powers of decision. Indeed, the impacts of decisions on people currently excluded from membership may well lead these excluded others themselves to demand inclusion in the relevant communities or in their decision-making processes. Besides this, the very boundaries of economic institutions like transnational corporate firms may themselves be unclear, or, even if clear, often involve extensive interaction and close cooperation with other firms, as in global supply chains or in the case of subsidiaries. Likewise, the informal communities brought into being with contemporary internet technologies may themselves be not only cross-border but also amorphous in their boundaries, without clearly defined notions of membership. If these transnational contexts involve decision making, appeal to the All-Affected Principle can help to set reasonable boundaries for who should be able to participate in these decisions or policy making.

Besides these various uses as a heuristic and corrective guide for the reach of democratic norms, the application of the All-Affected Principle can also lead to calls for new institutional design to give affected outsiders concrete opportunities for democratic input into relevant decisions. In fact, I propose that the main function of the All-Affected Principle is to address just these sorts of exogenous impacts of decisions. It demarcates the affected others, and argues for the need to give them democratic input to these decisions, if not fully equal participation rights. The cases here range from calls for powerful collective actors to simply take into account the effects of their decisions on others in their own decision processes, to the need to hear from these affected outsiders directly through such means as democratic forums, to more stringent requirements of granting these others full participation rights proportional to their affectedness, and in some cases, to according them fully equal participation rights.

I suggest that, in practice, the contemporary power of the All-Affected Principle resides particularly in giving us a way to address the increasingly dispersed, or even global, impacts of decisions, which I pointed to at the outset. The principle is thus central to dealing with these exogenous effects, where existing powerful states, global governance institutions, and transnational corporations increasingly set policy that impacts populations around the world. Inasmuch as these decisions, policies, rules, and laws affect the basic life chances of people who are not members of the institutions or communities in question, these affected outsiders should have rights of what I have called *democratic input* into the decisions in question.[5] As noted, this democratic input may sometimes consist in full participatory rights or representation, but in other cases it may suffice to enable opportunities to affect the deliberation processes of these institutions without granting fully equal participatory rights. It may also be necessary to design entirely new institutions to remedy the defects of the existing institutions of global governance, or even to create new democratic assemblies at regional or global levels.

However, given the extraordinarily wide scope of those potentially affected by decisions and policies of these powerful actors, we need to find some way to delimit and to specify the set of those who should be given opportunities to provide democratic input into these decisions. I have argued elsewhere that we need an understanding of those we could regard as "importantly affected." I have further suggested that this set should be taken to include those people seriously impacted in their ability to fulfill or realize their human rights, and in the first place their basic human rights.[6] The principle can accordingly be formulated as follows: Whenever people are prospectively seriously affected in their possibilities for fulfilling their basic human rights by a given decision or contemplated policy, these people have rights of democratic input into the decisions in question. It is insufficient, in my view, for decision makers to simply imagine the effects of their decisions on distant others, as is often recommended by stakeholder theory. Instead, they need to hear from these affected others concerning their interests and needs. Indeed, in some cases where others can be expected to be more affected than the decision makers, these affected others would need to have full rights of participation or representation in the decisions in question. I have delineated some of the implications of this requirement for global governance institutions in other work,[7] but it also has important implications for labor and labor rights, which I will sketch in the following parts of the chapter.

We can observe that such democratic rights for those affected are required by the very principle of equal positive freedom that I have proposed supports equal rights of democratic participation in the case of common activities. Insofar as people are impacted in the possibilities of human rights fulfillment, where this is clearly an important condition for their self-transformation or self-development over time, they require (some shared) access to determining the course of these conditions. I have elsewhere argued that human rights claims are not in the first instance to be understood as holding against the state, as on traditional interpretations. Instead they fundamentally hold as claims on others to set up and support institutional forms to help realize them, and these institutions would have to be responsive to people's own understanding of their basic needs and enable ways of hearing from them as to the effective means of meeting these needs or fulfilling their rights. Although the democratic rights that are entailed here are, at a level of generality, equal across persons, the specific ways that rules or policies affect particular groups or individuals necessarily give rise to differentiated rights of access into the various decisions and institutional contexts in question, since these touch people's lives in multifarious ways. I suggest that these sorts of differentiated effects and their correlative of differentiated rights of input are not pernicious when the All-Affected Principle is interpreted to apply to participation based on the external impacts of decisions, whereas to my mind it would tend to undercut political equality and the equality of membership in institutions if it were taken as the general and exclusive basis for democratic participation.

If we reflect on the way that the All-Affected Principle, like the common activities one, follows from the principle of equal positive freedom in the approach here, we can see that the norm of democracy is closely related to that of justice. However, it is certainly not coextensive with justice, which implies other requirements that go beyond the scope of either democratic principle. Among these implications of the principle of justice is the critique of domination and exploitation, including in forms of structural injustice. This in turn suggests that for a full account of labor rights, or for such desiderata as the regulation of market externalities, or of the economy more broadly to make it more responsive to people's fundamental interests or rights, we need to appeal to considerations of justice, and not only to the democratic considerations posited in the All-Affected Principle. While one could conceivably construe that latter principle such that nondomination and overcoming structural injustice would be a special case of it – since domination or exploitation violates the principle to the degree that it does not give scope to the collective will of those affected by exploitative or dominating forms of activity – to my mind, this would take the principle beyond its proper home in democratic theory. Instead, many social and political harms are best addressed with reference to principles of justice, rather than by relying only on democratic norms. Needless to say, these various principles also interact in practice in ways important to the account here. For example, increases in justice and equality in social and economic life can conduce to a better and more effective democratic politics. Indeed, meeting economic human rights to a decent standard of living is itself a prerequisite to viable democratic processes in the political sphere.

APPLICATION OF DEMOCRATIC CRITERIA TO LABOR

We can now move to the outlines of a democratic approach to dealing with the difficult impacts of economic globalization and of capitalist economic organization on labor. In my view, the application of the All-Affected Principle globally, along with the common activities criterion, requires a radical rethinking of work and labor, and more fundamentally, the relation of democracy to economic life, although we will only be able to consider these issues schematically here. In this part, I will take up the core requirement of self-management at work, or what has been called workplace democracy, and in the subsequent part explore some of the other applications of the All-Affected Principle to labor and labor rights. In both parts, the reflections and proposals will be largely normative, and admittedly difficult to envision concretely and to apply in practice. Nonetheless, I believe that it is important to clarify these normative democratic dimensions so they can be of some help in guiding practical transformation going forward.

The need for self-management has been a core thesis in my previous writing, given the requirement of overcoming domination and exploitation at work, along with the constructive democratic implications of the norm of equal positive freedom, or equal rights to the conditions required for free activity.[8] I will briefly note the arguments for self-management in this part and then discuss some of the problems arising from the need for worker-managed firms to implement the All-Affected Principle in their own policies and plans. In the third part of this chapter, where I take up some other implications of the All-Affected Principle for giving labor more of a say in global economic contexts, I will build on previous work concerning the democratic deficit in global governance institutions. I have advanced proposals for adding regular human rights impact assessments to the environmental and technological ones currently in use, and the inclusion of INGOs advocating for the global poor and of representatives of labor within the deliberations and decision processes of existing global governance institutions.[9] Other proposals have concerned the need for the development of regional forms of democracy, and for the reduction of the democratic deficit and of bureaucracy within existing regional associations, notably the EU.[10] I have also argued for more democratic forms of decision making within civil society organizations and even within social movements themselves (some of which have already moved to implement democratic forms of solidarity). It is clear, however, that these changes, though helpful, will not suffice to deal with the degradation of labor under the conditions of globalization or to rectify labor's lack of input and control in regard to the extensive range of corporate and governmental decisions that affect it. Deeper transformations are needed to address the democratic deficit in regard to labor, taking guidance from both criteria for democracy stated above.

Turning now to the requirement of self-management in firms and to rights of democratic management where full worker control cannot be achieved, we can consider how these requirements follow from both criteria of democracy, but most especially from the Common Activities Principle. Among the various stakeholders in a firm's activities – including suppliers, consumers, the surrounding community, etc. – employees are distinctive in being part of the firm itself. As members of it, taking it as a common activity, they properly have rights of codetermination over the firm's planning and policies. Seen in this light, their situation has many parallels with membership in a political community, understood as entailing equal rights of participation. Admittedly, this understanding of firms elides the customary distinction between the political as public and the economy as private. But corporate firms operate under a charter or other legal recognition granted by the public to corporations,[11] and under the aegis of publicly instituted property rights, and I suggest that these firms can also be viewed as quasi-public in the mode of their institutional functioning. Conceiving them within the frame of common activities defined by shared goals regards them as more than merely profit-seeking institutions, looking to the ways they function as productive group agents, though ones that involve institutionalized roles and practices through which they operate and make decisions. In this view, the steering of these firms normatively properly belongs to all the members who collectively should be enabled to decide their course rather than being restricted to a small group of directors and managers, as at present.

The democratic requirement most certainly does not imply that all those who work in a firm need to make all decisions, but rather that the managers need to be accountable to the workers and, in the strong case, should be chosen by them. Ideally, all who work in the corporate firm should be given ownership and management rights, though they may delegate responsibilities to managers, that is, authorize managers to assume them. The democratic rights for members can be vested in them after some initial waiting period, thereby avoiding counterarguments, e.g. concerning "scabs" potentially having voting rights, or even having to give them to workers who turn out to be ill-suited to the job at hand. We can also acknowledge that democratic management is a desideratum that can be implemented to various degrees short of full self-management. In such cases, it comes closer to what has been called participative management, although the latter has tended to be understood in theories of management and business ethics to include only a weak set of requirements.[12]

The All-Affected Principle supports rights of democratic participation similar to that implied by the common activities criterion, since clearly workers are very deeply affected by a firm's policies and plans, almost always considerably more so than other stakeholders, both in terms of intensity and consistency of these effects. However, I think the common activities criterion remains the dominant criterion here, inasmuch as it casts workers as members equally with managers and, in the strong case, generates full rights of participation rather than only democratic input into decisions.

The All-Affected Principle has important consequences for the other stakeholders of a firm (including distantly situated ones). It supports the introduction of forms of democratic input for these stakeholders, and in cases where they are directly and forcefully affected, requires even fuller forms of participation and representation. Although it is true that distant others increasingly contribute to a firm's production or activity more generally, e.g. by way of global supply chains, nonetheless it is still possible to distinguish members from importantly affected nonmembers. Those who labor in the firm can be identified as members, whereas other stakeholders are affected or impacted by it, but do not constitute the firm itself in the relevant sense.

The normative requirement for firms to consider the impacts of their policies on distant stakeholders would apply to worker-controlled as to existing hierarchical firms. To a modest degree, the need to take stakeholders into account is already recognized by current theories of business ethics, whether in terms of the notion of corporate social responsibility or in terms of stakeholder theory itself. However, this taking into account is usually envisioned as simply a matter of managers imagining the impacts on these stakeholders. A somewhat stronger requirement would be the introduction of human rights impact assessments to supplement the existing technology or environmental impact assessments. Yet, this too falls short of actually hearing from those impacted others beyond the firm. To accomplish that, it might be possible to include representatives of distant stakeholders within the firm's decision-making processes.

However, much of the required democratic input would undoubtedly need to take place within institutions above the level of the firm, assumed to exercise some democratic sway over them. Ideally, workers or their associations would elect the members of these high-level supervisory bodies. In the nearer term, they are more likely to take the form of regulatory institutions within elected democratic governments. Even these would require eliminating the power of lobbyists and others who advocate for narrow corporate interests, if the concerns of affected workers are be taken seriously. It would also require more generally removing the power of money from politics – a difficult prospect indeed. The influence of wealth and corporate power in contemporary politics clearly undermines political equality and its elimination is a prerequisite for gaining real equality for labor and other currently marginalized groups.

The proposal here for self-managing firms is of course incomplete as it stands. They would be likely have to operate within a market framework, though not necessarily a market in labor of the sort we have at present. Further, as theorists like David Schweickart and others have argued, transitioning to a system of self-managing firms would require new sources of loans, including from governments, for starting up new firms.[13] New firms could be encouraged to have a Green mandate, and their introduction could also help to deal with the problems posed by ever-growing degrees of automation in manufacturing, if funding were made available for these purposes. Needless to say, an economy of self-managing firms raises new questions, especially concerning the possible disinclination of such firms to take on new workers as equal members. Nonetheless, the importance of eliminating existing domination and exploitation within the work process and of introducing greater degrees of participatory decision making in those contexts provides motivation for addressing these new issues. It can be noted finally that participation at work would likely have a salutary effect on politics, both in terms of providing opportunities to practice participation[14] and because of the empowerment of workers that it entails, an empowerment sorely lacking at present.

THE ALL-AFFECTED PRINCIPLE AND
CONTEMPORARY LABOR RIGHTS

The reach and application of the All-Affected Principle for labor extends beyond the workplace. Its use points to the fact that labor is most often not adequately represented in decisions and policy making that affect its onerousness or the dangers it poses to workers' health and safety. And the principle can ground labor rights to collectively bargain with owners in existing contexts of contemporary capitalism. We can consider in this final part some further applications of the principle, by way of a list, and take note of how these would enhance the situation of labor and serve to extend and deepen labor rights.

1. The International Labor Organization (ILO), a unit of the UN, is tasked with improving labor conditions and helping to generate work opportunities around the world. It promulgates international labor standards, e.g. regarding child labor, forced labor, etc. However, it is primarily representative of governments, along with employers, and labor (in equal measure). One major problem is that the ILO has no real power to regulate the use of labor to accord with these standards, despite its declarations of them. In view of the impact such standards would have for people's work activity, a prospective change would be to at least make the ILO more fully representative of labor, as the group most closely affected by standards or their absence. It would also be essential to endow this more fully representative body with effective powers not only to regulate work so as to eliminate child labor and forced labor, but also to protect collective bargaining. In the long term, the organization could also support and facilitate democratic management within firms. Granted, this is more of a wish list for the ILO (or a similar organization) rather than an immediately realizable scenario, but movements towards this sort of transformation would be important.

2. A related change would involve gaining input from workers and distantly affected people in institutions of global governance like the WTO, which deeply affect their life chances. Such a change would aim to at least counterbalance the power within them of wealthy states and corporate interests and include a new focus on meeting workers' needs. An even deeper structural transformation would involve replacing some of these institutions by new ones explicitly representative of labor internationally and fully responsive to developing states.

3. The right to form and join unions for the protection of people's interests is included among the human rights enunciated in article 23 of the Universal Declaration (1948). That right would seem to require also a second right, namely, to collective bargaining over wages and conditions of work. Indeed, the UDHR article also specifies a right "to just and favourable conditions of work," to "equal pay for equal work," and to "just and favourable remuneration" providing for the worker and the worker's family "an existence worthy of human dignity." Clearly, these are examples of rights that are dependent for their form on a particular stage and type of institutional development. Nonetheless, I believe that these rights, including the right to form unions, are responsive to the

even more basic right to an adequate level of material well-being, as well as to the conception of the freedom and dignity of all humans that underlies the Declaration.

We can see that, short of worker management or control, collective bargaining is a crucial tool for the improvement of the conditions of work and the achievement of material well-being and equal social status for labor. It can be seen as required by both the common activities and the All-Affected Principle, inasmuch as it enables participation and representation in regard to labor's affected human interests in the sphere of work. One concrete proposal would be to make the recognition of the right of collective bargaining a condition for all trade agreements and for all foreign direct investment. This would extend the notion of human rights conditionality in a more progressive direction to include an under-appreciated human right. Needless to say, in the United States, the rights to form unions and to collective bargaining have been eroded over time rather than becoming more fully recognized and established over the years. Short of the introduction of self-management, however, unions and collective bargaining constitute crucial means for ameliorating the effects of capitalist political economy on labor, both domestically and in international contexts.

4. It is sometimes suggested that free trade is bad for workers but that protectionism will be good for them. However, I think we need to recognize that both free trade and protectionism as presently constituted for the most part operate to benefit corporations and wealthy interests rather than workers, who nonetheless are deeply affected by these policies. So it is necessary to address and assess trade from the standpoint of its impact on labor. In addition to questioning the functioning of the WTO and its lack of representation of the interests of workers, it would also be helpful to consider the connection of both labor and capital to borders. Capital presently is quite free to move across borders, while workers are most often bound by them, and in any case find it difficult to move. Some modest control on finance capital, or at least forms of taxation of it, should be contemplated. Besides this, enforceable labor standards can be attached to trade deals, to try to prevent the "race to the bottom." Indeed, such standards would be helpful at an international level, although the problems posed by their disparate impact on developing countries would need to be addressed. Implementing these standards would thus require concomitant efforts to address global inequalities, for example, through some (modest) forms of global taxation, as well as by more open immigration policies.

5. An account of labor rights given the effects of globalization on workers would be insufficient without an acknowledgement of the unemployed. They are deeply affected by economies and markets, but have little opportunity for input or for participation. Policies that affect the

unemployed are enacted politically so the All-Affected Principle would here seem to require their active participation in politics. But a basic precondition for such political participation is in jeopardy if the unemployed lack the basic essentials of life. This suggests the need to support them by way of guaranteed basic income (or other modalities of material support), in addition to the more standard directions of job training and job creation.

6. Related considerations of the role of economic well-being as a crucial condition for participation in democratic politics, which so deeply affects laborers and sets conditions for their activity, point to the need for a living wage, and its status as a central contemporary goal for labor. Of course, the call for a living wage also follows from the intrinsic importance of an adequate level of material well-being as a human right.

7. The All-Affected Principle helps to call attention to the impact of work on reproduction activity in the home and on the status of gender in work both in that sphere and on the job. Economic and development policies undoubtedly can have differential and often problematic effects on housework and caring labor, the burdens of which have traditionally been assumed mainly by women. As a form of labor, housework has tended to be uncompensated, despite its substantial value. Alternative ways of providing it and/or compensating for it need to be assessed not only in economic terms, but through a consideration of its differential impacts on women. Alleviating their unequal burden remains a requirement for full gender equality. Moreover, caring work and housework require reevaluation and valorization as equally essential forms of work in comparison with standardly compensated types. The All-Affected Principle specifically requires that women, and care workers more generally, be represented in processes of legislation and policy making that affect their care work and, more mundanely, their housework, and that the needs of all care workers should be taken into account in deliberations concerning the policies that affect them as workers.

Beyond these proposals, it is clear more generally that focusing on all those affected by the modes of functioning of contemporary economies helps to call our attention to the disparities in power relations that characterize the sphere of politics and economics. It calls for a more inclusive approach on the part of policy makers and citizens that would cut through ideological or epistemically unjustified biases, and requires instead considering the entire set of people and groups impacted by a proposed law or policy. I have suggested that labor is prominent among such groups and that it is often marginalized in such decision-making processes. However, it is not the only such group disadvantaged by capitalist economic organization and existing globalization processes, or by governments that often reflect the interests of the wealthy and powerful. Indeed, conflicts have arisen, and can be expected to continue to emerge, between labor and other affected groups, for example, Indigenous people, or the unemployed. The All-Affected Principle does not directly provide guidance toward resolving such conflicts, although if sensitively applied, it can help provide guidance for whose interests need to be taken into account in any given case.

CONCLUSION

It is useful to observe that conflicts between labor and other groups in fact presuppose, and are likely exacerbated by, the existing social and economic context, one marked by separation among various groups, each of which is taken to have quite different interests. While we can expect that some sorts of variations in the interests of diverse groups will undoubtedly persist through all social formations, the proposal made above for self-management and more democratic economies could function to moderate some of the most pernicious differences and conflicts among groups. It would involve a degree of structural transformation, with the potential result that a broad subsection of the population as a whole would be understood to fall under the heading of labor. In this transformation, an empowered labor would not be understood as it is at present as limited to a "working class" sharply distinguished from a "middle class" or from the "upper class." Rather, if full worker control were to prevail, with few exceptions people would be considered to be – and would take themselves to be – workers or laborers (and also managers). Of course, some groups, e.g. the unemployed or those who cannot work, would still need to be treated separately.

I suggest that this transformation would likely endure even as work itself becomes less prominent over time (at least in its traditional forms), given the increased automation of work processes. We can expect that the concept of work will itself undergo a transformation, to include more than remunerated production and service activities. It would extend to creative, caring, and community service work as well. However, the application of the All-Affected Principle to that new context would need to be further explored, in ways that go beyond the present chapter. In the near term, this principle clearly requires that workers be given much greater opportunities to address the potential consequences of automation, both in their own workplaces and in the political sphere. Indeed, this same requirement can also be seen to follow from the core proposal for democratic management developed earlier in this chapter. It is evident, in any case, that both of the principles considered here – the Common Activities Principle and the All-Affected Principle – have multifarious and interlocking implications for enhancing the role and status of labor in contemporary political economy and in our political societies more generally.

NOTES

* Prepared for presentation at the Harvard University Ash Center Workshop on the All-Affected Principle, June 15, 2017. I would like to thank Melissa Williams, Archon Fung, Sean Gray, and the other workshop participants for their helpful comments on earlier versions of this paper.
1 On the common activities criterion, see Carol C. Gould, *Rethinking Democracy: Freedom and Social Cooperation in Politics, Economy and Society* (Cambridge: Cambridge University Press, 1988), especially Chapter 1. On the All-Affected Principle and its relation to the democratic deficit and globalization, see Gould, *Globalizing Democracy and Human Rights* (Cambridge: Cambridge University Press, 2004), especially Chapters 7 and 9. On the implications of both principles for global governance institutions and transnational democracy, see Gould, "Structuring Global Democracy: Political Communities, Universal Human rights, and Transnational Representation," Special Issue on Global Democracy and Political Exclusion, *Metaphilosophy* 40, no. 1 (January, 2009): 24–46; and Gould, *Interactive Democracy: The Social Roots of Global Justice* (Cambridge: Cambridge University Press, 2014), especially Part III, which also includes a discussion of international labor rights and democratic management.
2 Gould, *Rethinking Democracy*, especially Chapters 1 and 8, and *Interactive Democracy*, especially Chapters 1–4.
3 Robert E. Goodin, "Enfranchising All Affected Interests, and Its Alternatives," *Philosophy and Public Affairs* 35, no. 1 (2007): 40–68. See also Goodin (this volume).
4 Archon Fung, "The Principle of Affected Interests: An Interpretation and Defense," in *Representation: Elections and Beyond*, ed. Rogers M. Smith and Jack H. Nagel (Philadelphia: University of Pennsylvania Press, 2013), pp. 236–68.
5 See Gould, "Structuring Global Democracy;" and Gould, *Interactive Democracy* (2014).
6 Gould, "Structuring Global Democracy."
7 Gould, *Globalizing Democracy and Human Rights* and "Democracy and Global Governance," in *Oxford Handbook of International Political Theory*, ed. Chris Brown and Robyn Eckersley (Oxford: Oxford University Press, 2018).
8 Gould, *Rethinking Democracy*, Chapter 1 and *Interactive Democracy*, Chapter 4 and 14.
9 Gould, "Structuring Global Democracy," and *Interactive Democracy*, Chapter 13.
10 Carol C. Gould, "Regional vs. Global Democracy: Advantages and Limitations," in *Global Democracy: Normative and Empirical Perspectives*, ed. Daniele Archibugi, Mathias Koenig-Archibugi and Raffaele Marchetti (Cambridge: Cambridge University Press, 2012), pp. 115–31, and *Interactive Democracy*, Chapter 15.
11 See David Ciepley, "Beyond Public and Private: Toward a Political Theory of the Corporation," *American Political Science Review* 107, no. 1 (2013): 139–58; and "Member Corporations, Property Corporations, and Constitutional Rights" (unpublished manuscript).
12 See, for example, P. L. Koopman and A. F. M. Wierdsma, "Participative Management," in *Personnel Psychology: Handbook of Work and Organizational Psychology*, ed. P. J. D. Drenth et al. (Hove, East Sussex, UK: Psychology Press, 1998), pp. 297–324;

   Soonhee Kim, "Participative Management and Job Satisfaction: Lessons for
   Management Leadership," *Public Administration Review* 62, no. 2 (2002): 231–41.
13 David Schweickart, *After Capitalism* (Lanham, MD: Rowman & Littlefield,
   2002).
14 See Carole Pateman, *Participation and Democratic Theory* (Cambridge: Cambridge
   University Press, 1970).

The All-Affected Principle and Global Political Legitimacy

In Defense of Democratic Realism

Terry Macdonald

My aim in this chapter is to offer an interpretation of the All-Affected Principle that captures important intuitive sources of its appeal for democrats in the pluralist institutional landscape of global governance practice.[1] Here I take the AAP to be an institutional principle for distributing the political power contained within governance institutions (in shorthand, "political inclusion"), as distinct from an ethical principle for guiding the discretionary "considerations" of powerful decision-making elites.[2] Thus understood, the AAP provides an alternative to the more common democratic claim that political inclusion should be distributed in accordance with the scope of egalitarian moral solidarities – whether these are understood in "communitarian" terms as national in scope,[3] or in "cosmopolitan" terms as globally all-inclusive.[4]

In what follows I present a normative interpretation of the AAP, as a democratic principle for distributing political inclusion, which incorporates answers to three key questions. First, what distinctive democratic values does the AAP advance, in contrast to the solidaristic egalitarianism of cosmopolitan or communitarian principles? Second, what follows institutionally from the AAP, in relation to the institutional sites in which political inclusion is to be sought, the types of institutionalized governance power that political inclusion is to distribute, and the basis on which particular individuals are to be politically included within particular institutional sites? Third, what does an endorsement of the AAP imply for our broader theoretical understanding of the normative role and limitations of democracy as a global political project? The answers I offer to these questions are guided by what I call a "realist" normative conception of democracy. Some influential philosophical defenders of the AAP have presented it as an ideal-theoretic democratic principle – with institutional implications that are "wildly impractical."[5] Here I offer a rival interpretation that accounts for its role as a realist democratic principle for distributing political inclusion. Whereas ideal-theoretic democratic principles identify criteria for judging institutions to be morally justifiable (or "just"), realist democratic principles instead identify criteria for judging institutions to be politically legitimate, in the normative sense of being worthy of political support by real political actors in some concrete operational context.[6] Here I take the broader concept of democracy to denote a governance practice that institutionally empowers the self-determining political agency of some collective or collectives (the "*demos*" or "*demoi*"),[7] on terms that are politically inclusive of individuals.[8] As such, articulating a realist conception of democracy requires consideration of which forms of political inclusion best strengthen the real-world support-worthiness of governance institutions, as instruments of collective political empowerment.

I develop and argue for this realist interpretation of the democratic AAP in three steps, answering each of the above key questions in turn. First, I argue that the distinctive democratic value of the AAP derives from its concern with institutionally empowering those valuable dimensions of individuals' political agency that are expressed through participation in the practical performance of global governance functions, alongside those expressed through deliberative or aggregative social "choice" procedures. By aligning political inclusion with political "affectedness" rather than moral solidarity, the AAP recognizes that the collective activities constituting existing governance practices (rather than philosophers' ideals of political community) constitute the politically legitimate starting point for democratic political projects. Second, I argue that this interpretation of the normative point of the AAP supports a pluralist, rather than a cosmopolitan, institutional approach to democratic inclusion; the sites, types, and constituencies of inclusion should vary across institutional contexts, depending on their real-world consequences for the empowerment of individuals' capacities to advance their interests through institutional collaboration with others.[9] Third, I elaborate the broader "realist" conceptions of global democracy and political legitimacy that are implied by this interpretation of the AAP, and highlight some advantages and limitations of the realist account.

THE DEMOCRATIC VALUE OF THE ALL-AFFECTED PRINCIPLE

To understand the distinctive democratic value of the AAP as a principle of political inclusion, it is instructive to begin with some further reflection on what it means to be included in a democratic process. Central to the concept of democracy, as characterized here, is the idea of empowered collective agency: democracy is an inclusive process of collective self-determination, empowered through shared governance institutions. As such, the meaning of political inclusion in a democratic process must be derived from an underlying conception of the kind of empowered collective agency in which inclusion is sought.

Since ideas of power, collectivity, and agency are some of the broadest in the modern political lexicon, the conceptual space within the idea of democratic inclusion is in principle very wide. Among most contemporary democratic theorists, however, there is convergence on a much narrower conception of empowered collective agency – as the operation of social choice procedures within some formal institutional process of political decision making. Here the notion of social "choice" denotes either the aggregation of individuals' formal preference signals in the form of electoral "vote," or collective agreement arising from the mutual articulation of individuals' reasons in the form of deliberative "voice."[10] Corresponding with this conception, the democratic idea of political inclusion is typically identified narrowly with participation in aggregative or deliberative political decision-making procedures.

The normative appeal of this conception of empowered collective agency rests on two implicit theoretical commitments, both of which have been influential through the modern historical period in which contemporary democratic theories have developed. The first is a normative commitment to a rationalist model of political agency, which attributes value to the democratic self-determination of collectives as a function of the value placed on the strategic rationality of individual voting behaviour, or the communicative rationality of public deliberation. The second is an empirical commitment to a hierarchical model of political governance, which assumes democratic social choice procedures can be "plugged in" to some institutionally subordinated governance instruments with the requisite material capabilities (resources, technologies, and administrative infrastructures) to implement democratic decisions – as is envisaged, paradigmatically, within constitutional democratic states or functionally equivalent cosmopolitan governance institutions.

If we understand the empowered collective agency at the heart of the democratic project in this way, what follows for democratic principles of political inclusion? This social choice-focused democratic conception of empowered collective agency can be straightforwardly reconciled with traditional principles of political inclusion based on morally solidaristic (communitarian or cosmopolitan) conceptions of political community, simply by prescribing the construction of constitutional democratic states to align with moral solidarities at either national or global levels. It is much more difficult, however, to reconcile it with the AAP as a principle of political inclusion. If it is assumed that all of democracy's empowered collective agency is located within the social choice procedures for which the AAP regulates inclusion, then the prescriptive implications of the AAP appear to be either indeterminate or circular. The AAP cannot generate determinate institutional prescriptions unless we can first determine what set of people will possibly or probably be affected by some specific decision-making process. Yet we cannot even begin to speculate about what range of people will possibly or probably be affected unless we have some substantive idea about the content that its decisions will possibly or probably have. But if we counter this indeterminacy by specifying in advance some range of substantive decisions, we encounter a new problem of circularity – insofar as settling some decisions in advance seems to call for pre-judgment on the very matters that democratic decision-making procedures are supposed to settle.

In one influential interpretation of the AAP, Robert Goodin proposes a way of escaping both the indeterminacy and the circularity just described. His proposal is to assume all decision-making processes to be entirely open regarding the range of their possible decisions, such that any decision-making outcome is assumed to be possible, in any decision-making process. This avoids the charge of circularity by making no substantive assumptions of the kind that would prejudge a democratic decision-making process, since all possible decisions remain in the set available for a *demos* to decide upon. It also provides determinacy by prescribing universal inclusion, such that "(at least in principle) we should give virtually everyone a vote on virtually everything virtually everywhere in the world."[11]

But while this proposal escapes the problems of indeterminacy and circularity, it encounters two new problems: impracticality and prescriptive non-distinctiveness. The first of these problems is straightforward: as Goodin himself recognizes, his proposal for universal inclusion in all decision-making processes is "wildly impractical,"[12] and untenable as a real-world prescription for democratic institutional design. The second problem is that this interpretation of the AAP as an institutional principle effectively collapses it into a variant of cosmopolitan solidarism, insofar as claims to political inclusion follow directly from cosmopolitan moral concern for individuals' interests, conditioned only by an extremely broad background assumption of (possible if not actual) global social interconnectedness. While talk of "affectedness" here may help to justify the cosmopolitan institutional claim that universal political inclusion follows as a prescriptive corollary of cosmopolitan moral solidarity, this "affectedness" talk does not generate any prescriptive institutional principle that is distinct from solidaristic cosmopolitan inclusion.

Here I propose an alternative normative interpretation of the AAP that preserves its prescriptive distinctiveness as an institutional principle of political inclusion, while further escaping the problems of indeterminacy, circularity, and impracticality. My proposal is that the AAP's directive to align political inclusion with political "affectedness" is prescriptively distinctive in virtue of directing democrats to recognize existing institutional practices of governance (rather than philosophers' communitarian or cosmopolitan moral ideals of political community) as the politically legitimate starting points for democratic political projects. In concrete prescriptive terms, this means that the AAP directs democrats to pursue political inclusion of the affected not only through formal social choice procedures linked to hierarchical state-like administrations, constructed to align with national or global moral solidarities. Rather, the AAP prescribes the expansion of political inclusion within a much wider set of institutionalized governance practices, incorporating non-state organizations such as corporations and NGOs alongside more institutionally complex market and networked governance activities, which perform significant governance functions within real global political practice.

In addition to achieving prescriptive distinctiveness, this interpretation of the AAP helps to solve the problem of indeterminacy: since the AAP prescribes inclusion through governance institutions that already exist in concrete forms, empirical analysis of institutions' functions and impacts can help inform political efforts to map out circles of "affectedness." It also helps to moderate objections to the practicality of the AAP. Any democratic project must confront substantial practical challenges, which are inherent to its emancipatory and egalitarian political ambitions. But the prescription to start by engaging institutions within existing governance practice at least gives democrats some concrete political agencies to "go to work on" – as Nagel puts it in a related argument about global justice[13] – rather than contemplating the task of engineering a revolutionary overhaul of the global institutional order.

Beyond these analytical advantages of my proposed interpretation of the AAP, we must also consider what substantive theoretical commitments are required to support its normative appeal as a democratic principle of political inclusion. The claim that real governance practices constitute the right starting point for the pursuit of democratic inclusion can draw some preliminary support from well-established empirical literatures highlighting various functional limitations of "hierarchical" state-based governance instruments, and corresponding functional advantages of the disaggregated "network" and "market" governance instruments[14] that play substantial roles in existing "private,"[15] "complex,"[16] and "liquid"[17] global governance institutions.[18] But normative claims about the democratic value of real governance practices must rest on more than empirical assessments of their distinctive functional capabilities; it must rest further on normative assessments of the substantive political interests that real governance institutions have functional capabilities to advance. So here we need a further account of how and why practice should have primacy in defining the democratic "common interests" that governance institutions should strategically pursue.

One well-known account, derived from pragmatist political thought, goes some of the way by demonstrating the special epistemic value of experimental forms of political action found within some real governance practice.[19] But such epistemic justifications for the primacy of practice are not adequate alone, since they account only for the instrumental value of certain forms of governance practice in identifying how best to advance substantive "common interests" (albeit allowing that understandings of these interests may themselves shift as experimentalist practice develops). A normative argument for the primacy of practice in defining governance problems must go further, by accounting also for the role practice should play in defining the substantive content of these "common interests."

On my proposed account of this role, the "common interests" advanced through the functions of existing governance practices have democratic value insofar as participation in the constitution of institutions' material governance capabilities, alongside participation in institutions' deliberative or aggregative "social choice" procedures, can constitute meaningful expressions of individuals' political agency, of the kind that democratic projects aim to respect and empower. The claim is that political value judgments concerning common interests are not always expressed communicatively – in the rationally articulated forms of vote or voice that contribute directly to decision making within formal social choice procedures. Rather, they are often expressed behaviourally[20] through individuals' behavioural patterns of adaptation, support, and resistance towards institutions within real political practice, which over time and in the aggregate contribute substantially to shaping the functional capabilities embodied in governance institutions.[21]

Relevant political behaviours here may include institutional rule-compliance, or conversely rule-evasion, "foot-dragging," or "false compliance,"[22] resource allocations towards or away from particular institutional activities, cultural expressions of institutional endorsement or disapproval, or patterns of attentional engagement or disengagement with institutions. Such behaviours vary in their degrees of communicative articulateness: some, such as financial donations to institutions, or organized protest actions against them, may be both intended and interpreted as clear communications of political value judgments articulated explicitly elsewhere. But others – in particular those involving more "everyday" (ad hoc, low-stakes, and unprincipled) interactions with institutions – express less articulate judgments, based in part on non-cognitive evaluative faculties such as attentional and emotional responsiveness or motivational energies, which are more dissimilar from the intentional modes of "choice making" envisaged by rationalist normative models of democratic political agency.[23]

On this interpretation, the forms of political inclusion prescribed by the AAP are democratically valuable insofar as they provide individuals with access to powerful institutional avenues for collaboratively advancing the interests that they judge to be most valuable – whether these judgments are politically expressed through rationalized voice and vote within institutions' decision-making procedures, or alternatively through the less articulate everyday behaviours that help shape the range of powers accumulated within real institutions, and thereby the scope of their decision-making impacts. The political value of democratic institutions is still understood to be derived from their role in politically empowering the exercise of collective self-determination; but this collective self-determination extends beyond collective choice making to incorporate empowered collective agency more broadly conceived.[24] Rather than viewing "social choice" decision-making procedures as the sole sites of democratic collective agency – with the functional capabilities of "public power" cast as mere instruments for executing these decisions, via a hierarchical subordination of "public power" to the decision-making authority of a *demos* – here democratic collective agency is viewed instead as more highly diffused across more complex social processes for constituting as well as deploying institutional power.

Some democrats may object that this normative interpretation of the AAP cannot fully overcome the circularity objection, since limiting inclusion to those affected by existing governance practices may reinforce a range of injustices supported by the existing institutional boundaries of governance capability and impact, and rig global political decision-making processes against more just political decisions.[25] I will return to the larger theoretical questions raised by this challenge in the final section of the chapter. But for now it is enough to point out that it is perfectly coherent to recognize that many existing global governance practices perpetuate (and are to some degree products of) injustices – and moreover to protest these injustices strongly – while nonetheless insisting that governance practices can embody some valuable expressions of collective political agency.

On the interpretation I have outlined here, the application of the AAP as a principle of political inclusion provides a normative bridge between practice-based and philosophically based dimensions of democratic collective agency, by defining a division of labour between them within an overarching institutional framework for democratic global governance. Governance practice produces its animating institutional material, in which the functional capabilities of governance institutions are structurally embodied, while social choice procedures perform the secondary role of rationalizing and moralizing this collective agency, through filtering some important dimensions of it through the philosophically justified procedures of public deliberation and egalitarian preference aggregation.

THE INSTITUTIONAL IMPLICATIONS OF THE ALL-AFFECTED PRINCIPLE

Having thus established a rough interpretation of the distinctive democratic values advanced by the AAP, the next question to consider is: what follows institutionally from this interpretation of the AAP? There are three institutional questions in particular that must be addressed in further detail than I have considered so far. In what institutional sites is political inclusion to be sought? What types of institutionalized governance power is political inclusion to distribute? And on what basis are particular individuals to be politically included within particular institutional sites? I will consider these questions in turn – arguing overall for what I describe as a pluralist institutional approach to political inclusion.

Pluralist Institutional Sites of Political Inclusion

The institutional account that follows from my normative interpretation of the AAP is pluralist, first, with respect to the institutional sites in which it prescribes democratic political inclusion. This institutional pluralism is not prescribed as a political ideal, or as a logically necessary corollary of the AAP; rather, it follows from the normative imperative to respond democratically to empirical facts about existing global governance practices. Existing global governance practices are pluralist in the sense that the sites of political agency within them are institutionally diffused, and not structurally linked through any unifying functional logic or authoritative hierarchy of the kind that characterizes a constitutional state. Following from the normative argument I have just presented, it is all of these plural institutional sites of existing political agency in which the AAP prescribes political inclusion of the affected.

Many of these diffused sites of global institutional agency take the familiar form of formal organizational "decision making" – albeit dispersed across multiple organizational entities and types, including not only sovereign states and international organizations, but also transnational corporations and NGOs.[26] But much of the political agency exercised through other institutional forms of global governance is diffused not only across plural organizational decision-making procedures, but out of such procedures and into institutional structures of other kinds. Within the market and network institutions noted above, for instance, political agency is diffused outside of formal organizational decision-making procedures with respect to both: the processes through which actors express and coordinate value judgments – for instance, purchasing decisions in markets, or negotiations within networks; and the processes through which these value judgments are converted into political outcomes through the exercise of power – for instance, through the economic pressures of market incentives and rewards, or the social pressures of network interdependencies and socialization.

In some global governance contexts political agency is diffused even further, through complex problem-solving processes in which outcomes are shaped in part through the interactional dynamics operating among multiple types of organizations and institutional structures.[27] Together, these constitute what are sometimes described as institutional "ecologies," as distinct from rule-based structures.[28] To illustrate this kind of dynamically diffused political agency within global governance processes, we can consider the example, explored in some detail elsewhere,[29] of transnational business regulation focused on managing company–community land disputes in the land-intensive palm oil sector. Here, the regulatory outputs from governance processes depend not on the operation of any formal institutional procedures or structures, but rather on complex and informal interactional dynamics among multiple organizational participants – including companies, local community representatives, local and national government actors, and transnational organizations such as the World Bank Group's International Finance Corporation Compliance Advisor Ombudsman (IFC-CAO), and the multi-stakeholder Roundtable on Sustainable Palm Oil (RSPO) – each of which is embedded, in turn, within its own wider (sovereign, market, or network) institutional schemes.

In governance contexts where political agency is so widely diffused, it can sometimes be difficult to identify clear institutional sites where political inclusion could be formally "plugged in," to achieve democratic empowerment for affected populations. One democratic response to these difficulties – advocated by Hayward (this volume) – is to shift the focus of democratic inclusion from institutional "decision making" towards "structural power," understood as "collective norms" that elude decisional control of particular agents in virtue of their institutionalized, objectified, motivationally internalized, and habituated modes of operation. Rubenstein (this volume) similarly argues that the AAP requires sites of democratic inclusion to track real-world power dynamics, but she directs attention beyond "structure" to include more linear "chains" of influence operating among multiple governance actors (such as NGOs and donors). But while the AAP does imply that such real-world dynamics of political power or influence should provide the starting point for situating democratic inclusion, it does not follow that all existing forms of power or influence can serve equally well as sites for democratic politics. Assuming that democracy is valuable insofar as it inclusively empowers collectives to act together through shared institutions, then what matters is not only where power can be located, but moreover where power can be institutionally harnessed by mobilized political collectives and put to work in the advancement of common interests.

Sometimes groups' empowerment can best be strengthened by tracing existing institutional power structures and chains of influence, and seeking greater access to them: in the above example of transnational business regulation, for instance, local communities can achieve some democratic empowerment by seeking greater influence within national or international rule-making processes with powers to shape social and economic structures of land ownership and control, or within transnational corporate decision-making networks.

Other times, however, harnessing the power of existing structures and influence "chains" will first require reconstruction of established institutional agencies or establishment of new ones, with functional capabilities better tailored to serving the interests of disempowered groups. In the same transnational business regulation case, this may require more self-conscious political mobilization and institution-building efforts among local communities and their global allies in land disputes with transnational business, to create (rather than just locate) empowering sites for democratic inclusion. But new institution-building efforts of this kind will nonetheless remain compatible with the AAP's prescription to locate sites for democratic inclusion within real governance practice, insofar as these efforts are incrementalist in character – aimed just at moralizing and rationalizing, rather than wholly supplanting, the pluralistic governance functions and structures of global political life.

Pluralist Institutional Types of Political Inclusion

A difficulty raised by this prescription to pursue direct political inclusion of affected populations within diffused institutional sites of governance agency is that established democratic institutional models of political inclusion have been designed instead for organizational decision making. More specifically, they have mostly been focused on inclusion within participatory social choice procedures of the aggregative or deliberative varieties discussed earlier – or alternatively forms of political representation that can stand in for these under certain conditions.[30] But this focus cannot adequately capture what it would mean to expand political inclusion in relation to those dimensions of agency that are expressed through behavioural participation in the constitution of institutions' material governance capabilities, of the everyday and sometimes inarticulate kinds discussed earlier.

As such, the idea of "political inclusion" cannot be restricted to familiar democratic institutional models of participation or representation in social choice. Instead, we need to expand our institutional conception of political inclusion to reflect a wider understanding of what kind of collective political agency, or self-determination, democracy is concerned with: we should shift our institutional focus from social choice to the broader idea of social empowerment.[31] In doing so, we may bring the meaning of democratic inclusion closer to what Josiah Ober has argued was an element of its original classical meaning. Whereas contemporary democrats typically understand democracy's etymological root "*kratos*" as power in the sense of rule through some pre-existing institutional apparatus, Ober argues that this interpretation is more closely linked to the alternative Greek "*arche*" regime-type suffix; "*kratos,*" on the other hand, is better interpreted as "power in the sense of strength, enablement, or 'capacity to do things.'"[32] *Demokratia* thus means not "rule by the demos" but rather "'the empowered demos' – it is the regime in which the demos gains a collective capacity to effect change in the public realm," in part through creating new institutions rather than merely redistributing access to the old.[33]

Understanding democratic inclusion in these broader empowerment terms has important institutional implications for the democratization of diffused global governance practices. Inclusive social choice procedures, plugged into hierarchical rule-making procedures of formal organizations, should endure as crucial instruments of empowerment within many organizational sites. But a commitment to inclusive empowerment further requires expansion of institutional responsibility taking in wider social domains – as required to support individuals' capabilities to exert direct behavioural influence on the operation of institutions and the evolution of their governance functions. The range of capabilities required for empowerment in this broader sense includes the forms of social and economic capital and physical security required to express settled interests through everyday institutional engagements and pressures. They further include the freedoms and resources required to create new interests through innovation, collaboration, and mobilization with others outside of formal organizational structures – and in so doing, to help creatively construct new governance functions and institutional forms.

Such expanded institutional responsibility taking for individual's political capabilities can incorporate a mix of both "positive" and "negative" responsibilities, where the former involve active provision of institutional support to individuals and the latter involve institutionally secured noninterference. To illustrate more concretely, consider again the example of diffused governance agency within multi-stakeholder business regulation processes, discussed earlier. A participating corporation may exercise "positive" responsibilities through extending social and economic support within broader corporate social responsibility (CSR) programmes to local community stakeholders, aimed at combatting social hierarchies and economic inequalities that may inhibit individuals' opportunities for political activism. And it may exercise "negative" responsibilities by institutionalizing prohibitions on interference in oppositional organizing by community activists or others. Similarly, state participants may exercise "positive" responsibilities by extending access to their legal instruments to non-citizen stakeholders, such as through opening access to national judicial grievance mechanisms; and they may exercise "negative" responsibilities by permitting citizens access to external (non-state and international) governance processes and grievance mechanisms – thus according some freedoms to "exit" from the exclusive jurisdiction of territorial authorities.[34] Overall, such expansions of institutional responsibility for the inclusive empowerment of the affected may necessitate substantial functional departures from organizational mandates established by founders, and sufficient flexibility in the institutional mandates to allow for ongoing responsiveness to the dynamic functional demands of empowering the affected.[35]

Matching Affected Individuals to Sites and Types of Political Inclusion

Given the pluralist institutional sites and types of political inclusion that the AAP prescribes, the final institutional question is: on what basis are particular individuals to be politically included within particular institutional sites, in order for all affected interests to be considered adequately included overall? In principle, my interpretation of the AAP deems an individual to be "affected" by any governance process with consequences for their interests – as they define them through a mix of both explicit articulation and less-articulate judgment and behavioural expression in practice. Identifying affected constituencies entitled to inclusion within any given institutional site must accordingly involve a dynamic political process engaging both governance institutions, and individuals staking political claims to inclusion on the grounds of affectedness, whom we can call "stakeholders." On one side, governance institutions – such as the corporations and states in the above example – must make good-faith efforts to identify affected populations, based on independent interpretive judgments about stakeholder interests. And on the other, affected populations themselves must not only make efforts to articulate interests clearly, but further work actively and creatively towards identifying and behaviourally supporting opportunities for functionally advantageous institutional development.

Given the extent of political interdependence within a globalized world order, a political process of this kind may seem to push towards a very expansive (perhaps even cosmopolitan) account of individuals' democratic claims to political inclusion. It is important to appreciate, however, that in judging claims for political inclusion – whether from the standpoint of governance institutions or activist stakeholders – the AAP directs us to consider not only who is affected by particular governance processes, but also which institutional sites provide consequential avenues for political empowerment of these affected individuals. This follows from the interpretation I have given of the normative point of democratic inclusion of all affected interests – which is providing individuals with access to powerful institutional avenues for advancing their interests. Once we take proper account of considerations concerning the likely efficacy of particular inclusions, I contend that we arrive at a considerably more restrictive set of individual democratic entitlements: the AAP does not oppose all institutional exclusions of affected individuals, but only those that exclude individuals from governance institutions with substantial functional capacities to advance their particular interests.

One assumption we might be tempted to make here is that inclusion is likely to be most consequential at the decision-making levels most geographically or socially proximate to the effects of decision-making outcomes on that individual. To take an example, we might suppose that if an individual is affected by the environmental impact of some corporation's operations within their local community, the most consequential decision-making site for them to be granted political inclusion in is the one with the most direct causal link to the effects they are experiencing – which in this case would be the corporation's internal decision-making processes. But what a proximity criterion misses is that the degree of influence that a particular governance process has on producing a political outcome is not the only factor in determining the degree of power that a particular individual participant in that process will gain from inclusion. The empowerment of an individual depends further on the extent to which their individual interests are aligned with those that the decision-making process in question is functionally empowered to advance. Including an individual in a particular governance process will have little value as an instrument of empowerment if that process has capacities to advance only interests that are fundamentally opposed to their own.

Looking again at the corporate example, a key reason that corporate strategies of "stakeholder inclusion" and "community consultation" commonly result in little more than public relations window dressing is that corporate organizations are not functionally equipped to serve all (or even most) of the interests of external communities that they affect. Environmental standard setting, for example, requires engagement with complex policy problems that corporations are often neither technically nor morally equipped to resolve alone. To the extent that a corporation lacks the functional capacity to produce a particular environmental outcome, then granting affected individuals access to its internal decision-making processes will prove an ineffectual instrument for empowering them to pursue that outcome.

In some cases, incremental reforms to corporate operations may be sufficient to generate the requisite functional capabilities; but in other cases, more consequential forms of political inclusion can be achieved by shifting away from direct engagement with corporations towards alternative institutional sites. For example, if a corporation were willing to support stronger environmental standards but lacked the technical expertise to support standard setting and compliance, then a more consequential institutional site for advancing environmental interests may be that of an emergent multi-stakeholder governance process, whereby states, IOs, and NGOs may lend technical expertise to improve corporate environmental performance. Or alternatively, if the corporation lacked even in-principle support for stronger environmental standards, then a more consequential site for advancing environmental interests may be that of a new regulatory governance process, through which strategies could be developed among like-minded external actors to impose political pressures for corporate compliance.

This example thus points us towards a different kind of criterion for linking individuals to institutional sites of empowerment: inclusion is likely to be consequential not only where the institution has proximity to experienced impacts, but further where there are sufficient common interests shared with the institution's other participants to enable the included individual to pursue their interests through institutional collaboration with others. This recognition prompts us to remember – when thinking about political inclusion – that the political agency democracy seeks to empower is always collective in character: when democratically linking individuals to institutions, we must take account not only of the "vertical" impact of decision-making powers on the particular interests of single individuals, but also of the "horizontal" relationships among the interests of the many individuals who must be willing and able to act together through this governance process, in a project of democratic collective action.[36]

JUSTICE, LEGITIMACY, AND DEMOCRATIC EMPOWERMENT: A REALIST ACCOUNT

The normative democratic interpretation of the AAP advanced here is vulnerable to moral critique in two key dimensions. First, it is vulnerable to critique in terms of procedural moral principles, which are central to familiar moral ideals of democratic social choice. Applying my interpretation of the AAP within pluralist global governance practices undercuts procedural moral principles insofar as it permits some erosion of the political authority of democratic "social choice" procedures, which are structured in accordance with rational and egalitarian principles. By prescribing political inclusion through diffused institutional sites of global governance that lack these procedural characteristics, the AAP compromises the forms of collective rationality[37] that formal and public procedures of preference aggregation and deliberation can support, and may also make it harder to operationalize and institutionally assure political equality within global governance processes.[38]

It is vulnerable to additional moral critique in terms of substantive moral principles of liberal-egalitarian social justice, which are often identified as justificatory philosophical grounds for democratic procedural principles.[39] At a minimum, some of the political exclusions permitted by the AAP may leave unchallenged unjust forms of social and economic inequality and domination that shape existing governance practices, and thus influence the substantive interests advanced by status quo institutional functions. In some cases these political exclusions could even reinforce social injustices, insofar as the democratization of established governance institutions serves to bolster their sociological (as distinct from normative) legitimacy, and thus strengthen their functional capabilities to advance unjust collective political agendas. I regard these moral critiques as sound, and do not dispute the charge that my normative interpretation of the AAP should be regarded as non-ideal from the perspective of a liberal-egalitarian conception of justice.

One way to defend my interpretation, in light of this concession, would be within the framework of a "non-ideal" theory of justice[40] – arguing that the AAP provides the most effective democratic instrument for pursuing justice under non-ideal social conditions. Here, however, I set aside altogether the philosophical assumption that conceptions of justice are the right place to look for the normative grounds of democratic political principles and projects. Instead, I contend that these grounds are located in the conceptually distinct value of political legitimacy, understood as an institutional virtue of normative acceptability or "support-worthiness."[41] As such, the normative role of democratic principles is not to articulate some institutional dimensions of a moral ideal of justice, but rather to identify criteria for judging institutions to be politically legitimate, in the normative sense of being worthy of political support by real political actors in some concrete operational context.

There are many competing accounts of the normative sources of political legitimacy in general, and correspondingly, of the role of democratic principles in legitimizing governance institutions. One family of theories views political legitimacy as distinct from justice in the character of the moral values each captures; such accounts link political legitimacy to special procedural[42] or non-ideal standards of justice,[43] or with other independent moral values.[44] A second views political legitimacy as distinct from justice insofar as it captures epistemic, alongside moral, virtues of political institutions.[45] A third views political legitimacy as derived from some distinctly political value – such as solving complex political problems of order[46] or "meta-coordination,"[47] or institutionalizing a political conception of collective "self-determination"[48] or "collective agency."[49]

It is a variant of this latter political conception of the value of political legitimacy that I invoke here to account for the normative grounds of the democratic AAP. On my favoured account, principles of political legitimacy are grounded in the value of the collective political agency they help to empower, through the governance institutions to which they are applied. Different normative theories of political legitimacy invoke varying substantive normative conceptions of valuable "agency" and "collectivity" – with varying normative commitments to rationalism, egalitarianism, cultural norms, and so on. Here democratic institutional principles serve as distinctive standards of political legitimacy insofar as they empower the exercise of collective political agency on terms that are inclusive of affected individuals. This collective agency account of the sources of normative political legitimacy thus provides the overarching conceptual framework within which my earlier arguments – concerning the legitimacy of practice-based versus social choice-based models of collective political agency – play out. By empowering practice-based alongside social choice-based dimensions of collective political agency, the AAP expands the scope of inclusive political empowerment, and in so doing strengthens the political legitimacy of global governance institutions.

The scale of the prescriptive gap between an AAP grounded in a practice-based collective agency conception of political legitimacy and a democratic principle of inclusion grounded instead in a philosophically based moral conception of justice will depend on how exactly a more comprehensive account of the practice-based dimensions of collective agency is fleshed out. It will depend first on what range of agents' real motivations towards institutional adaptation or resistance are viewed as valuable forms of agency and admissible as normative sources of political legitimacy; and it will depend further on how far this agency departs from the idealized constructions of "rational" and "reasonable" political agency that frame the justificatory structures of liberal-egalitarian theories of justice.[50] But however our fine-grained normative conceptions of agency are filled out, what deeply differentiates justice-based and legitimacy-based accounts is that the concept of political legitimacy accommodates a more realistic account of political agency, which prescribes respect for more motivationally and contextually diverse dimensions of political judgment than ideal-theoretic moral alternatives. It is in this respect that my account can be labelled as "realist" and linked broadly to an extended family of realist political theories that emphasize the importance of motivationally engaged and contextually sensitive approaches to the justification of political institutions.[51]

A key virtue of this realist account is that it preserves a useful division of labour between two distinct normative problems: the search for principles that can galvanize real institutional projects of collective action – which is the problem of political legitimacy; and the search for principles that can illuminate and sensitize political agents to the demands of moral reasons – which is the problem of justice. If we analytically conflate these two problems, we politically deflate the potency of both – diminishing the action-guiding utility of principles of political legitimacy, as well as the critical force of principles of justice. The "realist" normative interpretation I have provided here of the AAP preserves this important distinction: the democratic AAP directs institution builders towards appropriate criteria for expanding the scope of political boundaries, as an instrument of empowerment; while the challenge of expanding the boundaries of moral concern and imagination is preserved intact within the separate theoretical jurisdiction of justice.

CONCLUSION

The arguments I have presented here, in support of a "realist" democratic interpretation of the AAP, are important in part because they push us to confront a larger set of questions about both the concept of democracy and the sources of political legitimacy in contemporary global politics. In thinking about the concept of democracy, and the fundamental values that support it, it must be acknowledged that the interpretation I have set out here takes us a very long way from both the institutional models of "closed" democratic societies and the moral ideals of political rationality and equality that have been traditionally linked to the democratic idea. It is a difficult question – worthy of more extensive reflection – whether this merely stretches the concept of democracy, or whether it more irretrievably breaks it, and thus calls for a fresh conceptual framework that can more freely and directly capture the organizing political values of a complex global governance order.

In thinking about the sources of political legitimacy in global politics, my arguments push us to reinvigorate normative debates about the role of substantive "common interests" in the constitution of political legitimacy, and to consider how these can be reconciled with the value placed on empowering collective political agency that drives democratic conceptions of legitimacy. In particular, more attention must be given to unpacking the sources of the value that is often implicitly attributed in theories of legitimacy to practice-based constituents of collective political agency, around which real democratic projects are mobilized. These are both large theoretical questions, which set a challenging theoretical agenda for democrats in the years to come.

NOTES

1 By "governance" practice I mean all institutionalized processes of social coordination and control that are structured to advance some "common interests" shared among members of some collective. Definitions of "common interests" and the "collectives" that share them are often politically contested – and resolving such disputes is a key task for normative standards of political legitimacy, such as those advanced by democratic theories.

2 To put this in the terms set out in the volume's Introduction, my interpretation of the AAP is thus concerned with the distribution of institutional "input" in the currency of "power": that is, it is a principle for empowering affected individuals *directly*, rather than merely identifying individuals as subjects for consideration by others – whether by institutionally empowered political decision makers, or by otherwise empowered elites with the capacity to "constrain" institutional decision makers. But whereas the introductory discussion describes democratic empowerment of the affected as giving them a "say" in the formulation of "rules" (whether through formal "decision-making processes," or through more diffuse forms of political influence), I link the AAP to a broader conception of political empowerment, which I will elaborate and defend in what follows.

3 David Miller, *On Nationality*. (Oxford: Clarendon Press, 1995).

4 David Held, *Democracy and the Global Order: From the Modern State to Cosmopolitan Governance* (Stanford: Stanford University Press, 1995); Daniele Archibugi, *The Global Commonwealth of Citizens: Toward Cosmopolitan Democracy* (Princeton, NJ: Princeton University Press, 2008).

5 Robert E. Goodin, "Enfranchising All Affected Interests, and Its Alternatives," *Philosophy and Public Affairs* 35, no. 1 (2007): 40–68, at p. 64.

6 Terry Macdonald, "Sovereignty, Democracy, and Global Political Legitimacy," in *Oxford Handbook of International Political Theory*, ed. C. Brown and R. Eckersley (New York: Oxford University Press, 2018).

7 By "political agency" I mean politically consequential activity guided by some set of judgment-based *political attitudes* broadly construed.

8 This broad conceptualization of democracy is closely related to the collective "self-rule" idea invoked by Warren and Gray (this volume); though as I explain further below my conception of empowered collective political agency is institutionally broader than typically associated with the concept of political "rule."

9 I understand "interests" throughout as the ends each individual judges worthy to advance through political action. This is a subjective and political conception of interests, which dovetails with my conception of political agency: interests are understood as the ends advanced by political agents.

10 Christian List and Mathias Koenig-Archibugi, "Can There Be a Global Demos? An Agency-Based Approach," *Philosophy and Public Affairs* 38, no. 1 (2010): 76–110; Iris Marion Young, *Inclusion and Democracy* (New York: Oxford University Press, 2000).

11 Goodin, "Enfranchising All Affected Interests," p. 64.

12 Goodin, "Enfranchising All Affected Interests," p. 64.

13 Thomas Nagel, "The Problem of Global Justice," *Philosophy and Public Affairs* 33, no. 2 (2005): 113–47, at p. 146.

14 R. A. W. Rhodes, "The New Governance: Governing Without Government," *Political Studies* 44, no. 4 (1996): 652–67; Lawrence S. Finkelstein, "What Is Global Governance?" *Global Governance* 1, no. 3 (1995): 367–72.

15 A. Claire Cutler, Virginia Haufler, and Tony Porter, *Private Authority and International Affairs* (Albany: State University of New York Press, 1999).

16 Thomas G. Weiss and Rorden Wilkinson, "Rethinking Global Governance? Complexity, Authority, Power, Change," *International Studies Quarterly* 58, no. 1 (2014): 207–15.

17 Nico Krich, "Liquid Authority in Global Governance," *International Theory* 9, no. 2 (2017): 237–60; Kate Macdonald and Terry Macdonald, "Liquid Authority and Political Legitimacy in Transnational Governance," *International Theory* 9, no. 2 (2017): 329–51.

18 Some have argued that the functional benefits of such alternative governance instruments are best realized "in the shadow of hierarchy" such that some mix of governance instruments may be functionally optimal. See Adrienne Héritier and Dirk Lehmkuhl, "The Shadow of Hierarchy and New Modes of Governance," *Journal of Public Policy* 28, no. 1 (2008): 1–17.

19 Michael C. Dorf and Charles F. Sabel, "A Constitution of Democratic Experimentalism," *Columbia Law Review* 91, no. 2 (1998): 267–473; Grainne de Búrca, "New Governance and Experimentalism: An Introduction," *Wisconsin Law Review* 2 (2010): 227–38; Grainne de Búrca, Robert O. Keohane, and Charles F.

Sabel, "Global Experimentalist Governance," *British Journal of Political Science* 44, no. 3 (2014): 477–86.

20 Raymond Geuss, "What Is Political Judgement?," in *Political Judgement: Essays for John Dunn*, ed. R. Bourke and R. Geuss (New York: Cambridge University Press, 2009); Mark Philp, *Political Conduct* (Cambridge, MA: Harvard University Press, 2007); Jonathan Floyd, "Normative Behaviourism and Global Political Principles," *Journal of International Political Theory* 12, no. 2 (2016): 152–68.

21 Here I assume that while social power is not typically distributed *equally* among individuals (even in strong democracies), nor is it typically *monopolized* by a single "sovereign" ruler, or ruling class; as such, the functional capabilities of institutions cannot be engineered in a wholly "top-down" fashion, but must rather depend in part on the forms of "bottom-up" support or resistance they can attract.

22 James C. Scott, *Weapons of the Weak: Everyday Forms of Peasant Resistance* (New Haven: Yale University Press, 2008).

23 Macdonald, "Sovereignty, Democracy, and Global Political Legitimacy"; Terry Macdonald, "Democratizing Global 'Bodies Politic': Collective Agency, Political Legitimacy, and the Democratic Boundary Problem," *Global Justice: Theory, Practice, Rhetoric* 10, no. 2 (2018): 22–42.

24 Terry Macdonald, "Institutional Facts and Principles of Global Political Legitimacy," *Journal of International Political Theory* 12, no. 2 (2016): 134–51.

25 Raffaele Marchetti, "Models of Global Democracy: In Defence of Cosmo-Federalism," in *Global Democracy: Normative and Empirical Perspectives* (New York: Cambridge University Press, 2012).

26 Jan Aart Scholte, "Civil Society and Democratically Accountable Global Governance," *Government and Opposition* 39, no. 2 (2004): 211–33; Steven Bernstein and Benjamin Cashore, "Can Non-state Global Governance Be Legitimate? An Analytical Framework," *Regulation & Governance* 1, no. 4 (2007): 347–71; Terry Macdonald, *Global Stakeholder Democracy: Power and Representation Beyond Liberal States* (New York: Oxford University Press, 2008).

27 Kenneth W. Abbott and Duncan Snidal, "Strengthening International Regulation through Transnational New Governance: Overcoming the Orchestration Deficit," *Vanderbilt Journal of Transnational Law* 42 (2008): 501–38; Thomas Gehring and Sebastian Oberthür, "The Causal Mechanisms of Interaction Between International Institutions," *European Journal of International Relations* 15, no. 1 (2009): 125–56.

28 Kenneth W. Abbott, Jessica F. Green, and Robert O. Keohane, "Organizational Ecology and Institutional Change in Global Governance," *International Organization* 70, no. 2 (2016): pp. 247–77.

29 Macdonald and Macdonald, "Liquid Authority and Political Legitimacy."

30 Mark E. Warren, "What Can Democratic Participation Mean Today?" *Political Theory* 30, no. 5 (2002): 677–701; John Dryzek, *Deliberative Global Politics: Discourse and Democracy in a Divided World* (London: Polity Press, 2006); Young, *Inclusion and Democracy*; Macdonald, *Global Stakeholder Democracy*.

31 This shift resonates with also with the suggestion of some contemporary democratic theorists that democratic agency can be expressed through forms of social and cultural influence that extend beyond formal "voice" in formal political decision-making institutions. See Danielle Allen and Jennifer S. Light, ed., *From Voice to Influence: Understanding Citizenship in a Digital Age* (Chicago: University of Chicago Press, 2015).

32 Josiah Ober, "The Original Meaning of 'Democracy': Capacity to Do Things, Not Majority Rule," *Constellations* 15, no. 1 (2008): 3–9.

33 Ober, "The Original Meaning of 'Democracy'," p. 7.

34 Macdonald and Macdonald, "Liquid Authority and Political Legitimacy."

35 Kate Macdonald and Terry Macdonald, "Towards a 'Pluralist' World Order: Creative Agency and Legitimacy in Global Institutions," *European Journal of International Relations* 26, no. 2 (2020): 518–44.

36 This recognition resonates strongly with Rubenstein's argument (this volume) that "affectedness" can in part be constituted, not merely articulated, through the collaborative responsibility-taking of organized political activism; and it resonates further with Gould's and Stilz's arguments (this volume) about the normative character of democratic collective action, and self-determination, respectively.

37 Jack Knight and James Johnson, "Aggregation and Deliberation: On the Possibility of Democratic Legitimacy," *Political Theory* 22, no. 2 (1994): 277–96; Seyla Benhabib, "Deliberative Rationality and Models of Democratic Legitimacy," *Constellations* 1, no. 1 (1994): 26–52.

38 Brian Barry, "Is Democracy Special?" in *Democracy and Power: Essays in Political Theory* (New York: Oxford University Press, 1991); Charles R. Beitz, *Political Equality: An Essay in Democratic Theory* (Princeton, NJ: Princeton University Press, 1989).

39 John Rawls, *Political Liberalism* (New York: Columbia University Press, 1993).

40 Laura Valentini, "Ideal vs. Non-ideal Theory: A Conceptual Map," *Philosophy Compass* 7, no. 9 (2012): 654–64.

41 Allan Buchanan and Robert O. Keohane, "The Legitimacy of Global Governance Institutions," *Ethics & International Affairs* 20, no. 4 (2006): 405–37; Allan Buchanan, *The Heart of Human Rights* (New York: Oxford University Press, 2014); Macdonald, "Institutional Facts and Principles"; Macdonald and Macdonald, "Liquid Authority and Political Legitimacy."

42 Rawls, *Political Liberalism*.

43 Laura Valentini, "Assessing the Global Order: Justice, Legitimacy, or Political Justice?" *Critical Review of International Social and Political Philosophy* 15, no. 5 (2012): 593–612.

44 Eva Erman, "Global Political Legitimacy Beyond Justice and Democracy?" *International Theory* 8, no. 1 (2015): 29–62.

45 Joshua Cohen, "An Epistemic Conception of Democracy," *Ethics* 97, no. 1 (1986): 26–38.

46 Bernard Williams, *In the Beginning Was the Deed: Realism and Moralism in Political Argument* (Princeton, NJ: Princeton University Press, 2005).

47 Buchanan, *The Heart of Human Rights*; Buchanan and Keohane, "The Legitimacy of Global Governance Institutions."

48 Miller, *On Nationality*.

49 Macdonald, "Institutional Facts and Principles."

50 Elsewhere, I have argued that conceptions of valuable political agency should be expanded beyond influential rationalist accounts to include additional *creative* faculties; but it is beyond the scope of this chapter to elaborate that substantive view. See Macdonald, "Democratizing Global 'Bodies Politic';" Macdonald and Macdonald, "Towards a 'Pluralist' World Order."

51 Williams, *In the Beginning Was the Deed*.

11

Markets, Fairness, and the All-Affected Principle

Thomas Christiano

In this chapter I will explore the idea that an important realization of the All-Affected Principle is the idea that persons ought to have capacities for participating in voluntary exchange. This realization occurs in the context where decision making is decentralized. Normally, the All-Affected Principle is meant to give people power over decisions in which their legitimate interests are at stake. And this is usually thought to mean that persons ought to have a say in a centralized collective decision procedure. But centralized decision making is not the only context in which this principle can be realized. It can also be realized in situations in which decisions are more properly made in a decentralized way, allowing different persons to pursue their own interests in their own way, as John Stuart Mill thought.

There are several contexts in which decentralized decision making seems especially appropriate. One, reasonably open markets are desirable ways of organizing production in society because they tend to put resources to their best use. Two, states make decisions by negotiating agreements with one another. Three, relations between persons in clubs, associations, friendships and other groups are created through voluntary agreements. And finally, the relations between various associations and clubs are also often determined by voluntary agreement.

Centralized and decentralized decision making do not come in all-or-nothing forms. A main component of markets are firms, which are centrally organized; and markets are usually properly heavily regulated in a centralized way so as to overcome the ill effects of unequal endowments and market imperfections such as externalities, asymmetries of information, high transaction costs, natural monopoly or monopsony as well as the forms of unfairness typical of imperfect and incomplete markets. International negotiation among states is often – though not often enough – constrained by procedures and methods that are meant to overcome the problems of imperfect information and unfairness through multilateral conferences. And many states are federally organized, which makes room for decentralized agreement making among the federal units. And democratic processes also depend in large degree on decentralized decision making in the form of citizens creating and joining associations such as political parties and interest group associations for democratic purposes or for the purpose of expressing ideas.

I will argue that in some circumstances the capacity for voluntary agreement making can be an adequate realization of the All-Affected Principle. The basic idea is that one can, with this capacity, attempt to advance one's interests by entering into voluntary agreements with others. The All-Affected Principle can be satisfied if persons are able to enter into agreements with those whose actions affect them or with those who can advance their interests. Persons should have an equal say or a say proportionate to their legitimate interests and this can be realized in voluntary agreement making, or so I shall argue.

In what follows, I attempt to explain and vindicate this proposition. I start by drawing an analogy between democratic decision making traditionally conceived and voluntary agreement making. This helps us see how we can define appropriate procedural norms for the evaluation of processes of voluntary agreement making in both market and international contexts. I argue that fair voluntary agreement in markets and international decision making is a realization of the same principle as fair collective decision making in democracy, only one is for decentralized decision making and the other is for centralized decision making.

I then lay out the Proportionality Principle, which I take to be the fundamental principle underlying both fair collective decision making and fair voluntary agreement making. I give some examples of when the Proportionality Principle departs from equality. And I defend the principle. We can see, however, that there is a deep puzzle about voluntary exchange that makes it especially prone to unfairness. I then say something about institutions that can realize the principles above. The democratic conception of fair voluntary exchange actually can help us see when voluntary exchange needs to be regulated or even replaced in order to achieve the realization of the Proportionality Principle.

VOLUNTARY AGREEMENTS AND DEMOCRATIC PARTICIPATION

The immediate object of agreements are arrangements of rights (understood broadly to include liberties, claims, powers, and immunities) and duties among those who make the agreement. The participants can set up a system of rules of interaction, which establish a complex of rights and duties and to which they are committed. Or they can merely exchange rights (and the associated duties) to particular things. Further purposes of the agreement consist in a change in the division of labor and the production of benefits and burdens among the parties. The parties shape the social world they live in in terms of basic rights and duties, the division of labor, and they alter it so as to bring about benefits and burdens that the social world can achieve. We can think abstractly about the benefits minus the burdens as the surplus the agreement brings about above the level of benefits the status quo realizes. The transaction takes place in the context of a prior set of conditions, which might be thought of as conditions of the process of transaction. Among these are the absence of force and fraud and other background conditions that enable the participants to treat each other as equals. When a person engages in making agreements, contracts, and other arrangements with other people, they are in effect attempting to shape the social world they live in.

If a person buys a house, they rearrange the social world in that others are now excluded from this house unless the owner consents to their coming in and is able to conduct activities in this particular space as they wish, with or without others. The owner has rearranged the social world in that now there is a space in the world that others can only enter with their consent, whereas before there was none. The owner has revised the relationships they have with others. When a person takes a job, they agree to work for a certain reward. They have rearranged the social world in that certain others now work with them under certain conditions and resources are transferred to them while they employ their skill in producing with others certain kinds of goods.

These different transactions have various effects in shaping the social world the person lives in by altering the rights, duties, and powers that different people have in relation to that person. And if we think of the whole series of agreements a person enters into in the course of a life, we can see that they shape the whole social world they live in through this activity. A person constructs the conditions of their life through this activity of rearranging the rules in their social world. They do this, to be sure, with other people who are also engaged in the activity of shaping their lives with others. And the activity of determining a person's social world is, of course, constrained by the activities of others, both because they have to make agreements with others and because they must respect the social arrangements that others have created. The social world is an aggregate product of all these different activities of social shaping. It is the product of coordination and it is the product of separate activities that are not coordinated but that mesh together, because the activities are engaged in side by side and within the context of a common legal system.

There is an important similarity between the activity of citizenship and the activities of persons in the processes of agreement making with others. Just as a citizen participates in shaping the overall character of the society they live in by participating in collective decision making about the overall collective features of the society, so the ordinary person in everyday life shapes parts of the social world in which they live by engaging in agreement making with others – the difference being that in the case of citizenship each has a small voice in a very large activity, while in private life each has a large voice in relatively small issues.

The justification of these different powers of shaping the social world is grounded in common liberal concerns. Persons have different interests that conflict and they disagree on how best to shape their social worlds; indeed, they are often uncertain about their own interests. We think that people ought to be able to make the basic decisions about how their society is organized, and how their lives with others are organized, by exercising the power to advance their legitimate aims in accordance with their own judgments. They need this power both because they do not want to be imposed upon by people with less understanding and concern for their interests and because they need to explore their interests.

The analogy of democratic citizenship with the activities of persons in decentralized settings is not meant to imply that these decentralized settings ought to be centralized and democratized in the traditional way. My intention is to show that there is an analogy between democratic citizenship and the activities of persons in decentralized settings, not to suggest that we should eliminate the decentralized settings. There are many important values that are realized in decentralized settings that make them unsuitable for at least complete collectivization. The values involved in personal relationships and development and the distinctive values that arise from people cultivating their particular talents and ideas must be given some significant protection from collectivization. And I think, with the tradition of economic theory of Adam Smith and John Maynard Keynes, that some kind of open market system is important for putting resources to productive uses. Furthermore, any effort to replace decentralization in international politics with serious centralization in the near-term future is likely to lead to very unhappy and tyrannical government. The integrity of states, so essential to the realization of the basic interests of persons, must be preserved for a significant time into the future.

Nevertheless, that the democratic idea has a realization in decentralized settings as well as centralized settings will shed light on how we ought to think normatively about voluntary exchange. It will help us develop some basic principles for how to evaluate a system of exchange and provide us with a way of thinking about when and how to reform or change institutions. I elaborate next a picture of the basic idea of fairness in exchange that builds on the democratic analogy.

FAIRNESS IN INDIVIDUAL TRANSACTIONS

The conception of fairness in individual exchange here articulated attempts to avoid the classical natural law approach of equal exchange in value[1] and attempts to develop a procedural conception of fair exchange that goes beyond the standards of absence of coercion and fraud.[2] The reason for the procedural approach is that the benefits of transactions can be quite heterogeneous and hard to compare outside the points of view of each of the participants. So, it may be very unclear in many circumstances whether the goods exchanged are equal in value in some more objective sense.

Let us first think of an individual exchange as if there were only one exchange for each person's whole life. The appropriate background fairness conditions for such an exchange consist in the realization of equal capacities for that exchange. This breaks down into two components: equal cognitive conditions, including equal access to information relevant to discerning one's interests and concerns and abilities to negotiate desirable arrangements, and equal opportunity for exiting or refusing entry into the arrangement.

When we extend the principle to the usual case in which each person engages in a series of many exchanges, the persons must have equal capacities globally in the sense that they start from background conditions that ensure equal capacities for all. This equal background condition need not be fully maintained throughout the series, because earlier agreements persons enter into may curtail opportunities they have in later agreement making. If this is done knowingly, the later agreement making in which there may be some inequality of opportunity is not unfair. Furthermore, individuals may choose to focus on some agreements in which they think of themselves as having much at stake and focus less on other exchanges in which they think of themselves as having a lot less at stake. This stake sensitivity in agreement making will have some importance later.

This realizes a kind of democratic value in everyday life, because the two conditions in the one-shot case specify circumstances in which persons have an equal say in the structuring of their relations with each other. And the global principle of equal capacity gives persons a kind of equal say in the formation of their social lives together with others regarding the contents of the series of agreements they enter into.[3] It specifies a kind of condition of global equal bargaining power between parties such that each person has an equal say overall. It does not imply equal bargaining power in each agreement-making context but only over the sum of agreements a person enters into.

This principle of equal capacity is meant to give persons equal power in the process of the creation of the informal social world they live in. Their interests are, roughly speaking, equally at stake in the system of agreement-making overall. This is like the idea of equality in democratic collective decision making in which persons are to have equal power because we think that, for the most part, their interests are equally in play in the political system.

We achieve this condition of equal power in agreement making by making sure that people have the education and resources that enable them to discern their interests and exit or refuse transactions and enter others that advance their interests. Education, basic needs provision, and other goods give people opportunities to choose among transactions by enhancing their bargaining power.

The principle of equal opportunity for exit is meant to be a special principle for societies like the modern nation-state in which there is a rough equality of stakes for persons overall in the process of agreement making, at least for the great majority of people. There are a number of qualifications that need to be explained concerning this principle. First, we need to say what kinds of things can produce inequality in the outcomes of the processes of agreement making. One, those who knowingly exert themselves and make use of their opportunities for the sake of a particular good are more likely to achieve that good, other things being equal, than those who knowingly do not exert themselves for the sake of that good. Two, more controversially, it makes sense for differences in natural talent to bring about some inequalities in social power that arise from occupying different positions in the division of labor. With Rawls, we should not accept that differences in talent should bring about significant differences in income or wealth. But two people who are competing for a particular social position may justly end up in different positions in the division of labor if differences in their natural talents imply that they should occupy those different positions, even if one of the positions is more desirable and interesting than the other.

The question is, what can justify this? It can be justified by the principle that we ought to think inequality can be justified over equality when all are better off and by the idea that it is important that people be able to realize their talents. The realization of natural talent implies that persons are benefited when they exercise those talents. To require that people not be able to exercise their talents so that they have no more bargaining power than others would be to make others worse off as well as the person who is deprived of the opportunity to exercise talent. There is injustice here, but it is desirable in order to avoid leveling down.[4]

THE PROPORTIONALITY PRINCIPLE

The second observation is that the principle of equal opportunity is really a special case of a more general principle, which also governs collective decision making. The more general principle is that persons ought to have a say in a transaction in proportion to the legitimate stakes they have in the transaction.[5] This principle is narrower than Mark Warren's principle of proportionality in this volume. His is a more general principle of equity and includes distribution in proportion to need or desert. My principle only regulates the distribution of power. The principle of equal opportunity is a principle that respects this more general principle for the special case of overall equal legitimate stakes.

The stakes a person has in an agreement or set of agreements consists of the range of potential legitimate interest affecting outcomes of that agreement. This includes the effect on interests if there is no agreement and the effects on interests of the various agreements available in the circumstances. We must distinguish between, on the one hand, *ex ante* stakes a person has in a transaction or system of transactions and, on the other hand, the actual stakes in a particular transaction. *Ex ante* stakes are the extent to which the transaction or the system can advance the legitimate interests of each party independent of the distribution of resources among the parties. This varies according to context in the sense that it depends on the real possibilities of the system or the transaction. Actual stakes will depend on the interests in the transaction as well as the distribution of resources among the parties, which will determine what each party brings to the transactions. In the context of a particular transaction, a person with very few resources will have higher actual stakes in the agreement because they have fewer resources to fall back on or to offer others in alternative transactions. The transaction matters all the more. A person with a lot of resources has less need of the particular transaction and so has a lesser stake.

This principle applies to democratic decision making as well as voluntary exchange. In the case of democratic decision making, the stakes are the range of interests affected by plausible outcomes that can be achieved by the collective decision process. The equal distribution of power is a special case of its proportional distribution.[6] In the case of democratic decision making we see the application of proportionality in two ways. First, some decisions in a federalist system are made in a way that gives all persons an equal say; other decisions give greater weight to persons in local jurisdictions. A natural interpretation is that when people's interests are affected in a roughly equal way overall, they have an equal say, and when some persons' interests are much more affected than others (as in local political decisions), they have significantly more say. This is institutionalized in the system of federal institutions.

Second, proportionality operates at the level of individual democratic decisions as well, but only informally and according to the judgment of the individual. That is, when people with equal political power think that some issue is of great importance, they devote many more resources to that issue and fewer resources to things that matter less. The democratic process overall, on the assumption that the differences cancel each other out when all issues are taken into account, gives people broadly egalitarian opportunities to trade with people through logrolling. It is equality of stakes in the collective decision making overall that justifies the equal vote.

Voluntary agreement making is different from collective decision making. There are usually two distinct dimensions: one is whether to make an agreement at all, and the other is what the content of the agreement is. It is for this reason that the definition of stakes is different from that of collective decision making. The basic determinant of relative stakes in the case of particular actual voluntary exchange is the relative significance of the non-agreement point. This means that how much a person benefits from an agreement need not determine stakes. How the surplus of the agreement is divided up will depend on what the parties agree to. But the initial condition of the agreement, which are the values or disvalues of no agreement for each of the parties, is external to the agreement and thus can provide an external reference point for determining the stakes.

The principle of equal capacity is based on the idea that persons have equal *ex ante* stakes in a system of transactions. In society virtually all the fundamental interests we have (with respect to voluntary exchange) are in play in the whole system of voluntary exchanges. The non-agreement point is essentially life outside society. It then requires that the distribution of resources be adjusted so as to achieve equal capacity. This is a special case of the more general principle that persons ought to have capacities that are proportionate to their *ex ante* stakes. Someone who has a lot less stake in a transaction ought to have less power over it than one who has more stake.

The principle of proportionality is qualified in the two ways of the equal capacities principle above. A further qualification results from a worry, pointed out by Nozick, that this gives people power over the intimate choices of others. If one person loves another deeply and the other chooses to marry a third person, then the first person has great stakes in the second person's choice. Does this mean that the first person ought to have a say in the choice? This seems really implausible. We should allay this worry with the idea that some interests are protected interests in the sense that a person may choose to fulfill these interests without the leave of others. This might be the case, for example, in choices of friends or life partners and perhaps choices about basic questions of conscience.[7]

A clarification is in order here. I take stakes to be defined in terms of well-being and I think of well-being as being essentially an objective state. But the stakes involved in the Proportionality Principle in a pluralistic society must proceed with a fairly generic conception of the interests of persons, since there is likely to be significant disagreement and uncertainty regarding what particular interests persons have. Persons have interests in health, friendship, resources, education, and other generic goods and the principle of proportionality allows them to explore those interests with the power that it assigns them.

SOME CASES IN WHICH THE PROPORTIONALITY PRINCIPLE APPLIES

I have already pointed out that sometimes proportionality applies to politics in a non- egalitarian way. But there are important contexts in which persons or groups come together to make important agreements where they are not really part of an extensive and unified system of agreement making and in which they have different stakes.

First, states with different populations make negotiated agreements. Larger societies have a greater stake than smaller societies in their negotiations. The democratic principle in voluntary exchange, as in the case of collective decision making, is an individualistic principle. Hence the theoretical challenge is to aggregate the interests of the members of the society in a way that is relevant to defining the stakes each society has.

Second, agreement making among states in the making of international law is fairly modest compared to the domestic legislation states engage in and relatively modest compared to the amount of agreements individuals enter into in modern societies. In climate change negotiations, we can see that certain societies have much more at stake in these negotiations than other societies.

The average Bangladeshi has a great deal more at stake than the United States citizen in the medium short run, which is a function of the extent to which the society is affected by non-agreement. Proportionality would suggest that Bangladesh has more of a say in the content of its agreement with the United States on climate change (abstracting from difference in size of population).

Third, people enter into contractual arrangements across different societies, such as when a firm from a wealthy society sets up shop in a poor country to employ relatively cheap labor. The poor person has a significant amount at stake in this activity, presumably more than the members of the company and its consumers. The members of the company do have an important stake in setting up desirable arrangements because they must make sure that the company's costs do not go too high. The consumers have an interest in paying lower prices and this is what is partly driving the move to sweatshop labor. But perhaps here the consumer's interest in lower prices is a far lesser stake than the poor person's interest in having a decent wage. Of course, even here there is a lot more complexity: some poor consumers may have a pretty big stake in low-priced goods such as shoes.

ARGUMENT FOR THE PROPORTIONALITY PRINCIPLE

Intuitively, when we are setting up an arrangement with another person whom we know well and we know that the other person has a lot at stake while we have less, we often give more say to that person over the arrangement: "This matters more to you [or for you], so you should decide."

There are really two main connected theoretical arguments for this principle that start from the All-Affected Principle, suitably modified. The first argument is essentially a welfarist argument. The idea is that people have an important interest in taking care of their own interests. The basic reasons are that they know their interests better than others do, they have incentives to concern themselves with their own interests, and they have the capacity to learn from mistakes about their own interests. To the extent that more is at stake in an agreement for a person than for others, they have more of their interests at stake and so there is reason for them to take greater care. But this also gives reason to others to give them a greater say in the agreement. The welfare of persons is better advanced when they have a greater say in those issues in which they have a greater interest.

There is an egalitarian argument for this as well, at least under normal circumstances with normal people. The idea is that a principle that extends a greater say to those who have more interests at stake in agreements will, over the long run, equalize the say of persons over the matters that affect their interests. This is based on the idea that over the long run normal people have roughly equal stakes in how the external world is organized. The principle gives people an equal say over the external world they live in when we think of its global application.

One question that we cannot address here is whether the principle we are defending is essentially an instrumentally defended principle or whether there may be some intrinsic value to implementing the principle. The arguments above suggest an instrumental cast, but the democratic interpretation of equality of opportunity offered above suggests that there may be intrinsic value in implementing the idea.

Before moving on, I want to address three important concerns. First, the principle I have defended is an individualistic principle in a limited sense. It focuses on the distribution of power to individuals in the process of exchange and whole systems of exchange. In this respect it is much like the democratic principle for collective decision making. And it is committed to a kind of deeper individualism, which asserts that the ultimate values that we are dealing with are the well-being of the individual and justice among individual persons. Even the notion of the common good will have an individualistic interpretation on this account. But the principles of justice are not individualistic; they specify a collective order with the proper distribution of benefits and burdens among persons. I also reject individualism regarding the content of well-being. I want to argue that many, or perhaps most, of the important interests people have consist in their social relations with others. Friendship is an obvious case of this, but so is the interest in being recognized and affirmed as an equal and the interest in making the world a home for oneself, or the interest in seeing that one is making a contribution to valuable cooperative activities. The social nature of our interests is compatible with the democratic conception of voluntary exchange.

A second clarification has to do with the nature of the duties people have with regard to this principle of the proportional distribution of power in the system of exchange. The principle applies in the first instance to institutions just as much as conventionally democratic collective decision-making principles. Another departure from individualism obtains here because individuals have jointly held duties to bring about, maintain, and improve these institutions. Since the duties are jointly held, each person has a duty to do their fair share in bringing about, maintaining, reforming, and complying with the institutions that distribute power. In reasonably well-functioning institutions, individuals may go about pursuing their partial interests as they see fit.

One important question is: What kind of duties do people have to take up the slack when others fail to do their share? It is not the case that each person must do everything possible to make up for every inequality of power they have not produced, but they do have duties to do their share – but what is that when others fail to do theirs? I do not have a complete answer for this, and it will depend on the specific problem confronting a person. If a particular person is in dire straits, an agent may have the duty to do quite a bit. If a particular person unjustly has less power than other persons, it is not clear what it is fair to ask a better-situated person to do. But it is not normally everything that can be done. The duties are jointly held and so fairness in the distribution of duties plays a role even in the case of taking up the slack.

A final clarification repeats what I have already said. The principle I have defended is a principle of equal distribution of power among individuals. But much of decentralized decision making involves interactions between groups such as firms or states and sometimes between these and individuals. I do think the individualistic principle still applies here, but it is not between the firm and the person as if these are two individuals. The firm is a group of persons and so the question of power ultimately comes down to the distribution of power between the persons in the firm and the persons the firm is negotiating with. For a complete analysis of this kind of interaction we will need a method of aggregating the persons' stakes to arrive at an account of the proper distribution of power between the firm and the person. And this method will vary depending on the institution in question. For example, something close to an additive method may be acceptable in the case of the relations between states with different populations. But additivity will not work in the case of firms as they are constituted in the United States, where there is significant conflict between the different elements. An account of the proper methods of aggregation of stakes is absolutely essential to the full articulation of the principle I am defending in this paper, but I am not in a position to offer one now.[8]

THE PUZZLE

One of the most fundamental puzzles in a system of free transactions is that the principle of power proportionate to stakes is prone to violation in many normal circumstances. For example, if you have two persons who depend on making an agreement to advance certain interests, the one who has the least stake will often have more power. This is because they can more easily afford no agreement. But this means that power is inversely proportioned to stakes in a scheme of free transactions, while the normative principle tells us that power ought to be proportioned to stakes.[9] This is the fundamental puzzle that Marx pointed to in the relations between capital and labor. The laborer has a great deal at stake in a transaction since their life depends on it, while the capitalist has a lot less at stake. The consequence is that the capitalist has more bargaining power.[10]

A scheme of equal opportunity in a context of equal *ex ante* stakes provides a unique resolution to this problem. Power cannot be inversely proportioned to stakes in this context overall. Proportionality can still continue to function in this context but it is informally applied by the parties. For example, if two parties have equal capacity overall and one party has more at stake in a particular transaction than another because of difference of interest, the usual consequence is that the one with less at stake will devote less attention to the issue (in order to devote more time to other issues) while the one with more at stake will devote more time. To the extent that each has overall equal stakes and capacities, the disproportions will cancel out. In this way, the overall proportion between capacity and interest is maintained.

What Marx was concerned with was that the capitalists, who have less actual stake in each particular transaction with a particular worker, also have many more resources to devote to the making of the transaction. This compounds the initial disproportion.

INSTITUTIONS

It looks like this problem does occur in perfectly competitive and complete markets but only in a highly attenuated way. In markets where there are lots of buyers and sellers and no impediments to exchange and there is no incompleteness so that credit and insurance are available to everyone, there is no difference in bargaining power. And a genuine inequality of stakes only obtains as a result of unequal initial endowments, but this difference may not normally count for much when there is unlimited availability of credit and insurance. Only when there is extreme difference of endowments, including natural endowments, will complete markets be very unfair to participants.

The puzzle is nevertheless a deep one, because in fact we always observe significant divergence from complete and perfect markets. And many of the principal institutions in what we call the market are specifically designed to overcome imperfections in actual markets. Indeed, one of the central institutions of modern capitalism, the firm, is essentially a response to market imperfections.[11] At the same time, some form of a system of voluntary transactions is a highly effective tool in figuring out how to allocate resources to their most productive uses. We do not have a clear idea of an alternative system for the allocation of scarce resources that does not involve the use of voluntary market exchange playing a central role.

The question is, how can we make use of this tool for allocating resources in an efficient way but without sacrificing fairness? There are really four basic kinds of mechanisms that we can introduce to try to ensure a kind of fairness in the process of making agreements. The first is redistribution so as to achieve a kind of background distribution of resources that enables people to meet each other on reasonably equal terms. The second is direct regulation of the employment relation. The third is direct regulation of the bargaining process so as to help achieve a kind of balance between worker and employer. The fourth involves some kind of collectivization in the decision making in economic institutions. Here we replace bargaining with collective decision making among the parties and try to achieve equality in the collective decision process. We can think of a number of institutions that might help to alleviate the disproportionality involved in voluntary transactions.

One basic mechanism for overcoming the problem is redistribution of resources from those who have low stakes to those who have high stakes so as to equalize the stakes as much as possible, or so as to provide some kind of basic floor of resources to protect those who have very few resources and thus lessen the stakes for the less well positioned. The welfare state comes to mind as a complex of institutions that are designed to lessen the stakes for workers when they choose where and how to work.

The provision of public education is a way to ensure that persons are able to develop their abilities so as to participate as equals in economic life. Unemployment insurance and income maintenance programs imply that the alternative to work at a particular job is not starvation or penury but some kind of minimally decent life. It is important to notice one distinctive function of the welfare state is that it enhances the power of persons to shape their social world. It enhances people's power to shape their work conditions and wages. The dismantling of the welfare state is in effect a kind of authoritarian strategy to disempower workers.

A second mechanism is direct regulation of the employment relation. Minimum wage legislation, legislation concerning working conditions, legislation concerning hours of work, and legislation constraining how workers can be fired are all direct regulations imposed by the political society. They do this because workers tend to be at a bargaining disadvantage in negotiating the work agreement with employers. These constraints on work conditions increase the bargaining power of workers by decreasing the bargaining power of the employer since they lessen the alternatives available to employers.

The third kind of mechanism is direct regulation of the bargaining process. Here the idea is to make use of facts that are already present without having to redistribute resources such as the great number of workers and their potential for organization. One institution for altering the conditions under which agreement to work is made to avoid great unfairness is union organization. The effect of union organization is not to lessen the stakes of the worker in work, but to increase the stakes of capital in refusing terms of work by requiring capital to deal with a lot of workers at the same time. Unions do this by themselves, but the state can help by setting up rules for negotiation that are favorable to unions. Notice that this mechanism introduces elements of voluntary agreement and elements of collective decision making. Workers participate in unions as participants in a collective decision-making process, but that collective agent then bargains with employers.[12]

A fourth kind of mechanism is local collectivization. I do not mean here to say that the whole structure of society is collectivized. I am assuming some kind of decentralized market system for allocating resources to their most efficient uses. The idea here is to replace the process of bargaining with all its inequalities with a collective decision-making method that includes unions, laborers, managers, and capitalists.[13] This seems to be the mechanism at work in the German codetermination system. The particular value of the approach I have taken makes egalitarian voluntary exchange and egalitarian collective decision making derive from a single basic principle. They are two distinct types of realizations of the principle of proportionality. What this approach suggests is that one kind of decision making can conceivably be a remedy for a deficiency in the other. I have in mind, for example, various kinds of workplace democracy. Workplace democracy can be a partial remedy for imperfections in the market that put workers at a serious disadvantage in the bargaining process. Consider the familiar case of partial monopsony in which there are lot of workers but it is not easy for them to move from job to job, either because they have to make asset-specific investments or because they have imperfect information or because of high transaction costs in moving from one job to another. And let us further suppose that the circumstance workers find themselves in is not the result of a set of fully understood choices made earlier. The workers are at an unjust disadvantage. The consequence of this is that they tend to have relatively little say in the process of agreeing to a work contract. They have little say over the conditions of work. We can possibly rectify this deficiency by giving them more direct and locally collective power over the conditions of work, as in workplace democracy. The approach I am suggesting has this as a result, and I think it is a good result.

But the approach I am suggesting is not a general argument for workplace democracy, because the conditions under which the argument above works are not general conditions. In fact, I think that there is continuity here. We can imagine partial deficiencies remedied by partial requirements for workers' participation. In cases where the deficiencies are great, the requirement of fairness suggests a greater say. In case where they are present but not so great, they suggest a lesser say. Union organization is in some ways a lesser form of participation and it may be defensible as a response to lesser problems.

CONCLUSION

I have attempted to present here a vindication of the idea that the possession of a capacity to enter voluntary exchange is a realization of the All-Affected Principle. It is a way in which one can try to advance one's interests in the context of other persons. And I have tried to show that the fundamental principle for evaluating voluntary exchange is the principle of proportionality and that this is the same principle for evaluating collective decision making. I have tried also to show what some of the benefits of thinking of exchange in this way are.

NOTES

1 See, for example, Aristotle, *Nicomachean Ethics*, trans. Roger Crisp (New York: Cambridge University Press, 2014), Book V; Thomas Aquinas, *Summa Theologica*, trans. Thomas Gilby (New York: Cambridge University Press, 2008); Karl Marx, *Capital, Vol. 1*, trans. Ben Fowkes (New York: Penguin, 1990); Alan Wertheimer, *Exploitation* (Princeton, NJ: Princeton University Press, 1996).

2 For example, Robert Nozick, *Anarchy State and Utopia* (New York: Basic Books, 1974).

3 Thomas Christiano, "Equality, Fairness and Agreements," *Journal of Social Philosophy* 44, no. 4 (2013): 370–91.

4 Thomas Christiano and Will Braynen, "Inequality, Injustice and Leveling Down," *Ratio* 21, no. 4 (2008): 392–420.

5 Harry Brighouse and Marc Fleurbaey, "Democracy and Proportionality," *The Journal of Political Philosophy* 18, no. 2 (2010): 137–55.

6 For a discussion see Gray (this volume).

7 See Nozick, *Anarchy, State, and Utopia.*

8 Thomas Christiano, "Legitimacy and the International Trade Regime," *San Diego Law Review* 52, no. 5 (2015): 981–1013.

9 Thomas Christiano, "The Tension between the Nature and the Norm of Voluntary Exchange," *Southern Journal of Philosophy* 54, no. S1 (2016): 109–29.

10 Marx, *Capital Vol. 1.*

11 Ronald Coase, "The Nature of the Firm," in *The Firm, the Market and the Law* (Chicago: University of Chicago Press, 1988); Oliver Williamson, *The Economic Institutions of Capitalism: Firms, Markets and Relational Contracting* (New York: Free Press, 1985).

12 Richard Freeman and Edward Lazear, "An Economic Analysis of Works Councils," in *Works Councils: Consultation, Representation, and Cooperation in Industrial Relations,* ed. Joel Rogers and Wolfgang Streeck (Chicago: University of Chicago Press, 1995).

13 Richard Freeman and James Medoff, *What Do Unions Do?* (New York: Basic Books, 1984); see also Gould (this volume).

12

The All-Affected Principle and Climate Change[*]

Melissa Lane

Discussions of the history of the All-Affected Principle (AAP) frequently locate it in a procedural maxim of Roman private law known by the tag *quod omnes tangit* ("what touches all"), a maxim that became, in various formulations, a more expansive principle of medieval canon and civil law.[1] One representative locus of this maxim is in a law passed under Justinian in 531 and included in the second edition of the *Codex* that forms part of his *Corpus Iuris Civilis*, that where several different *tutores* (tutors) were appointed as guardians for a single ward or an undivided guardianship (*tutela*), all of them must consent to any legal proceeding to terminate the joint guardianship. The relevant part of the law reads: "it is necessary that all of them give their authorization so that something which touches them all in the same way is approved by all of them (*necesse est omnes suam auctoritatem praestare, ut, quod omnes similiter tangit, ab omnibus comprobetur*)," the *quod omnes ... tangit* serving as the familiar tag.[2] I begin this contribution with reflections on the significance of this particular legal origin as inspiration for the All-Affected Principle, before going on to deploy these reflections to assess the relevance of the principle for the case of climate change. (For clarity, I will refer to *quod omnes tangit* in its various formulations as "the maxim" or "maxims," and to contemporary formulations of the AAP as "the principle" or "principles." I focus on those versions of the principle that adhere relatively closely to the original maxim.)

THE ROMAN LAW MAXIM: "QUOD OMNES TANGIT"

While the All-Affected Principle "has migrated into democratic theory" in a broad wave of scholarship over the last several decades, as Mark Warren observes in his contribution to this volume, the relevance of the Roman law formulation has been disputed by Jürgen Habermas, who argues that as a maxim of judicial procedure (a context of norm application), it is not relevant to the principles governing the fundamental justification of norms [note that this volume uses "justification" and "application" in related ways].[3] One might think to bolster Habermas' case by pointing out the private law context of the original maxim. How could a maxim governing court procedure for legal guardians be relevant in any more than a homonymic way to broad issues of normative democratic theory?

In fact, the history of political thought has already been deeply marked by Roman private law as a source of maxims migrating into the realm of political theory and eventually democratic theory, as Daniel Lee has argued in his work on the emergence of the idea of popular sovereignty.[4] Already in the medieval period, the *quod omnes tangit* maxim had begun a migration into the public domain, for example in the English royal approach to the defense of the realm in a "'case of necessity,'" in which it was held that "all must consent to such extraordinary taxes as were justified by the emergency."[5] So while differences in contexts are of course significant, a brief overview of the history of *quod omnes tangit* and related maxims indicates that many of the dilemmas marking the AAP today share commonalities with the Roman and medieval uses, and debates, about the varied forms of the original maxim.

Within Roman law, variants of the maxim were implicitly or explicitly formulated in a number of contexts. In addition to the law that was noticed above (of the multiple guardians (*tutores*) appointed to share a single guardianship (*tutela*) who must all agree to a proceeding to terminate that guardianship), another case discussed by Ulpian in the *Digest* was that of the users of the water of a given aqueduct, all of whom were entitled to be heard in relation to certain decisions about its management.[6] As these cases suggest, a first commonality between the original Roman context of the maxim and contemporary versions of the principle lies in the interaction of the procedural and the substantive. Construing the AAP within the ambit of its Roman law origins points to a procedural focus in the sense of discursive input. The maxim originated in the context of judicial procedure and the scholar Gaines Post summed up what it required in the contexts to which it applied: "all must be given a hearing and a defense of their rights."[7] Such a procedural right clearly depends on a prior specification of moral claims in at least two respects: first, who has the right to be heard in a given proceeding, and second, on what basis (in virtue of what specific other rights or other morally relevant attributes) that right to be heard is attributed. So in the case of the Roman guardianship law mentioned above, each guardian's right to be heard in any legal proceeding to terminate the guardianship depended on their having been previously named in that role and so attributed the bundle of rights to act on behalf of the ward that such a role entailed.

Thus, the very specification of procedural rights relied on a previous set of substantive rights, themselves assigned or recognized through other procedures. The AAP as a maxim was, as it were, an auxiliary or supplementary framework that depended on a body of wider law to give it point and meaning.

Moreover, the guardianship law accommodating multiple guardians of a single ward's interests and rights underscores the relevance of the procedure in relation to giving voice to some on behalf of the interests of others. This is also a potentially promising feature for modern versions of the AAP to emphasize: discursive input may be given procedurally by empowering some to speak on behalf of the moral claims of others.

A second important commonality lies in the need to achieve closure of a procedure that could otherwise seem quite open-ended, and in which a dilatory or evasive attitude to the summons, or a demand that still others putatively affected also be summoned, could threaten to extend a court case indefinitely. One such danger that became especially evident in medieval times was this: that the right to have rights considered could be exercised as a capacity to block or obstruct the resolution of justice. Distance, in particular, such as for those "overseas or in the Holy Land [presumably on crusade]," was one factor that often came into play.[8] This led to the need to achieve "a synthesis of voluntary and procedural consent."[9] Procedural rights to be heard had to be made to comport with procedural devices to close hearings and resolve cases. While an open-ended procedure might have value as a regulative ideal, in institutional legal and political contexts, a procedure is most practically useful when it can be conclusively resolved. Closure does not require unanimous consent, but rather, only compliance with the required procedure, just as majority decision procedures need not be interpreted as representing the will of the minority or of the whole, but only as serving to determine a binding decision to be followed.[10]

This general point may help to explain some of the important variations that developed in the statement of the maxim itself, building on variant formulae found already in the corpus of the Roman law. In particular, as Gaines Post observes, the great common law authority Bracton followed popes such as Innocent III and sovereigns such as Edward I in their related formulations in never using either the word *similiter* ("in the same way") or the phrase *ab omnibus comprobetur* ("must be approved by all").[11] By leaving out *similiter*, on the one hand, Bracton opened the door to a recognition that those who are touched may not all be touched in the same way, an important feature for contemporary developments of the principle. By leaving out *ab omnibus comprobetur*, on the other hand, and preferring weaker formulations requiring only that all those touched be summoned to a hearing (*vocandi sunt*),[12] he transmuted an absolute consent requirement into a summoning procedure in which verification that one had had the opportunity to be heard could suffice.[13] In so doing, Bracton's uses of the maxim suggest ways in which the AAP might be likewise reformulated for new purposes today, while also limiting its reach and power to what one might call having a voice, rather than even a potential veto – a point that has been made by others in criticizing the AAP and related principles and to which I return in my conclusion.[14]

The third point of comparison, which may initially appear to be a disanalogy to many contemporary applications of the AAP, will lead directly into my

discussion of climate change. It pertains to the significance of the private law
context of the original *quod omnes tangit* maxim. The maxim presupposes the
existence of rights (in particular, though not exclusively, rights related to property) that have been already established by a different part of the legal code and
already acknowledged as held by those to whom the maxim applies. The "all"
in *quod omnes tangit* is not an open-ended, indeterminate group of people, but
rather a specific and already separately identifiable group who possess already
acknowledged rights. The procedures to which *quod omnes tangit* applies are
those which give force to, and are based on, preexisting rights, rather than
serving to establish rights *ab initio*. Indeed, it is this sort of point that is likely
to have inspired Habermas' remark, noted earlier, dismissing the relevance of
quod omnes tangit to the justification of norms, even though the burden of this
chapter is that such relevance can nevertheless be defended.

As I turn now to consider whether the maxim can underpin a version of the
AAP as a principle relevant to a moral and political response to the anthropogenic role in causing climate change through greenhouse gas emissions, the
potential disanalogy just noted may seem to present a roadblock. For it may
seem that there are no preexisting rights or claims in the area of property that
are relevant to climate change and that could thus underpin an application
of the maxim-based principle. In the next section, however, I will argue that
this is not the case. Rather, there are grounds to identify moral rights to a fair
per capita share of a total global carbon budget, which could then underpin
an application of the AAP. Such an application could involve any version of
that principle adhering closely to the procedural force – in allowing discursive
input – of the original maxim ("what touches all similarly must be approved
by all," or the variations noted above and considered further below). In the
subsequent section I will consider the case for another (additional or parallel)
application of the AAP, not on the basis of moral rights to a kind of property,
but on the basis of moral rights against the unjust imposition of harm or the
risk of harm. Then, in the final section, I will consider a range of procedural
and institutional possibilities for taking account of both of these kinds of rights
in embodying the AAP in moral, legal, or political expectations and practices.

CLIMATE CHANGE AND THE AAP: THE CASE FOR MORAL
RIGHTS TO A KIND OF PROPERTY

To think about whether the AAP is helpful in the context of climate change,
one must think first about the value of focusing on procedural forms of
expressing discursive input into the establishment or modification of a moral
or legal order. The presumptive value would include rectifying some inequities
in causal and political power and so potentially allowing for better substantive
outcomes in the domain of the harms caused by climate change than is currently the case. In order to realize any such procedure, we must consider the
underlying substantive rights on which it would have to rest: whether there

are recognizable rights or claims that some group of "all affected" hold, and whether that group can be properly identified. While one might leap to the issue of "future generations" here – and indeed we will come on to that issue below – I think that it is more helpful to inquire first, as the above discussion of the maxim suggested, into the sense in which there might be in this context a group of "all" with preexisting rights or claims that a principle such as the AAP can acknowledge.

One argument that would support the application of the AAP would be to accept arguments that have been made for the atmosphere as a global commons as the basis for the preexisting moral rights on the basis of which a claim to discursive input for all affected could be founded.[15] This moral idea takes as a starting point the idea of a global "carbon budget" of greenhouse gases in the atmosphere, set at a point that is likely to be compatible with keeping the increase in the earth's mean surface temperature within a certain tolerable range. That total accumulation – understood as a sum of carbon sources and sinks – is a total for all time. It has been driven most dramatically (though not solely) by fossil fuel emissions in the period of the Industrial Revolution, and its rate of increase is expected to eventually slow, stop, and gradually decline, as future energy and other needs can be supplied instead by non-fossil fuel and non-greenhouse-gas emitting activities. On the global commons argument, this total accumulation is understood as a kind of negative commons, one to which no individual or country had preexisting property rights or could rightfully establish a squatter's claim to keep out others from making equal fair use of the same commons.[16]

For present purposes, consider the players in the Industrial Revolution period of the dramatic increase in the accumulation in terms of countries or nation-states, divided into richer countries that have emitted far more and poorer countries that have emitted far less per capita, and in many cases less also in absolute terms.[17] Countries are also the dominant (though not the only) players in the politics of potential mitigation in the critical period of the next decades in collectively determining whether a sustainable path to a tolerable likely global mean temperature rise will be achieved. Thus the concept of a global carbon budget for fossil fuel emissions is assigned per capita to the populations of countries between, say, 1880 and 2050, providing something akin to "property rights" as a moral basis for the applicability of a version of the AAP.[18]

This cumulative carbon budget of fossil fuel emissions has been calculated as 820 GtC, of which just over 400 GtC have been already emitted since 1880 (using 2010 data).[19] Yet in 2011, one billion of the people living in the poorest countries emitted less than 1 percent of the total global carbon emissions that year.[20] Working the numbers, one could calculate the proportion of emissions in the full period likely to be attributable to the richest countries versus the poorest countries. That has been done by the Global Carbon Project for a slightly different time period (1870–2015), for cumulative emissions from fossil fuels and cement, showing the United States to be responsible for 26%, the EU28 for 23%, China for 13%, Russia for 7%, Japan for 4%, India for 3%, and all other countries for the remainder.[21] A further adjustment for populations over that time period would confirm, broadly speaking, that the "property rights" attributable on the basis of the global carbon budget to the poorer countries, and people within them, have been usurped to a considerable extent by the richer, who have taken up far more than their fair share of the carbon budget to date, while the poor are far more vulnerable to its effects.[22] (The Global Carbon Project data just cited shows that the United States and the EU28 are jointly responsible for just under half of the total.)

Of course, these rights are moral, not at present legal, but as often in the history of rights claims, the former can provide a basis for eventual political and sometimes ultimately legal claims. Indeed, Susan James has argued that even moral rights must be conceptually understood to require an "effective method of implementation," judgments about which will be "partly shaped by our moral beliefs about the urgency of the right in question."[23] This brings the AAP itself into focus. The AAP can be understood as a moral insistence that all affected have a right to be heard, implying a procedure – whether actual or counterfactual – that is capable of reaching some conclusive outcome such that the right to be heard can be brought to bear in relation to some decision or outcome. As the right to a fair share of the global commons has never been implemented and its absence is having dire consequences for many, especially in the Global South, the impetus to develop a version of the AAP that can inform a moral procedure and ultimately a legal or political one (however imperfectly on each level) is considerable.[24]

Such a procedure would ideally include the summoning of all affected in some form (whether as a thought experiment, or through some institutional means, the possible implementation of each of which is discussed below) in order to redress the balance of so-called property rights through mechanisms of compensation as well as mitigation and support for adaptation. Carbon footprint calculations can help to establish broad divisions among those who are using up more than their fair share of the global carbon budget (the term in ancient Greek would be *pleonexia*, or greedily grasping more than one's fair share). This can establish the baseline for compensation, while institutional arrangements for forms of trusteeship (canvassed below) can help to forestall further such usurpation, drawing on the AAP's origins (or at least originating encapsulation) in the Roman law maxim that allows and enables some to speak on behalf of the moral claims of others.

Setting an end date in defining the global carbon budget has the further advantage that it can obviate some of the conceptual difficulties about future generations that otherwise arise when considering the ethics and politics of climate change and the AAP more generally. The AAP must always contend with the problem of whether "possible" people – including those whose very existence is contingent upon the decisions made to which the AAP is being applied – are relevant to its application, or whether only "actual" people in the actual world that materializes as a result are so relevant. While Robert E. Goodin's original reasons for construing the principle in terms of those who are "possibly affected" remain theoretically cogent, the imposition of an end date for the global carbon budget calculation helps to limit the scope of possibility, albeit without resolving the theoretical difficulties entirely.[25] Indeed, the need to consider an indefinitely long sequence of future generations, each composed (barring a catastrophe of human extinction or near-extinction) of very large numbers of people, is difficult more generally for consequentialist reasoning as for democratic theory.[26] Being able to posit that future generations beyond a certain point should not need any longer to emit carbon from burning fossil fuels, and should be able to drastically reduce their remaining emissions into balance with natural or artificially created carbon sinks, enables us to remove them from consideration of the All-Affected Principle in terms of the agency of those who will go on doing the affecting. They still remain, of course, in the pool of "all affected" by the ongoing effects that anthropogenic climate change, even if such change is eventually to be slowed or stopped, will have upon them. That brings me to the next section, on the AAP as a principle applied to moral rights against wrongful harm or the risk of such harm.

CLIMATE CHANGE AND THE AAP: THE CASE FOR MORAL RIGHTS AGAINST UNJUST HARM

As just discussed, unjust usurpation of moral "property rights" is one way of construing the morally salient way in which some agents "touch" or "affect" others by means of greenhouse gas emissions and so make the AAP potentially relevant to climate change. A more general explanation for the wrongs done by anthropogenic climate change – wrongs that will continue well beyond the date set for contributions to the global carbon budget – lies in the wrongful imposition of harm or the risk of harm. An agent (individual or collective, but I shall focus on the former here for simplicity) emits greenhouse gases or in some relevantly responsible way induces or acquiesces in their being emitted as a means, or side-effect, of pursuing the agent's ends. And these emissions contribute to the imposition of serious harm on others, when that harm could be avoided (either by reducing emissions, though not possible in all cases, or by providing compensation).[27]

By imposing this unnecessary and disproportionate harm, all those who emit – or more precisely, those who emit above a relevant fair threshold and without perfect compensatory offsetting, if such a thing is technically feasible to a sufficiently high epistemic standard – are contributing to a grave moral injustice against all those affected by their emissions. That is, against all present and future persons, all of them subject to the changing climate that emissions contribute to engendering, as well as, on some accounts, other constituents of the biosphere.[28] Not only are all present and future persons, and living (and indeed nonliving) natural entities, affected, but all past and present persons have contributed to some extent to affecting others in this way (even people in the far distant past emitted greenhouse gases in the course of living their lives, though their moral responsibility for having done so may be limited by fair-share as well as epistemic considerations). Carbon footprint analysis and sectoral studies, as well as country-level analyses, can help to distinguish those who are proportionately most responsible in generating emissions.

Here a number of problems have been flagged in the literature. One is whether what emissions impose is actual harm, or a "risk of harm." John Broome refers to the latter at one point,[29] but what he means by this is that "there is only the tiniest possibility that your emissions harm no one," presumably having in mind questions about thresholds or timing that he has discussed earlier. (He relies upon a continuous harm function and one to which all emissions potentially, and almost certainly actually, contribute, even if in infinitesimal amounts.) But one might wonder, first, whether emissions that are necessary for a certain standard of living (to be philosophically or politically determined) should count as doing harm at all, insofar as they do not cross an accepted threshold for interpersonal (and ideally reciprocal) interaction. And one might wonder, further, whether the risk involved should not be taken more seriously, in its potentially differential effects. Broome argues that even if one's emissions engender only "minuscule, imperceptible harms," nevertheless on a global scale "the amounts add up."[30] Here I pass over the controversy over whether so-called "imperceptible" or "negligible" harms can in fact be understood as contributing, causally or in some other relevant sense, to a significant collective harm, one that I have discussed elsewhere.[31] My interest at present, relative to the AAP, is in the differential effects of such contributions as well as their differential causes.

The key point is this: those affected will not all be affected *similiter*. On the contrary, the modifications in ecological conditions effected by climate change will (almost certainly) affect present and future people, and other constituents of the biosphere, in dramatically different ways and to significantly different extents, both because of the altered extent of exposure to hazardous changes and because of social as well as natural factors shaping differential vulnerabilities.[32] A few lucky people may find previously extreme climates become more temperate (though even they will also be affected by drastic climate-induced changes of various kinds); far more will see their livelihoods evaporate with parched fields, or their villages or countries inundated by rising sea levels (this was seen catastrophically in the flooding of Pakistan in the summer of 2022). And because the "patients" of the harm done will suffer its consequences in these very different ways and extents, the "agents" of the harm done must be treated as causing very different kinds and levels of harm to different patients. The generic contribution that a marginal emission of greenhouse gases makes to climate change (even if we posit that it is generically equal, which may not be the case, for example, if an aviation emission at altitude does more harm because of radioactive forcing than the same marginal emission would do emitted elsewhere) is not equivalent to a generic imposition of equal harm. Thus, to the broad division between rich and poor in causing climate change must be added the inverse vulnerability to suffering its effects.

To be sure, just how emissions link to harm is a matter of ongoing scientific debate and increasing capacity for precisification. While the causal link between greenhouse gas accumulation and global mean temperature is well established in basic science on the basis of observations, models, and historical records, the effects of an increase in global mean temperature on the complex systems that shape the biosphere and so result in increased risk of harm to many of its constituents (while also in some cases benefits to some) are far more complicated to trace. Scientists have in recent years made great progress in being able to conduct attribution studies that can quantify the increased risk of certain events occurring (extreme weather events, severity of hurricanes, and so on) as a result of the changed background conditions shaped by global warming (in its turn shaped crucially by anthropogenic greenhouse gas emissions). It is now possible to quantify how changes in climate (to which individual agents contribute) make certain effects (such as hurricanes) more likely, or more likely to be more destructive, and so to have expected greater levels of affectingness on individuals.[33] Studies also demonstrate how changes in climate, such as temperature rises, lead to differential likelihoods of individual and group actions such as conflict and violence.[34] In light of these studies, we can move beyond the individualized causal framework that has dominated philosophical debates about imperceptibility in assessing contributions to climate change, at least when seeking ways of thinking about "all affected" and "all affecting" rather than answering questions of individual moral responsibility.[35] Rather than seeking to individuate the likelihood of an individual emission causing, or contributing relevantly to, some harm to some specific other persons, we can explore other paradigms of affecting and affectedness. I shall canvass two: forms of tort liability on the one hand, and structural injustice that might be compared to racism and sexism (and other similar phenomena) on the other.

The tort liability paradigm can in some cases assess responsibility for causing a risk of harm to an entire community, even though that may not eventuate in a harm to a specific person. One might think of emitting greenhouse gases at least above a "necessary" threshold as like driving above the speed limit, knowing that by doing so one imposes the risk of harm on other drivers (and more problematically on pedestrians, cyclists, etc., as there the risk is not fully reciprocated). In such contexts, some have argued that public policy can and should, in assessing contributions to corrective justice, include those who have negligently or otherwise wrongly imposed risks of harm, even where those harms do not eventuate – for example, by setting up a fund for all motorists (or all caught on speed cameras, even if not ticketed) to contribute to compensation for those who are in the event harmed by car accidents. Catriona McKinnon has drawn this analogy in advocating a "corrective justice" approach to greenhouse gas emissions. As she suggests, adopting such an "ex ante view of responsibility" – in the way that some have argued should be done for tort liability – would provide "a justification for extracting resources for reparation from a liable agent (or her insurers) now even though those their actions put at risk exist in the distant future and, indeed, even if many of those distant strangers are never in fact harmed by the action."[36]

The tort liability paradigm, however, does not break with the individualizing paradigm of harm on which harms are still generally treated as assignable to discrete persons as both agents and patients, even if the risk of harm affected a class of persons generally before its materialization as an actual harm. An alternative paradigm could seek to model the harms posed by climate change as akin to contributions to structural injustices such as racism, sexism, and other forms of domination. One reason to consider climate change to be "structural injustice" is that it is hard to separate the "affecters" from the "affected": very many people are doing the affecting, though some much more extensively and culpably than others, and everyone now or in the future alive (as well as other beings and the earth itself) is in the group of those affected, though again not necessarily *similiter*, given the ways in which exposure and vulnerability are seamed and structured by political, social, and economic inequalities. And this means, further, that there are no clear lines from the actions of one individual or discrete group to the harm suffered by another, an ambiguity that is further heightened by the complexities of climate science itself, in terms of the multiple and sometimes countervailing effects that increased concentrations of greenhouse gases have on various aspects of the dynamics of the climate system. Instead, the actions of the affecters collectively constitute conditions that make harm likelier without making it individually predictable or assignable (even if group-level probabilistic predictions may be feasible).

To be sure, contributions to greenhouse gas emissions are not exactly like contributions to sustaining racism and sexism. It is beyond the scope of this chapter to provide a full analysis of the similarities and differences; instead I will simply point to some commonalities. One is that in all these contexts, actions that might be *prima facie* (or "facially": on their face) innocent and legitimate can instead have unjust effects, harming distinct individuals but also further embedding unjust domination into the social and sometimes physical fabric of society. As Luke Cole and Caroline Farrell have argued, in an article that both compares and links pollution and racism, because "racism ... is ... structural ... [f]acially neutral decisions" can reinforce it, as when business owners choose the site of a polluting factory based on the criteria of "appropriate zoning, access to transportation, and cheap land."[37] Other work on the production and reproduction of identities, including identities shaped by domination, suggests that people tell, institutionalize, and objectify (build into the material civic fabric) the stories that construct these identities.[38] Others still suggest that it is our "habits" that shore up oppression and inequality, as for example the "racial habits" that shore up racism.[39] In these cases, it would be both impossible and unnecessary to try to individuate a discrete harm or causal chain – from one person's facially neutral decisions; telling, institutionalizing, or objectifying of stories; or racial habits – to a specific measurable harm suffered by another who is affected by those actions or dispositions.

In structural cases, people contribute to harm by playing a role in the social constitution of conditions and dispositions that make it likely or effect it. Neither insiders nor outsiders can penetrate or dissolve that social web to identify either the harm caused by individual agents or that suffered by individual patients, much less to link them directly. Nevertheless, one might be able to attempt "attribution studies" of a similar kind in the social sphere to those now being pursued in climate science. Do increases in background expressions or toleration of racist attitudes, for example, create a climate in which acts of racist hatred and racially motivated violence become measurably more likely? If so, one could establish varying levels of responsibility, from that of individual perpetrators of specific acts, to that of those who more actively facilitate the formation of structural conditions, to that of all people who serve as contributors by tolerating the continued existence of those conditions and failing to intervene actively to attempt to change them.[40] The same kind of broad scale of responsibility can be applied to the harms caused or risked by climate change. Those who contribute to its background conditions – especially and disproportionately those who are on a global scale relatively wealthy, measured both as individuals and also as countries (though the latter requires further analysis of the distribution of responsibility internally) – are responsible in one way. Those who more actively facilitate the formation of structural conditions, such as by promoting the continuation rather than the phasing out of especially polluting industries, are responsible in another way. There may be relatively few equivalents in the domain of climate change to the individually identifiable perpetrators of individual racist or sexist acts. But that only means that the responsibility of the contributors and facilitators is all the more urgent to address.

CLIMATE CHANGE AND THE AAP: PROCEDURAL AND INSTITUTIONAL ARRANGEMENTS

I have argued so far that the AAP can embody procedural recognition, at least morally speaking, of those who have preexisting moral claims, whether analogous to property rights (in the moral domain), or against being subjected to wrongful harm or the risk of harm. Yet as observed earlier, even in the original development and application of the maxim *quod omnes tangit*, the entitlement of all affected (or touched) to give their consent to the proposal in question had to be modified in the medieval period's more expansive applications of it to allow for procedural closure. Bracton, as was noted above, dropped the call for all touched to consent, instead calling only for them to be summoned – giving them the presumptive opportunity to be heard, but depriving them of an effective veto should they fail or refuse to respond to that opportunity. That turned the maxim in judicial contexts into something closer to a compulsory consideration of potentially affected interests and rights in the context of a conclusive procedure. In other words, it gave those affected the opportunity to exercise their voice, but not the opportunity to exercise a veto at their discretion (as the original Roman guardianship cases may have envisaged, though even there the need for procedural closure was significant).

In the context of climate change, such a move would suggest the institutionalization of procedures enabling the compulsory consideration of all potentially affected interests and rights, within the relevant domain (so bounded by an end date for the "property rights" of the global carbon budget, but extending indefinitely into the future for the risks of harm). A number of institutional mechanisms have been canvassed in the literature for such purposes. Some of these would introduce the voice of otherwise unrepresented parties into present-day proceedings by means of representation. For example, the model of ombudspersons appointed in democratic assemblies to represent the interests of nonhumans, distant humans, or future humans is potentially promising. We might also take a leaf out of Bracton's focus on judicial settings to think about the potential for guardian ad litem positions, modelled on those "appointed as an 'arm of the court' to protect children who are unable, because of age or other incapacity, adequately to express their wishes," though in this case those being protected would not necessarily be minors.[41] Indeed, as noted earlier, a Roman law in the context of which the *quod omnes tangit* maxim was articulated involved the several guardians (*tutores*) of a single ward. Empowering some to speak on behalf of the moral rights of others, who would otherwise go unheard, would be broadly in keeping with the spirit of the original maxim and its historical evolution (even though in that law it was the rights of all the guardians to be heard that was in question).

Another institutional route would be to protect the moral claims to "property rights" in the global commons of the carbon budget, in the form of actual commons trusts.[42] Such trusts have been canvassed elsewhere in environmental law. Issuing "shares" in the carbon budget whose use would require the consent of the trust would be akin to cap and trade mechanisms, but could operate at a more dramatic and symbolic level of global politics. More broadly, the idea of trusteeship for future generations – both for their own capacities and institutions for democratic self-governance, as argued by Dennis F. Thompson, and perhaps also more broadly for their environmental capacities and institutions, political as well as ecosystem-related – again seems a natural extension of the original context of guardians at stake in the *quod omnes tangit* maxim.[43]

CONCLUSION

Whatever institutional arrangements are pursued for particular purposes will carve up the world of interactions in a particular way. Models of affectingness and affectedness are always shaped by judgments of salience, within the scope of existing knowledge, and must also allow for closure if they are to be institutionally and even, in many cases, morally relevant. It behooves those concerned with climate change to broaden the horizon of the AAP to include the intricate patterns of interaction, inequality, dependence, expectation, and "normality" within which the effects of climate change are shaped, and also to seek institutional and theoretical mechanisms that can impose principled closure on those patterns relevant for specific purposes.

At the same time, in light of the grave failure of national and international institutions so far to rise fully to the challenges of mitigation and adaptation on the existential scale that is urgent, the lack of a veto to accompany the voice granted by the AAP is of increasing concern. As Pakistan Senator Mustafa Nawaz Khokhar wrote in the *Guardian* about the catastrophic climate change-induced flooding of 2022, "Pakistan contributes less than 1% in global emissions and yet it is one of the countries most at risk due to climate change and global heating ... We're now living through a crisis that wasn't of our making."[44] Being guided by the original uses, contexts, and variations of the Roman law maxim *quod omnes tangit* may open the door to a richer, more variegated, and more objectively discernible horizon of understanding the AAP – who is affecting whom, and what follows from that – when it comes to climate change. Yet as with all matters to do with the ethics and politics of the AAP and climate change alike, there are no easy ways out.

NOTES

* I am grateful to Susan Brison for encouraging me to think about harm in relation to climate change on the model of structural injustice and domination; Colleen O'Gorman for her thinking and research on contributions to the structural injustice of domination in the context of sexual assault; Anastasia Repouliou, Emily Salamanca, and Ian Walling for research assistance supported by Princeton University; Wolfgang Ernst, during my stay at All Souls College in Hilary 2018, for stimulating discussions of the *quod omnes tangit* principle and for sharing his expertise and research in Roman law; Dennis Thompson and Melissa Williams for their thoughtful comments on earlier drafts of this chapter at the Harvard AAP workshop, and all the participants therein; the helpful work of the editorial team, variously including Danielle Allen, Archon Fung, Sean Gray, and Tomer Perry; Steve Pacala for inviting me to co-teach the Environmental Nexus course in Spring 2017 with him, Marc Fleurbaey, and Rob Nixon, as well as Ian Campbell for superb teaching assistance that extended to intellectual camaraderie about these questions; and the Climate Futures Initiative at Princeton University, which I currently co-convene with Rob Socolow, and which has been supported over time by Princeton University's High Meadows Environmental Institute, Andlinger Center for Energy and the Environment, Princeton Institute for International and Regional Studies, and University Center for Human Values, for providing a fruitful context for this strand of my research.

1 For example, Christian List and Mathias Koenig-Archibugi cite it in the form *quod omnes tangit ab omnibus approbetur*, as famously used by Edward I (see footnote

following herein); Johan Karlsson Schaffer cites it in the form *quod omnibus tangit, ab omnibus tractari et approbari debet,* used *inter alia* by Innocent III and Boniface VIII. See Christian List and Mathias Koenig-Archibugi, "Can There Be a Global Demos? An Agency-Based Approach," *Philosophy and Public Affairs* 38 (2010): 76–110, at 81 n.12. The Roman law origins are noticed by others, including Johan Karlsson Schaffer, "The Boundaries of Transnational Democracy: Alternatives to the All-affected Principle," *Review of International Studies* 38 (2012): 321–42, at 323.

2 C. 5, LIX, 5, 2, cited from the Latin and English in *The Codex of Justinian: A New Annotated Translation, with Parallel Latin and Greek Text,* based on a translation by Justice Fred H. Blume, general editor Bruce W. Frier, 3 vols. (Cambridge: Cambridge University Press, 2016), vol. 2, pp. 1358–9. See also the older edition of the Paulus Krueger, ed., *Corpus Iuris Civilis,* 11th ed. (Berolini [Berlin]: apud Weidmannos [Weidmann], 1954), 3 vols, vol. 2 [*Codex Iustinianus*], p. 231. The passage is cited in Yves M.-J. Congar, "Quod omnibus tangit, ab omnibus tractari et approbari debet," *Revue historique de droit français et étranger* 35 (1958): 210–59, at pp. 210–11. It is worth noting that in the previous section (C. 5, LIX, 5, pr.) the law had laid down that "the authorization even of one tutor shall be sufficient for all *tutores,* where the management is not divided according to geographical area or portions of the estate," contrary to previous practice for certain kinds of tutorial appointments (1356–7). So the case of terminating the guardianship is an exception to a more general rule which did, in some cases, allow one *tutor* to act in a way that bound others.

3 Jürgen Habermas, *Between Facts and Norms: Contributions to a Discourse Theory of Law and Democracy,* trans. William Rehg, 2nd ed. (Cambridge, MA: MIT Press, 1996), Postscript n.11, at pp. 565–6. Habermas cites Niklas Luhmann,"Quod omnes tangit … Anmerkungen zur Rechtstheorie von Jürgen Habermas," *Rechtshistorisches Journal* 12 (1993): 36–56.

4 Daniel Lee, *Popular Sovereignty in Early Modern Constitutional Thought* (Oxford: Oxford University Press, 2016).

5 Gaines Post, "A Romano-Canonical Maxim, *Quod Omnes Tangit,* in Bracton and in Early Parliaments," in *Post, Studies in Medieval Legal Thought: Public Law and the State, 1100–1322* (Princeton: Princeton University Press, 1964), pp. 163–238, at 217.

6 Ulpian, D. XXXIX, 3, 8, cited by Congar, "Quod omnibus tangit," p. 211; the Latin can be found in Iustinianus, *Digesta Iustiniani,* available at http://latin.packhum .org/loc/2806/2/0#261, last accessed September 24, 2023, or in the *Corpus Iuris Civilis,* 16th ed. (Berolini [Berlin]: apud Weidmannos [Weidmann], 1954), 3 vols, vol. 1 [*Institutiones* and *Digesta,* the latter ed. Theodor Mommsen and rev. Paulus Krueger], p. 647.

7 Post, "A Romano-Canonical Maxim, *Quod Omnes Tangit,* in Bracton and in Early Parliaments," p. 170.

8 Post, "A Romano-Canonical Maxim, *Quod Omnes Tangit,* in Bracton and in Early Parliaments," p. 205.

9 Post, "A Romano-Canonical Maxim, *Quod Omnes Tangit,* in Bracton and in Early Parliaments," p. 171.

10 This point is made both about *quod omnes tangit* as a Roman law maxim which makes a demand for a certain kind of unanimity or consensus, but not an absolute one, and more generally about Roman and medieval appeals to the *maior pars*

as a decision procedure, by Wolfgang Ernst, "Maior pars – Mehrheitsdenken in der römischen Rechtskultur," *Zeitschrift der Savigny-Stiftung für Rechtsgeschichte (Romanistische Abteilung)* 132 (2015): 1–67, at 54–5.

11 Post, "A Romano-Canonical Maxim, *Quod Omnes Tangit*, in Bracton and in Early Parliaments," p. 223. As Post observes there, Edward I in one famous intervention preferred the formulation *quod omnes tangit ab omnibus approbetur;* this is functionally nearly identical to *ab omnibus comprobetur.*

12 In doing so, Post observes ("A Romano-Canonical Maxim, *Quod Omnes Tangit*, in Bracton and in Early Parliaments," p. 223), he was "probably influenced by the decretalists, who frequently stated the principle of procedural consent in such words as *omnes quos causa tangit vocandi sunt* ['all those whom the case touches must be summoned', as glossed by Post elsewhere in the same volume, at 172] and referred to Justinian without saying *ab omnibus comprobetur.*"

13 Post, "A Romano-Canonical Maxim, *Quod Omnes Tangit*, in Bracton and in Early Parliaments," p. 223.

14 One such critique is advanced by Minh Ly, "A Human Right to Deliberative Justification," *Journal of Politics* 80, no. 4 (2018): 1355–68, who argues that "It is not enough for people to be merely consulted or given the chance to offer feedback on a policy that cannot be changed. Consultative mechanisms ... are insufficient. Instead, people must be able to challenge policies in a way that leads to human rights violations [the specific rights on which he focuses] being prevented or stopped" (p. 1356).

15 The idea of common atmospheric ownership and equal emissions entitlements is explored and defended, albeit as being most cogently based on libertarian as opposed to egalitarian presuppositions, by Darrel Moellendorf, "Common Atmospheric Ownership and Equal Emissions Entitlements," in *The Ethics of Global Climate Change*, ed. Denis G. Arnold (Cambridge: Cambridge University Press, 2011), pp. 104–23. Moellendorf is responding to a critique of the idea by Simon Caney expressed *inter alia* in "Climate Change, Energy Rights, and Equality," pp. 77–103 in the same volume. In this contribution I limit myself to proposing how the AAP could make sense on the basis of a global atmospheric commons view, without being able here to defend such a view in full.

16 I am indebted to Stephen Pacala's lectures in an undergraduate course that we co-taught (with Marc Fleurbaey and Rob Nixon) at Princeton University in Spring 2017 (ENV 200: The Environmental Nexus), for the broad outlines and specific references to the science in relation to the carbon budget and, below, to attribution studies.

17 It should however be noted that there are rich people in poor countries for whom any institutional solution based in theory on a per capita basis should ideally account. See S. Chakravarty, H. de Conink, S. Pacala, R. Socolow, and M. Tavoni, "Sharing Global CO_2 Emission Reductions among One Billion High Emitters," *Proceedings of National Academy of Science* 106, no. 29 (2009): 11884–8, for discussion of which I am grateful to Rob Socolow.

18 In the five years between the first drafting of this chapter in fall 2017 and its commitment to press in fall 2022, the proposal considered in the original draft of a closing window of 2100, has already come to appear implausibly late.

19 SBC Energy Institute, 2015, in order to achieve the Paris Agreement path of warming (one of the RCP paths from IPCC AR5) that would be likely to keep warming

less than 2°C and have atmospheric CO_2 accumulation not increasing after midcentury [2050].

20 Stephane Hallegatte et al., *Shock Waves: Managing the Impacts of Climate Change on Poverty* (Washington, DC: World Bank, 2016), p. 193.

21 Corinne Le Quéré et al., "Global Carbon Budget 2017," *Earth System Science Data Discussions* 10 (2018): 405–48, at 426 (Figure 5): https://doi.org/10.5194/essd-10-405-2018 (last accessed September 24, 2023).

22 Hallegatte et al., *Shock Waves*.

23 Susan James, "Rights as Enforceable Claims," *Proceedings of the Aristotelian Society* 103 (2003): 133–47, at 136, 138 respectively.

24 Again, some, such as Minh Ly (cited above, n. 14), would contend that the AAP route of giving a hearing and a voice, but not a veto (or even the procedural potential to argue for a veto), is inadequate.

25 Robert E. Goodin, "Enfranchising All Affected Interests, and Its Alternatives," *Philosophy and Public Affairs* 35, no. 1 (2007): 40–68, argues that the "actually affected" interpretation of the principle must be rejected as it engenders "incoherence" (p. 52). Archon Fung distinguishes "two related but distinct potential difficulties here: endogeneity and indeterminacy," but argues that these difficulties can be ameliorated by taking the principle as "a regulative principle for continuously adjusting the boundaries of inclusion" through political processes: see Archon Fung, "The Principle of Affected Interests: An Interpretation and Defense," in *Representation: Elections and Beyond*, ed. Rogers M. Smith and Jack H. Nagel (Philadelphia: University of Pennsylvania Press, 2013), at 247 and 248 respectively.

26 For an argument that a Rawlsian approach can do better than deliberative democracy in taking account of future generations, see Clare Heyward, "Can the All-Affected Principle Include Future Persons? Green Deliberative Democracy and the Non-Identity Problem," *Environmental Politics* 17 (2008): 625–43. For a more general defense of both the possibility and the moral imperative of considering future people in an open-ended way, see William MacAskill, *What We Owe the Future* (New York: Hachette Press, 2022).

27 For a survey of seven factors that support the thought that greenhouse gas emissions unjustly cause harm – roughly, that these emissions as done by most people in the rich world are actions (not omissions), and that the harm they do is serious, not accidental, generally uncompensated, done for one's own benefit, not fully reciprocal between the global rich and the global poor, and could easily be reduced – see John Broome, *Climate Matters: Ethics in a Warming World* (New York and London: W.W. Norton and Company, 2012), pp. 55–9.

28 For the case of animals, see Pablo Magaña, "Nonhuman Animals and the All Affected Interests Principle," *Critical Review of International Social and Political Philosophy* first published online (July 15, 2022): https://doi.org/10.1080/1369823 0.2022.2100962.

29 Broome, *Climate Matters*, p. 79.

30 Broome, *Climate Matters*, pp. 75, 76.

31 Melissa Lane, *Eco-Republic: What the Ancients Can Teach Us about Ethics, Virtue, and Sustainable Living* (Princeton: Princeton University Press, 2012), pp. 66–9 and *passim*; Melissa Lane, "Uncertainty, Action, and Politics: The Problem of Negligibility," in *Nature, Action and the Future: Political Thought and the Environment*, ed. Katrina Forrester and Sophie Smith (Cambridge: Cambridge

University Press, 2018), pp. 157–79. My contentions have been criticized by Ewan Kingston, and Walter Sinnott-Armstrong in "What's Wrong with Joyguzzling?" *Ethical Theory and Moral Practice* 21, no. 1 (2018): 169–86; I had originally targeted them in part against Walter Sinnott-Armstrong, "It's Not My Fault: Global Warming and Individual Moral Obligations," in *Perspectives on Climate Change: Science, Economics, Politics, Ethics*, ed. Walter Sinnott-Armstrong and Richard B. Howarth (Amsterdam et al: Elsevier, 2005), pp. 285–307. I am grateful to Ewan Kingston, as well as Richard Tuck, for discussion of these points.

32 The distinction between exposure and vulnerability is central to environmental disaster research. For an application within the United States, see Eric Tate et al, "Flood Exposure and Social Vulnerability in the United States," *Natural Hazards* 106, no.1 (2021): 435–57. I am grateful to Michael Oppenheimer for helping me to appreciate this distinction.

33 Friederike E. L. Otto, Geert Jan van Oldenborgh, Jonathan Eden, Peter A. Stott, David J. Karoly, and Myles R. Allen, "The Attribution Question," *Nature Climate Change* 6, no. 9 (September 2016): 813–16. https://doi.org/10.1038/nclimate3089. They write: "Scientists can now provide reliable answers to the question of whether anthropogenic climate change has altered the probability of occurrence of classes of individual extreme weather events, which often is a relevant question. The emergence of a set of complementary approaches deepens our confidence in these results and paves the way to provide robust answers to questions from stakeholders and the public in the immediate aftermath of an extreme weather event. When communicating these results, it is important to clearly state the probabilistic framing of the attribution question, how the event is defined and the level of confidence in the findings based on physical understanding. If the attribution question is being asked to provide guidance from the present on what the future may hold, in general approaches accounting for the full change in probability provide useful answers" (p. 816).

34 See generally T.A. Carleton and S.M. Hsiang, "Social and Economic Impacts of Climate," *Science* 353, no. 6304 (2016): https://doi.org/10.1126/science.aad9837, and as illustration, R.P. Larrick et al., "Temper, Temperature, and Temptation: Heat-Related Retaliation in Baseball," *Psychological Science* 22 (2011): 423–8.

35 There is a large literature on what I called in *Eco-Republic* the problem of negligibility, in relation to causation and in particular in relation to climate change, my own contributions to which are cited above. See more generally Derek Parfit, *Reasons and Persons* (Oxford: Clarendon Press, 1984), pp. 67–86, who was building on an earlier article by Jonathan Glover, "It Makes No Difference Whether or Not I Do It," *Proceedings of the Aristotelian Society, Supplementary Volumes* 49 (1975): 171–209; Shelly Kagan, "Do I Make a Difference?," *Philosophy & Public Affairs* 39, no. 2 (2011): 105–41; and for a commentary on Kagan focusing primarily on the understanding of "imperceptibility," Julia Nefsky, "Consequentialism and the Problem of Collective Harm: A Reply to Kagan," *Philosophy & Public Affairs* 39, no. 4 (2011): 364–95.

36 Catriona McKinnon, "Climate Change and Corrective Justice," *Jahrbuch für Recht und Ethik / Annual Review of Law and Ethics* 17 (2009): 259–75, at 266.

37 Luke W. Cole and Caroline Farrell, "Structural Racism, Structural Pollution and the Need for a New Paradigm Poverty, Justice, and Community Lawyering: Interdisciplinary and Clinical Perspectives," *Washington University Journal of Law & Policy* 20 (2006): 265–82, at 277.

38 Clarissa Rile Hayward, *How Americans Make Race: Stories, Institutions, Spaces* (Cambridge: Cambridge University Press, 2013), p. 2.

39 Eddie S. Glaude, Jr., *Democracy in Black: How Race Still Enslaves the American Soul* (New York: Crown/Archetype, 2016).

40 For the distinction between perpetrators, facilitators, and contributors, I am indebted to the work of Colleen O'Gorman, *Lessons from Emily Doe: A Survivor-Centric Approach to Sexual Assault,* a thesis presented to the Department of Politics, Princeton University, in partial fulfillment of the requirements for the degree of Bachelor of Arts, April 4, 2017.

41 Linda Gunsberg and Paul Hymowitz, *A Handbook of Divorce and Custody: Forensic, Developmental, and Clinical Perspectives* (Hillsdale, NJ: The Analytic Press, 2005), p. 22.

42 See the general discussion of commons trusts in environmental management, with further references to studies in environmental law, in Alex Zakaras, "Democracy, Children, and the Environment: A Case for Commons Trusts," *Critical Review of International Social and Political Philosophy* 19 (2016): 141–62.

43 See Dennis F. Thompson, "Representing Future Generations: Political Presentism and Democratic Trusteeship," *Critical Review of International Social and Political Philosophy* 13, no. 1 (2010): 17–37.

44 Mustafa Nawaz Khokhar, "Rich Countries Caused Pakistan's Catastrophic Flooding. Their Response? Inertia and Apathy," *The Guardian*, September 5, 2022: www.theguardian.com/commentisfree/2022/sep/05/rich-countries-pakistan-flooding-climate-crisis-cop27; his summary final sentence compresses the interaction of exposure and vulnerability, and the multiple determinates of each.

PART IV

AUTONOMY, AFFECTEDNESS, AND ASSOCIATIONS

13

Cities, Structural Power, and the All-Affected Principle

Clarissa Rile Hayward

"People should have a hand, and they should have an equal hand, in shaping the collective norms that significantly affect them." This statement of the All-Affected Principle (AAP) is a rough one, and deliberately so. Scholars who work on the AAP disagree about not just the principle's validity, but also the sense in which the relevant affecting might be significant, and the most appropriate way to cash out the multivalent ideal of political equality. In this chapter, although I touch on these issues, my principal focus is the notion of "shaping ... collective norms." My central claim is that those who would apply the AAP should articulate it in a way that is attentive to structural power. Doing so requires a focus on not decisions, but power relations. It directs attention to not just the definition of political boundaries and the allocation of votes, but more generally the conditions that enable and constrain multiple forms of political action.

The chapter proceeds in three parts. In the first, I sketch a series of familiar critiques of the AAP (that it threatens freedom of association, political identification, and collective self-determination) and introduce a case (public school desegregation in the contemporary American metropolis) for which these concerns are minimized. Here my aim is to introduce a new critique: to show that the AAP is largely inattentive to structural power. In the second section, I develop that critique. I make the case that people can be significantly affected not only by the decisions that other people make, but also by structural constraints, which are defined by institutionalized and objectified collective norms. In the third section, I suggest that those who would apply the AAP should focus not exclusively on decisions, but more broadly on relations of power, because people can be significantly affected by nondecisions, by doxic norms, and by positioning in systemic relations of domination. My argument recommends a reformulation of the AAP, one that broadens it, even if at the cost of rendering it less realizable: *People should have an adequate and equal social capacity to shape the power relations that delimit their fields of possible action.*

THE AAP AND LOCAL POLITICAL BOUNDARIES

In its standard formulation, the All-Affected Principle identifies those agents who should be included in democratic processes; it is a normative principle that explains how to draw political boundaries, and how to allocate votes.[1] The AAP is often interpreted as supporting forms of transnational democratization that are radically at odds with the geopolitical status quo.[2] In addition, some proponents of the principle recommend applying it to domains where democratic rights typically are not protected, such as workplaces, civic associations, families, and other economic and social institutions.[3] That the AAP pushes us to interrogate settled beliefs about democracy's confines is among its strengths. The world we inhabit is characterized by profound cross-national interdependencies. Relations of power – by which I mean relations among social actors who have the capacity to shape one another's fields of possible action[4] – do not stop at the political boundaries that define nation-states. Instead, actions taken in one political society often significantly affect people who live outside its borders, as well as nonmembers who reside within. Hence putatively democratic institutions and practices that base political rights on citizenship-as-membership can have anti-democratic implications.

The AAP decenters membership. It pushes against the logic of citizenship as the basis for rights, especially rights of political participation, challenging what Linda Bosniak calls the "normative nationalism" that often informs (and often only *implicitly* informs) democratic theory – the assumption, that is, that "the territorial nation-state is the rightful, if not the total world of … normative concern."[5] The inclusion of all affected can require unbundling the rights and privileges attached to membership in a territorially based political society and linking them to multiple, overlapping regimes of governance – regimes that traverse the boundaries that delimit political communities. What is more, because power relations not only cross political borders, but also exceed formal institutions of governance, they are not contained by the boundaries that divide public from private, and state from society and economy. If people should have a hand in shaping the collective norms that affect them – rather than only the laws and the policies to which governments subject them – then democrats must think creatively about procedural and institutional mechanisms that give significantly affected persons political voice at home, at work, and in other social and economic realms that are not administered by states.

Its intuitive appeal notwithstanding, the AAP has been challenged by critics who find it problematic for at least three analytically distinct reasons. First, some worry that if the principle recommends democratization across political boundaries and within nonpolitical associations, then it conflicts with the right to freedom of association.[6] Just as no one but me should help decide whether I marry and, if so, whom (the argument goes), so no one but "us" – the members of our political society, or our association – should help decide where we draw our boundaries and what we do within them. Much like the institution of arranged marriage, these critics charge, the AAP violates the right *not* to associate with particular others, including others (like the potential partners I choose not to marry, or the would-be members our association does not admit) who are significantly affected by the exercise of that right.

Critics worry, second, that applying the AAP might undermine people's capacities to identify with a political society or with another cooperative association. Within this group of critics, some see identification as instrumentally valuable. David Miller, for example, claims it is critical for motivating people to participate in cooperative schemes that involve self-sacrifice.[7] Others view it as intrinsically valuable – a process that enriches people's lives by defining what Michael Walzer calls "communities of character," that is, "historically stable, ongoing associations of men and women with some special commitment to one another and some special sense of their common life."[8] Political identification need not be rooted in ethically thick understandings of who "we" are; instead, it can be rooted in constitutional principles, including principles of constitutional democracy.[9] In any case, the concern is that if others outside our collectivity have a say in what we decide and how we act, they can alter the very practices, values, and principles according to which we define our shared identity. They can change *who we are*, jeopardizing our capacity to identify with our political society, or with the other associations through which we "[pursue] in common the objects of common desires."[10]

The third concern derives from the first and second. Some worry that the AAP extends democracy's reach at the cost of undermining what is arguably *the* core democratic value: collective autonomy. For people to author the laws and the other norms with which they govern themselves, they need boundaries within which they can decide those norms, absent outside interference. In addition, they need to identify politically – to experience themselves as part of a "we" for the sake of which they are willing to "moderate their [self-interested] claims in the hope of finding common ground on which to base political decisions."[11] Absent such identification, the worry is, "rule by the people" may devolve into the coercion of the minority by the majority – a form of government under which citizens do not experience themselves as having authored any collective decisions except those they explicitly endorsed.

For these (as well as for other, more pragmatic) reasons, some critics of the AAP suggest that affectedness should trigger not the right to *participate* in political decision making, but merely the right to have decision makers afford one's interests consideration. People may have duties to those whom their decisions affect, the idea is, but they can discharge those duties without granting votes to outsiders, and without opening the borders that delimit their communities and define their associations. Thus, Kit Wellman writes that he is "inclined to agree that the emerging global infrastructure entails that virtually all of us have increasingly substantial relationships with people all over the world," but emphasizes that people can discharge their "duties to those outside of [their] borders … without necessarily allowing those to whom [they] are duty bound entry to [their] country" or political voice.[12]

I return to these critiques near the end of this chapter. But for the greater part of it, I bracket them, because my principal aim is to introduce a separate concern about the AAP: its inattention to structural power. As a first step toward explicating this problem, I want to introduce a case for which worries about threats to freedom of association, communal identification, and collective autonomy are minimal, because the power relations involved are subnational, rather than transnational, and situated within not a private association, but a nearly universally agreed-upon sphere of democratic governance. The case is that of school desegregation in the post-Civil Rights era United States.

Perhaps the best place to start is with the famous 1974 US Supreme Court case, *Milliken v. Bradley*, which addressed a proposed interdistrict school desegregation plan in metropolitan Detroit. The key point to note with respect to this case is that, had the desegregation program at issue been implemented, it would have crossed political – in this case, school district – boundaries. The Detroit Board of Education had proposed the plan two years prior, in response to an order by the US District Court for the Eastern District of Michigan, which had argued that, by that point in the city's history, only plans that included suburban districts could be effective in desegregating Detroit's schools. The District Court had ruled, and the Sixth Circuit Court of Appeals had affirmed, that desegregation plans need not respect local school district boundaries, since those jurisdictions are no more than "instrumentalities of the state created for administrative convenience."[13] In other words, school districts are quite unlike Walzer's "communities of character." It seems uncontroversial to claim they are not crucial sites of either political identification or collective self-determination. Although Americans identify politically, and they practice collective self-government, in local communities like townships and municipalities, as well as at the level of the nation-state, this is significantly less the case in single-function administrative units like school districts.

Nevertheless, the US Supreme Court disagreed with the lower courts. Writing for the majority, Chief Justice Warren Burger expressed concerns that interdistrict desegregation would undermine collective autonomy by entitling citizens who live in one district to vote in school board elections in another. In a lengthy series of rhetorical questions, he asked, in part:

[Were the inter-district plan to be adopted, w]hat would be the status and authority of the present popularly elected school boards? Would the children of Detroit be within the jurisdiction and operating control of a school board elected by the parents and residents of other districts? … Who would construct attendance zones, purchase school equipment, locate and construct new schools, and indeed attend to all the myriad day-to-day decisions that are necessary to school operations affecting potentially more than three-quarters of a million pupils?[14]

Local control over the educational process" the Chief Justice underscored, "affords citizens an opportunity to participate in decision-making.[15]

I quote this passage at length because the anxieties to which Chief Justice Burger gives voice – not only his practical worries about implementing cross-jurisdictional governance, but also his normative concern about detaching democratic rights from extant political jurisdictions – mirror those of many critics of the AAP. However, in the context of American urban politics, these anxieties are curious. Surely the state of Michigan could centralize to the metropolitan level, or to some intermediate unit of government between the local school district and metropolitan Detroit, both electoral control over public school officials and collective decision making about attendance zones, educational equipment, infrastructure, and the like. People can and do form bounded political communities, they can and do identify politically, and they can and do exercise collective autonomy at levels of government considerably more centralized than local public school districts. The normative claim that an interdistrict desegregation plan would undermine collective autonomy is dubious.

Yet it is also revealing. The parallel between Burger's worries and those of many critics of the AAP suggests that part of what some find jarring about the principle may be simply that it problematizes jurisdictional boundaries that are taken for granted, because they are relatively long-standing, because they are attached to physical spaces that are the sites of differential patterns of investment and disinvestment, and because (to borrow Charles Mill's language) they are "normed" to populations that are constructed as socially or culturally different.[16]

THE AAP AND STRUCTURAL POWER

Milliken v. Bradley reinscribed the jurisdictional boundaries at issue. In a decision that would hamstring efforts to desegregate American schools for decades to come, the Supreme Court reversed the lower court's judgment. It ruled that federally imposed desegregation plans cannot cross school district lines, except in those cases in which decisions made in one district are shown to have caused segregation in another, or in which it is proven that the district boundaries themselves were drawn with the intent to promote segregation. There is an obvious sense in which the ruling pushed against the logic of the All-Affected Principle. It reified extant political boundaries, asserting that democratic processes (here, the popular control of school boards through local elections) must be tied to territorially based political jurisdictions. At the same time, it implied, implausibly, that the status quo delineation of school district boundaries mapped onto and contained the effects of the "myriad day-to-day decisions" that regulate access to educational opportunity in metropolitan Detroit.

That said, there is a sense in which the majority decision was *not* at odds with the AAP, or at least with many influential formulations of that principle. The court emphasized not only limits to cross-jurisdictional responsibility for racial segregation and racial inequality in Detroit's schools, but also limits to responsibility for racial inequalities that are structurally induced. The majority underscored that "[t]he boundaries of the Detroit School District, which are coterminous with the boundaries of the city of Detroit, were established over a century ago by neutral legislation when the city was incorporated."[17] Justice Stewart, in a concurring opinion, stressed that Detroit and its public school system had become "predominantly Negro" due not to decisions that had been made by identifiable individual or collective agents, but instead to "unknown and perhaps unknowable factors such as in-migration, birth rates, economic changes, or cumulative acts of private racial fears."[18] On the majority's view, the focus of efforts to desegregate Detroit's schools should be the effects of clearly identifiable decisions. It should *not* be the effects of uncoordinated, large-scale social processes that interact in ways that are "unknown and perhaps unknowable."

Of course, the Court's aim in *Milliken* was not to apply the All-Affected Principle, it was to interpret and apply the principles of the US Constitution. Yet there is a slippage in the majority's reasoning that I want to suggest can be instructive for those who aim to specify the AAP in a way that enables its application: a mismatch between, on one hand, the goal of tying "significant affecting" to democratic control, and on the other, an exclusive focus on the explicit decisions that individual and collective agents make. In Detroit in the 1970s, "significant affecting" not only traversed the jurisdictional boundaries that defined local public school districts, it also exceeded the control of agents who were positioned to make decisions informed by the intent to discriminate. Racial segregation in late twentieth-century Detroit was produced and reproduced, in significant part, through the uncoordinated actions of multiple actors pursuing reasonable ends (parents seeking the best education possible for their children, for example, or elected officials acting to advance their constituents' interests) in a context of structural racial inequality.

As the Detroit case illustrates, people can be significantly affected by the interaction of large-scale structural processes, and yet it can be exceedingly difficult – at the limit, it may be impossible – to isolate the decisions that constitute those processes. If the ethic informing the AAP is a deeply democratic one, if the AAP urges that people should have a hand in shaping *all* the collective norms that significantly affect them, then the principle requires attention to structural power.

Let us define structural power as a network of collective norms that are, to varying degrees (1) institutionalized, (2) objectified, (3) internalized as motivational systems, and (4) embodied as what Pierre Bourdieu calls relatively enduring dispositions (*habitus*).

In order to clarify how structural power is relevant to the All-Affected Principle, I will expound briefly on each of these four ideas.[19]

1. When norms are *institutionalized*, they are built into rules, laws, and other institutional forms, which distribute rewards and sanctions that reinforce them. An example relevant to the case of twentieth-century

Detroit is the underwriting standards that were created by the US Federal Housing Administration (FHA) beginning in the mid-1930s. From that time, and for three decades after – a period during which the agency not only insured mortgages for a third of new housing in the nation, but also profoundly shaped the private mortgage insurance market – the FHA required that the estimate of a property's value reflect the presence in the surrounding area of what it called "Adverse Influences," which it defined to include "incompatible racial and social groups."[20]

2. When norms are *objectified,* they are built into material forms (or object forms) that people experience corporeally as they engage in practical activity. A case in point is racialized urban and suburban space in post-war Detroit. Consider, for instance, the suburb of Grosse Pointe, which borders the city and is headquarters to one of the fifty-three school districts involved in the proposed desegregation plan at issue in *Milliken.* As of the 2010 census, Grosse Pointe was 93 percent white, and just 3 percent black.[21] According to the nonprofit Edbuild, in 2016, the border between the Grosse Pointe and Detroit public school districts marked the single largest socioeconomic disparity between any two public school systems in the United States.[22] Grosse Pointe touts its public schools on its homepage, where it announces, in bold letters, "Excellence is our proud tradition!" It elaborates:

The City of Grosse Pointe is a community nestled along the shores of Lake St. Clair … a place where lovely homes grace tree-lined streets. Residents are afforded a scenic waterfront park with two outdoor swimming pools and a private marina. Our community takes pride in its excellent private and public schools. The City strives to offer an environment that is safe for both young and old.[23]

But *why* is Grosse Pointe "lovely," "scenic," and "safe"? Why is it home to "excellent" schools, while neighboring Detroit, with a poverty rate close to 50 percent, has a public school system that has been in a state of financial emergency since 2009? Because political decisions – like local decisions to zone to require large lots or to limit the construction of multi-family housing, as well as state and federal decisions to channel public investment toward suburban exclaves, and away from older cities – produce norms that become objectified in material form.

Think of the detached, single-family house or the "tree-lined street." Objectification depoliticizes. It makes "loveliness," "safety," and "excellence" appear to be qualities that emanate from physical forms, obscuring the collective decisions that produce political effects like the creation of the stark disparities between Grosse Pointe and neighboring Detroit.

3. When social norms are institutionalized, they define incentive structures that agents *internalize as motivational systems.* Imagine a white homebuyer who wanted a government-backed mortgage for a house in Detroit in the postwar years. To qualify, they would have had to buy in a racially

exclusive white enclave. In Detroit, as in other American cities, white buyers responded to this incentive by moving en masse to the housing developments that were built with generous federal subsidies in the new postwar suburbs. It is deeply misleading to depoliticize this phenomenon by psychologizing it: by characterizing it as "cumulative acts of private racial *fears*." It is equally misleading to privatize it: to characterize it as "cumulative acts of *private* racial fears." No doubt it is true that racist attitudes informed the decisions many individual whites made to exit from cities like Detroit. Yet, at the same time, "white flight" was the predictable result of the public subsidy of suburban home ownership in a dual housing market.

4. When social norms are objectified, they form the material context of people's practical activity. Hence, competent social actors master them implicitly. That is to say, they learn to conform to them, not just through conscious decisions, but also through a kind of practical know-how that powerfully supplements judgment and choice. Bourdieu characterizes such know-how as "a feel for the game." "Action guided by a 'feel for the game,'" he writes, "has all the appearance of the rational action that an impartial observer, endowed with all the necessary information and capable of mastering it rationally, would deduce." He continues:

> And yet, it is not based on reason. You need only think of the impulsive decision made by the tennis player who runs up to the net to understand that it has nothing in common with the learned construction that the coach, after analysis, draws up in order to explain it and deduce communicable lessons from it.[24]

Much like Bourdieu's tennis player, the contemporary resident of Grosse Pointe, Michigan can master the common sense of racial practice even if they do not endorse, even if they are never consciously aware of, the collective decisions that helped to create it.

TRACK POWER, NOT DECISIONS

A decision that is "neutral" in the sense in which Chief Justice Burger says the definition of school district boundaries was in nineteenth-century Detroit, when institutionalized and/or objectified, can interact with other social structures to shape large-scale processes (like the migration processes and the urban economic restructuring that Justice Stewart calls "unknown and perhaps unknowable"): processes that significantly affect what people can do and be. Those who are committed to the democratic principle that people should have a hand in shaping the collective norms that significantly affect them must subject institutionalized and objectified norms, along with social processes that produce systematic inequalities, to the same scrutiny to which we subject decisions. What would that entail? I want to suggest that articulating the AAP in a way that is attentive to structural power requires attending to not only decisions, but also (1) nondecisions, (2) doxic norms, and (3) systemic relations of domination.

Let me say something more about each of these ideas.

1. I borrow the term "nondecision" from the postwar literature on power's so-called "second face."[25] E. E. Schattschneider famously argued that "[s]ome issues are organized into politics while others are organized out."[26] However, what Schattschneider called the "mobilization of bias" is not simply a matter of agenda-control; it is not only in effect when agents make decisions that intentionally delimit the terms of political conflict. It is also a matter of the inertial force of institutionalized collective norms, and of the political interests that institutionalized norms construct.

   Think of the definition of public school district boundaries to coincide with the definition of municipal boundaries in mid-nineteenth-century Detroit. Over the course of the following century and a half, this institutional arrangement would interact with interregional migration and urban economic restructuring to incentivize "white flight" to Detroit's racially exclusive suburbs. Multiply that incentive by the fifty-three suburban districts that would have participated in the proposed school desegregation plan, and by the thousands of residents of each of those fifty-three districts, and you have a wide-ranging set of socially constructed racial interests, centered on home ownership, property values, and restricted access to well-funded, high-performing schools. Now it is not just decisions, but also nondecisions – *not* deciding to intervene to countervail the flight of jobs and capital from city to suburb, for example, or for that matter, *not* deciding to desegregate across school district boundaries – that significantly affects the residents of contemporary Detroit.

2. I borrow the term "doxa" from Bourdieu, who uses it to signify collective norms that function as background assumptions: taken-for-granted expectations about aspects of the social world that many people experience as natural or otherwise inevitable.[27] The idea is closely related to his notion of *habitus* (discussed above), since agents internalize doxic norms in the form of intersubjectively shared cognitive, perceptual, and affective dispositions, or what William Sewell calls "schemas."[28] Sally Haslanger writes that schemas "are embodied in individuals as a shared cluster of open-ended dispositions to see things a certain way or to respond habitually in particular circumstances." She elaborates: "Schemas encode knowledge and also provide scripts for interaction with each other and with our environment."[29]

   For an example of a doxic norm that people internalize as an intersubjectively shared schema, recall the jurisdictional boundary that divides Detroit from neighboring Grosse Pointe. The discussion in the previous section suggests that some people experience that boundary not as a socially produced norm that helps create and maintain inequality, but as a physical frontier that merely *reflects* (pre-political) differences between what is "lovely," "safe," and "excellent," and what is not.

3. Social structures that create patterned inequalities can position people in
   relations of systemic domination. They can do so, I want to underscore,
   even if no agent directs or controls them, and even if none intends the
   relevant outcomes. I use the word "systemic" to contrast my view with
   that of many contemporary neo-republicans, who understand nondomination as "resilient noninterference" – that is, as one agent's capacity
   to act without being subjected to the will of another.[30] On this view,
   although domination need not involve actual interference (it entails only
   the *possibility* of interference within some specified range of action), it is,
   necessarily, an agent-centered phenomenon – that is, it consists in a direct
   relation between an agent who dominates and one who is dominated. To
   quote Philip Pettit, domination "cannot be the product of 'a system or
   network or whatever'."[31] In this respect, neo-republicans echo theorists
   of power's "third face," for whom power ends where structure begins.[32]

I disagree. Structural forms of constraint, like the school district boundaries at issue in *Milliken*, are social in origin, and they can limit people's fields
of action no less so than can decisions made by other people. Steven Lukes
famously worried that attention to structural power can make it difficult to
theorize *responsibility* for unjust power relations.[33] My own view is consonant with that of Iris Marion Young, who argues that people can be subject
to systemic forms of domination for which no identifiable agent is *causally*
responsible, but emphasizes that attention to structural power highlights what
she calls the "forward-looking" *political* responsibility to act with others to
change unjust structures.[34]

In sum, attention to social structure directs democrats to re-specify the All-
Affected Principle. It directs us to track not decisions, but power. Granted,
one aspect of having "an adequate and equal social capacity to shape the
power relations that delimit one's field of action" is having adequate and equal
decision-making power. The view I recommend is one that supplements, rather
than supplants, those that emphasize decision making. For this reason, the
implications of the All-Affected Principle that have been sketched by some
scholars of local government law remain apposite. Consider Gerald Frug's
proposal that people be legally empowered to cross jurisdictional boundaries
and to cast votes in the elections of any local government in the metropolitan
areas in which they live.[35] Frug makes the case for granting each voter multiple votes, which they can cast in the local election(s) of their choice. Thus, a
resident of the city of Detroit who wanted to influence the zoning regulations
that prevent them from moving to Grosse Pointe and sending their children to
its "excellent" schools might cast some, or even all, of their votes in Grosse
Pointe's local elections. Of course, a voting system like the one Frug proposes
could have perverse effects. It might further empower the already-privileged,
by enabling affluent suburban voters to coordinate to vote in Detroit's elections, influencing city politics in ways that exacerbate existing inequalities.

The practical challenge for those who focus on decision making is to develop governance regimes that grant all affected persons – especially those who are marginalized by the status quo – an adequate and equal capacity to help shape collective decisions.

As I have argued throughout this chapter, an additional challenge for those who would apply the All-Affected Principle is that "shaping" power relations is not reducible to participating in formal decision making. If people are significantly affected by nondecisions, by doxic norms, and by systemic relations of domination, then democrats must think creatively not only about how to reform voting laws and other institutions, but also about how to promote people's capacities to reshape political agendas and to problematize the taken-for-granted. For this reason, the AAP can recommend political changes that have nothing to do with voting. These might include, for example, providing aid to the relatively powerless to help them bring claims in court; protecting and enhancing people's capacities to organize collectively, to protest, and to engage in a wide range of direct actions, including strikes; and devoting collective resources to supporting forms of public expression, such as public art, that problematize the dominant terms of discourse and unsettle doxic beliefs.

Although interventions like these have not been the principal focus of most theorizing about the AAP, they can play a critically important role in giving people an adequate and equal hand in shaping the norms that significantly affect them. How would an approach that moves away from an exclusive focus on voting and boundary drawing fare in light of the three objections to the AAP cited at the start of this chapter? The first, recall, was the worry that applying the AAP would undermine the right to freedom of association. The fact that the principle need not dictate how to define membership in political societies alleviates this concern. To return to the marriage analogy, in my own case, I did decide to marry a person who (happily) decided to marry me. No other people can compel us to admit them to our union. That does not mean, however, that no one does or should have the capacity to help shape other-regarding facets of our relationship. To cite one obvious example, the US government taxes my income today at a different rate than it did before I married. It seems entirely unobjectionable, from a concern about freedom of association, that my spouse and I do not independently decide the tax bracket to which we are assigned.

Second, if the AAP does not require forcing people to allow others to join their associations, but instead recommends giving them the capacity to shape the power relations that affect them, regardless of the definition of associational boundaries, then applying the principle need not undermine people's capacities to identify with "communities of character." If there is something about identifying as an American that is instrumentally and/or intrinsically valuable – or for that matter, if there is something valuable about identifying as a resident of Grosse Pointe, Michigan – then the challenge for democrats is to find ways to support and enable identification, while at the same time institutionalizing members' responsiveness to outsiders' legitimate claims. Suppose what is distinctive about "us" as residents of Grosse Pointe is that we value excellence in public education. If that means no more than that we devote a substantial percentage of our fair share of public resources to building schools and paying to staff them, all well and good. Perhaps a neighboring community, comprised entirely of elderly residents without school-aged children, will channel its fair share of resources toward some other end. But the fact that we value excellence in public schooling does not license us to pursue said excellence on the backs of our neighbors. If "pursuing in common the object of [our] common desires" affects the significant interests of people outside our association, then democratic norms demand that those others have a say in how we pursue our ends. One way to support communal identification in a case like the one at hand would be to detach some rights and/or benefits from communal membership. For example, perhaps Grosse Pointe should not have the right to collect property taxes and use them to fund local public services. If what is at stake is truly a communal valuation of education over other public goods, then a tax-revenue sharing system might preserve local decision making about priorities, while at the same time reducing the extent to which Grosse Pointe residents' decisions affect people in neighboring Detroit.

Third, although the concern that applying the AAP might undermine collective self-determination is valid, it is worth underscoring that collectivities' rights to self-determination, much like the self-determination rights of autonomous individuals, are not absolute. As I type these words, part of the lawn in the front of my house has been torn up by the local water utility, which has scheduled a water main replacement project in my neighborhood. Because I write from home, and because the noise distracts me as I write, I would prefer for them not to dig on my property at this time. Were I to realize that preference, however, it would delay the project, affecting my neighbors' significant interests. My property rights are abridged in this instance, and rightly so, because I live in a community with other people who would be significantly affected were that not the case. In a similar vein, collectivities' rights to self-determination can and should be abridged when the decisions they make are not purely self-regarding. In the case of school desegregation in the contemporary metropolis, Chief Justice Burger may be right that "[l]ocal control over the educational process affords citizens an opportunity to participate in decision-making." That said, funding can be centralized without undermining people's capacities to shape many local decisions about curriculum, pedagogy, and other educational concerns.

CONCLUSION

By way of conclusion, I want to say something about what I see as the principal strength, and the principal drawback, of the approach to theorizing the AAP sketched in this chapter. I am reminded of the advice that my son's chess coach gave him many years ago, when he used to play competitive chess. The coach would emphasize that, to grow as a player, he needed to think imaginatively, sometimes even in ways that seemed counter-intuitive. The coach advised that, while considering his next move, my son should think not only about what he might do, and what his opponent's likely response would be to each possible move, but also about what he might do were he to find himself in a different tactical situation than the one he currently faced. "Ask yourself fanciful questions," he would prompt, "like: 'What if that rook weren't there?'"

My central aim in this chapter has been to draw attention to the significance of structural power for specifying and applying the All-Affected Principle. In the case of US school desegregation post-*Milliken*, realizing that principle would require nontrivial changes not only to how Americans organize school districts and other subnational governments, but also to how they understand their rights (as students, as parents, as property owners), their interests, and their identities. It would require changes that would challenge longstanding hierarchies and threaten the privilege of those who benefit from the status quo. If it is difficult to imagine building the political will among the American citizenry to enact such change, that difficulty highlights an unfortunate ramification of my argument. Rather than rendering the AAP more attainable, I have suggested a reformulation that makes it more elusive. My argument pushes not toward neat, or even obviously feasible policy applications, but instead toward "big think" about structural change.

I am of two minds about this outcome. On the one hand, I appreciate the need for a realistic specification of the AAP, if the goal is to move closer to actualizing it. The more expansively the principle is defined, the more challenging it becomes to apply and to realize. At the same time, however, I want to make a plea that political theorists not become so hemmed in by concerns about feasibility that we fail to consider applications that might work only were we to find ourselves in a different tactical situation than the one we currently face (only "if that rook weren't there"). Politics, like chess, requires not just strategy, but also imagination.

NOTES

1 See, for example, Robert A. Dahl, *After the Revolution? Authority in a Good Society* (New Haven: Yale University Press, 1970); Robert E. Goodin, "Enfranchising All Affected Interests, and Its Alternatives," *Philosophy and Public Affairs* 35 (2007): 40–68.
2 David Held, *Democracy and the Global Order* (Cambridge: Polity Press, 1995); Iris Marion Young, *Inclusion and Democracy* (New York: Oxford University Press, 2000); Goodin, "Enfranchising All Affected Interests."
3 For example, Young, *Inclusion and Democracy*; Archon Fung, "The Principle of Affected Interests: An Interpretation and Defense," in *Representation: Elections*

and Beyond, ed. Rogers M. Smith and Jack H. Nagel (Philadelphia: University of Pennsylvania Press, 2013); Carol C. Gould, *Interactive Democracy: The Social Roots of Global Justice* (New York: Cambridge University Press, 2014).

4 See Clarissa Hayward, *De-facing Power* (New York: Cambridge University Press, 2000).

5 Linda Bosniak, *The Citizen and the Alien: Dilemmas of Contemporary Membership* (Princeton, NJ: Princeton University Press, 2006), p. 134.

6 See, for example, Christopher Wellman, "Immigration and Freedom of Association," *Ethics* 119, no. 1 (2008): 109–41.

7 See David Miller, *On Nationality* (New York: Oxford University Press, 1995) and *Citizenship and National Identity* (London: Polity Press, 2000).

8 Michael Walzer, *Spheres of Justice: A Defense of Pluralism and Equality* (New York: Basic Books, 1983), p. 62.

9 See, for example, Jürgen Habermas, "The Postnational Constellation and the Future of Democracy," in *The Postnational Constellation: Political Essays*, trans. and ed. Max Pensky (Cambridge, MA: MIT Press, 2001) pp. 58–112.

10 Alexis de Tocqueville, *Democracy in America*, ed. J. P. Mayer, trans. George Lawrence (New York: Harper and Row, 2006 [1840]), p. 514.

11 Sarah Song, "The Boundary Problem in Democratic Theory: Why the Demos Should Be Bounded by the State," *International Theory* 4, no. 1 (2012): 39–68, at 47.

12 Wellman, "Immigration and Freedom of Association," pp. 124–5.

13 *Bradley v. Milliken* (1973) 484 F.2d at 246.

14 *Milliken v. Bradley* (1974) 418 US at 743.

15 418 US at 742.

16 Charles Mills, *The Racial Contract* (Ithaca, NY: Cornell University Press, 1997), p. 42.

17 418 US at 748.

18 418 US at 756, n. 2.

19 For a more detailed explication, see Clarissa Hayward, "On Structural Power," *Journal of Political Power* 11, no. 1 (2018): 56–67, on which this discussion draws.

20 Federal Housing Administration, *Underwriting Manual: Underwriting and Valuation Procedure under Title II of the National Housing Act* (Washington, DC: US Government Printing Office), 1938, par. 937; see also, Clarissa Hayward. *How Americans Make Race: Stories, Institutions, Spaces* (New York: Cambridge University Press, 2013).

21 https://factfinder.census.gov/faces/tableservices/jsf/pages/productview.xhtml?src=CF, accessed February 27, 2018.

22 http://viz.edbuild.org/maps/2016/fault-lines/, accessed February 27, 2018.

23 www.grossepointecity.org, accessed February 27, 2018.

24 Pierre Bourdieu, "Fieldwork in Philosophy," in *In Other Words: Essays Toward a Reflexive Sociology*, trans. Matthew Adamson (Stanford, CA: Stanford University Press, 1990), p. 11.

25 Peter Bachrach and Morton Baratz, "Two Faces of Power," *American Political Science Review* 56, no. 4 (1962): 947–52; "Decisions and Non-decisions: An Analytical Framework," *American Political Science Review* 57, no. 3 (1963): 632–42.

26 Elmer E. Schattschneider, *The Semisovereign People: A Realist's View of Democracy in America* (Chicago: Holt, Rinehart, and Winston, 1960), p. 69.

27 Pierre Bourdieu, *Outline of a Theory of Practice*, trans. Richard Nice (New York: Cambridge University Press, 1977).

28 William Sewell, "A Theory of Structure: Duality, Agency, and Transformation," *American Journal of Sociology* 98, no. 1 (1992): 1–29.

29 Sally Haslanger, *Resisting Reality: Social Construction and Social Critique* (New York: Oxford University Press, 2012), p. 415.

30 For example, Philip Pettit, *Republicanism: A Theory of Freedom and Government* (New York: Oxford University Press, 1997) and *On The People's Terms: A Republican Theory and Model of Democracy* (New York: Cambridge University Press, 2012); see also, Frank Lovett, *A General Theory of Domination and Justice* (New York: Oxford University Press, 2010).

31 Pettit, *Republicanism*, p. 52; see, however, Philip Pettit, *Just Freedom: A Moral Compass for a Complex World* (New York: Norton, 2014), which moves away from this view.

32 Steven Lukes, *Power: A Radical View*, 2nd ed. (New York: Palgrave, 2005); see, however, Clarissa Hayward and Steven Lukes, "'Nobody to Shoot?' Power, Structure, and Agency: A Dialogue," *Journal of Power* 1, no. 1 (2008): 5–20.

33 Lukes, *Power*; Lukes and Hayward, "'Nobody to Shoot?'"

34 Iris Marion Young, "Responsibility and Global Labor Justice," *Journal of Political Philosophy* 12, no. 4 (2004): 365–88; Iris Marion Young, "Responsibility and Global Justice: A Social Connection Model," *Social Philosophy and Policy* 23, no. 1 (2006): 102–30; Iris Marion Young, *Responsibility for Justice* (New York: Oxford University Press, 2011); see also, Clarissa Hayward, "Responsibility and Ignorance: On Dismantling Structural Injustice," *Journal of Politics* 79, no. 2 (2017): 396–408.

35 Gerald Frug, "Voting and Justice," in Clarissa Hayward and Todd Swanstrom, eds., *Justice and the American Metropolis* (Minneapolis: University of Minnesota Press, 2011).

14

Philanthropy and the All-Affected Principle

Emma Saunders-Hastings and Rob Reich

The All-Affected Principle (AAP) in democratic theory claims that all who are affected by a decision should be able to have a voice in that decision. Questions immediately arise: How wide is the scope of the principle and what are its grounds? In this chapter, we focus initially on a question concerning scope. The AAP is most frequently assumed to apply to formal political decision making. We explore whether the principle should have any purchase in a particularly prominent and powerful extra-governmental domain: philanthropy. Should the All-Affected Principle be an important norm of good philanthropic practice?

If the AAP is understood modestly, then perhaps this is already the case. Donors and grant-making foundations often acknowledge the importance of learning from the feedback of two groups affected by their decision making: the grantees whose activities may be shaped by donor preferences and conditions (the strings attached to grants), and the beneficiaries whose interests those grantees attempt to advance. However, there is reason to doubt this modest application of the AAP. In foundation philanthropy, it remains rare to provide unrestricted general operating support to grantees, and many of the most prominent foundations deploy a decidedly technocratic approach (sometimes called strategic giving) that relies on highly targeted grant making. This approach treats grantees as subcontractors whose task it is to carry out a particular component of a vision or theory of change developed by philanthropists. The voices of beneficiaries and the knowledge possessed by grantees are routinely neglected.[1]

In general, foundations pay lip service to the notion of empowering grantees and beneficiaries, while reserving the right to define for themselves the interests and effects that are relevant to their objectives in grant making. An honest assessment of the AAP as applied to philanthropy reveals that the ways that most foundations have attempted to incorporate grantee and beneficiary voice fall very far short of the kinds of democratic reforms that the AAP envisions.

In what follows, we provide an example of the kind of dispute that can arise from foundations' technocratic orientation, and we use the case to reflect on whether the AAP should be applied to philanthropic decision making. Thinking about the AAP in the case of philanthropy invites exploration of the scope of the All-Affected Principle (and its application to nongovernmental actors). Against common interpretations of the AAP that apply it only to formal political decision making, we argue for extending to philanthropy the AAP's demand that affected parties be included in decision-making processes. We do so without relying on an expansive reading of the AAP that interprets it as applying to *all* kinds of decisions, public and private. Rather, we argue that the reasons we have for endorsing the AAP – for thinking that it is wrong for people to be denied influence over exercises of power that affect them – do not pick out formal political decision making as a uniquely important site of inclusion. Parallel reasons apply to philanthropy and some, we think, have particular force in that domain.

Our revisionary argument about the scope of the AAP also illuminates questions concerning the principle's grounds. Philanthropy is an interesting test case for our intuitions about the grounds of the AAP, because it calls attention to important differences between two ways that the AAP is often framed: as a demand to *consider* affected interests in decision making, or as an obligation to *enfranchise* the bearers of those interests. Of course, enfranchising affected interests is often an important instrumental strategy – probably the most reliable one – for ensuring that the relevant interests *are* considered: often, the goals of considering and enfranchising affected interests will overlap. But in the case of philanthropy, they often come apart: in general, philanthropists are attempting to consider and advance the *interests* of their intended beneficiaries, but *not* to grant beneficiaries or grantees control over how their interests are advanced. The case of philanthropy therefore provides resources for considering whether the AAP is instrumental to the consideration or advancement of substantive interests, or also grounded in respect for the autonomy of the people who bear those interests. By considering the appropriate scope of application of the AAP, we hope to underscore the broad implications of a commitment to democracy for the organization of social and political relationships in circumstances – as is the case of philanthropy – of unequal power.[2]

CASE: PHILANTHROPIC EFFECTS WITHOUT INCLUSION

The Bill and Melinda Gates Foundation's global health grant making in Africa has attracted criticism for its starkly technocratic orientation. Consider the case of Botswana, a democracy whose rate of HIV/AIDS prevalence has consistently ranked among the highest in the world.[3] The Gates Foundation launched a pilot program for HIV/AIDS prevention and treatment, the African Comprehensive HIV/AIDS Partnerships (ACHAP), in Botswana in 2000. By 2005, deaths from AIDS had fallen significantly (although prevention efforts showed less success).[4] However, over the same period, pregnancy-related maternal deaths and child mortality both increased. This led to concerns that the foundation's initiative had drained many doctors away from primary care and into the foundation's areas of priority (Gates-supported salaries in the HIV/AIDS sector were significantly higher).[5] In response to criticism, the director of the Global Fund to Fight AIDS, Tuberculosis, and Malaria (a Gates partner) acknowledged that their interventions may have had a "distorting effect," but said, "we're a Global Fund for AIDS, TB, and malaria. We're not a global fund that funds local health."[6] The Global Fund reserved the right to determine the effects in which it was interested and for which it owed justification.

The Gates Foundation, like many large foundations, expresses a commitment to the empowerment of its beneficiaries; its announcement of the ACHAP grant is titled "Working *with* Botswana to Confront its Devastating AIDS Crisis" (my emphasis). However, in the face of complaints that democratically elected Batswana officials were excluded from decision making around the program,[7] Gates Foundation officials have defended selective interventions delivered outside countries' general health systems and targeted to the foundation's areas of focus. The stated rationale is that they do not want government departments to become dependent on foundation money. Dr. Tadataka Yamada, the executive director of the Gates Foundation's global health program from 2006–2011, explained that "What [the Foundation] can't do is fill the gaps in government budgets … It's not sustainable."[8] Rather, "What we do is we catalyze … We are not replacement mothers."[9]

Such comments, like those of the Global Fund director, reflect a potentially troubling combination of impulses: on the one hand, philanthropists' desire for impact; on the other, a reluctance to assume responsibility for effects (direct or indirect) that lie outside specific program goals. Philanthropists and foundations that have been exceptionally generous in giving money for the relief of global poverty and related problems have been less willing to cede control over how that spending is allocated and evaluated. This reflects a more general resistance, on the part of philanthropists, to characterize their relationships with beneficiaries as *political* relationships that involve significant differences in power. Many large foundations assume that the relevant knowledge resides primarily in the foundation itself, whose leaders and staff have their own theories about how to produce social change and strategies to test and measure those theories through grants. Democratic norms of inclusion and accountability are exactly what the foundation seeks to avoid. Put differently, foundations represent a form of technocratic or expert voice within democratic institutions and civil society. The question is whether this represents a problem from the point of view of democratic governance.

APPLYING THE ALL-AFFECTED PRINCIPLE TO PHILANTHROPY

On virtually any interpretation of the AAP, it will already be obvious that Batswana citizens ought to have a voice in decisions that affect their interests as significantly as healthcare allocation does. But it is also unclear how this principle affects the obligations of the Gates Foundation. Most discussions of the All-Affected Principle focus on formal *political* decision making, at the level of state and interstate institutions.[10] The normative claim is straightforward: people whose interests are (significantly) affected by political decision making should have the opportunity to influence those decisions by, minimally, having their preferences consulted or, more ambitiously, by directly participating in the decision making. But should the AAP apply outside of formal political institutions?

Perhaps not. One possible reaction to the case discussed in the previous section is that democratic institutions, at the national, sub- and supranational levels, ought to ensure that citizens have a voice in the decisions that affect them. But in the absence of such institutions (or perhaps, in the domestic case, against the backdrop of democratic institutions), private actors operating on a voluntary or commercial basis are entitled to act as they like, provided they follow the rules set by political actors. In the philanthropic case, this means that the Gates Foundation, and any other philanthropic entity, is entitled to act in such a way *to produce the effects that it thinks are desirable* (and that may really *be* desirable). The framework is one of private contract: the foundation offers a grant, it is entitled to attach whatever strings it wishes in order to carry out its vision, and the potential grantee can either accept these strings or reject the grant altogether. To the extent that grantee or beneficiary voice is present at all, it is at this moment of initial negotiation and contract. Construed in this manner, provided they follow the rules set by political actors, the prerogative of foundations to discount or ignore the voices of beneficiaries and grantees is straightforward. If there is a problem here, it exists at the level of background institutions, and we should focus on resolving the problem at that same, political, level.

We question this argument. Private actors (and not only states and intergovernmental organizations) can acquire duties to allow the *people* affected by their decisions real influence over those decisions (and not, as is now common practice, simply to take those decisions with reference to the *interests* of the people affected). There are two principal reasons to apply a principle of affected interests to the activities of philanthropists.

First, the claim that private actors would be entitled to exercise broad discretion against the backdrop of distributively and politically just international institutions does not imply that they enjoy the identical moral discretion absent such institutions. In ideal theory, the AAP is generally understood as a principle regulating higher-order lawmaking and the design of political institutions, not as a requirement that individuals have a say in *each and every* decision that affects them. (Nozick's example – proposing that all hopeful suitors have a say in the decision of whom, if anyone, a woman should marry – is a famous *reductio* of the latter possibility.)[11] This restriction of democratic principles to higher-order institutions is a common feature in democratic theory, and the priority of equal influence over *political* institutions is clear enough, at least when we are operating in ideal theory. As Kolodny puts it, "if we do have equal influence over political decisions, and those decisions have final authority over nonpolitical decisions, then that itself contributes to moderating the threat ... posed by unequal influence over nonpolitical decisions," since in such a society "whatever hierarchy there may be is ultimately regulated or authorized from a standpoint of equality."[12] This might seem to provide a rationale for restricting the AAP to higher-level public institutions – ones capable of regulating the downstream, nonpolitical distribution of influence. The practice of philanthropy would be such a downstream location, and the inclusion of beneficiaries in decisions about the targets and terms of donations might then be supererogatory. At the ideal end of the ideal–nonideal spectrum, the presence of just background conditions may make plausible a contractual framework of transacting parties in a voluntary exchange.[13]

In nonideal circumstances, this position is untenable. There is a case for applying the AAP to the activities of philanthropists, *even if* one thinks that, in ideal theory, the AAP could justifiably be restricted in its application to political institutions. This argument does not rest on the implausible claim that there is a first-order normative obligation to give all people affected by *any* decision a say in making that decision. Rather, when there are serious defects in either distributive or political justice, either globally or domestically, the AAP's demands for inclusion and empowerment can devolve on actors on whom it might not otherwise be binding.

One important reason for treating the AAP as a norm of philanthropic practice concerns the devolution of responsibilities of inclusion in contexts where democratic domestic and/or transnational institutions are missing. To return to the Botswana case that we've been discussing: if global institutions were arranged in compliance with the AAP, such that the international political order was as responsive to the interests of Batswana citizens as it is to those of citizens of any other country, matters would look different. But it's clear that foundation officials driving a hard bargain can *not*, in the real world, excuse themselves by pointing out the prior opportunities for Batswana citizens and officials to shape the rules and norms that distribute global economic and political power. While Botswana itself is a stable and functioning democracy, its officials and citizens are constrained by injustices and power asymmetries in the international system. On one interpretation of the AAP, which makes it solely a principle of ideal theory, this is just one way of restating the injustice of the international system (and perhaps of trying to motivate change). But on another interpretation, this changes the obligations of secondary actors: acknowledging the failure of political institutions at the transnational level, domestic political institutions and private actors may be morally constrained to grant rights of participation. Put simply, the case for restricting the AAP to higher-level institutions in ideal theory does not suffice to insulate secondary actors from responsibility for directly satisfying the principle in nonideal theory, where the just division of institutional labor envisioned in ideal theory is inoperative. If the AAP is a genuine ethical or political principle (and not just a diagnostic tool), then we ought to consider its implications for individuals and private actors under conditions of injustice (which is to say, under all actually existing conditions).[14]

In a world where the All-Affected Principle was realized at the level of political institutions, people would (by assumption) have a say in the scope for action and political regulation of private actors. In nonideal circumstances, absent such higher-level principles of political inclusion, private actors exercise their superior power in a way that lacks full democratic authorization and legitimation. Against the backdrop of distributive unfairness and the presence of unjustly vulnerable or disadvantaged populations, the efforts of private actors through philanthropy to ameliorate inequality, to secure the dignity of the vulnerable, or to improve the prospects of the disadvantaged are often laudable. But charity is no substitute for justice. And even if charity is a second-best response to injustice, the standing of private actors to direct their charity as they please, and to exercise their discretion without including the voices of those whom they seek to affect, may not hold. To the extent that one holds a normative commitment to the All-Affected Principle, the failure to realize that principle through political institutions affects the downstream normative standing of private actors. This point applies broadly, for example to the activities of for-profit private actors.[15]

Second, separable from the presence of background injustice, there is a particularly strong case for applying a principle of affected interests to *philanthropic* decision making. It arises from the fact that, in the case of philanthropy, it is often *the very interests of the people affected* that foundations and NGOs invoke when defending the effects produced. This is different from what generally occurs in the case of for-profit multinational corporations. Of course, it might still be troubling when corporations produce effects (especially negative effects) on people in ways that those people are not able to influence. But one might argue for something like a version of the doctrine of double effect here: perhaps private actors pursuing their own interests are entitled (within some range) to produce negative effects on others, so long as they do not specifically intend those negative effects.

But the intentional structure of philanthropy is different, in ways that should encourage us to reflect on the kinds of effects that ground claims for inclusion in decision making. It is especially disrespectful to exclude people from influence over decisions that affect them *while claiming that one is promoting the interests of those people.* For most liberals, the normative standards for seeking to affect or influence someone for her *own* benefit are actually *more* stringent than the standards for affecting her as a by-product of the pursuit of one's own interests. And so a commitment to anti-paternalism could ground a particularly strong case for enfranchising affected interests in philanthropic contexts. The case of philanthropy invites conversation both about the domain of application of the All-Affected Principle, and the *kinds* of interests that ground claims for inclusion and influence.

Our argument does not require thinking (implausibly) that philanthropic action is distinctively likely to cause harm; we assume as overwhelmingly likely that profit-seeking corporate activities produce more negative effects than do those of philanthropists. Nor does our argument require thinking that philanthropies like the Gates Foundation produce more harm than good: it is likely that the good effects of Gates Foundation activities far outweigh the bad. Rather, we challenge the assumption that it is primarily the risk of *negative* effects that grounds people's claims to inclusion in decision making. The *reasons* underlying the pursuit of different effects also have a place when assessing claims for inclusion. On this argument, one need not think that all people potentially affected by Bill and Melinda Gates's philanthropy are entitled to a say in how they spend it, *before* they take any decisions about where to donate: the anti-paternalist argument is compatible with thinking that donors enjoy wide discretion as to whether and where to give. An anti-paternalist specification of the principle of affected interests focuses rather on *how* one gives and on how control of philanthropic funds is distributed between the donor, beneficiaries, and other affected interests.

Put differently, considering whether the AAP should apply to extra-governmental domains such as philanthropy opens up a conversation not just about the scope of the principle but about its very grounding.

INSTRUMENTAL AND INTRINSIC JUSTIFICATIONS
FOR THE AAP

Why exactly ought the interests of those affected by a decision be included in the decision-making process? In the case of philanthropy, one answer is that doing so is very likely to produce better outcomes: by incorporating the voices of grantees and beneficiaries, philanthropic interventions are improved. On this view, the AAP has an *instrumental justification*: its application in philanthropic decision making tends to improve what it is that philanthropists or NGOs seek to produce.

Within the world of philanthropy and NGOs, this is not an especially controversial view, at least when expressed as an aspiration or as a general principle. Foundations often claim that they aim to incorporate the voices of grantees and their beneficiaries in their decision making for the simple reason that doing so is a basic condition for learning how to improve philanthropy and produce better outcomes. Foundations that seek to be learning organizations will routinely look to their grantees and beneficiaries as the sources of local knowledge and try to access that knowledge through organizational processes that routinize grantee feedback. However, given the obvious power imbalance between foundations and their grantees, creating meaningful feedback loops and learning mechanisms is structurally difficult. And foundations lack substantive forms of accountability for their performance (they neither have competitors, as do firms in the for-profit marketplace, nor governance structures, as do government agencies in a democratic society, that could force the replacement of leaders through regular elections[16]), so they can easily operate *without* incorporating grantee or beneficiary voice. And apart from these considerations, in an age of highly technocratic philanthropy there is ample reason to doubt whether foundations do more than offer hollow gestures to the importance of grantee voice. The AAP might have an instrumental justification in the domain of philanthropy, but abiding by or operationalizing it in practice is evidently difficult if it is endorsed just as a norm of good practice. And this despite its being in the interest of donors, assuming that donors actually seek to produce good outcomes and to improve their grant-making practice over time.

We believe that the philanthropic context also reveals a potential *intrinsic justification* for the AAP. Suppose one believed that there are clear benefits to purely technocratically driven philanthropy (accepting that neglecting grantee and beneficiary voice is compatible with, or even necessary to produce, good outcomes), and suppose further that philanthropy was undertaken in the presence of fully just background conditions, giving philanthropists a wide discretion to practice grant making as they wish. Even so, we have reason to endorse an application of AAP to philanthropy.

The argument here is the anti-paternalism case we have briefly developed. Technocratic philanthropy might deliver uncontroversially good outcomes for grantees and beneficiaries, with those outcomes acknowledged by both grantees and beneficiaries. But in acting paternalistically, philanthropists wrong the agents they intend to benefit. Such paternalism is morally objectionable, and all the more so when we view philanthropy dynamically, as more than a one-off interaction between one donor and one grantee.

The germ of the argument can be seen in a cliché often invoked by grantees or critics of philanthropy: that philanthropy is something that should be *done with* rather than *done to* the people who benefit from it. Some of these cases can be understood on the instrumental argument that we discussed above, or as exposing the pitfalls of hierarchically organized social practices. But we can also understand the undemocratic practice of philanthropy as objectionable in itself, on anti-paternalist grounds that speak to the grounds of the AAP (and of democracy) more generally.

THE AAP AS AN ANTI-PATERNALIST PRINCIPLE

One reading of the moral principle underlying the AAP is this: that each person's comparably important interests deserve equal consideration.[17] This interpretation of the grounds of the AAP makes the AAP something close to a principle of justice. What's fundamental is the obligation to consider and promote the interests of all; *how* this is to be done is a downstream question.

We believe that a different premise grounds the appeal of the AAP: that people should be treated as both competent and entitled to articulate and promote their *own* interests, rather than, in the worst case, being vulnerable to powerful actors who can negatively affect their interests with impunity or, in the best case, relying on technocratically benevolent but unaccountable external actors to promote their interests on their behalf. Democratic decision making is not merely instrumental to the protection of people's substantive interests (grounded in the empirical claim that if people are denied a say in the decisions that affect them, their objective interests are likely to be underserved). It is also required by respect for autonomy: affected people need to be able to define for themselves what their interests are. This interpretation of the AAP (unlike the one calling for equal consideration) makes it a fundamentally democratic principle: the *grounds* of the principle are not just about an open-ended commitment to the equal moral worth of persons but also about *how* we implement equal consideration (that is, by giving power to the people we want to be considered). On our reading, commitment to the AAP implies commitment to anti-paternalism: *hierarchically* organized consideration of affected interests is insufficient to satisfy the AAP.

We use the term paternalism broadly, to refer to attempts to influence an agent's decisions or actions that express the judgment that the agent's ability to choose or act well on her own behalf is deficient or inferior in some relevant respect. Our focus is therefore on the insult that paternalism expresses toward the person paternalized.[18]

We do not restrict our definition of paternalism to cases where the paternal-izer engages in coercion or where there is otherwise some defect in the consent of the person paternalized. This is a controversial choice: some will judge it overinclusive, and instead wish to restrict the definition of paternalism to cases where the paternalizer coerces the person paternalized or otherwise infringes on her rights.[19] On the latter, more restrictive definition of paternalism, it will generally be difficult to see how the activities of philanthropists could count as paternalistic, since philanthropists are usually understood to be *adding* to the options available to beneficiaries rather than removing any preexisting options. Perhaps one could argue that background conditions are so flawed that the offers extended by philanthropists count as coercive (since grantees or beneficiaries lack any acceptable alternative) or that the grantees or benefi-ciaries are incapable of genuine consent. While we accept that such conditions might sometimes obtain, we do not believe that classifying philanthropy as paternalistic depends on accepting such claims.

Paternalism is not, on our understanding, a subset of coercion but a broader category of wrong: it is objectionable not (or not only) as an unjustified liberty restriction but as a failure to show respect for autonomous agents and a threat to relations of equality. It can be expressed not only where paternalizers unilat-erally intervene in ways that restrict liberty relative to a pre-intervention base-line, but also where they attempt to put in place structures to restrict the *future* scope for choice of beneficiaries (even if beneficiaries consent to those struc-tures). Suppose that a prospective beneficiary B has X range of liberty or scope for choice at time T. At time T+1, philanthropist A offers B a benefit, conditional on restricting B's scope for choice to X–Y at time T+2. On our reading, what is relevant to the assessment of paternalism is not only whether there is any coercion or liberty-infringement at time T+1 (we assume there is not: that B's scope for choice at T+1 is actually *greater* than X, because of the added option that A offers), but A's reasons for seeking to constrain B's scope for choice at time T+2. If those reasons refer to B's inability to judge or act well on her own behalf, A's action can be paternalistic even if B is better off overall at time T+2 and if her consent to receive the benefit with the attached conditions was genuine.

To motivate the possibility of noncoercive, non-rights-infringing, consensual paternalism, consider the following example. Suppose that wealthy parents set up a trust for their children, which is designed to be unlocked in stages over the life spans of the children: they come into an initial bundle of money at age 18, another at age 30, another at age 45, and so on. At each stage, there are conditions that specify whether the child is entitled to the money, and perhaps also conditions on how the money may be used (e.g. only for education, housing, or childcare). Stipulate that the adult children are not owed this money as a matter of justice: the parents have fulfilled their duties of care, the children are now self-sufficient, and by not receiving the money in the trust they would not be left badly off in absolute terms (we might even think that the money they receive through the trust may, in the big picture, leave them unjustly *well*-off).

It is easy to see that complying with the conditions in order to access the trust makes the adult children better off in welfarist terms – at least in one way (i.e. in respect of money) and presumably overall (since they have the option of refusing to comply with conditions that they judge to be too onerous, and of forgoing their claims to the money in the trust if they judge that the tradeoffs aren't worth their while). We can assume that the adult children's consent to the terms of the trust (if they accept them) is genuine and unforced. Still, we take it that such a trust represents an expression of distrust of the agency of the adult children, and that the parents in this case act in an insultingly and objectionably paternalistic way. (One might think this *even* if one still thought the parents had a moral and legal entitlement to dispose of their property as they see fit; we are not arguing that all forms of paternalism are all-things-considered impermissible or that they should all be legally barred.)

The reason for this intuition – and something important about paternalism that this case helps bring out – is that paternalism is often a feature of ongoing *relationships,* and not always of one-off transactions. Part of what can be objectionable about paternalism is the attempt to put oneself in a position of longer-term authority over an autonomous agent, even if that attempt proceeds by getting the agent to *agree* to defer to another person's judgment about the agent's best interests.[20] Assessing the consensual or noncoercive character of individual transactions does not always give us sufficient information to assess whether or not a social or political relation is objectionably paternalistic: we need more information about the ongoing patterns of interaction between the relevant actors, in particular regarding whose judgments are taken as authoritative in making decisions about an agent's important interests.

This understanding of paternalism has significant advantages for evaluating paternalistic treatment in globalized contexts of widespread injustice, where entitlement claims may be complex and obscure. Standard liberal definitions of coercion focus on the behavior, aims, and intentions of the coercer, not on the range of options or subjective experience of the person putatively coerced. While coercion does not require the exercise of force, it does require that the coercer have the intention and the ability credibly to threaten to make some of your preexisting options less attractive if you fail to act in the ways that they want.[21] Whether or not something is coercion also depends on the background structure of rights and entitlements. If I threaten to withhold something that you have a claim on unless my terms are met, that is coercion; if I offer you something that you do not have a claim on, subject to conditions, it becomes a noncoercive offer. In the case of international philanthropy, whether a philanthropist's action is coercive or not – and, derivatively, whether it is objectionably paternalistic or not – will depend on whether or not putative recipients have a claim on the good in question, and whether that claim is assignable to the philanthropist making the threat or offer. Often the answer will be mixed: for example, it will often seem plausible to say that potential recipients have a claim on *someone* for resources to meet basic needs, but that the claim is assignable to their own governments (or perhaps, derivatively, to the international community) and not to any particular philanthropist or group of philanthropists. So although aid recipients may encounter an unjustly constrained set of options, this is a fact that philanthropists are at worst *exploiting* rather than creating or threatening to create. *Relative to the no-donation baseline*, they are not coercing the recipients. And yet from the point of view of beneficiaries and an evaluation of their relationships, this seems beside the point; background injustice plays a significant role in motivating beneficiaries' consent to restrictions on their autonomy, and we should be able to register the unfair and insulting character of the resulting relationships. This requires a diachronic understanding of paternalism that shifts attention from the character of the paternalizer's infringement (at the moment of intervention) to ongoing curtailments of the paternalizee's autonomy.[22] The AAP is a useful anti-paternalist guide because it provides a better heuristic for avoiding paternalism than do calls to avoid coercion.

In summary, then, we believe that the case of philanthropy can be useful in illuminating both the scope of the AAP (and, in particular, how the democratic demands of that principle can devolve from public institutions to secondary actors in nonideal theory, where choice sets are tainted by background injustice) and its grounds (in particular, the insufficiency of a hierarchical organization of consideration).

CONCLUSION

How might enfranchising affected interests work in the case of philanthropy? Here there is a spectrum of possible responses. At the weak end, recognizing democratic deficits at the institutional level and incorporating commitments to anti-paternalism could encourage donors and foundations voluntarily to expand the kinds of nonbinding community "consultation" that they sometimes currently engage in. They could also choose to channel gifts through (rather than outside) democratic governments where those exist; where democratic institutions are absent, they could expand unconditioned gifts to civil society groups and individuals – more general operating support rather than targeting grant making. These are ways of incorporating a commitment to enfranchising affected interests as a matter of *ethical* theory – that is, of converting it into moral advice for donors.

As a matter of *political* theory, there are also ways that we might try to challenge the presumption that *donors* are entitled full discretion in controlling and assessing their spending. There are a range of possible mechanisms by which we could attempt to accomplish this, in ways that do not rely on distributing all control to *governmental* actors: for example, we could adjust tax incentives for philanthropic donations to favor unconditioned giving. We could insist upon community representation on the governance boards of foundations. We could demand greater transparency in grant making so that both grantees and beneficiaries have the opportunity to examine the records of past and current foundation activities. The challenge of implementation here is to increase people's control over the decisions that affect them, in ways that do not rely on exaggerated estimations of the democratic responsiveness of either philanthropists or actually existing states.

As the trust case we sketch above suggests, paternalism can occur even in the presence of consensual transactions that make the paternalized better off. Paternalism can be morally objectionable even under such conditions. But consent does make some difference, politically; the same respect for agents that moves us against paternalism should make us hesitate to block genuinely voluntary transactions, since to do so would be to prevent agents from pursuing what they take to be the best options available to them. In the Botswana case, for example, it would seem outrageous for the US government to block the Gates Foundation's philanthropy, given that the terms of the aid were in this case accepted by democratically elected and accountable officials in Botswana. In addition to bearing its share of responsibility for international distributive injustice, the United States would then be responsible for the added injustice of preventing Batswana officials from accessing remedial options that would otherwise be available to them.

However, there can nevertheless be reasons to adjust voluntarily (and, where possible, politically regulate) the terms of voluntary transactions with a view to equalizing bargaining power. The case for this does not require arguing that the consent of putatively paternalized agents (or representatives of paternalized agents) is not genuine. We can think that people really are *choosing* the best option available to them, but that the option set from which they are choosing is itself unfair. This in turn introduces unfairness into an outcome

that is nevertheless chosen (and chosen in a way that makes a real moral difference). The appropriate response is not to block the people paternalized from
choosing what they wish, but to try to improve their bargaining position. This
might be attempted in a range of ways: most weakly, by making ethical (or
merely instrumental) appeals to philanthropists; more strongly, by incentiv-
izing unconditional giving (unconditional cash transfers, for example, to the
unjustly disadvantaged and their representatives) and by subjecting to public
criticism giving that exploits the unfair inequalities in bargaining position that
currently obtain internationally.

Philanthropy, especially big philanthropy as practiced by large foundations
that seek to ameliorate inequality or respond to injustice, is characterized by –
perhaps defined by – a situation of unequal power. One clear upshot of our
arguments here is that philanthropists deserve scrutiny, not just gratitude, in
exercising their power. Such scrutiny is warranted not merely for the reason
that we should wish for philanthropists to be effective in ameliorating inequality or responding to injustice, and that scrutiny may contribute to effective
philanthropic projects. It is warranted because we should recognize and illuminate the paternalism that is often at the core of big philanthropy.

Beyond scrutiny, however, we have argued more demandingly that the All-
Affected Principle has purchase in the extra-governmental domain of philanthropy. This is so for instrumental and intrinsic reasons. Incorporating the
voices of affected grantees and beneficiaries in philanthropic decision making
is instrumentally valuable in bringing about more effective philanthropy. And
incorporating the voices of grantees and beneficiaries in philanthropic decision
making is intrinsically valuable in mitigating a situation of deeply unequal
power and responding to potentially morally objectionable forms of paternalism at the heart of philanthropic relationships. The case of philanthropy
thereby reveals important dimensions of the scope and grounds of the AAP.

NOTES

1 Foundation officers themselves sometimes criticize foundations for failing to learn
  from the experiences of beneficiaries or incorporate the local knowledge of grantees; see for e.g. "The Future of Foundation Philanthropy: the CEO Perspective,"
  Center for Effective Philanthropy, 2016, p. 23, http://research.effectivephilanthropy
  .org/the-future-of-foundation-philanthropy. On the other hand, the years since this
  chapter was originally written (in 2016–17) have seen a flurry of high-profile unrestricted giving (notably by MacKenzie Scott) and a broader interest in developing
  new models of "trust-based philanthropy." These developments have the potential
  to grant more power to affected interests, although it remains too early to tell how
  far that potential will be realized.
2 For other recent works investigating how democratic principles apply to philanthropy, see Rob Reich, Lucy Bernholz, and Chiara Cordelli, ed., *Philanthropy in
  Democratic Societies: History, Institutions, Values* (Chicago: University of Chicago
  Press, 2016); Chiara Cordelli, *The Privatized State* (Princeton: Princeton University

Press, 2020); Theodore Lechterman, *The Tyranny of Generosity: Why Philanthropy Corrupts Our Politics and How We Can Fix It* (Oxford: Oxford University Press 2021); Rob Reich, *Just Giving: Why Philanthropy Is Failing Democracy and How It Can Do Better* (Princeton: Princeton University Press, 2018); and Emma Saunders-Hastings, *Private Virtues, Public Vices: Philanthropy and Democratic Equality* (Chicago: University of Chicago Press, 2022). This chapter builds on arguments developed by the authors in the latter two works.

3 This paragraph and the next draw on Saunders-Hastings, *Private Virtues, Public Vices*, pp. 154–60, where this case is discussed in more detail.

4 See Bill and Melinda Gates Foundation, "Working with Botswana to Confront Its Devastating AIDS Crisis," Bill and Melinda Gates Foundation, June 2006, https://docs.gatesfoundation.org/Documents/achap.pdf; John Stover et al., "Estimated HIV Trends and Program Effects in Botswana," *PLoS ONE* 3, no. 11 (November 2008), www.plosone.org/article/info%3Adoi%2F10.1371%2Fjournal.pone.0003729; and Ilavenil Ramiah and Michael R. Reich, "Public-Private Partnerships And Antiretroviral Drugs for HIV/AIDS: Lessons From Botswana," *Health Affairs* 24, no. 1 (March/April 2005): 545–51. Both the Stover and the Ramiah and Reich studies were funded by grants from ACHAP itself.

5 Charles Piller and Doug Smith, "Unintended Victims of Gates Foundation Generosity," *Los Angeles Times*, December 16, 2007: http://articles.latimes.com/2007/dec/16/nation/la-na-gates16dec16.

6 Piller and Smith, "Unintended Victims of Gates Foundation Generosity."

7 See Ramiah and Reich, for statements from Festus Morgae, then the Batswana president, as well as from the health minister serving at the time. Their objections are discussed in more detail in Saunders-Hastings, *Private Virtues, Public Vices*, pp. 158–9.

8 Piller and Smith, "Unintended Victims of Gates Foundation Generosity."

9 Piller and Smith, "Unintended Victims of Gates Foundation Generosity."

10 For an important exception, see Archon Fung, "The Principle of Affected Interests: An Interpretation and Defense," in *Representation: Elections and Beyond*, ed. Rogers M. Smith and Jack H. Nagel (Philadelphia: University of Pennsylvania Press, 2013).

11 Robert Nozick, *Anarchy, State, and Utopia* (Oxford: Basic Books, 1974), p. 269.

12 Niko Kolodny, "Rule Over None II: Social Equality and the Justification for Democracy," *Philosophy and Public Affairs* 42, no. 4 (2014), p. 306.

13 But see Ruth Grant, *Strings Attached: Untangling the Ethics of Incentives* (Princeton: Princeton University Press, 2012) for an argument that the attachment of strings to a potential gift should be analyzed not as a straightforward choice situation between transacting parties in a voluntary exchange but as an exercise of power. The relevant question is whether the power relationship is deeply unequal. We return to this question later in our chapter.

14 It is an interesting question to consider whether philanthropy is best understood as a remedial activity, a second-best mechanism for responding to injustice that would be rendered wholly unnecessary if just background arrangements were secured. Donations to a soup kitchen or the private distribution of vaccinations for domestic or global health might be morally worthy endeavors, but such philanthropy, one might argue, should seek its own elimination by striving to end hunger or to create an adequate public health system. An alternative view of philanthropy leaves a place for it even in fully just conditions; it is a first-best activity for the production of

certain goods. For more, see Reich, "What are Foundations For?" *Boston Review*, 2013.

15 See Chiara Cordelli, "Reparative Justice and the Moral Limits of Discretionary Philanthropy," in *Philanthropy in Democratic Societies: History, Institutions, Values,* ed. Rob Reich, Lucy Bernholz, and Chiara Cordelli (Chicago: University of Chicago Press, 2016); "The Institutional Division of Labor and the Egalitarian Obligations of Nonprofits," *Journal of Political Philosophy* 20, no. 2 (June 2012): 131–55; and "How Privatization Threatens the Private," *Critical Review of International Social and Political Philosophy* 16, no. 1 (2013): 65–87, for arguments about how institutional duties of justice can devolve on private actors.

16 See Rob Reich, "Repugnant to the Whole Idea of Democracy? On the Role of Foundations in Democratic Societies," *PS: Political Science and Politics* 49 (July 2016): 466–70.

17 This would align with a "broad" or "substantive" interpretation of the AAP, which interprets the AAP as mandating the *consideration* rather than the *enfranchisement* of affected interests. While we do not claim that the AAP commits us to a particular or strongly egalitarian procedure (e.g. to majoritarian voting with equal opportunity for influence), it does, in our view, require efforts to grant affected people *a say over decisions* that affect their interests, and not just that people's *substantive interests be considered.*

18 For similar accounts of paternalism, see Seana Valentine Shiffrin, "Paternalism, Unconscionability Doctrine, and Accommodation," *Philosophy & Public Affairs* 29, no. 3 (Summer 2000): 205–50; Jonathan Quong's "judgmental definition" of paternalism in *Liberalism without Perfection* (Oxford: Oxford University Press, 2011), p. 80; and Nicolas Cornell, "A Third Theory of Paternalism," *Michigan Law Review* 113 (June 2015): 1295–336. Shiffrin and Quong's definitions turn on the motives of the (putative) paternalist while Cornell (like us) focuses on the external meaning of the paternalist's actions, but there is significant overlap on the centrality of insult or negative judgment (rather than classes of actions, e.g. coercive or noncoercive) to paternalism. See also Saunders-Hastings, "Benevolent Giving and the Problem of Paternalism," in *Effective Altruism: Philosophical Issues,* ed. Hilary Greaves and Theron Pummer (Oxford: Oxford University Press, 2019) and *Private Virtues, Public Vices,* chapter 4.

19 However, the claim that paternalism can be noncoercive does not depend on accepting an insult-based account (or critique) of paternalism; for an influential defense of noncoercive paternalism, see for Richard H. Thaler and Cass Sunstein, *Nudge: Improving Decisions about Health, Wealth, and Happiness* (New York: Penguin, 2009).

20 See Saunders-Hastings, *Private Virtues, Public Vices,* pp. 105–6.

21 See for e.g. Robert Nozick, "Coercion," in *Philosophy, Science, and Method: Essays in Honor of Ernest Nagel,* ed. Sidney Morgenbesser, Patrick Suppes, and Morton White (New York: St. Martin's Press, 1969), pp. 440–72.

22 Our concern with paternalism overlaps with the complaint about undemocratic exclusion that Sean Gray (this volume), following Patchen Markell, calls "usurpation."

15

International Non-Governmental Organizations, the All-Affected Principle, and Social Justice Organizations

Jennifer C. Rubenstein

"Why do I, as the black woman, have to fix that? ...

I want white men to make the noise."

– Bozoma Saint John[1]

According to the All-Affected Principle (AAP), all and only those individuals who are significantly affected by a decision should have a say in, or influence over, that decision.[2] This principle is typically applied to questions about the boundaries of political communities and the scope of government institutions (Warren, this volume). Some scholars, however, have argued that it should be applied more broadly, for example to philanthropic foundations (Saunders-Hastings and Reich, this volume) and workplaces (Gould, this volume).[3] Fung characterizes this extension as a shift from "governments" to "governance." "We should," he argues, "interpret the [all-affected] principle as applying not only to legislatures but also to administrative agencies, private corporations, civic organizations, and governments of other societies."[4]

In this chapter I take up this invitation by considering whether and how the AAP ought to be extended to large-scale, Western-based INGOs such as Oxfam, Care, and Doctors Without Borders. These INGOs undertake humanitarian, development, and/or advocacy work across borders, either directly or by funding other organizations. I focus on the AAP's relevance not to INGOs' internal governance structures, but rather to their "external"[5] relationships with their intended beneficiaries,[6] donors, local community members, host governments, domestic NGOs and civic organizations in the countries where they work, and people affected by their advocacy campaigns (see Gould, this volume).

While they are sometimes celebrated as saints or heroes, these INGOs are also frequently criticized for being, in effect, undemocratic. As one prominent report based on thousands of interviews with aid recipients and community members in dozens of countries concluded,

The nuances are different, but the message is the same: humanitarian action is a top-down, externally driven, and relatively rigid process that allows little space for local participation beyond formalistic consultation. Much of what happens escapes local scrutiny and control. The system is viewed as inflexible, arrogant, and culturally insensitive ... Never far from the surface are perceptions that the aid system does not deliver on expectations and is "corrupted" by the long chain of intermediaries between distant capitals and would-be beneficiaries.[7]

What leverage does the AAP offer for recognizing and grappling with these sorts of issues? Would greater compliance with the AAP be a good way to address them? In response to these questions, I argue that efforts to extend the AAP to INGOs (and other non-state actors that engage in governance) almost always analogize them to governments. This analogy deploys what I call the AAP's "inclusive face": it tells us that like conventional governments, INGOs should include those they significantly affect in their decision making. For example, Oxfam should include those significantly affected by its advocacy campaigns in its decisions about those campaigns. Yet because inclusion is a rather conservative political project, the AAP's inclusive face offers only a limited basis for critique.

There is, however, another way to extend the AAP to INGOs that has gone virtually unacknowledged: rather than analogize INGOs to governments, we can analogize them to unaffected individuals (or any other unaffected entity). This analogy deploys what I call the AAP's "exclusive face." It tells us that INGOs such as Oxfam should *not* have a say in or influence over decisions that *do not* significantly affect them; they should be excluded.[8] The AAP's exclusive face offers a more radical basis for critique of INGOs than its inclusive face.

However, even the AAP's exclusive face has serious limitations in the context of INGOs. These limitations are due to INGOs' social position as elites seeking to address social problems that they have good reasons to help address, but that primarily affect others. INGOs in this position run up against what I call the *involvement/influence dilemma*: they can be involved in addressing social problems or they can avoid undue influence, but it is difficult for them to do both simultaneously.[9] I therefore turn to three organizations that directly and intentionally address the question of how elites should help address social problems that primarily affect others: SURJ, Thousand Currents, and the Solidaire Network. These organizations do not fully reject the AAP, but they reinterpret and recast it in ways that are relevant to, and generative for, other entities in a similar situation, such as Western-based humanitarian, development, and advocacy INGOs.

Before turning to the argument, I briefly sketch how I am interpreting the AAP for the purposes of this chapter. I interpret "affected" to mean having one's *basic* interests *significantly* affected. I also conceive of affectedness as *proportional*: the more one's basic interests are affected, the more influence one should have. While still quite vague, these specifications help to prevent the AAP from having highly regressive and inegalitarian implications, such as wealthy US corporations having a say in Mexican environmental policy because it will slightly reduce their profits.

As noted above, the AAP is typically taken to apply to formal decisions. However, if the point of the AAP is to give people meaningful influence over the forces shaping their lives, limiting its scope to formal decisions – like limiting its scope to conventional governments – is too narrow.[10] In response to this worry, Hayward recommends a "focus on, not decisions, but [structural] power relations" (this volume). While Hayward acknowledges that her conception of the AAP is so broad that it might be difficult to implement, some expansion of the AAP beyond formal decision making is necessary for the principle to have force or relevance in the context of INGOs. I thus adopt a *wide conception of decision making* that extends beyond discrete decisions. (I discuss what this might look like in more detail below.) To summarize, I conceive of the AAP as a claim that people should have influence over decisions (and other processes and practices) that significantly affect their basic interests, to a degree that is roughly proportional to how much their basic interests are affected.

THE AAP'S INCLUSIVE FACE AND THE GOVERNMENT ANALOGY

The AAP is, most obviously, a principle of inclusion; Dahl calls it "very likely the best principle of inclusion you will find" (see the introduction to this volume). The AAP's "inclusive face" focuses on bringing individuals into decision-making processes that affect them; it offers remedies for members of disenfranchised groups (e.g. women and African Americans in the US context), colonial subjects, and individuals harmed by the activities of foreign governments.

Scholars who extend the AAP to non-state actors have focused almost exclusively on the AAP's inclusive face. This is because they analogize INGOs to governments. The logic of this *government analogy* proceeds as follows: the AAP applies to conventional governments. Some non-state actors function like conventional governments in that they engage in governance. Humanitarian INGOs, for example, are sometimes said to engage in "humanitarian governance."[11] Just as individuals should have a say in decisions made by conventional governments that significantly affect them, they should also have a say in governance decisions by non-state actors that significantly affect them.

While they do not necessarily use the vocabulary of the AAP, many INGOs have tried to comply with its inclusive face. They have done this by, for example, hiring and promoting employees from among the populations with which they work, consulting more closely with (reasonably) legitimate political leaders of those populations, and holding "listening sessions" with members of especially vulnerable social groups, such as disabled or lower-caste people. They have instituted complaints mechanisms and local ombudspersons, and undertaken surveys to solicit feedback. While some of these efforts have had little practical effect – e.g. complaints mechanisms sometimes go unused because they require literacy in places where literacy rates are low – they have, on the whole, gone some ways toward addressing the criticisms of INGOs cited at the outset of this chapter. But beyond whether it suggests incremental steps in the right direction, does the government analogy leading to the AAP's inclusive face offer a compelling and persuasive vision for how INGOs might act more consistently with democratic norms?

In one sense, the answer to this question is clearly yes. For at least three decades, scholars, aid practitioners, and others have argued that INGOs are not merely collections of well-intended, virtuous individuals engaged in acts of charity. They are, instead, political actors that engage in governance activities.[12] Analogizing INGOs to governments brings this argument to life. It suggests that INGOs should be analyzed as political actors and held to democratic norms such as transparency and accountability.

In the context of the AAP, however, analogizing INGOs to governments has at least two drawbacks. First, the idea that INGOs should govern more inclusively normalizes governance by INGOs. Focusing on *how* INGOs govern (i.e. more versus less inclusively), shifts attention away from *whether* they should be engaged in governance in the first place and how to reduce their governance role. This is troubling because compared to conventional governments, INGOs are severely limited with regard to both their democratic legitimacy and their ability to provide services at large scales for extended periods.[13] Even if INGOs are the only entities able and willing to serve a governance function in a particular place at a particular time, a focus on making their governance activities more inclusive can further entrench their governance role and undermine relationships of responsiveness and accountability between populations and their conventional governments.[14]

Second, as noted above, the government analogy deploys the AAP's inclusive face, and inclusion – while sometimes crucial[15] – is in many respects a rather limited and conservative political project.[16] As one commentator wrote, echoing more academic critics of inclusion:

[I]nclusivity at its heart never aims to shift the status quo. Bringing underrepresented voices into a previously constructed process that was never designed by or for them simply does not work. The power dynamics set up by the premise of inclusion don't welcome new ideas.[17]

While this statement is perhaps overly sweeping, it captures the ways in which inclusion as a political project frequently leaves too much unquestioned and unchanged.

THE AAP'S EXCLUSIVE FACE AND THE INDIVIDUAL ANALOGY

Given the limitations of the AAP as a principle of inclusion, it is noteworthy that the AAP is also a principle of *exclusion*: it tells us not only that individuals who *are* significantly affected by a decision *should* have a say in that decision, but also that those who are *not* significantly affected should *not* have a say. Both intrinsic and instrumental justifications for including the affected in decision making are undermined if the unaffected are also included.[18] This exclusive face of the AAP focuses on excluding unaffected individuals (and other entities) from decision-making processes that don't affect them; it rejects unwanted meddling by outsiders, e.g. unwanted "humanitarian" military intervention.[19]

While analogizing INGOs to governments leads to the AAP's inclusive face, analogizing INGOs to unaffected individuals (or simply recognizing that they are themselves not relevantly affected) leads to its exclusive face; just as individuals should not have influence over governments' decisions if they are not affected by those decisions, non-state actors such as INGOs should not have influence over governments' decisions if they are not affected by those decisions. (An exception is if INGOs are acting as legitimate representatives of those who are significantly affected.) This *individual analogy* flips the government analogy on its head. While the government analogy demands that Oxfam include people who are affected by its decisions, the individual analogy demands that Oxfam be excluded from decisions that don't affect Oxfam.

To summarize the argument so far: the government analogy centers INGOs' governance role and says that those who are significantly affected by their decisions should be included in those decisions. It invokes the AAP's inclusive face, articulating a complaint about exclusion, the remedy for which is inclusion. In contrast, the individual analogy centers governance by conventional governments. It says that if INGOs are not significantly affected by those governments' decisions, it should not have a say in those decisions. Invoking the AAP's exclusive face, it articulates a complaint about meddling and interference, the remedy for which is exclusion. While INGOs more frequently acknowledge and seek to demonstrate their compliance with the AAP's inclusive face, they also sometimes acknowledge and seek to demonstrate their compliance with its exclusive face. For example, human rights and humanitarian INGOs sometimes describe themselves as (1) witnesses engaged in *témoignage* who simply report what they see, (2) technical experts, (3) "microphones" that "amplify" the voices of those who are significantly affected by a given issue, and/or (4) connectors that help other actors find and network with each other. These formulations of INGOs' role suggest that they exercise limited independent power and influence.

There are, however, limits on how much INGOs can comply with the exclusive face of the AAP, even when they construe their role in these ways. That is, there are limits on how much they can limit their own influence. This is because it is difficult for powerful elites be involved without also having influence. Like King Midas they change what they touch, in ways that sometimes undermine their intentions. For example, in part to reduce their own influence, INGOs frequently fund local organizations. But in so doing, they empower some organizations but not others, and create incentives for local organizations to anticipate and conform to INGOs' own expectations and preferences.[20] Likewise, INGOs that try to "amplify" the voices of others choose which voices to amplify. One striking example of this phenomenon is cash transfer programs. Cash transfer INGOs such as GiveDirectly are explicitly committed to the value of non-paternalism and minimizing their own influence. However, even cash transfer programs can have unintended negative effects; there is some (contested) evidence that people who do not receive cash transfers, but who live near people who do, experience reduced life satisfaction, asset holdings, and consumption.[21] GiveDirectly is also involved in policy discussions with governments about cash transfers, efforts to test universal basic income programs, etc. There is not necessarily anything wrong with this – but it does mean that GiveDirectly has influence.[22] The broader point is that virtually all involvement by the powerful entails influence, with the result that it is difficult for INGOs to be involved without violating the AAP's exclusive face.

If this is right – if INGOs cannot be involved without also exerting influence – then the AAP's exclusive face has much more radical implications than its inclusive face. The AAP's exclusive face suggests that in some circumstances INGOs should simply not exist, at least not in anything like their current form, because they can't avoid exerting influence even when they are not significantly affected. INGOs addressing important issues should instead be replaced by local organizations run by people who are significantly affected by those issues.[23]

While its implications are radical, the exclusive face of the AAP also does not offer adequate guidance to INGOs. As this chapter's epigraph implies, there are sometimes good reasons for privileged entities to help address social issues that don't significantly affect them. For example, INGOs and their donors (which can be individuals, governments, corporations, foundations, etc.) sometimes cause, contribute to, benefit from, and/or exacerbate the large-scale problems that INGOs seek to address.[24] They also sometimes have an especially strong or specialized capacity to address these issues. These can be good reasons for INGOs and/or their donors to be involved in addressing them, by contributing resources, time, expertise, or labor, or taking on some of the risk involved in doing so.

If this is right, then the implication of the AAP's exclusive face – that unaffected INGOs should not have any influence – is not only too simple, it might let would-be donors off the hook from helping to address problems they helped to create. INGOs therefore face what I call the *involvement/influence dilemma*: a choice between a) being involved, and thereby exerting undemocratic influence, or b) abstaining from any influence, but as a result not doing what they (or their donors) should to address large-scale problems.

The foregoing two sections suggest two conclusions. First, anyone seeking to extend the AAP to INGOs via the government analogy should explain why the government analogy is more appropriate than the individual analogy. That is, why, from a democratic perspective, is making INGOs more inclusive better than excluding them? Second, even if the exclusive face of the AAP offers more critical leverage than its inclusive face, it does not offer sufficient guidance for navigating the involvement/influence dilemma. In the next section I turn to some organizations that have grappled with this dilemma and offer some helpful guidance in how to do so. First, though, I mention two additional aspects of the AAP that exacerbate the involvement/influence dilemma and are also problematic in their own right.

First, the AAP is entirely forward-looking. It asks, at t_1, who will be affected at t_3 by a decision at t_2. This approach excludes, or at least downplays, the relevance of the past for who should have what kind of influence in the present. This is objectionable insofar as histories of exclusion matter for how influence should be allocated in the present and the future. Not only do these histories remind us of patterns of exclusion and domination that have been perpetuated over time, but for political reconciliation to be achieved, compensatory or rectification-based allocation of influence might sometimes be necessary.[25] It is beyond the scope of this chapter to show that it *is* necessary; my point is just that the AAP leaves no space for incorporating considerations of past exclusion or injustice into determinations of how to allocate influence in the present or future.

Second, the AAP is dyadic. Especially when "decision" is interpreted more narrowly, the AAP conjures a series of dyadic linkages between discrete individuals and a given decision. Those individuals should each have a say in the decision if they will be affected by it; they should not have a say if they will not be affected. The lines of connection run between each individual and the decision, like spokes of a wheel or arms of a starfish; they do not run among individuals, understood as individuals or as members of social groups. The AAP thus downplays ongoing relationships among actors, including structural relationships of domination and oppression. Rather than seeing decisions themselves as *effects* that emerge out of ongoing power relations, the AAP focuses on the "downstream" question of who should have a say in those decisions once they are being made. (This problem is less acute when we adopt a "wide" conception of decision making, but as Hayward notes in this volume, widening the AAP too much can make it difficult to apply.)

I have argued that the involvement/influence dilemma, future orientation, and emphasis on dyads are all serious limitations of the AAP. However, these limitations do not – to my mind at least – nullify the democratic intuition at the heart of the AAP: the idea that everyone should have a say in matters that affect their basic interests. Rather, these limitations of the AAP suggest the need to think more about how it might be enacted in ways that are responsive to the complexities of influence and involvement under conditions of extreme power inequalities, historic injustice, and ongoing oppressive relationships.

SOCIAL JUSTICE ORGANIZATIONS AND INGOS
AS OUTSIDER ELITES

To take up this task, I turn to three social justice organizations that explicitly thematize the role of powerful elites in addressing social problems: Showing Up for Racial Justice (SURJ), a "national network of groups and organizations organizing white people for racial justice";[26] Thousand Currents, an NGO that "funds grassroots groups led by women, youth, and Indigenous Peoples in the Global South";[27] and, Solidaire, a "community of individual donors and foundation allies … [that] work together to address the deep systemic causes of injustice and inequality [by increasing] resources for those who are fighting for a world where everyone can live with dignity."[28] All three organizations are based in the United States and participate in or fund activist social movements in the United States and elsewhere.

These organizations differ from each other and from the INGOs that are my main subject here. They vary in their purposes, structures, and funding sources; they operate at different scales and in different political and social contexts. But despite these differences, they wrestle explicitly with a question that, I have argued, INGOs also confront: How might the AAP's central democratic intuition be recast in a way that is sensitive to the difficulties that arise when relatively privileged elites seek to address social problems that primarily affect others?

SURJ, Solidaire, and Thousand Currents' responses to this question are relevant to INGOs not as models to be rigidly replicated, but rather as exemplars that INGOs might learn from and build on creatively. In particular, these organizations suggest how the AAP might be revised in ways that move (1) from the involvement/influence dilemma to accountability for influence, and (2) from forward-looking and dyadic to temporally expansive and relational. The reconstruction that I offer here most closely tracks arguments made by SURJ, but elements of it run through the statements and practices of Solidaire and Thousand Currents as well.

From the Involvement/Influence Dilemma to Accountability for Influence

Social justice organizations dissolve the involvement/influence dilemma for themselves in a few different ways. First, they do not insist that being affected by an injustice is a necessary precondition for being involved in addressing it. Instead, they acknowledge or remain open to other possible grounds and motivations for involvement, including having caused or benefitted from the injustice, or having the capacity to help address it (though they tend not to mention these grounds or motivations specifically).

Second, they recognize that elite involvement entails influence. Rather than denying this influence or trying to eradicate it completely, they seek to moderate and temper elites' involvement in ways that make their influence more democratic, solidaristic, and accountable. One way they do this is by guiding privileged activists toward experiences and ways of seeing that help them to recognize their *shared interests* with members of oppressed groups, without resorting to false equivalencies. For example, SURJ seeks to "organize out of mutual interest."[29] It argues that "the system of white supremacy harms all of us – including white people, though in very different ways than people of color." "We [white people] must find our stake – our mutual interest – in joining these fights." One way white people can do this is proleptically, by taking action; as SURJ notes, "[i]t is important to make sure new people have a chance to become leaders ... Action is how we create commitment to our work!" Solidaire likewise argues that "Only massive social movements, woven together in solidarity, are mighty enough to save the future *for us all*."[30]

A second way that these social justice organizations seek to shape and constrain elite involvement is by making elites accountable to activists from oppressed groups who are themselves accountable to other members of those groups. Thus, SURJ argues that in taking action to end white supremacy, white people should be "in relationship with and take direction from people of color ... who are doing racial justice work in the movement and who are accountable to a group of people." However, this form of accountability-to-the-accountable "doesn't mean waiting by the phone for a person of color to tell us exactly what to do. It means developing plans to organize in the white community and seeking feedback. Sometimes people of color are too busy organizing in their own communities to provide us feedback. We should act in those cases and not wait for permission." For SURJ, then, accountability does not mean acting mechanistically as a tool or extension of organizations led by people of color. It means exercising creativity, agency, and discretion, but taking political responsibility for doing so. White people should "[t]ake risks, make mistakes, learn, and keep going."[31] In this way, SURJ avoids both horns of the influence/involvement dilemma: it neither a) eschews all involvement in order to avoid having influence, nor b) gets involved in ways that have excessive or unwarranted influence. Instead, SURJ remains true to the democratic spirit of the AAP by requiring that elites' influence be constrained by and responsive to those whose basic interests are most significantly affected.

Thousand Currents takes a similar approach. It holds that "[t]he people who can solve [social problems] best are the people whose lives are most affected by them."[32] It therefore structures its grant-giving activities in ways that limit its own influence and that of its donors. Thousand Currents gives long-term "grants with no strings or conditions attached. That means we don't dictate what activities and strategies [grantees] use, freeing them up to listen more closely to the community. If our partners want to pay the light bill, or start a new program, it's up to them."[33] At the same time, it acknowledges and takes responsibility for its influence by asking its grantees to evaluate it.[34] In this way, Thousand Currents, too, is accountable to organizations that are comprised of, and accountable to, those most affected by the issues it addresses.

Likewise, Solidaire states that it "look[s] forward to bringing more of our practices in line with our value of standing with the leadership of those most affected by the issues of our time."[35] It does this by, among other things, incorporating past grantees into decision-making processes to identify new grantees.

What might accountability to the accountable look like in the context of humanitarian, development, and advocacy INGOs?[36] We can begin with the idea, discussed above, of shared interests as a basis for action. While appeals to pity or sympathy are more common, humanitarian and development INGOs have sometimes appealed to donors' self-interest in, for example, avoiding Ebola, terrorism, or an influx of refugees. Yet because they cast the very people whom INGOs seek to assist as threats to donors' self-interest, these sorts of appeals don't invoke *shared* interests. The example of social justice organizations suggests that the difference between self-interest and shared interests is crucial, and that a deeper analysis of the issues that INGOs address might bring the shared interests of INGOs, donors, and the people whom INGOs seek to assist more clearly into view. Because of the importance of avoiding false equivalences, it is vital that this conception of shared interests centers on shared aims shaped by those most affected, rather than shared experiences.[37]

Alongside efforts to recognize and forge a sense of shared interests, there is also the matter of INGOs and their donors taking political responsibility for their influence. The INGO GiveDirectly, discussed above, tells potential donors that by donating to GiveDirectly they "send money directly to people living in extreme poverty."[38] But of course the donations go to GiveDirectly, which in turn decides how to allocate and otherwise use the money it receives. GiveDirectly's commitment to anti-paternalism is salutary. But by denying that it exerts independent influence, it reduces its accountability for that influence. In contrast, SURJ, Thousand Currents, and Solidaire acknowledge and take responsibility for their influence.

Beyond acknowledging influence, there is also accountability for that influence. The type of accountability that SURJ and the other social justice organizations model – accountability to the accountable – is fairly indirect, and so cannot replace accountability directly to the people INGOs seek to assist. It is also informal, and so cannot entirely replace more institutionalized and formalized accountability structures within and among INGOs, e.g. "safeguarding" measures to avoid hiring aid workers with a history of sexual abuse. Accountability to the accountable might also be difficult to implement in situations where there are no mobilized groups comprised of and accountable to those most significantly affected, or where it is difficult for INGOs to determine which of these groups is accountable to people affected by INGOs' actions.[39] That said, broader aspects of the accountability-to-the-accountable approach are relevant to INGOs. When they can, INGOs should create accountability relationships not only with those they most significantly affect, but also mobilized legitimate representatives of those they most significantly affect. Even if they are informal, such relationships can function as an effective complement to more formalized and direct accountability mechanisms. For example, accountability to the accountable could help INGOs ensure that their formal safeguarding procedures don't have the unintended negative effect of excluding local organizations.[40]

From Forward-Looking and Dyadic to Temporally Expansive and Relational

I argued above that the AAP is forward-looking: it allocates influence over a decision to those who will be most significantly affected by that decision *in the future*. I also argued above that the AAP is dyadic: it emphasizes relationships between a given individual and the decision(s) that affect that individual, not relationships among those who are affected.

The three social justice organizations that I have been discussing tamp down these aspects of the AAP. They agree that, roughly speaking, the most affected should have the most say. But rather than give the most say in a decision only to those who *will be* most affected by that decision, they support and follow the lead of mobilized groups comprised of and accountable to those who *are and have been* most affected by the oppressive social structures that give rise to or exacerbate the problems that they are seeking to address. In other words, because their approach is more attentive to ongoing social structures rather than one-off decisions or events, their sense of how power should be allocated is less focused on future effects. For example, Thousand Currents' Buen Vivir fund aims "to shift the economy by transferring control of capital to communities *most affected by racial, economic, and environmental injustices*"[41] (my emphasis). By allocating influence with an eye toward ongoing relationships and structures of oppression and domination, rather than who will be most affected in the future by a specific decision, social justice organizations take the idea of giving a say to those who are most affected in a direction that is more temporally expansive and relational/structural than does the AAP as it is usually conceived (and is more aligned with Hayward's account [see Hayward, this volume]).

In the context of INGOs, this formulation suggests that rather than consulting with those who are likely to be affected by any given decision they take, INGOs should seek to cede power in a more ongoing way to oppressed and disenfranchised groups. While this sometimes won't be possible, it suggests a somewhat different normative guidepost than what is offered by the AAP in its more conventional forward-looking and dyadic instantiations. Conversely, it suggests that a main reason to exclude INGOs from decision making is not only that they are unaffected by particular decisions, but also that they and their donors sit atop social hierarchies.

CONCLUSION

The idea at the heart of the AAP – that everyone should have a say in decisions that significantly affect them, and not interfere excessively in decisions that don't – is a powerful democratic ideal. I have argued that what it actually implies, in the context of INGOs, depends on whether it is extended to them *via* the government analogy, which deploys the AAP's inclusive face, or the individual analogy, which deploys its exclusive face. The latter offers a more radical basis for critique than the former. But because INGOs are elites seeking to address social problems that primarily affect others, even the AAP's exclusive face does not provide them with adequate critical tools or normative guidance. In particular, it doesn't acknowledge or offer tools for navigating the involvement/influence dilemma, it is too forward-looking, and it is too dyadic.

Turning to three social justice organizations that explicitly thematize the involvement/influence dilemma – SURJ, Solidaire, and Thousand Currents – I argued that they recast the AAP in ways that are generative for INGOs. In particular, they suggest the importance of accountability for influence to organizations that are themselves accountable to, and comprised of, people who are significantly affected by the issues that INGOs address. This chapter has only scratched the surface of what humanitarian, development, and advocacy INGOs might learn from social justice organizations such as SURJ, Thousand Currents, and Solidaire. While there are significant differences between and among them, both types of entities face the question of how elites should address social issues that primarily affect others. Future work might look in much more detail at both types of organizations to understand what the former might learn from the latter, and what the insights and experiences of both can tell us about the AAP.

NOTES

1 http://fortune.com/2018/03/12/tech-diversity-uber-bozoma-saint-john-sxsw/.

2 For helpful comments on previous versions of this chapter, I thank the other participants in the workshops on the AAP from which this volume emerged, as well as Hayley Elszasz, Matthew Frierdich, Jennifer Petersen, Allison Pugh, and Denise Walsh.

3 See also, Elizabeth Anderson, *Private Government: How Employers Rule Our Lives (and Why We Don't Talk About It)* (Princeton, NJ: Princeton University Press, 2017).

4 Archon Fung, "The Principle of Affected Interests: An Interpretation and Defense," in *Representation: Elections and Beyond*, ed. Rogers M. Smith and Jack H. Nagel (Philadelphia: University of Pennsylvania Press, 2013).

5 "External" is in quotations here because INGOs' own "borders" are somewhat ill-defined. For example, some INGOs serve as, in effect, implementing arms of governments or other funders, and they often employ aid recipients.

6 I use the term "intended beneficiaries" rather than "beneficiaries" to leave open the possibility that aid recipients don't benefit from aid; I use "intended beneficiaries" rather than "affected population" to leave open the possibility that some people who are affected by the issue at hand (e.g. a civil war) or by aid provision itself do not receive aid. I use "intended beneficiaries" rather than "aid recipients" to focus

on INGOs' intentions rather than characterize the people to whom they provide aid as passive.

7 Antonio Donini, Larissa Fast, Greg Hansen, Simon Harris, Larry Minear, Tasneem Mowjee, and Andrew Wilder, *Humanitarian Agenda 2015: The State of the Humanitarian Enterprise* (Friedman School of Nutrition Science and Policy, Tufts University, 2008); see also, Michael Maren, *The Road to Hell: the Ravaging Effects of Foreign Aid and International Charity* (New York: Free Press, 1997); Alexander De Waal, *Famine Crimes: Politics & the Disaster Relief Industry in Africa* (Bloomington: Indiana University Press, 1997).

8 Suzanne Dovi, "In Praise of Exclusion," *Journal of Politics* 71, no. 3 (2009): 1172–86; cf. Michael L. Frazer, "Including the Unaffected," *Journal of Political Philosophy* 22, no. 4 (2014): 377–95.

9 I use the word "dilemma" here in its informal, colloquial sense to mean a tension or likely tradeoff; I do not mean to indicate a necessarily insoluble conflict.

10 Fung, "The Principle of Affected Interests."

11 Michael N. Barnett, "Humanitarian Governance," *Annual Review of Political Science* 16 (2013): 379–98; Jennifer C. Rubenstein, *Between Samaritans and States: The Political Ethics of Humanitarian INGOs* (New York: Oxford University Press, 2015).

12 Rubenstein, *Between Samaritans and States*; De Waal, *Famine Crimes*; Barnett, "Humanitarian Governance"; Thomas Risse, Tanja A. Borzel, and Anke Draude, (eds) *The Oxford Handbook of Governance and Limited Statehood* (New York: Oxford University Press, 2018).

13 Some INGOs recognize this dynamic and resist taking on a governance role for this reason. See Rubenstein, *Between Samaritans and States*.

14 De Waal, *Famine Crimes*; but, cf. Simone Dietrich, Minhaj Mahmud, and Matthew Winters, "Foreign Aid, Foreign Policy, and Domestic Government Legitimacy: Experimental Evidence from Bangladesh," *Journal of Politics* 80, no. 1 (2018): 133–48.

15 Jumana Farouky, "The Foundation that Wants Women to Ditch Handicrafts and Get Political." Online at www.newsdeeply.com/womensadvancement/community/2018/03/02/the-foundation-that-wants-women-to-ditch-handicrafts-and-get-political. Retrieved on April 21, 2018.

16 Danielle Allen, "Invisible Citizens: Political Exclusion and Domination in Arendt and Ellison," In *NOMOS XLVI: Political Exclusions and Domination*, ed. Melissa S. Williams and Stephen Macedo (New York: New York University Press).

17 Ari Sahagun, "What It Means to Trust the Process and Why We Do It." Online https://thousandcurrents.org/impact/what-it-means-to-trust-the-process-and-why-we-do-it/. Retrieved on April 23, 2018.

18 See Gray, Stilz (this volume); cf. Frazer, "Including the Unaffected."

19 Rainer Bauböck, *Democratic Inclusion: Rainer Bauböck in Dialogue* (Manchester: Manchester University Press, 2017); Stilz (this volume).

20 Reich and Saunders-Hastings (this volume).

21 Johannes Haushofer, James Reisinger, and Jeremy Shapiro, "Your Gain is My Pain: Negative Psychological Externalities of Cash Transfer." Working Paper, 2015. Retrieved from www.princeton.edu/haushofer/publications/Haushofer_Reisinger_Shapiro_Inequality_2015.pdf.

22 In a recent book Rafanelli seeks to distinguish between acceptable and unacceptable influence across borders. See Lucia Rafanelli, *Promoting Justice across Borders* (New York: Oxford University Press, 2021).

23 Swarna Rajagopalan, "Funding Small Non-Profits Can Be a Giant Step for Development." Online at http://idronline.org/funding-small-nonprofits-giant-step-for-development/#comment-538.

24 David Miller, "Distributing Responsibilities," *Journal of Political Philosophy* 9, no. 4 (2001): 453–71; Richard W. Miller, *Globalizing Justice: The Ethics of Poverty and Power* (New York: Oxford University Press, 2010); Michael Goodhart, "Interpreting Responsibility Politically," *Journal of Political Philosophy* 25, no. 2 (2017): 173–95.

25 Catherine Lu, *Justice and Reconciliation in World Politics* (Cambridge: Cambridge University Press, 2017).

26 www.showingupforracialjustice.org/. Retrieved on June 7, 2017.

27 https://thousandcurrents.org/. Retrieved approximately 2017.

28 https://solidairenetwork.org/. Retrieved approximately 2017.

29 https://surj.org/about/our-values/. The rest of the quotations in this paragraph are from the same source. Retrieved on September 24, 2023.

30 Solidaire, "Annual Report," 2014. Online at https://solidairenetwork.org. Retrieved on April 20, 2019.

31 Capitalization altered.

32 https://thousandcurrents.org/our-model/. Retrieved approximately 2017.

33 https://thousandcurrents.org/does-thousand-currents-walk-the-talk/. Retrieved on September 24, 2023.

34 https://thousandcurrents.org/does-thousand-currents-walk-the-talk/. Retrieved on September 24, 2023.

35 Solidaire, "Annual Report," 2016. Online at https://solidairenetwork.org. Retrieved on April 20, 2019.

36 Over the past twenty years, the term "accountability" has gone from being hailed as a "magic bullet" in humanitarian and development circles to being ridiculed as an overused, ambiguous buzzword. There is therefore ample room for it to be re-thought. See Nicholas De Torrente and Eric Stoebbarts, "MSF and Accountability: From Global Buzzwords to Specific Solutions," 2008. Online at https://odihpn.org/magazine/msf-and-accountability-from-global-buzzwords-to-specific-solutions/.

37 cf. Wendy Brown, *States of Injury: Power and Freedom in Late Modernity* (Princeton, NJ: Princeton University Press, 1995), p. 49.

38 www.givedirectly.org/. Retrieved on April 14, 2018.

39 For a sense of these challenges see Michael Agier, *Managing the Undesirables* (Cambridge: Polity Press, 2011).

40 Mary-Rose Romain Murphy, "Safeguarding: Reflections of a Global South Leader Amid #Aidtoo," 2018. Online at https://medium.com/globalgoodness/safeguarding-reflexions-of-a-global-south-leader-amid-aidtoo-8edac8c26d7c.cs.

41 https://thousandcurrents.org/impact/what-it-means-to-trust-the-process-and-why-we-do-it/ (my emphasis). Retrieved approximately 2017.

Index

Printed in the USA
CPSIA information can be obtained
at www.ICGtesting.com
CBHW020415261124
17997CB00003B/156

9 781009 454001